MediaSport

As we enter the twenty-first century, sport increasingly dominates the international media. Daily newspapers, television channels and local news feature ever more sports coverage, often at the expense of political and community news. At the same time, cable and satellite networks are building their global expansion strategies on sports programming as they accelerate penetration into new markets.

MediaSport provides a comprehensive assessment of the ways in which sport and varied forms of media interact with culture, and is written by leading experts from around the world in the fields of sports studies, media studies, journalism and cultural studies.

Among the subjects covered are:

- marketing and commodification of sports
- media treatment of gender, race, and sport
- nationalism and the globalization of sports
- violence, fanship, and audience experiences
- postmodern mediation of sport and the Internet

Clearly written and wide-ranging, *MediaSport* provides essential insights into the latest thinking on the relationship between global sport and the world of communication.

Contributors: Robert V. Bellamy Jr, Jennings Bryant, Pamela J. Creedon, Laurel Davis, Margaret Carlisle Duncan, Walter Gantz, Janet C. Harris, Othello Harris, Sue Curry Jansen, Mary Jo Kane, Kathleen M. Kinkema, Helen Jefferson Lenskyj, Stephen R. McDaniel, Jim McKay, Margaret MacNeill, Michael A. Messner, Toby Miller, Arthur A. Raney, Michael R. Real, David Rowe, Don Sabo, Christopher B. Sullivan, Leah R. Vande Berg, Lawrence A. Wenner, Garry Whannel, David Whitson, Dolf Zillmann.

Lawrence A. Wenner is Professor of Communication and Director of the Sports and Fitness Management Graduate Program at the University of San Francisco. His previous publications include *Media, Sports,* and *Society*, and he is a former editor of the *Journal of Sport and Social Issues.*

ROUTLEDGE

LONDON AND NEW YORK

GENERAL REFERENCE

MediaSport

■ Edited by Lawrence A. Wenner

First published 1998 by Routledge
11 New Fetter Lane, London EC4P 4EE

Simultaneously published in the USA and
Canada by Routledge
29 West 35th Street, New York, NY 10001

Typeset in Times by Florencetype Ltd,
Stoodleigh, Devon

Printed and bound in Great Britain by
T.J. International Ltd, Padstow, Cornwall

*British Library Cataloguing in Publication
Data*
A catalogue record for this book is available
from the British Library

*Library of Congress Cataloguing in
Publication Data*
MediaSport / edited by Lawrence Wenner
  p.   cm.
    Includes bibliographical references and
   index.
   1. Mass media and sports.
   2. Sports–Social aspects.
   I. Wenner, Lawrence A.
  GV742.M337   1998
  070.4′49796–dc21   98–2658
                    CIP

ISBN 0–415–14040–4 (hbk)
ISBN 0–415–14041–2 (pbk)

Contents

Part two

MEDIASPORT INSTITUTIONS

Part three

MEDIASPORT TEXTS

Part four

MEDIASPORT AUDIENCES

About the Contributors

Robert V. Bellamy, Jr. is Associate Professor of Media Studies and Communication at Duquesne University. His current research seeks to document how and why sport is the best exemplar of the 'product' necessary to the ongoing globalization of media industries. He is the co-author of *Television and the Remote Control: Grazing on a Vast Wasteland* and the co-editor of *The Remote Control in the New Age of Television*, both with James R. Walker.

Jennings Bryant is Professor of Communication and Director of the Institute for Communication Research at The University of Alabama. He is the author or editor of 15 scholarly books, including *Media Effects* and *Media, Children, and Family*. His primary research interests are in entertainment theory, media effects, and communication processes and theory.

Pamela J. Creedon is Director of the School of Journalism and Mass Communication at Kent State University. She has been active in sports journalism research for more than a decade. Her recent book *Women, Media and Sport: Challenging Gender Values* details the history of women in sports journalism, broadcasting and marketing. With experience in corporate public relations and college sports information, her writings explore the social dimensions of women's sports magazines and the promotion of women's intercollegiate sports.

Laurel R. Davis is Assistant Professor of Sociology at Springfield College in Springfield, Massachusetts. She recently published a book called *The Swimsuit Issue and Sport: Hegemonic Masculinity in 'Sports Illustrated'*. Her work has appeared and she has served on the editorial boards of such journals as *Sociology of Sport Journal* and the *Journal of Sport and Social Issues*. Her interests include sociology of sport, media, gender, sexuality, race, and class.

Margaret Carlisle Duncan is Associate Professor of Human Kinetics at the University of Wisconsin, Milwaukee. She is former editor of *Play & Culture* (and its later incarnation, *Play Theory and Research*), and has served as President of

The Association for the Study of Play and the North American Society for the Sociology of Sport. Her research on media portrayals of female athletes and women's sports and on mediated sport spectatorship has been widely published in sociology, sport studies, and communication journals.

Walter Gantz is Professor and Chair of Telecommunications at Indiana University. His research focuses on the uses and impact of the media in everyday life, with special attention to the ways couples accommodate each other's media preferences and usage patterns.

Janet C. Harris is Professor of Exercise and Sport Science at the University of North Carolina at Greensboro. Her books include *Athletes and the American Hero Dilemma; Play, Games, and Sports in Cultural Contexts* (with R.J. Park); and *Introduction to Physical Activity* (with eight other authors). She is former editor of *Quest*. Her interests in sport include audience interpretations, community and youth development, and global/national/local relations.

Othello Harris is Associate Professor of Physical Education, Health and Sport Studies and Black World Studies at Miami University. His research interests include race and sport involvement, especially the extent to which sport enhances or impedes opportunities for social mobility for African Americans. His work has been published in journals such as *The Black Scholar*, *Sociology of Sport Journal*, *The Journal of Social and Behavioral Sciences* and *Sociological Focus*. He is the author of chapters in numerous books.

Sue Curry Jansen is Associate Professor of Communication at Muhlenberg College, Allentown, Pennsylvania. Her recent books include *Censorship: The Knot That Binds Power and Knowledge* and *Embodying Knowledge: Essays on Communication, Culture, and Society.*

Mary Jo Kane is Director of the Center for Research on Girls & Women in Sport and Associate Professor in the College of Education & Human Development at the University of Minnesota. She is holder of the Dorothy Tucker Chair for Women in Exercise Science & Sport. Her research focuses on the media's treatment of female athletes, particularly as such treatment contributes to homophobia and hetero-sexism in women's sports.

Kathleen M. Kinkema is an Assistant Professor of Kinesiology and Recreation at Western State College in Gunnison, Colorado. Her scholarly interests focus on audience interpretations of mediated sport.

Helen Jefferson Lenskyj is a Professor at the University of Toronto in the School of Physical and Health Education and the Ontario Institute for Studies in Education. She has written three books and numerous articles on sport, gender and sexuality.

Stephen R. McDaniel is an Assistant Professor in the Department of Kinesiology and Director of the Graduate Program in Sport Management at the University of Maryland College Park. His work appears in journals such as the *Journal of Sport Management*, *Journal of Promotion Management* and *Psychology & Marketing*. His interest in sport communication is focused on sport sponsorship and consumer behavior related to sport media.

Jim McKay is in the Department of Anthropology and Sociology at The University of Queensland, Australia. He is the author of *Managing Gender: Affirmative Action and Organizational Power in Australian, Canadian, and New Zealand Sport,* and the Editor of the *International Review for the Sociology of Sport.* His research and teaching interests include popular culture, men's studies, and ethnic relations.

Margaret MacNeill is an Assistant Professor at the University of Toronto in the School of Physical and Health Education and Graduate Studies in the Department of Community Health. She has presented media and marketing workshops internationally to athletes and fitness professionals. Her research interests include studies of the political and cultural economies of Olympic media production, athletes' rights, and gender issues in health communication.

Michael A. Messner is Associate Professor of Sociology and Gender Studies at the University of Southern California. He is co-editor of *Men's Lives* and *Sport, Men, and the Gender Order: Critical Feminist Perspectives* and *Through the Prism of Difference: Readings on Sex and Gender.* He is author of *Power at Play: Sports and the Problem of Masculinity* and co-author of *Sex, Violence, and Power in Sports: Rethinking Masculinity* (with Don Sabo). His latest book is *Politics of Masculinities: Men in Movements.*

Toby Miller is an Associate Professor of Cinema Studies at New York University. His books include *The Well-Tempered Self: Citizenship, Culture, and the Postmodern Subject, Contemporary Australian Television* (with S. Cunningham), *The Avengers,* and *Technologies of Truth: Cultural Citizenship and the Popular Media.* He edits the *Journal of Sport & Social Issues.*

Arthur A. Raney is a doctoral candidate in mass communication at The University of Alabama. His chief interest is the effect of media messages on perceptions of social justice. His research to date has focused on television violence, sports, religion, and children's television programming policy.

Michael R. Real is Professor and Director of the School of Communication at San Diego State University. His books include *Exploring Media Culture, Super Media* and *Mass-Mediated Culture.* His articles have appeared in dozens of scholarly and popular publications and he has directed a variety of local, national, and international research and production projects. The focus of his work is on media, culture, and social responsibility.

David Rowe teaches Media and Cultural Studies in the Department of Leisure and Tourism Studies at The University of Newcastle, New South Wales, Australia. He has published in several international journals, including *Cultural Studies, Media, Culture & Society, Leisure Studies, Sociology of Sport Journal* and the *Journal of Sport and Social Issues,* and is a frequent media commentator on cultural matters. His latest book is *Popular Cultures: Rock Music, Sport and the Politics of Pleasure.* Dr. Rowe's academic interests lie in the broad field of popular culture, especially music, sport, television and the print media.

Don Sabo is Professor of Social Sciences at D'Youville College, Buffalo, New York. His recent books include *Sex, Violence & Power in Sports: Rethinking*

Masculinity (with Michael Messner) and *Men's Health & Illness: Gender, Power & the Body* (with David Gordon). His current research focuses on the contributions of sports and physical activity to the health of girls and boys, and linkages between athletic participation and reproductive behavior. He is a trustee of the Women's Sports Foundation.

Christopher B. Sullivan is a Senior Management Analyst in the Florida Division of Workers' Compensation. Dr. Sullivan has conducted studies on the use of communication technologies in the Florida legislature, state agencies and universities, the local community and the military. His work is published in journals such as the *Journal of Business Communication*, *the Florida Communication Journal*, and *Advances in Telematics*. His research focuses on electronic mail, computer mediated communication and decision-making, telecommuting, and telecommunication policies.

Leah R. Vande Berg is Professor of Communication Studies at California State University, Sacramento. Her books include *Organizational Life on Television* (with Nick Trujillo) and *Critical Approaches to Television* (with L.A. Wenner & B.E. Gronbeck). Her research appears in journals such as *Critical Studies in Mass Communication*, *Communication Monographs*, and *Journalism Quarterly*. Currently, she is the Editor of the *Western Journal of Communication*. Her research interests include television, media and cultural values, and images of women and men in media, arts, and sports.

Lawrence A. Wenner is Professor of Communication and Director of the Sports and Fitness Management Graduate Program at the University of San Francisco. He is former editor of the *Journal of Sport and Social Issues*. His books include *Media, Sports, and Society* and *Critical Approaches to Television* (with L.R. Vande Berg & B.E. Gronbeck). His interest in sports focuses on audience experience and the effects of the commodified sport environment.

Garry Whannel is a Reader in Sport and Culture, and Co-Director of the Centre for Sport Development Research, at Roehampton Institute in London. He is the author of *Fields in Vision: Television Sport and Cultural Transformation* and *Blowing the Whistle: The Politics of Sport* and co-author of *Understanding Sport*. His current research examines sport stars, masculinities and moralities.

David Whitson is a Professor of Canadian Studies, Department of Political Science, University of Alberta, Canada. His previous books include *Hockey Night in Canada: Sport, Identities, & Cultural Politics* (with Rick Gruneau) and *The Game Planners: Transforming the Canadian Sport System* (with Don Macintosh). His research interests focus on Canadian popular culture, and globalization in the entertainment industries.

Dolf Zillmann is Professor of Communication and Psychology and Senior Associate Dean for Graduate Studies & Research at the University of Alabama. He has a longstanding interest in the psychology of sports spectatorship.

Preface

The mediation of sport cannot be missed on the contemporary cultural horizon. A daily newspaper without a sports section is an anomaly. Local news broadcasts feature sports far more prominently than they do coverage of local politics. Traditional television networks lose even more of their foothold on the market when they lose contractual rights to broadcast a popular sport. Cable and satellite networks build their ever more elaborate plans for global expansion on the ability of sport-related product to penetrate new markets and cross national borders with ease. Manufacturers of athletic apparel, such as Nike, spin marketing plans out of cultural sensibilities about sport. They aim at larger leisure and lifestyle markets and leave a large ideological footprint along the way.

One does not need to appreciate sport to realize that its world has content that is more compelling to many than other artifacts and responsibilities of daily living. Sport, too, has always been a conduit or medium through which feelings, values, and priorities are communicated. As we enter the twenty-first century, sport, both as content and as medium of communication, has reached new heights. This book explores this heightened sport as communication that is unique in how it interacts with the broader public sphere. The cultural fusing of sport with communication has resulted in a new genetic strain called *MediaSport*.

The world of *MediaSport* is examined by a distinguished group of scholars who have graciously shared their expertise in this volume. I wish to thank them for their contributions. The world that they look at is shaped at institutional, textual, and experiential levels. *MediaSport Institutions* include almost all of the significant players in the global communication, entertainment, and leisure complex that has come to dominate postmodern experience. *MediaSport Texts*, ranging from the super to the ordinary, are suspended in the hyperreal world of sport while they interact with the broader crossroads of identities rooted in notions of race, gender, nation, and the heroic. *MediaSport Audiences* have experiences that tint gender relations and family life, are shaped by the ritualized violence on the stage of sport, and grapple with fanship and involvement as sport enters cyberspace. You will find that many of the essays in this volume provide treatment of a side of *MediaSport* in a way that surely will be seen as landmark. Still, while the essays that are included in this volume cover much ground, the world of *MediaSport* and its implications cast a much longer cultural shadow. I hope others will join with us in exploring its contours.

I would like to thank Routledge, and my editor Mari Shullaw, for their patience and confidence in this project. They have trusted my judgment and it has been a pleasure working with them. The University of San Francisco and my graduate students in the Sports and Fitness Management Program have provided unyielding support for *MediaSport* that has been much appreciated. Finally, my wife Susan, with whom I share many sporting passions and far more of others, has provided much encouragement for me to see this book out the door and into the world. Susan remains my greatest fan, and I remain hers.

Lawrence Wenner
San Francisco

The MediaSport
Playing Field

Playing the MediaSport Game

Lawrence A. Wenner

Super Bowl Sunday has become the single most important day for the export of American culture to a globe amazingly eager to absorb the marketing fineries of consumer capitalism.

William Wong (1997, p. A21)

Now there's really only one true communal ritual left. To merely say that the Super Bowl is far and away America's biggest television event isn't enough. To call it a "manufactured holiday" doesn't do it, either. You can argue now that it has become our pre-eminent secular holiday . . . statistically, Hallmark Cards says, Super Sunday generates more social gatherings than any other occasion.

Richard Turner (1997, p. 62)

The roads are empty. The shopping malls are bare. It's Super Bowl Sunday in America. Straddled between two national holidays in the United States, Martin Luther King's birthday and President's Day, the late-January Super Bowl day that pits American professional football conference champions pales both in capital and cultural significance. It is one of the big dances on the 'MediaSport' board game. Like other big dances such as the Olympic Games and the World Cup, all are invited and those who do not come to the dance floor are viewed with scrutiny. Big time 'MediaSport' played well can be a compelling game. The monies involved stagger the imagination and rival small national economies. What may at first seem a national preoccupation takes on global implications. What starts as a sporting contest played between lines becomes transformed into spectacle that seems to have no bounds.

In this volume, selected dimensions of the MediaSport landscape are considered. We will examine how the cultural footprint of sport has grown significantly in the media age. Some years ago, Robert Lipsyte (1975) coined the term

'SportsWorld' to describe the powerfully compelling alternative world of sport in modern times. While the sanctum of sports still offers refuge, the world of sports is no longer other-worldly. It is at the crossroads of much daily commerce and provides the foundation to many of the shared cultural symbols that are left in what often seems a disjointed postmodern existence. The "joys" that theologian Michael Novak (1976) suggested came in experiencing sport as a "sacred" experience often seem to be overshadowed by the "profane" aspects that sport takes on as it becomes a media product. Many of Robert Lipsky's (1981) observations about why sports "dominate life" remain true, but the rules of "how we play the game" have changed.

Much change may be traced to the corporate landscape that has come to define the upper echelon of what can only be called MediaSport. The global "integrated marketing" strategies of the Time-Warner-Cable News Network-*Sports Illustrated* combine, the Disney-ABC-ESPN brands, and the Rupert Murdoch-News Corp. leveraging of the Fox television imprimatur through sport have only been the most recent sightings on the horizon (Adams, 1996). In other areas, major players such as Nike, who appear first on the scene as sporting goods manufacturers and "just advertisers," have transformed their cultural role and influence by "doing it" through sports at virtually every level across the globe. Other advertisers in categories as diverse as automobiles, finance, and alcohol rely on sports as a mediated vehicle to polish their global image and market products.

FROM THE SUPER TO THE ORDINARY

The case of the Super Bowl illustrates many basic elements of MediaSport in dramatic fashion. With a domestic audience of 140 million, the game broadcast dominates the "top ten" list of all-time best rated television programs. In a festive viewing climate where Super Bowl parties are common, advertisers use the broadcast as a way to roll out new products or to demonstrate that they are a major player in the consumer environment. Such advertising statements come with a hefty price tag. Companies such as Visa, Pepsi, Coca-Cola, and Intel often spend $500,000 to $1 million just to produce special Super Bowl messages. In 1997, with sponsors paying up to $2.4 million per minute, the $40,000 second had arrived (Emert, 1997). Formalizing what for years had been the case anyway, the Super Bowl has become a beauty contest for advertisers. The post-game show now features the results of *USA Today's* Super Bowl Ad. Meter competition, an on-the-fly poll of viewers, to name the top three commercials aired during the game broadcast (Carman, 1997; Turner, 1997).

Rupert Murdoch's nascent but growing Fox Television Network, which has spent $1.6 billion to outbid CBS for four years of rights to broadcast regular season games of the National Football League's senior conference, was using the Super Bowl in 1997 as a way to reinforce the network's "coming of age" in the global broadcast and data communications markets (Tyrer, 1994). The Fox program schedule was heavily promoted in a day that featured some five hours of "pregame" programming to hype what is typically a three hour long game where the ball is actually in play for a very few minutes (Real, 1975). With the Super Bowl broadcast destined to be the most highly-rated program in the ten years of the Fox Network, the benefits to the Fox "brand" were considerable (Carman, 1997).

The game broadcast offers an exciting narrative text in a friendly, ritual-laden setting. However, the "text" for any Super Bowl begins far before any game. The "meta-texts" for championship-level play in other sporting contexts and for earlier Super Bowl games frame meaning. Print and broadcast press coverage leading up to the game set a tone by hyping the contest and specifying what conflicts are worthy of conjecture. In terms of cultural analysis, this "stage setting" about how to look at the meaning of an event such as the Super Bowl may be more important than is what is actually contained in the text of the game broadcast (Wenner, 1989c). Still, a plowing of the textual field of an event such as the Super Bowl can yield much rich cultural "dirt" (Wenner, 1991, 1994b). Gender is very much on stage, with only men on the field and women on the sidelines. Race, too, interacts in the mix, with African-American players often typed, and white faces dominating decision-making positions on and off the field. And, of course, the values of blatant consumerism are always well-dressed and never questioned. The game itself, framed as the heroic use of strategic aggression and force to acquire territory and thereby "win," may be seen as analogous to the ideals that undergird American marketplace ideology. Real's (1975, p. 42) observations, some twenty years ago, hold true today:

> The structural values of the Super Bowl can be summarized succinctly: *North American professional football is an aggressive, strictly regulated team game fought between males who use both violence and technology to gain control of property for the economic gain of individuals within a nationalistic entertainment context.* The Super Bowl propagates these values by elevating one game to the level of a spectacle of American ideology collectively celebrated.

As these comments suggest, the meanings associated with mediated sport texts often extend well beyond the archetypal heroic myths of the playing field to offer lessons about cultural priorities and the current state of power relations.

Audience experience with media events such as the Super Bowl tend to be out of the ordinary. More women join men in viewing. The heightened activities that surround the game serve as the foundation to what becomes a cultural "high holy day" (Katz, 1980). A two week break in competition that precedes the Super Bowl fuels anticipation, knowledge, conjecture, and increased betting in association with the big game. An extensive line-up of pre-game programming provides encouragement for people to make more elaborate preparations for viewing. People are more likely to share in Super Bowl rituals by viewing in groupings of family and friends that often join together on other holidays and social occasions. Food is more likely to be elaborately prepared with more drink consumed in the celebratory atmosphere that often results (Rothenbuhler, 1988, 1989a). After the game, there appear to be higher risks than usual. In the home cities of winning teams, spontaneous victory celebrations often become combustible as emotions and alcohol interact in crowded public settings. Disappointments over a team's losing, lost money in bets, and resentment by one family member over the high priority that viewing has taken for another can all fuel domestic conflict and even violence.

While MediaSport super events signal an easily seen cultural "time-out," the story of everyday experience with mediated sport may be more important. While the cumulative effects of the constant drip of sports in everyday experience outweigh the influence of any one event, they may be much more difficult to see. So much mediated sport fills the cultural landscape that it has blended into the backdrop. The sensibilities of sport on the public stage have been naturalized to a degree that they are little pondered in the course of daily living.

Sports journalism and the commentary that takes place during games has little room for social reflection. In these camps there seems no more than an obligatory nod to the fact that the largesse of the MediaSport combine creeps almost daily to new heights. Certainly, there are knowing winks to the breathtaking and ever increasing salaries paid to élite athletes that are fueled by media monies. However, apart from an occasional rap on the knuckles of an athlete who has stepped out of line or a professional team owner who has drawn ire for overstepping the bounds of public subsidization of a private business, the stories of MediaSport are seen as diversions from everyday life that offer much cause for celebration and ongoing engagement.

The game of MediaSport is widely seen as a harmless party providing important social release and cohesion in chaotic and harried postmodern times. Because, almost without exception, public discourse about sport comes from voices inside the MediaSport combine and from those who stand to benefit as the stakes get higher, the story that is most often told is "welcome to the party." Standing on the sidelines, the voices in this book tell another set of stories. They tell stories of **MediaSport Institutions** and how marketplace dynamics build on cultural sensibilities about sport. They tell stories about **MediaSport Texts** and how they influence our realities about heroism, nation, race, and gender. Finally, these voices reflect on the most common way most of us experience sport, as members of **MediaSport Audiences**. Before considering the contours of each of these areas, it is worthwhile to take a quick look at the road taken to approach MediaSport.

APPROACHING MEDIASPORT

"Discovering" MediaSport was much like discovering America. It was fairly large and hard to avoid. There were already people there, too. However, it is worth pondering why it took so long for a "critical mass" to form at the gates of MediaSport inquiry. The small mob that first began to hover at the gates came largely from two quarters, media studies, in the discipline of communication, and sport sociology, an area that split time between the fields of both physical education and sociology. Influences and pressures in the disciplinary cultures of both areas may have impeded the discovery of sport in media studies and media in sport studies.

Sport in Media Studies

In the comparatively new communication and media studies disciplines, sport was largely off the disciplinary map as recently as 15 years ago. Looking back to the time of an earlier review (Wenner, 1989b) that attempted to provide a fairly comprehensive look at social research on media and sports, there were only about a dozen works by scholars that had communication or media studies as a home discipline. About a third of these come from the Bryant and Zillmann group (see their chapter in this volume) with an experimental focus on violence and enjoyment of sports, and about another third are traceable to a symposium of articles on sport published in a 1977 issue of the *Journal of Communication*, a journal that earlier published Michael Real's (1975) now classic essay on the Super Bowl. At that time, apart from the *Journal of Communication*, there was no other communication journal with a regular record of publishing research on sport.

There are a variety of ways to explain the early absence of sport in media and communication studies. First, the communication discipline was a relatively new derivative from far-flung quarters. Thus, early on it borrowed traditional social science models of inquiry from psychology and sociology and focused on the propagandizing effects of political communication. However, it also had a "professional" side to its education that raised eyebrows with members of the social science community, who were generally suspicious of and perhaps a little embarrassed by professional education, especially that in service of the entertainment industry. As a result, communication scientists may have compensated by focusing on "more serious" questions centered around politics, violence, and children. Sport, considered more peripheral, or even "frivolous," was little considered.

Questions of culture were largely deferred until increasing amounts of communication scholars discovered cultural studies in the 1980s. Like sport, it had been around for some time before its discovery by communication. The "critical turn" that American communication studies took in the 1980s enabled new projects in aspects of communicative culture in areas, that up until that point had received little treatment, such as popular music (Lull, 1988) and sport. This new willingness to put popular communication cultures on the agenda led to the publication of *Media, Sports, and Society* (Wenner, 1989a), a collection that, arguably, was the first to attempt to define and showcase the contours of the relationship between media and sport and its influence on social and cultural life. *Media, Sports, and Society* helped legitimize inquiry into media and sport, and fueled many of the more recent studies from both communication and sport sociology that are treated in this volume.

Media in Sport Studies

The story of media in sport studies has many parallels to sport in media studies. While sport may have seemed inconsequential to many as communication and media studies unfolded, media, as strange as it may seem, had little to do with how disciplinary agendas around the social side of sport were unfolding in physical education and sociology. It is important to note that sociology of sport, as an area of inquiry and as coursework had a tradition of being peripheral to both the fields of physical education and sociology. In physical education, praxis of the physical took center stage. Around this core were studies of exercise science, kinesiology, motor learning and the like. Here, social approaches to sport often enriched the core education of students aiming to be practitioners. If the culture of sport was being studied, it was largely being studied in reference to actually doing or administering the sporting activity. In any case, sociology of sport courses, often complemented by a sport psychology course centered on the knowledge and techniques of performance optimization, and were likely to be the only social science-oriented courses in the curriculum.

While in departments of physical education (that were increasingly being reframed as kinesiology or exercise science) these courses were often initially taught by a faculty with little formal social science training; in sociology departments the occasional sport sociology course that was offered was even more of a novelty. Because concern with sport, in and of itself, was often viewed with scorn by "serious" sociologists, sport was initially studied in the context of more established sociological traditions in social organization, stratification, and occupational sociology. While in the typical sport sociology course there would likely be a section on the economy, or even political economy of sport, the media component of sport commodification received little attention. This was likely traceable to the traditions of media study in sociology largely being transplanted to communication and media studies units in the 1960s and 1970s. The net result was that by the time big media met big sport, little media study remained in departments of sociology.

The cumulative effects of these cultural circumstances were that mediated sport was little examined in the circles that formed around the sociology of sport. In comparison to the dozen or so works traceable to communication scholars, little more than a handful of works from either physical education or sociology addressed mediated sport at the time *Media, Sports, and Society* appeared on the scene. The bulk of this work considered media in the context of a larger focus on hooliganism and violence (c.f., Coakley, 1988–89; Hall, 1978; Murphy, Dunning, & Williams, 1988; Whannel, 1979; Young, 1986). Others (c.f., Eberhard & Meyers, 1988; Therberge & Cronk, 1986), with focus on the sports journalism, drew on traditions in occupational sociology. Even so, concern over other issues, such as gender (Duncan & Hasbrook, 1988; MacNeill, 1988) could be spotted on the horizon. What is most striking about the literature seen in the three main sociology of sport outlets (*Sociology of Sport Journal, Journal of Sport and Social Issues, International Review for the Sociology of Sport*) is how little media-centered work appeared prior to the publication of *Media, Sports, and Society* (Wenner, 1989a). The breadth of that work, and the relatively parallel "discovery" of cultural studies and its help in legitimizing critical research in both sport sociology and media studies, have contributed to the virtual explosion of post-1990 MediaSport inquiry that fuels the chapters that follow.

MAPPING MEDIASPORT

The world of MediaSport comes about through the interaction of institutions, texts, and audiences. This basic drawing mirrors models drawn in both traditional communication research and cultural studies. It is not surprising, then, that the three most overarching reviews of the areas (Kinkema & Harris, 1992, and their essay in this volume; Wenner, 1989b) are organized largely along these lines. While traditions in media and communication research have often led to individual studies being contained to one of the areas, more recent influence from the cultural studies approach suggests that the lines are more realistically blurred. In any case, it seems desirable for studies to attempt to assess links between areas, and, over time, for research programs to theorize in the broader set of relations among institutions, texts, and audiences. A brief sketch of the priorities and challenges within these areas is offered below.

MediaSport Institutions

What is sometimes called the sports/media production complex (Jhally, 1989) can be broken down into what may appear to be discrete categories. For example, one may be tempted to distinguish between media organizations and sport organizations (Wenner, 1989b) and to focus on the coalitions they fuel. However, in more recent times these lines blur as global conglomerates such as Disney and Time-Warner mix media and sport holdings in an overall entertainment and leisure strategy. Still, there is a dance between organizations that hold sport product and those organizations that need it in its transformation as media product. These latter organizations are the owners of not only the broadcast and cable networks, satellite superchannels, and local radio and television stations, but also newspapers, magazines, and other outlets. In any case, macro-level political-economic analyses of these organizations form the backbone of MediaSport institutional analysis.

At a more micro-level of analysis, case studies of MediaSport production workers offer a different perspective of institutional dynamics. Here the focus is often on the tensions between creativity and constraint that face media workers who attempt to balance the standards and ethos of professionalism with the pragmatics of production under time and budgetary pressures. Ethnographic and other studies of sports journalists and the broadcast production process that grow out of occupational sociology offer fruitful insights into the priorities and compromises of professionals in the heat of decision-making.

The range of institutions, organizations, and individuals that interplay in the production of mediated sport is considerable. MediaSport organizations and their workers exist in broader social, political, and legal climates. As MediaSport crosses borders, local, national, and international bodies will necessarily interact and have conflict. Because of this, there is a real need for broader, more sophisticated conceptualizations of the MediaSport institutional climate. There may be no one "right" answer. However, a number of approaches may be fruitful. Amongst these are Dimmick and Coit's (1982) model of hierarchically-organized levels of media decision-making, Turow's (1992) "power roles" approach to media production, and Harvey, Rail, and Thibault's (1996) model of how a web of sport organizations interact in moves toward globalization.

MediaSport Texts

Analysis of the texts and content of MediaSport has been, by far, the most extensively examined area. There are a variety of reasons for this. First, selected texts are readily available for analysis. Second, troublesome or inequitable aspects are relatively easy to spot. Third, and perhaps most important, textual analysis is easier to do than either institutional or audience analysis, both of which have much more severe challenges in terms of access to data. In the institutional realm much of the more useful market data may be proprietary. Gaining access to media workers, and more significantly to candor about their relationship to their employers, can be problematic. Depending on the methodological strategy, audience study poses other obstacles. Ethnographic or observational studies require extensive time commitments. Gathering survey data reliably means careful and broad sampling which can be expensive and labor intensive and requires complex data entry and analysis. Experimental research in MediaSport usually necessitates producing media texts as the basis to test differing conditions on audiences.

MediaSport texts are plentiful and can be chosen using a variety of defensible strategies ranging from random to convenience to targeted sampling. Similarly, methods of textual or content analysis are diverse. To this point, much of the research is seemingly at the formative or "counting" stage. This sensibly begins to establish baselines to understand issues such as how racially or gender biased coverage may be, how much and what kind of sports violence or commercialization is featured, or how much nationalism or winning is emphasized. Other research on these same topics often focuses more on thick description, often in companion with ideologically-based semiosis. One risk, that is reflected in some of the research findings, is proving and reproving the obvious by all too often ruling out all but the preferred meaning. Learning when and how to get beyond the indisputable inequities, such as gender bias, found in MediaSport texts will be important as this research moves to the next stage. Given that textual and content analysis of MediaSport has been largely problem centered, one may deduce that scholars in this area are concerned with these problems not only in the abstract but also in connection to changes in policy and practice. In short, it seems they are largely looking to make media coverage of sport more equitable between the sexes and among races, and less violent, nationalistic, commercialized, and consumed with winning. Shouting these issues in a crowded theater of true believers will accomplish little. Textual analysis will need to be linked to understandings of the institutional dynamics before effective pressure may be brought to bear on policymakers and mediated sport decision-makers.

MediaSport Audiences

Textual analysis will also need to reach out to test its constructed realities with MediaSport audiences. There is little evidence to suggest that those armed with the stock tools of semiotics, hermeneutics, reader-oriented criticism or other critical text-based methods are raking through mediated sport in ways similar to spectators and fans in the audience. Audience study offers many ways to gain a hold on the variant understandings that come with experiencing mediated sport. Yet, there are real dangers here as well. Much in parallel to the tendency for textual analysis to gravitate to preferred meaning, ethnographically "inspired" audience study all too often gravitates to evidence for polyvalence in the text and correspondingly "subversive" or "empowering" reading positions. As the cultural turn in MediaSport audience study moves ahead, researchers using both culturally "sensitive" qualitative methods and those using more traditional survey methods or empirical analysis will need to recognize the artifacts that come with their methodological choices. In observational settings people are changed and in interview settings people often respond as they like to see themselves as opposed to how they really are. Hindsight, as it is often said, is "20/20." A corollary to this well may be that hindsight also sees far more polyvalence and resistance to texts than would be there without the researcher's query.

Just as audience research has some dangers, it has some real benefits. In particular, research on how fanship and gender interact with audience experience holds real promise. What are the contours of sports fanship and what role does media play in defining these? With rapid changes in how girls and women experience sport, how has this changed audience experience? In pursuing questions like these, it will be important to recognize that we will need to understand not only the texture of these experiences in limited qualitative settings, but do more to make generalizations based on broader survey samples. With the cultural turn, interest in qualitative methods has risen. This was long overdue. However, there remains a continuing need to understand how generalizable some of these thick snapshots are. As oxymoronic as it may seem to some, critically oriented survey research that is methodologically savvy and sensitive to nuance in "reading" the data may lead to our most useful understandings of the MediaSport audience experience.

READING MEDIASPORT

Following an introductory "Playing Field" section, the essays in this collection are placed in three sections, according to whether they most focus on MediaSport institutions, texts, or audiences. In pursuing cultural understanding, such distinctions are often artificial. Readers should join the authors in this collection in seeing MediaSport through linkages amongst institutions, texts, and audiences. While the contributors to this volume touch on major themes in MediaSport inquiry, the expanse of the field is far greater and touches many other cultural borders.

In getting started, the two essays that follow challenge readers to think about the breadth of the social shadow cast by MediaSport. In the first essay, Michael Real places the importance of MediaSport at the cultural crossroads of technology, commodification, and the postmodern condition. Real's essay provides a lens to view where MediaSport inquiry has been and where the "big picture" lies in its global future. The second essay, by Kathleen Kinkema and Janet Harris, rises to the challenge of reviewing and synthesizing broad research and writing on MediaSport. Their essay is an essential starting point for anyone interested in studying MediaSport as a cultural phenomenon. A first reading of the chapter will give you a "macro" view, while later, more selective re-readings of their review will help in framing institutional, textual, and audience issues addressed in later sections of the volume.

MediaSport Institutions are introduced by David Whitson in a chapter that traces fundamental cultural changes in sport to the integrated use of media by a corporate sphere that manufactures synergies to leverage and expand global markets. In the chapter that follows, Robert Bellamy amplifies many of these themes in examining what he calls a "new oligopoly" of media giants that use sport as a tool for vertical integration. In addition, his analysis highlights how sports organizations use media in their move toward global markets. Pamela Creedon's chapter on women, sport, and media provides important insight into how sport and media are both gendered institutions and how structural biases affect reception of women's sports. Creedon's analysis keys on how market tolerances compromise diversity in the public image of female athletes and their achievements. Margaret MacNeill's chapter on athletes' rights and the ethos of sports journalism raises important new questions to close out this section. MacNeill considers the differential ethos of journalists as they approach sport and coverage of athletes, and more importantly, points to strategic interventions that can help athletes in curbing journalistic abuses of accuracy, privacy, and human rights.

MediaSport Texts are examined in reference to the larger cultural discourses about national identity, celebrity and heroism, race and ethnicity, and gender. This section opens with provocative consideration of mediated constructions of nation and sport by David Rowe, Jim McKay, and Toby Miller. They consider the role of mediated sport in constructing national mythologies, in perpetuating citizenship differentiated by gender, and in co-opting ethnic identity in strategic ways. Leah Vande Berg examines one of MediaSport's key textual artifacts, the sports hero as celebrity. Vande Berg considers how sports heroism has moved other forms of heroism to the margins, and how the social push of marketing has facilitated the traditional modern hero giving way to decidedly postmodern constructions ready-made for the commodity market. Laurel Davis and Othello Harris focus on discourses about race embedded in media treatment of sports in the United States. In a most comprehensive treatment, they illustrate inequities in amount of coverage, the contours of stereotyping, interactions of the coverage of deviance with race, and the heralding of African-American sports success as evidence for the American Dream. Three chapters focused on how gender is constructed in mediated sports texts close this section. In the first essay, Margaret Carlisle Duncan and Michael Messner provide a comparative look at how women and men are treated in coverage by the sports media. Relying on their important series of studies sponsored by the Amateur Athletic Foundation of Los Angeles, Duncan and Messner outline how media differentiates the achievements of female and male athletes through differences in production values, portraits of athleticism, and the symbolic marking of athletes through naming and sexualization strategies. This last issue, the construction of gender identity and sexualities, is given more extensive treatment by Mary Jo Kane and Helen Lenskyj. They examine media treatment of female athletes, extracting how discourses on heterosexual femininity, homophobia, and lesbianism interact with cultural power. In the next chapter Don Sabo and Sue Curry Jansen provide counterpoint in their analysis of constructions of masculinity in the sports media. They use the cultural archetype of the Promethean myth as a point of departure to consider the "binary bind" of gender-typed analysis, the sport media connection to men's violence and the culture of pain, and the marginalization of gay and minority athletes in public discourses of masculinity.

MediaSport Audiences are approached in a variety of ways in the last section. Opening the section, Garry Whannel's chapter on reading the sports audience points to merits in a more critical, culture-based approach to audience experience with mediated sport. Whannel argues that sports consumption needs to be viewed in terms of broader domestic and leisure practices, through the lenses of gender, race, and class identities, and most importantly, in the context of pleasure and ritual. The intersection of sport and gender are addressed as Walter Gantz and I synthesize our most important findings in a longstanding research program on audience experiences with televised sport. Our analysis puts key questions and myths of gender differences, fanship, and marital turbulence in relation to viewing sports under the microscrope. How violence interacts with the enjoyment of mediated sport is explored by the two scholars most associated with this question, Jennings Bryant and Dolf Zillmann, who are joined by Arthur Raney in a chapter that contextualizes the experience in a broader social framework. Their analysis looks at the roots of sports violence, competing theories of spectatorship and enjoyment of violence, and the social implications of empirical evidence on reception of sports violence. In the closing chapter, Stephen McDaniel and Christopher Sullivan outline the contours of experience with "cybersport." They look at new mechanisms of delivery, offer tactical and terminological strategies to aid analyzing the new media technology and sport nexus, and provide a profile of audience experiences with cybersport.

MEDIASPORT VISTAS

As we enter the twenty-first century, there is almost no evidence to suggest that the recent patterns of unbridled growth that have recently characterized the MediaSport production complex will slow. Major players in the global communication market seem surefooted in their investments in sport as a tool to expand their markets. As a media product, much sport crosses borders with relative ease. The Internet will only make cross-border flow that much easier. It will also offer new ways to construct identities in experiencing and responding to sport. As spiraling interest in coverage of the Olympic Games suggests, identities formed at local and national levels can be strategically used in stimulating interest in global competitions. Globalization will undoubtedly fuel changes in MediaSport texts. It seems likely that many of these changes will purposefully open texts to broader markets. An artifact of this is that some texts will likely become more friendly to heretofore marginalized audiences for sports. Mass texts may move to be more inclusive of women who have not yet saturated the MediaSport audience. On the other hand, we will see specialized texts exploding in their growth and siphoning from the mass market. The interaction of the mass and the global with the specialized and the local will be important to watch as MediaSport enters a new era.

MediaSport: Technology and the Commodification of Postmodern Sport

Michael R. Real

The importance of mediated sports today is evident in both their scale and intensity. The huge scale of media sports appears in audience sizes of many millions for televised sporting events and media contracts for billions of dollars. The scale is there in the explosion of sport talk radio, sport magazines, Internet sport sites, and consequent global sport marketing, inflated salaries and endorsement contracts. It is there in a public obsession with sport that spills over into attitudes toward schools, politics, family, and daily life. The intensity of involvement with MediaSports appears in the manner in which individuals become totally absorbed in the mediated sporting event, arranging personal schedules around the events and integrating relationships and ritual activities into the obsession with sport. The sports media fan modifies patterns of clothing and decoration, searches out supplemental sources of information, enters pools and places bets, joins fantasy leagues, and in other psychological and visible ways expresses the central importance that mediated sports occupy in individual lives.

Institutions, the structured organizations of grouped power in society, connect the large-scale sports media event to intense individual involvement. In that decisive instant in 1994 when Roberto Baggio's penalty kick sailed above the goal to end the World Cup final and give Brazil victory, the structured institutions of sports and media made it possible for Brazilians at home to see it and go crazy, for Italians to see it and agonize, for the world to see it and experience emotions of ecstasy, despair, frustration, and satisfaction or dissatisfaction of all kinds. More than 100 countries had purchased television rights to the World Cup and upwards of a billion people had access to that missed penalty kick in the final shootout. Institutions of television broadcasting and international sports had created an event and global access to an event that brought together viewers through sophisticated systems of technology, finance, scheduling, and commodification.

In addition to questions of institutional scale and individual intensity, MediaSport today suggests other overarching questions, questions largely shaped by the institutional alignments of sports and media in the context of late capitalism. Has the integration of sports and media into a combined totality moved sports away from classical value assumptions and toward commercialization and profit? Is the relationship between mass media of communication and the world of sports one of exploitation (parasitic) or mutual benefit (symbiotic)? Is the commercialized ritual involvement of the individual and group in MediaSports without historical parallel, or is it foreshadowed in traditional theories of commodification, myth and ritual, particularly in the theory of "deep play?" Is the relationship of MediaSport to larger social forces random, or is it the logical result of "late capitalism" as identified in postmodern theory?

Wrestling with these questions (one cannot avoid sports metaphors even in scholarly writing) pits our powers of social analysis against the need to comprehend the power of institutions in society, the meaning of the media texts issuing from these institutions, and the creation of audiences participating at a distance through these powerful social rituals and institutions. These and the many specific questions addressed in the essays in this book are far more than mere "hobbyism" by academics engaging in popular slumming below the level of proper scholarly pursuits. These questions and issues are at the heart of virtually all the major concerns in social and cultural life today. Ignoring MediaSport today would be like ignoring the role of the church in the Middle Ages or ignoring the role of art in the Renaissance; large parts of society are immersed in media sports today and virtually no aspect of life is untouched by it. But the saturation with sport also makes MediaSport difficult to analyze; it is like asking a fish to analyze water. Those most involved in it often have the worst vantage point from which to comprehend it. It is essential that we "problematize" MediaSport by stepping outside it and asking questions that a remote anthropologist might ask about this strange and curious set of social texts, practices, and institutions.

WE KNOW A LOT MORE NOW BUT FAR FROM EVERYTHING: THE LITERATURE

Like many others writing in or reading this volume, I was raised in a sports-oriented family and community. Sports, sex, music, religion, and school vied for attention throughout my youth. By the time my career in media analysis developed, it had not occurred to me to explore the relation of media to sports. Then, in the early 1970s, it came to my attention that the number one annual event in American media was a sports event, the then-young Super Bowl. In examining the writing around sports and media up to that time I was shocked to find so little. There was extensive research and analysis of media and of sports, but there was simply no coherent body of literature that connected the two. Of course, the next several decades filled that gap with a vengeance as important work on sports and media proliferated. Many of the authors in this book – Wenner, Rowe, McKay, Whannel, Zillmann and Bryant, Creedon, Vande Berg, and the rest – were crucial in that effort, and the abundant literature cited in this book is the fruit of that proliferation.

Among the pioneering studies of media and sports were examinations of football on television in the form of British soccer (Buscombe,1975) and the American Super Bowl (Real, 1975). The 1980s saw intense international work. Studies of media and sport explored a variety of issues in Australia by Geoffrey Lawrence and David Rowe (1986a, 1990) and by John Goldlust (1987), in Canada by Richard Gruneau (1983) and Hart Cantelon and Jean Harvey (1987), in Great Britain by Jennifer Hargreaves (1982), John Hargreaves (1986), Alan Tomlinson and Garry Whannel (1984), and Steve Barnett (1990), in the United States by Benjamin Rader (1984), Lawrence Wenner (1989), and Allen Guttman (1978, 1986, 1988). Together they documented the awareness that sport is a powerful institutionalized ritual force accessed through the expressive potential of institutionalized media transmissions.

Within the developing literature two conflicting models, both borrowed from biology, characterize the opinions of many experts on the interaction between the institutions of media and sports (Lucas, 1984). In one model, television is a corrupting parasite that latches onto the host body, sport, and draws life support from it while giving nothing back in return (Rader, 1984). In the other model, television and sports are connected symbiotically so that each both gives and takes in the relationship, leaving each better off than it would be without the other. A growing number of sports/media critics argue vigorously for either the parasitic or symbiotic model in the case of numerous sports in the US, in England, and around the world (Whannel, 1992). Taking the modern Olympic Games as a model, what has happened in recent decades due to the institutional structures and priorities of sports and commercial media?

Massive and detailed international research projects have examined the complex and powerful place of television in the past two decades of the Olympics. A 1984 UNESCO sponsored study (Real, 1989), which I had the privilege of organizing, found great ambiguity in the sociocultural impact of the Olympics: the unifying internationalized rituals of the Olympics exist in tension with divisive nationalistic zeal among commentators and editors. An exhaustive study of the Los Angeles Games as a media event by Daniel Dayan and Elihu Katz (1992) found many positive functions. The Olympics, they concluded, constitute one of the most influential of the "high holidays" of secular culture today, creating domestic rituals in which family and close friends come together to eat special foods, share time together, and celebrate the athletic competition. Recent books on the place of television in the 1988 Seoul Olympics (Larson & Park, 1993) and the 1992 Barcelona Olympics (Moragas, Rivenburgh, & Larson, 1995) have identified in satisfying detail how the events in one city become through the mediation of communication technology and broadcast institutions a varied and intriguing television experience for people all over the world.

MediaSports interconnect vast numbers of people, even by the most conservative estimates. *Television in the Olympics* by Moragas, Rivenburgh, and Larson (1995), for example, clarifies the question of exactly how big the Olympic television audience really is. The figure of 3.5 billion viewers worldwide was widely cited during the Barcelona Games in 1992. *Television in the Olympics* notes that this would be possible only if 90 percent of the developed world watched, making 1.1 billion viewers, and 9.7 persons watched each of the 244 million television sets in the developing countries, making 2.4 billion viewers. The authors suggest a more realistic estimate of 4 to 5 people per television set in the developing world reduces the maximum potential world audience to 2.3 billion. They further suggest that realistic estimates of viewing for any single event, such as the Opening Ceremony, should be between 700 million and 1 billion, depending on such factors as local interest, timing, alternative program availability, number of viewers per set, and others. The same figure of 700 million to 1 billion is probably not exceeded by the World Cup Final.

Still, who could have imagined a century ago such a widely shared, peaceful coming together as the televised Olympics or World Cup? And is this huge involvement of individuals made possible by the institutional alignments of global sports organizations and global media parasitic or symbiotic, and what role does the postmodern context of late capitalism play?

THEMATIC ISSUES: TECHNOLOGY AND COMMERCIALISM IN MODERN SPORTS

No force has played a more central role in the MediaSport complex than commercial television and its institutionalized value system – profit-seeking, sponsorship, expanded markets, commodification, and competition. The example of steady change in the modern Olympic Games during the past one hundred years illustrates the shift from the "modernist" tradition to the "postmodern" condition. From 1896 to 1996, pressures of increasing media coverage, expanded technology, and commercial profit eroded classical Olympic ideals.

Traditional participant sports were theorized as positive influences in building character and teaching sportsmanship. In the ideals of Baron Pierre de Coubertin, who created the modern Olympic Games, we have the characteristic tenets of the classical modernism of early industrial society – the rational perfectible individual, progress, science, technology, and moral improvement (Real, 1996). With reason and technology, humankind can conquer obstacles and achieve happiness. The high hopes of Renaissance humanism, the industrial revolution, the theory of evolution, universal education and urbanization all came together in the modernist hope to create an efficient, abundant life for all, one periodically celebrated in the modern Olympic Games. This framework of Olympic ideals dominated the rhetoric of the Olympic movement from the first Athens games in 1896 until de Coubertin's death in 1937 following the Berlin games. Coubertin's successors, especially up to the death of Avery Brundage in 1975, continued the modernist ideals of amateurism and the celebration of the human body and élite physical culture as the foundations of modern Olympism.

Current postmodern theory contrasts sharply with this classical modernist view of sports media and the Olympics. Institutionalized commercial incentives in television marketing and, by association, in the expanded Olympic enterprise have shifted the emphasis. The steady escalation of media money is pervasive throughout major sports but especially obvious in the Olympics and the soccer World Cup. Rights to sell world television rights to the 2002 and 2006 World Cup were sold by soccer's ruling body, FIFA, to a private sports company in 1996 for $1 billion and $1.2 billion respectively.

Postmodernism contends that there is no longer any consensus around the modernist-defined historical conditions, human goals, and driving ideas. All is relative, commercialized, significant only in context and for the moment. Against the original well-articulated modern Olympic ideal, Jean-Francois Lyotard (1984) notes simply the demise of the modernist worldview and prospect. A countryman of de Coubertin and leading articulator of postmodernism, Lyotard ascribes the end of modernism and its replacement by postmodernism to the breakdown of the grand narratives of nineteenth-century science, reason, and progress. In their place is a sense of limits, of relativity, of varied styles and goals, of skepticism over progress and perfectibility. The idea of progress within rationalism and freedom has given way to "bricolage: the high frequency of quotations of elements from previous styles or periods (classical or modern)" (Lyotard, 1993, p. 171).

As Lyotard observes: "One can note a sort of decay in the confidence placed by the last two centuries in the idea of progress . . . in the certainty that the development of the arts, technology, knowledge and liberty would be profitable to mankind as a whole" (1993, p. 172). Too many signs point in the opposite direction in Lyotard's judgment: "Neither economic nor political liberalism, nor the various Marxisms, emerge from the sanguinary last two centuries free from the suspicion of crimes against mankind" (p. 172). The development of techno-sciences can increase disease as well as fight it, can destabilize human populations as well as protect.

Sports media in the Olympics and World Cup today retain a gloss of international idealism but are really organized around the institutions of late capitalism and the resulting values of postmodernism.

TRADITIONAL SPORTS IDEALS VERSUS THE CONSUMER CULTURE OF LATE CAPITALISM

The world of sports in the age of mass media has been transformed from nineteenth century amateur recreational participation to late twentieth century spectator-centered technology and business. The older traditions were not perfect, any more than current practices are entirely imperfect. The shifts are well illustrated in the Olympic movement. Even more than in other sports, aristocratic privilege, not commercial sponsorship, sustained the Olympic movement in its well-documented first decades, with no patronage more generous than from de Coubertin himself (Guttman, 1992; J. Lucas 1980, 1992; MacAloon, 1981). But when the games after World War I began to gather momentum as major international events with increasing press coverage and general recognition, public and commercial support became more prominent in maintaining the Olympics, first from sponsoring cities and later from television rights fees and corporate sponsorship. These institutions – the modern city-state and commercial businesses – could not pretend to float above the necessities of material existence as had the previous Olympic aristocracy.

With the release of Leni Riefenstahl's two-part *Olympia* film (Graham, 1986), as well as experimentation with television at the Berlin games, the intrusion of the moving image into the Olympics began. This increased from mid-century with the 1956 Melbourne organizing committee being the first to sell television rights to the games (R. Lucas, 1984). As broadcast networks in the United States and Europe boycotted the rights sale, the programming in the United States resulted in only six pre-recorded, half-hour programs presented on a scattering of independent stations; but the principle of commercial Olympic television had been established, and the Olympics would never again be the same. Perhaps no other single force has contributed more to the postmodernizing of the Olympics than television coverage in general and television rights fees in particular. They have created a new relationship between the public and the games at the same time as they have brought the dynamics of "late capitalism" (Mandel, 1975) into the Olympic movement.

The television rights fees for the Summer Olympics have increased several hundredfold in the second half of the twentieth century. The United States commercial networks have generally paid some 50 to 75 percent of the total Olympic revenue from television rights and production costs. Table 2.1 shows, in millions of US dollars, what the fees paid by US television have been (R. Lucas, 1984; J. Lucas, 1992).

After mid-century, television revenues quickly replaced Olympic ticket sales as the principle source of income from the Games. In 1960 television provided only 1 of every 400 US dollars of the cost of hosting the Summer Olympics. In 1972, 1 of every 50 dollars was from television; in 1980, 1 of every 15 dollars; and by 1984, 1 of every 2 dollars of Olympic host costs were paid for from television revenues (Real, 1989).

Table 2.1   US Television Olympic Rights Fees in Millions of Dollars, 1960–2008

Summer Games			*Winter Games*		
1960	Rome	CBS = 0.6	Squaw Valley	CBS = 0.05
1964	Tokyo	NBC = 1.6	Innsbruck	ABC = 0.59
1968	Mexico City	ABC = 4.5	Grenoble	ABC = 2.5
1972	Munich	ABC = 12.5	Sapporo	NBC = 6.4
1976	Montreal	ABC = 25.0	Innsbruck	ABC= 10.0
1980	Moscow	NBC = 95.5	Lake Placid	ABC = 15.5
1984	Los Angeles	ABC = 225.0	Sarajevo	ABC = 91.5
1988	Seoul	NBC = 305.0	Calgary	ABC = 309.0
1992	Barcelona	NBC = 401.0	Albertville	CBS = 243.0
1994			Lillehammer	CBS = 300.0
1996	Atlanta	NBC = 456.0		
1998			Nagano	CBS = 375.0
2000	Sydney	NBC = 705.0		
2002			Salt Lake City	NBC = 545.0
2004		NBC = 793.0		
2006				NBC = 613.0
2008		NBC = 894.0		

This immersion of the Olympics in the MediaSport world of television exposure and rights fees has been followed by rapidly increasing commercial sponsorship of the Games and teams themselves. The Olympic Program (TOP), formed in 1982 by the IOC, has combined with the marketing consortium International Sports and Leisure (ISL) to sell corporate sponsorships at a level approaching a 50–50 split with income from television rights. TOP contracts with Coca-Cola, Eastman Kodak, 3M, Ricoh, Matsushita, *Sports Illustrated*, Visa, and US Postal Express in 1992 brought in more than $120 million to the IOC (J. Lucas, 1992, p. 79). The 1984 Los Angeles Games pioneered this approach, even selling rights to one company to advertise itself as the "Official Olympic Specimen Carrier" because it transported the urine samples of athletes to laboratories. Television exposure and commercialization prepared the environment for this additional corporate commercial sponsorship, sponsorship which brought $179 million in 1996 to the IOC from one transnational corporation alone, the Coca-Cola company based in Atlanta (J. Lucas, 1992).

The intrusion of late capitalism's commercialism into MediaSports through television and sponsorships signals the economic shift from the modern to the postmodern Games. Echoed by hundreds of other critics, British historian Steven Barnett (1990, p. 134) warns: "The Olympic Games could be hijacked by an obsessively competitive American television industry, whose money will eventually corrupt completely the original spirit." The changes from the aristocratic but idealistic modern games of de Coubertin to the pragmatically profit-centered postmodern games point to the qualities of "late capitalism" as described by Fredric Jameson in his widely debated analysis of postmodernism.

EMERGING PROBLEM: THE COMMODIFICATION OF MEDIASPORTS IN POSTMODERN TIMES

Jameson (1991, p. xviii), following Adorno, Horkheimer, and the Frankfurt School, places us in a period called "late capitalism," a period which Jameson also refers to as "'multinational capitalism,' 'spectacle or image society,' 'media capitalism,' 'the world system,' even 'postmodernism' itself." Jameson emphasizes that this conception of postmodernism "is a historical rather than a merely stylistic one . . . I cannot stress too greatly the radical distinction between a view for which the postmodern is one (optional) style among many others available and one which seeks to grasp it as the cultural dominant of the logic of late capitalism" (pp. 45–6). Jameson argues that "culture is today no longer endowed with the relative autonomy it once enjoyed" (p. 48). In this sense, the (post)modern Olympic Games in all their commercialism are not aberrations but logical expressions of the age in which they exist. For those suspicious of the postmodern as jargon, Jameson concedes: "I occasionally get just as tired of the slogan 'postmodern' as anyone else, but . . . I wonder whether any other concept can dramatize the issues in quite so effective and economical a fashion" (p. 418).

Postmodern MediaSports pay off. In fact, the capital produced by the postmodern era's media has carried the Olympic movement through two major financial crises since World War II. First, having been near bankruptcy in the decade before, the IOC officially declared in 1970 that all television revenues belonged to the IOC rather than, as previously, to the host city. Second, when Tehran's was the only other bid to host the 1984 Games, the IOC was forced to accept the commercially sponsored 1984 Los Angeles plan without the usual guarantee of public monies. Both commercial turns proved so lucrative to the IOC that Olympic leadership is now as attuned to economic progress and success as it is to athletic achievement. These commercial changes, combined with Olympic hostage-taking and boycotts made attractive because of the Olympics' media prominence, led Jeffrey Segrave and Donald Chu in 1981 (p. 363) to conclude: "The politicization and commercialization of the modern Olympics has reached such a crescendo that few could deny that the idealistic intentions of the Games have become increasingly immersed in a sea of propaganda."

As technologies of communication have made possible the incredible media outreach of media sports such as the Olympics, they have also brought about an increasing commodification of everything associated with sports. "Commodification" reduces the value of any act or object to only its monetary exchange value, ignoring historical, artistic, or relational added values. In addition, commodification has a fetishistic quality in which the commodities, because they represent commercial advantage, take on a bloated psychological importance to the individual or group. In recent decades the postmodern Olympics have become a virtual circus of commodity values and fetishes. Corporate logos and sponsorship abound, Olympic memorabilia multiply, merchandising and marketing pre-occupy officials, shoe sponsors become powerful decision-makers, promotions begin months before the Games and suffuse their media presentation, and Olympic leaders and the public learn to accept this commodification as if it were part of the (post)modern Olympic creed.

THE BRAVE NEW WORLD: COMMUNICATION TECHNOLOGIES AND "PASTICHE" STYLE

As sports media are run as profit-seeking businesses using the most advanced technologies, they utilize marketing and the "pastiche" style characteristic of postmodern art. Saturation with technologies of communication is a characteristic feature of the postmodern landscape. Technology and media can be defined as any extension of the human sensory apparatus, and after we create them, they create us (McLuhan, 1964). Cyberpunk literature is only a more extreme imagining of the freewheeling digitized, imaged, on-line existence which comes more and more to occupy real daily life. Within this plugged-in environment, the greatest concentrations of electronic technology in the history of the world have not been the Gulf War, despite its popular characterization as the Nintendo war, nor the space launchings with all their futuristic accoutrements. Rather, the now biennial Olympic Games attract the most breathtaking display of our technological capacity to capture, refine, and transmit messages of all types and to all places.

Jameson (1991, p. 16) describes our media and art as engendering "the well-nigh universal practice today of what may be called pastiche." Pastiche is the combining together in one work of the disparate styles and contents from what would normally be presented as quite different artistic eras and messages. High classical combines with art deco and neo-impressionism in the same eclectic architectural or other creative work. Traditional distinctions between high art and popular culture disappear as all become "mass-mediated culture" (Real, 1977). Feminist critics and cultural studies note the characteristic hodgepodge of style that marks virtually all of television: the strip of programming juxtaposes programs, advertisements, promotions, and credits in an array of formats from news to comedy, from cartoons to music videos to sports to movies. The viewer surfs through these channels by remote control, making the sequence of television viewing a diffuse pastiche of cultural choices (Kaplan, 1988).

Marketing impetus and pastiche style mark all media sports. For example, the IOC's media policies have been directed by the goal of making the Games available "to the widest possible audience." While this dictates against reducing television coverage to a pay-per-view event, among other things, it has reinforced the commercial incentives to cooperate with television, film, radio, newspaper, magazine, and other media sources to consistently expand the "spectacle" aspects of this global media event. In recent decades, more media personnel than athletes have been officially accredited to attend the Games. Opening and closing ceremonies have become big-time show business without parallel. The athletic competitions occurring in the Games are overlaid with promotions, commercial interruptions, sponsor logos, celebrity chasing, abrupt transitions, and entertainment packaging emblematic of what proto-postmodernist Guy Debord (1970) decried as the "Society of the Spectacle."

The most advanced video, audio, and textual processing occurs in overwhelming abundance in the Olympic Games, even from the nearly arctic conditions of the Winter Olympics, such as at Lillehammer in 1994. Transnational corporations develop and employ their most refined technologies to bring strikingly differentiated versions of Olympic events to viewers scattered in every part of the globe. In 1936 Leni Riefenstahl took two years to edit her 4-hour film record of the Games; in 1960 CBS flew films from Rome to New York to squeeze in some delayed same-day television coverage. Today, simultaneous events from widely dispersed venues are instantly relayed to broadcast centers and digitized, rearranged, and transmitted in quite different versions to different national audiences through a complex array of cameras, video decks, editors, signal processors and compressors, microwave relays, satellite feeds, and related technologies all backed with massive managerial, legal, and economic systems. Science fiction fantasies of technological capabilities become real and transparent as media consumers everywhere access the competitions and entertainments mounted as Olympic spectacles. In addition to the television technology, data and text transmissions speed off to print media, and the very record-keeping and coordination of the Games themselves are based on massive arrays of computerized technology and organization.

This is precisely the technologically saturated environment that Jean Baudrillard (1983) describes as the postmodern world of "simulacra," or simulations and representations, a world made up of copies of which there is no original. Walter Benjamin's famous essay (1969) on "The Work of Art in the Age of Mechanical Reproduction" anticipated the problem facing the IOC: How do the Olympics maintain their integrity as a work of human creation in the context of endless media manipulation?

The Olympic events lend themselves to a pastiche style. They are not a single sport or event like the World Cup or Super Bowl. The Olympics are many events occurring simultaneously. Nationalist interests dictate that while Great Britain may prefer equestrian events, India wants field hockey and team handball. When a national broadcaster buys Olympic rights, the host broadcaster provides a clean video–audio feed from each event, to which the national service may add its own commentator and then may transmit live or may edit and transmit on a delayed basis. It is "designer" television in which the original event becomes customized for each of scores of different audiences. The Olympic ideal of uniting the peoples of the world around a single experience becomes fragmented and nationalized when converted for local use. In this regard, Official Olympic historian John Lucas (1992, p. 42) argues that he would change only one current Olympic ritual: the playing of the national anthems for winners. National anthems are played more than 400 times during the Summer Games, further tipping the scale away from internationalism and toward fragmented nationalism.

While television channels attempt to present the Olympics in coherent patterns and the viewer can make some sense of bewilderingly diverse Olympic messages, the Olympics are clearly a "pastiche" of cultural artifacts in the Jameson sense. The grand reliance on tradition to anchor what the Olympics are and mean may sound rather like Jameson's warning: "The producers of culture have nowhere to turn but to the past: the imitation of dead styles, speech through all the masks and voices stored up in the imaginary museum of a now global culture" (1991, p. 18). This historicism results in "the random cannibalization of all the styles of the past, the play of random stylistic allusion, and . . . the increasing primacy of the 'neo'" in the "new spatial logic of the simulacrum" (p. 18). The fast-paced Olympic television presentation of multiple events with on-screen graphics and announcer commentary is the opposite of the classical coherent single-author focused artistic experience. Underlying it is the commercial incentive to maximize viewing audience by promotion and titillation, by superlatives and historical allusions, by giving the audience something even fancier than it had hoped for.

ARE MEDIASPORTS PURE SIMULATION IMPOSED ON THE PUBLIC?

Sports do suggest distinctions that postmodernism may otherwise ignore. The sporting event, such as an Olympic competition, has an externally situated reality that pure entertainment programming does not; in this it resembles news programming more than scripted drama. Michael Oriard in his excellent historical and critical study, *Reading Football: How the Popular Press Created an American Spectacle* (1993), has argued this point against Jameson. Jameson (1979), following Baudrillard, contends that there are no primary texts in mass culture, only repetitions. Against this, Oriard sees football as a primary text, ultimately unpredictable no matter how complete its packaging may be. Never denying the hype and manipulation of late capitalism, Oriard nonetheless argues that "the games themselves are authentic in ways that no commodity can be" (p. 9): real people perform real acts, are injured, and win or lose in a story that has a reality beyond that of popular movies, music, and literature and is the source of the sport's cultural power. His detailed account of the negotiations in the late nineteenth century that resulted in what North Americans know as football manages to foreground this essential reality of the human contest, a contest that was being variously interpreted by journalists and others at the time.

Football was, therefore, not artificially imposed by a single commercial power as seen in pure postmodernism. Football's cultural narratives and meanings, Oriard argues, were not imposed or arbitrary but "were created by an interplay of producers (rule makers, college authorities, players); consumers (spectators and readers); intermediary interpreters (sportswriters); a medium of communication (the daily press and popular periodicals); political, social, economic, and cultural contexts; and the inherent qualities of the game itself" (p. 119). No single interest owned football in the beginning; today its media presentation is bundled into a pastiche alongside the most disparate alternatives. Football's high holiday, the Super Bowl (Real, 1977), like the Olympics, has a commercial infrastructure and is suffused with pastiche style and the drive to commodify. But in the case of football, there is a primary text – the game – and it was not imposed from outside onto the public by a single vested interest.

"DEEP PLAY": RITUAL CONNECTIONS BETWEEN THE EVENT, THE TECHNOLOGY, AND THE FAN

Although it is illegal and occasionally gets raided, the cockfight in the Balinese village attracts great interest as fighting cocks are pitted against each other amid considerable excitement, side-taking, and betting. As one cock slices another to death with the razor sharp blade attached to his claw, much is revealed about culture. The Balinese cockfight reveals and reinforces group alliances within the village, relative positions of status, willingness to risk often unwise bets, and, more than any other event, how villagers interact and understand themselves. They are engaged in "deep play."

(Geertz, 1973)

The most intense involvement of a viewer in an event has been labeled "deep play" by Clifford Geertz (1973). He developed the theory of deep play in his descriptions of the involvement of Balinese spectators in the popular ritual cockfight, an event in which social order and large bets are often at stake. Historically and culturally, the involvement of the sports fan in a mediated sporting event closely parallels this deep play. The sports fan has many conscious motives (Wenner & Gantz, 1989, and this volume) but also less conscious mythic goals. Watching sports on television illustrates how ritual participation today occurs in a technological, fully commercialized wonderland. The obvious difference between a Balinese cockfight and a televised ballgame is in the array of technology and advertising that mediates between the subject and the event. Given this, do media sports qualify as "deep play" in Geertz's meaning of the term?

Geertz (1973, p. 432) borrows the phrase from Jeremy Bentham to characterize "play in which the stakes are so high that it is ... irrational for men to engage in it at all." If a man wagers half his life's savings on an even bet, the disutility of his potential loss is greater than the utility of his potential gain. In deep play, both parties are "in over their heads" (p. 432), and the participants stand collectively to reap net pain rather than net pleasure. Bentham considered such activity immoral and preferably illegal. Geertz, however, notes that there are symbolic as well as utilitarian issues in deep play: "Much more is at stake than material gain: namely esteem, honor, dignity, respect ... status" (p. 433). Psychological as well as financial stakes increase the meaningfulness of it all, and Geertz calls on Max Weber to remind us that "the imposition of meaning on life is the major and primary condition of human existence" (p. 434).

The deep fan of contemporary media sports bears remarkable similarities to the participant in Geertz's Balinese cockfight. First, both the cockfight and sports provide double meanings and metaphors that reach out to other aspects of social life. Second, both are elaborately organized with written rules and umpires, although one can grant that presenting Wimbledon tennis to the world considerably outstrips organizing a local cockfight. Third, betting plays a major role in each; the Balinese wager serious amounts, and American sports attract an estimated $41 billion a year in gambling (Wilstein, 1993). Fourth, violence heightens the drama of each. Fifth, the presence of status hierarchies surpasses money in importance at the event, with corporate and political elites assuming central roles; competition between high status individuals makes the game "deeper" to Geertz. Sixth, each of the two, the cockfight and the media sporting event "makes nothing happen"; neither produces goods or directly affects the welfare of the people.

The big game on television works almost exactly like the cockfight: "The cockfight renders ordinary, everyday experience comprehensible by presenting it in terms of acts and objects which have had their practical consequences removed and been reduced (or, if one prefers, raised) to the level of sheer appearances, where their meaning can be more powerfully articulated and more exactly perceived" (Geertz, 1973, p. 443). A close Olympic finals competition, a well-matched World Cup game, a British FA Cup final between Liverpool and Arsenal (Barnett, 1990; Hornby, 1992), a college or professional season-ending championship game in your favorite sport, many of these imitate the cockfight in presenting "death, masculinity, rage, pride, loss, beneficence, chance – and, ordering them into an encompassing structure" (Geertz, 1973, p. 443). These events ironically become real in an ideational sense. Deep fan learns what the Balinese learns from the cockfight, "what his culture's ethos and his private sensibility . . . look like when spelled out externally in a collective text" (p. 449).

Symbolically, then, the deep play of the participant in a Balinese cockfight has become diffused in a pluralistic society into the varied spectator sports available for live or mediated participation by today's deep fan. Sports activities create between 1 and 2 percent of the gross national product of the United States (Samuelson, 1989, p. 49). But its symbolic or expressive importance is far greater than that for many because it provides a language or interpretive structure that at once reflects, explains, and interprets social life. MediaSport today operates in a specific historical arrangement of technology, advertising, and consumerism. These mass-mediated sports give the deep fan crucial expressive, liminal, cathartic, ideational mechanisms and experiences. They represent, celebrate, and interpret contemporary social life, warts and all. Understanding the ritual dimensions of media culture is essential to understanding how humans act as they are interconnected by MediaSport institutions, technology, texts, and experience.

FURTHER INQUIRY: THE BALANCE SHEET ON HOW MEDIASPORT IS GOOD OR BAD FOR SPORTS

How have sports and media changed in the postmodern era of MediaSport? When the 1984 Opening Ceremony featured eighty-four pianos playing Gershwin, Alan Tomlinson was led to conclude: "Televisual images do linger on; and those of the Los Angeles Olympics of 1984 can only be said to owe more to the spirit of Liberace than to that of de Coubertin" (1989, p. 7–9).

In essence, the postmodern culture of late capitalism links the commercial incentive of the producers of media sports with the conditioned pastiche tastes of the MediaSport consumer in a deep play spectacle of nationalistic technological representation. Assessing all the evidence, is television making significant positive contributions to sports? Yes. Are there problems and could television do better? Yes, again. Is television a parasite sucking life out of MediaSports? Probably not. However, the symbiosis between them that benefits both sports and media is a dynamic one that can easily become unbalanced and that warrants extensive further inquiry.

The crucial distinction is that media such as television are only one part, albeit the most prominent part, of a vast cultural seismic shift from the "modern" world of a century ago, with its simple Olympic ideals, to the "postmodern" world of today with its relativism, commercialism, technological saturation and diversity. To imply that television works alone to corrupt media sports is to over-simplify to the point of misrepresentation. But to say that the televised media sports – such as the Olympics, the Super Bowl, the Oscars, the World Cup, and others – play a leading role in celebrating and shaping our global culture is to begin to approach a realistic sense of the complex place of MediaSport in the world of today.

The institutions of MediaSport structure for us a world of excitement and mythical deep play. But they also shift us away from many positive humanistic values. They inundate us with commercial messages inseparable from the amoral condition of postmodern exploitation. In limited ways within a balanced and rational human life, MediaSports can make significant positive contributions. At the same time, not because of individual failures but because of institutionalized capitalist priorities, there is the danger of mindless, misdirected adoration and devotion toward activities and heroes that can so quickly become violent, exploitive, greedy, and narcissistic. Being critically self-aware of the negatives of media sports, coupled with an appreciation of the power and joy of those same media sports, provides a minimal basis for acceptance of media sports within a potentially wholesome, balanced, and satisfying human life. MediaSport scholarship provides the necessary scoresheets for these issues of cultural sensibilities surrounding sports in a media age.

MediaSport Studies: Key Research and Emerging Issues[1]

Kathleen M. Kinkema &
Janet C. Harris

Media representations of sport have exploded in the past fifteen years. Today's average American household receives approximately thirty-three broadcast and cable channels, and there are occasions when as many as ten sporting events are televised simultaneously. Over 8,000 sporting events are televised each year, an average of twenty-two per day (Gorman & Calhoun, 1994; Helitzer, 1996). Certainly much of what we know and understand about sport is shaped by the media. Relationships between mass media and sports are a prominent area of study for scholars of both mass communication and sport. Recent examples of this work include a special issue of *The Journal of International Communication* and several monographs dealing with media and sport relationships (Baughman, 1995; Blain, Boyle, & O'Donnell, 1993; Creedon, 1994b; R. Jackson, 1989; Larson & Park, 1993; "Olympic Communication", 1995; Wenner, 1989a; Whannel, 1992).

Work on sport and the mass media concerns three major topics: production of mediated sport texts, messages or content of mediated sport texts, and audience interaction with mediated sport texts (Kinkema & Harris, 1992; Wenner, 1989b). These form the major sections of this review, but at the outset it is important to acknowledge the lack of clear demarcation between them. Considerable overlap exists, and certainly it is difficult and somewhat artificial to discuss them separately, although efforts are made to explore linkages.

Most of the studies examined in the following pages focus on televised sport programming, although occasional references are made to studies of print media and other mass cultural products. Works dealing with other mass media portrayals of sport such as sport literature or sport films are generally beyond the scope of this report.

PRODUCTION OF MEDIATED SPORT

Production of mediated sport involves the political and economic context in which sport programming originates as well as the technical processes used to produce it. It is important to recognize that media sport texts are carefully crafted and engineered. Both live and taped segments are used to organize sport experiences for viewers. Like all media texts, they are shaped by a variety of forces including production conventions and techniques, politics and economics of broadcasting and print media production, and ideologies of the producers. The technical production of mediated sport cannot be isolated from the political and economic context within which it occurs, and it has only been very recently that investigators have examined them together. Technical production processes have received more scholarly attention than the political and economic context, although televised sport in the global marketplace is a burgeoning area of inquiry.

Political and Economic Context

Relationships between the sport industry and the mass media industry are not simply matters of mutual interests and dependencies among advertisers, media organizations, sport organizations, and the public (Bellamy, 1989; Bogart, 1995; Briggs, 1994; Butler, 1994; Gorman & Calhoun, 1994; Lobmeyer & Weidinger, 1992; Real & Mechikoff, 1992; Whannel, 1992; Wilson, 1994). The development of television, including cable and regional sports broadcasting, has especially contributed to the complexity of these relationships. Jhally (1989) and Wenner (1989b) refer to these relationships as the sport/media complex, arguing that spectator sports and the media, particularly television, have become so enmeshed that it is virtually impossible to separate the two. As an extreme example, owners of sport franchises are sometimes owners or shareholders of media corporations. For example, the Atlanta Braves baseball team is owned by Ted Turner, who also owns cable stations WTBS (which broadcasts most of the Braves games), CNN, and TNT. Turner Broadcasting System has recently become part of an even larger Time-Warner media conglomerate (Butler, 1994; Creedon, Cramer, & Granitz,1994).

The right to broadcast sporting events must be purchased from those who control them – sport leagues, team owners, National Collegiate Athletic Association, International Olympic Committee, and the like. Networks, in turn, sell advertising to sponsors on national, regional, and local levels aimed at specific demographic groups. Advertising has become an increasingly complex part of the sport and media relationship. Indirect advertising, including signage at arenas, on athletic equipment, and on athletes themselves contributes significant revenue to teams, sport organizations and players. In addition to bringing in advertising revenue, networks justify paying exorbitant rights fees in order to use sports coverage as a place to promote their prime-time programs. However, there is not much evidence suggesting this works. Eastman and Otteson (1994), in their analysis of ratings for prime-time shows promoted during the 1992 Winter and Summer Olympics, found little support for the promotional value of Olympic programming.

Soaring rights fees paid for big-time sporting events and advertising revenues generated by the broadcasts are obvious examples of the influence of television on sport media relationships. The NBC network paid $456 million for the American broadcasting rights to the 1996 Olympic Games in Atlanta, expecting that 90 percent of US households (approximately 200 million viewers) would tune into the games. Networks can afford to pay increasingly more expensive broadcast rights because of the huge sums they can command for commercial spots. Advertisers for US coverage of the 1996 Olympic Games had purchased close to $700 million worth of commercial spots just prior to the opening, at a rate of about $500,000 for 30 seconds (Carlson, 1996; Impoco, 1996; Poole, 1996).

It appears that the television industry holds the upper hand in relationships with élite spectator sport because the money paid for broadcast rights is an indispensable source of revenue for the sport industry. For example, over 50 percent of the total income for teams in the NFL comes from television rights fees (Bogart, 1995; Lobmeyer & Weidinger, 1992). At the same time television ratings for some sporting events, such as Major League Baseball, National Football League games, and National Collegiate Athletic Association men's basketball games have dropped slightly over the past few seasons. For example, it is thought that the CBS network lost between $500 and $600 million during their most recent 4-year $1.1 billion contract with Major League Baseball (Bellamy, 1993; Eastman & Meyer, 1989; Gorman & Calhoun, 1994). As audiences for network sports programming shrink in the face of competition from cable stations, networks have begun giving production responsibilities to independent producers in an attempt to reduce costs (Gorman & Calhoun, 1994; Wilson, 1994). One example is Raycom, which selects and produces games with high regional appeal. They pay less for rights to games than the networks, and they use non-union, freelance crews. The games, because of their strong regional appeal, generally attract large audiences.

The sport industry, in the face of softening rights fees, has also begun to adopt strategies to ensure its continued economic livelihood (Bellamy, 1993; Gorman & Calhoun, 1994). Some professional leagues, such as the National Basketball Association, have instituted player and team salary caps. Many schools in the National Collegiate Athletic Association rely heavily on revenues from television to finance their athletic programs and often make concessions to the networks in an effort to gain increased television exposure. For example, NCAA men's basketball games often have starting times of 9 pm EST or later to accommodate television. One of the most feared NCAA sanctions is denial of television exposure. The length of both the Winter and Summer Olympic Games has been expanded to sixteen days in order to cover at least three weekend viewing periods (Lobmeyer & Weidinger, 1992; Real & Mechikoff, 1992).

Some professional teams have also begun producing their own television broadcasts instead of selling rights to local stations. The Seattle Mariners franchise in Major League Baseball cleared close to $3 million in 1992 using this strategy, and the Boston Celtics of the National Basketball Association own their own radio and television stations (Creedon, Cramer, & Granitz, 1994; Gorman & Calhoun,

1994). In addition, Olympic Games governing bodies and intercollegiate sport governing bodies are actively seeking corporate sponsors. For example, Georgia Institute of Technology recently received $5.5 million from McDonald's Corporation in exchange for naming a square block of the campus "McDonald's Center at Alexander Memorial Coliseum," putting the McDonald's golden arches on the basketball floor, tickets, and programs, and allowing McDonald's to operate restaurants and concessions on the Georgia Tech campus (Blumenstyk, 1995).

The growth of cable television, regional broadcasting, closed-circuit viewing, and pay-per-view programming have had, and will continue to have, significant effects on the media and sport industries in terms of sport programming, public policy, and economic issues related to the media production of sport. Surprisingly, this is an area that has not received much attention from scholars (Eastman & Meyer, 1989; Gorman & Calhoun, 1994; Williams, 1994).

Analyses of mediated sport production processes have attempted to show the manner in which processes involved in the production of sport for television are manifestations of political, economic, and ideological pressures and limits. There are several excellent ethnographies of television production of sporting events. Gruneau's (1989) case study of Canadian Broadcasting Corporation coverage of a World Cup downhill ski race at Whistler Mountain in British Columbia, MacNeill's (1995, 1996b) ethnography of the Canadian Television Network's coverage of the 1988 Calgary Olympics, and Stoddart's (1994) analysis of Australian network coverage of professional golf all show how production practices were shaped by the various political, economic, organizational, and technical factors. All three of these studies found that media productions of sporting events are neither objective technical representations of live sporting events, nor are they ideologically deterministic creations orchestrated by an all-powerful media conglomerate. In all cases, the complex processes associated with producing a live sports event involved shared decision-making among several levels of workers under tremendous pressures and time constraints. Workers were often unable to articulate their rationale for making particular production choices. For example, respondents to Gruneau's questioning about production decisions often replied that decisions were based on instinct.

The production of sport has also been examined in the context of gender and race. Theberge and Cronk (1986) showed that the organizational structure for news gathering and reporting in a newspaper sports department contributed to the underrepresentation of women's sport coverage. Ordman and Zillmann (1994) found that female sports reporters (for magazines and radio) were perceived as less competent than their male counterparts by both male and female respondents.

Several studies have shown that women have been substantially excluded from the production ranks. The few female members of production staffs are sometimes denied access to locker-rooms, and they are often victims of sexual harassment, condescension, and even physical threats when they do gain entry (Cramer, 1994; Creedon, 1994a; Eberhard & Meyers, 1988; Kane & Disch, 1993). Interviews with female journalists and broadcasters reveal a sense of cautious optimism that opportunities for women in the production of mediated sport are expanding (Cramer, 1994).

Racial and ethnic minorities are also underrepresented in the production of mediated sport. In an analysis of television coverage of several international sporting events over a 5 year period, it was found that 92 percent of the commentators were white, 8 percent were black, and there were no Latino-Hispanic or Asian commentators. Interviewers were also predominantly white (52 percent) (Sabo, Jansen, Tate, Duncan, & Leggett, 1996).

Global Dimensions

Elite, commercial sports have become global enterprises because those who control sport are constantly looking for new ways to increase profits by selling broadcast rights and licensed products, and cultivating spectator interest. In addition, corporate interests use sport as a vehicle for introducing products and services around the world (Bellamy, 1993; Coakley, 1994; Williams, 1994). Larson and Park (1993) suggest that corporate sponsors use the Olympics to exploit an association between their corporate image and Olympic ideals of world peace and friendship. Although globalization is certainly not a new phenomenon, increases in numbers of transnational corporations, global communication technologies, and international competitions are prominent forces in the global expansion of sport.

Production of the Olympic Games comprises the bulk of research focusing on global dimensions of mediated sport (Brownell, 1995; Larson & Park, 1993; Larson & Rivenburgh, 1991; MacNeill, 1995, 1996b; Real, 1996; Real & Mechikoff, 1992; Rivenburgh, 1995). Olympic planning, event scheduling, and venue design are often dependent on the needs of television (Larson & Park, 1993; Louw, 1995). As previously mentioned, broadcast rights to the games are a major source of revenue. The payment of rights fees establishes a hierarchy among competing networks broadcasting the games, and global telecast rights have long been dominated by US commercial networks. The Olympic Games, as a single event, are broadcast simultaneously around the world to approximately three billion viewers. Many nations receive similar content because they rely on an international feed provided by the host broadcasters. According to the rules of the Olympic Games, the host nation must provide a live television signal consisting of "objective" visual coverage of all events, including necessary background sounds and effects. Various rights-holding broadcasters are then free to apply their own set of editorial preferences (e.g., amount of coverage, content of coverage, use of commercials, broadcast styles). For example, Brownell (1995) shows how national media production styles impact on the way in which a "global" event is actually "localized." She found that distinctive features of the Chinese telecast of the 1992 Barcelona Olympic Games resulted from a number of historical, cultural, and economic factors.

Media influence in the articulation of local and global sport relationships has become an important and lively area of inquiry within sport studies (Donnelly, 1996; Harris, 1995; Maguire, 1993b, 1994b). The role of the media has been investigated in the emergence of American football in Western Europe and basketball in England, Americanization of hockey in Canada and sport in Australia, the articulation of national identities in the Australia/England cricket rivalry, soccer in Britain, and the political, economic, and cultural changes in Korea that resulted from the Seoul Olympic Games (Goldberg & Wagg, 1991; Gruneau & Whitson, 1993; Jackson, 1994; Larson & Park, 1993; Maguire, 1990, 1991, 1993a, 1994a; McKay & Miller, 1991; Rowe, Lawrence, Miller & McKay, 1994; Williams, 1994).

Maguire (1991, 1993b) argues that the development of American football in Western Europe can be accounted for by interrelationships within the "media-sport production complex" (Jhally, 1989; Wenner, 1989b) comprised of sports organizations, media and marketing organizations, and media personnel. These interrelationships vary in nature and form within and between continents. For example, the emergence of American football in England results from an interweaving of interests from the NFL, Anheuser-Busch, and a British television company.

Technical Production

Although media institutions claim to present athletic events objectively, they engage in considerable selective construction and interpretation in the production phase before their programs reach an audience. Studies of technical aspects of production of mediated sport have evolved from simple descriptions of techniques used in broadcasting (Butler, 1994; Williams, 1977), to examinations of meaning-making aspects of various production techniques (Buscombe, 1975), to current investigations that attempt to situate discussions of production techniques in the context of various sorts of social arrangements and ideologies. For example, MacNeill's (1988) analyses of a televised women's body building championship and a televised aerobic workout show how particular aspects of patriarchal ideology were reproduced in these media texts. Camera angles and framing, use of scan, zoom, and focus tended to emphasize sexuality in aerobics and physicality in body-building. Objectification of female bodies was particularly evident in the aerobics program. The commentary reaffirmed traditional notions of femininity and sexual attraction for both sports.

Producers of mediated sport are recreating an athletic event in order to attract an audience and entertain spectators (Butler, 1994). This has important implications for the form of sports coverage. One of the most important techniques is storytelling, or narrative. Narratives are self-consciously employed by the media to dramatize things (Butler, 1994; Carlson, 1996; Chalip, 1992; Gruneau, 1989; Harris & Hills, 1993; Hilliard, 1994; Impoco, 1996; MacNeill, 1996b; Muller, 1995; O'Connor & Boyle, 1993; Oriard, 1993; Poole, 1996; Remnick, 1996; Swenson, 1995; Tudor, 1992; Whannel, 1982, 1990). The President of NBC Sports, Dick Ebersol, discussing NBC's upcoming coverage of the 1996 Atlanta Olympic Games stated "Story-telling is the absolute key . . . even more important than who wins or loses . . . We want to tell a story, tell it well and move on" (Poole, 1996, p. 2B). As part of their Olympic pre-production process the NBC network sent six teams of researchers and journalists to forty states and thirty countries to gather information for background features on competing athletes and nations, and Olympic history (Impoco, 1996). This allowed NBC to present targeted athletes as more robust characters, placed in historical context.

Television sports coverage exhibits many of the same melodramatic elements that characterize soap operas, and thus have been dubbed the "male soap opera" (O'Connor & Boyle, 1993; Poynton & Hartley, 1990). Stereotyped characters and storylines, creation and resolution of suspense or drama as a central plot unfolds, and exploration of particular themes are components of narrative that are often present in media portrayals of sport (Harris & Hills, 1993; Whannel, 1982). Muller

(1995) used a narrative framework to show how the media shaped the drama that developed around the trading of superstar NFL quarterback Joe Montana from the San Francisco 49ers to the Kansas City Chiefs.

Media sport narratives are usually framed around the question "Who will win?" Butler (1994) suggests that if a game becomes so lopsided that this question is answered, the game runs the risk of television death as viewers switch channels, and networks shift to another game (common practice in broadcasts of NFL football and NCAA men's basketball).

One technique that is increasingly used by networks to create and maintain a dramatic storyline is to combine live and taped segments. Producers can shape a story by going back and forth between live action and taped segments, often without the knowledge of television viewers (Gruneau, 1989; Poole, 1996). This allows for more choices so that the network can focus on the most dramatic events, and place the most popular events during primetime viewing periods. Taped background information about athletes can also be inserted to enhance dramatic appeal. The NBC television network coined the term "plausibly live" to refer to their use of this technique in the coverage of the 1996 Atlanta Olympic Games (Carlson, 1996; Impoco, 1996).

One of the reasons that sport narratives are so successful is that closure to the story is often incomplete. Most popular television sporting events consist of a season, or series of games leading to a championship. Daily or weekly games resolve the "Who will win?" question for a particular day, but they leave open the larger question of "Who will win?" over the course of a season. Butler (1994) hypothesizes that the lack of a definite season and final championship may contribute to the relatively small television audience for sports such as golf and tennis, but there is scant evidence to support this.

In summary, it is clear that there are important relationships between sport organizations and media institutions. Presently, the mass media industry appears to have more power to reshape or redefine sport, compared with sport organizations' power to reshape or redefine mass communication. Such powers are based on increasingly complex political and economic relations between the two, as well as on more specific technical production conventions developed by broadcasting professionals. Analyses of production should not be isolated from the content of the text or audience consumption. Several studies of sport media have linked production with the content of the text (Gruneau, 1989; Larson & Park, 1993; MacNeill, 1995, 1996b; Stoddart, 1994). For example, Larson and Park's (1993) case-study of television production of the 1988 Seoul Olympics included analyses of Korean nationalistic images found in the television text. Information about how these images were produced, coupled with the nature of the image in the text, allows for greater insight into portrayals of Korea by the media during the 1988 Olympic Games. New studies that reach beyond production analysis to broader cultural understandings are needed.

TEXTS OF MEDIATED SPORT

Most studies of mediated sport focus on the content of the programming using a variety of textual analysis strategies. This is by far the largest area of research. It is important to note, however, that media texts are inextricably linked to the processes by which they are produced, and any separation of these necessarily places somewhat arbitrary limits on the analysis (Duncan, 1993).

Although it is clear that audiences interpret media texts in a variety of ways, texts are thought to sway audiences toward particular interpretations rather than others (Fiske, 1987; Jhally, 1989). These "preferred" ways of understanding are usually found to be supportive of dominant ideologies. Occasionally, however, alternate or oppositional material is inserted into the texts during production. This content provides alternatives that people might use to make sense of television in ways that run counter to the "preferred" readings. Furthermore, it is clear that audiences can make sense of mass media texts in ways that run counter to what seem to be "preferred" by producers (Duncan & Brummett, 1993; Fiske, 1987; Lalvani, 1994).

A common approach to studying mediated sport texts is to examine particular broadcasts or a section of print media coverage with the goal of describing the preferred meanings. Ideological connections are then identified and explored. Studies vary considerably with regard to extensiveness of data, and also with regard to the level of systematic analytical rigor. Some include only passing reference to various production techniques, while others are based on detailed, systematic study.

Salient themes include:

1   global, national, and local relations;
2   race relations;
3   gender relations;
4   commercialization;
5   winning;
6   drugs; and
7   violence.

Together these encompass a large portion of the social issues embedded in mediated sport texts. The preferred view of sport produced by the media suggests desired directions for audiences to be swayed. In the sections that follow, each of these themes is described and illustrated. In some cases, material which opposes the preferred meaning embedded in the mediated sport text will be examined.

Global, National, and Local Relations

Mediated sport programs often reproduce dominant ideologies in the nations in which they originate, and world-wide transmission of sport programming from a few Western countries seems to have great potential to contribute to greater understanding of global, national, and local relations. Media coverage of the Olympic Games provides the most prominent display of nationalist ideology as well as a venue for discussions of international relations. The major context within which international sporting events such as the Olympic Games are presented concerns national identity and international relations (Hargreaves, 1992; Larson & Park, 1993).

Nationalistic images are prominent in media renderings of the Olympic Games opening ceremonies. Despite the importance of Olympic rituals and icons designed to symbolize world peace and friendship, Rivenburgh (1995) found that the parade of nations and performances designed to showcase the culture of Barcelona and Spain comprised the largest portion of the international feed to the opening ceremonies in the 1992 Olympics.

Analyses of American media portrayals of the Olympic Games have focused on the promotion of American ideals and values (Real, Mechikoff, & Goldstein, 1989; Riggs, Eastman, & Golobic, 1993; Rowe & Lawrence, 1986; Tomlinson, 1989; Wenner, 1994b). American television viewers see virtually every medal ceremony when American athletes win the gold medal. Rowe and Lawrence (1986) noted that when non-American nations won gold medals, television coverage of the ceremony was often preempted in favor of showing American athletes competing in other events.

Media representations of Olympic events that provide nationalistic images are important in ideological struggles. It has been suggested that these nationalistic images not only obscure existing ethnic, gender, and social class boundaries, but also undermine attempts to challenge or alter exploitive relations that exist within a particular nation, thus supporting the status quo (Clarke & Clarke, 1982; Hargreaves, 1986; Rowe & Lawrence, 1986). Running counter to images that stress national unity are oppositional messages that portray divisiveness within a country. The "black power" salute during the playing of the American national anthem at the 1968 Mexico City Games exemplifies such an image, symbolizing cleavages between black and white Americans, and offering hopes of an organized struggle for equality (Clarke & Clarke, 1982; Rowe & Lawrence, 1986).

Portrayals of international relations in Olympic media texts have often appeared as divisive clashes between nations or ideologies. The texts contrast the broadcasters' and/or print journalists' styles, nationalities, and other characteristics. For example, prior to 1992, American media coverage contextualized the Games in terms of the conflict between Western bloc and Eastern bloc powers using the image of "cold war ideology" (Kinkema & Harris, 1992). More recently, Riggs, Eastman, and Golobic (1993) found that the US Olympic television discourse, influenced by American foreign policy, treated the Unified Team of the former Soviet Union as a "fading enemy," while Unified Germany and Japan were constructed by the media as possible "emerging enemies."

One method often employed by the media to construct national identity involves the characterization of athletes from foreign nations in stereotyped ways (Clarke & Clarke, 1982; Gillet, White, & Young, 1996; Hargreaves, 1986, 1992; Larson & Rivenburgh, 1991; Tudor, 1992). Analyses of British coverage of the 1980 Moscow Olympics showed that the media portrayed Britain's opponents at the Games using blatant racist/ethnic stereotypes (Hargreaves, 1986). In a non-Olympic study, Tudor (1992) reported that British coverage of World Cup soccer relied heavily on ethnic and cultural stereotypes of competing nations to create the television narrative. In one case, the unexpected success of the team from Cameroon, initially stereotyped as "happy-go-lucky," "naive," and "unsophisticated," created a problem for the British media when they advanced in the tournament giving the English team a scare. Characterization of the Cameroons was reformulated to present them as more worthy opponents for the English team in an effort to explain their success.

Media representations of sport, particularly international sport and the Olympic Games, focus substantially on national unity and identity, championing the dominant values and ideals of the nations in which they originate. Oppositional messages such as the "black power" salute and the recharacterization of the Cameroon soccer team have been found in some media texts (Clarke & Clarke, 1982; Rowe & Lawrence, 1986; Tudor, 1992). However, it does not appear that systematic attention has been devoted to searching for oppositional material connected to global, national, and local relations.

Race Relations

There are few studies dealing with race relations in mediated sport texts. The work that exists primarily documents racist images of African American athletes in the United States. Stereotyped renderings of black athletes attribute their sport achievement to "natural" abilities and "instincts," while white athletes are portrayed as hardworking and intelligent (Andrews, 1996b; D.Z. Jackson, 1989, 1996; Murrell & Curtis, 1994; Rainville & McCormick, 1977; Rainville, Roberts, & Sweet, 1978; Sabo & Jansen, 1992, 1994; Wonsek, 1992).

Davis (1990) suggests that American society's preoccupation with questions of racial differences in athletic performance, based on faulty "common sense" notions of racially-linked genetic differences between black and white athletes, is in itself racist. She cites the 1990 NBC network news special, "Black Athletes – Fact and Fiction" as a blatant example of this racist preoccupation. According to Davis, focusing on "supposed" biological differences obscures the sociopolitical context of inequitable race relations in society, legitimating the present power structure. Several journalists and scholars have responded in similar fashion to the NBC network broadcast (Mathisen & Mathisen, 1991; Smith, 1990; Wiley, 1991).

D.Z. Jackson (1989) analyzed the television broadcast commentary for seven NFL games over two seasons and five NCAA college men's basketball games in an attempt to ascertain the extent of racial stereotyping by sportscasters. Utilizing categories of Brawn (running, leaping, size, strength, quickness), Brains (intelligence, motivation, leadership), Dunce (confused, emotionally out of control), and Weakling (lack of speed and size) to encompass descriptors of athletes made by television commentators, Jackson found that African American football and basketball players were most often described in a manner characterized as Brawn while White players were most often described using characteristics categorized as Brains. Over 80 percent of all Dunce comments made about professional football and college basketball players were attributed to African Americans while white players received 85 percent of the Weakling comments. A follow-up study, conducted during the 1996 NCAA men's basketball tournament, produced similar results (Jackson, 1996). Utilizing categories of Brains, Brawn, and Dunce, Jackson found that white athletes were less likely to be characterized as "brainy" than in the 1989 study, yet black athletes were twice as likely to be categorized as Brawn as they were in 1989. There was little change in the Dunce category. The implications of these stereotypes are serious and may help to explain why blacks are underrepresented in positions of leadership and in American sports.

Sabo, Jansen, Tate, Duncan, and Leggett (1996) examined whether the television coverage of seven international sporting events over a 5-year period differed according to the race, ethnicity, or nationality of the athletes. One of the strengths of this study is that the sample included black, white, Asian and Latino-Hispanic athletes. Results showed that efforts were generally made to avoid prejudicial treatment of minority athletes. Contrary to earlier studies, blacks were not characterized primarily by their physical attributes and skills more than athletes from other racial or ethnic groups. In fact, they were less likely to receive negative comments from sports commentators. Asian athletes were often described in stereotyped ways, such as "machine-like" and unemotional. Commentary focusing on Latino-Hispanic athletes was mixed. They were described using physical descriptors more than black or white athletes, although overall the treatment of Latino-Hispanic athletes by broadcast personnel was positive. According to the authors, lack of overt stereotyping and prejudicial comments about black athletes "suggests that media professionals have responded to past criticisms of prejudicial treatment of blacks in sport media" (1996, p. 13). Sabo and Jansen (1994) also report that media stories about black athletes are increasingly framed in positive ways (e.g., showing athletes engaged in community service, highlighting their academic achievement.)

Evidence of racism has been found in other aspects of media coverage of sporting events. Sabo, Jansen, Tate, Duncan, and Leggett (1996) found that blacks, Asians, and Latino-Hispanics were underrepresented as commentators and interviewers in the television broadcasts of international sporting events. Wonsek (1992), analyzing television coverage of twelve NCAA men's basketball games found that African Americans were overrepresented in the coverage as players, but underrepresented or nonexistent in other roles such as coaches, commentators, interviewers, cheerleaders, or actors in commercials. She suggests that the predominant image of blacks as athletes "may contribute further to the objectification of the black male as little more than a finely tuned machine ... whose role it is to provide entertainment for a viewing audience" (1992, p. 451). Davis (1993) argues that the lack of representation of people of color in the sports coverage and advertisements in *Sports Illustrated* suggests that the preferred spectator/consumer of the magazine is white.

Analyses of race relations portrayed in media representations of sport have documented the existence of racist images of black athletes. There is some evidence that these images are improving (Sabo et al., 1996), but very few efforts have been made to search systematically for additional messages that contradict racist ideologies.

Gender Relations

Most of the textual analyses of mediated sport have dealt with images of gender, primarily focusing on the underrepresentation of women and the stereotyped manner in which women are portrayed in sports (Blinde, Greendorfer, & Sankner, 1991; Crossman, Hyslop, & Guthrie, 1994; Daddario, 1992, 1994; Duncan, 1990, 1993;

Duncan & Hasbrook, 1988; Duncan, Messner, Williams, Jensen, & Wilson, 1994; Feder, 1995; Halbert & Lattimer, 1994; Hargreaves, 1994; Higgs & Weiller, 1994; Kane & Parks, 1992; Kinkema & Harris, 1992; Leath & Lumpkin, 1992; Lee, 1992; Lumpkin & Williams, 1991; McKay & Huber, 1992; Messner, Duncan, & Jensen, 1993; Sabo & Jansen, 1992; Shifflett & Revelle, 1994). The media are prime sites for the reproduction of gender definitions and gender relations, and media images of women and men in sport tend to follow prevailing gender stereotypes.

Analyses of media sport texts suggest that marginalization and sexualization of female athletes are primary means by which current societal patterns of patriarchy in sport are reproduced (Duncan, 1990, 1993; Duncan et al., 1994; Hall, 1993; MacNeill,1988). The media trivialize female athletes by devoting a disproportionately smaller amount of time to their performances as well as by highlighting their physical attractiveness or their domestic roles such as wife, mother, or supportive girlfriend of a male. Female athletes are evaluated partially in terms of the extent to which their physical characteristics or domestic roles correspond to dominant notions of femininity. Textual analyses of mediated sport in which images of male and female athletes have been examined have focused on the manner in which mediated sport defines notions of both masculinity and femininity, the ways in which the media portray male and female athletic performances, and the ways in which these are tied to the broader context of gender relations in society at large.

Daddario (1994) found that although television coverage of the 1992 Winter Olympics included women in sports that defy traditional stereotypes (e.g., luge, Alpine skiing), several strategies were utilized to marginalize the accomplishments of the athletes. Sexist descriptors, focusing blame for poor performances on individual athletes, diminishing the sexuality of athletes by reducing them to adolescent status and portraying athletes as cooperative rather than competitive, all served to trivialize the accomplishments of the women portrayed.

In an in-depth analysis of the ways in which the media construct images of women, MacNeill (1988) analyzed an aerobics program and a women's bodybuilding broadcast on Canadian television. While on the surface the physical activities of the women appeared to resist dominant patriarchal views, they actually served to produce and reproduce images of active women engaged in "feminine" activities.

Recent analyses of gender in mediated sport have led to cautious optimism on the part of researchers (Duncan et al., 1994; Messner, Duncan, & Jensen, 1993). Less overt sexist language and less sexualization of female athletes were found in television coverage of women's basketball and tennis, compared to previous studies. Also, preliminary observations suggest that there was increased coverage of female athletes in the US telecast of the 1996 Summer Olympics. However, we need systematic documentation of this as well as investigations of the ideological content of the programming.

Duncan (1993) argues that in subsequent analyses images of gender in mediated sport should not be isolated from the social structures and institutional practices that create the images. Objectification, commodification, and voyeurism were identified as formal media structures that contribute to sexism and stereotyping in the media, and she showed how each of these mechanisms occurs in the *Sports Illustrated* swimsuit issue. This study is an excellent example of linking production to text. Connections to audience are also made by acknowledging that readers of *Sports Illustrated* may not interpret the swimsuit issue in the preferred, patriarchal manner, though audience data is not provided.

Several recent analyses of gender in media sport texts have focused on hegemonic representations of masculinity (Gillet, White, & Young, 1996; Jansen & Sabo, 1994; Kane & Disch, 1993; Lalvani, 1994; Morse, 1983; O'Connor & Boyle, 1993; Poynton & Hartley, 1990; Sabo & Jansen, 1992; Trujillo, 1991, 1995). Jansen and Sabo (1994) showed that use of the war metaphor in the language of mediated sport idealizes masculinity, celebrating differences between men and women, ultimately trivializing and devaluing women and marginalizing men who appear weak or passive.

Trujillo (1991) shows how the print media portrayed Major League Baseball star pitcher Nolan Ryan as the embodiment of hegemonic masculinity. Ryan was constructed as the archetypal male athlete, capitalist worker, family patriarch, white rural heterosexual cowboy, all distinguishing features of hegemonic masculinity.

Images of women and men in media portrayals of sport have received considerable scholarly attention. Most of the findings suggest that marginalization of female athletes is the primary means by which patriarchy is reproduced in media coverage of sport. Although systematic efforts have generally not been made to document them, there are images in texts that run counter to dominant gender ideology. Duncan and Hasbrook (1988) found moments of resistance to the notion of female inferiority in their analysis of the text of the 1986 New York City Marathon. Duncan et al. (1994) found that some portions of television coverage of women's basketball and tennis were less sexist than previously documented. In studies of portrayals of men, images support dominant ideas about masculinity, and no messages were found that resist hegemonic masculinity in sport texts.

Commercialization

Commercialization is a salient theme in mediated sport texts, visible in commercials, corporate sponsorships, and media portrayals of sporting events and athletes. Use of commercials and commercial images in sport programming is especially important because, as discussed earlier, élite spectator sport has become increasingly dependent on corporate sponsorship. Real and Mechikoff (1992) report that during a 6-month period advertisers spent $1.1 billion for commercial time on network sports programming in the United States.

Commercials during sporting events often reflect the event that surrounds them (Duncan & Brummett, 1987; Jhally, 1989). For example, many advertisements during the 1992 Olympics featured the Dream Team (Wenner, 1994b) and commercials for McDonalds using a boxing theme were shown during 1984 Olympic boxing events. In addition, the Super Bowl has become as well known as a showcase of new commercials as it is a showcase for the National Football League's finest teams. Duncan and Brummett (1987) suggest the possibility that such commercials "blur the distinction between sport and advertisement, thus creating a link between sports and commodities in the viewer's mind" (p. 174). It is important to remember, however, that we have no evidence concerning how viewers actually interpret such advertisements.

Media sport texts often portray athletic stars as commodities in their own right (Brummett & Duncan, 1990; Duncan & Brummett, 1987; Dyson, 1993; Farrell, 1989). This occurs through commentaries about converting their talents and notoriety to cash, and also through portrayals of them as coveted objects that we are encouraged to look at and examine intensively.

Despite substantial connections between advertising and mediated sport, there is only a small body of scholarly work dealing with sport advertising. Strate (1992) argued that beer commercials, often shown during sporting events, reproduce hegemonic masculinity, presenting traditional stereotyped images of men and women. Wenner (1994b) found that commercials associated with the Dream Team televised during the 1992 Barcelona Olympics reinforced ideals of nationalism, youth sports dreams, and sports heroism.

Sage (1996) explored promotional strategies used by American professional team sports franchises. Professional team and sport league executives continually try to cultivate an image linking franchises and leagues, including the marketing of merchandise, to images of US patriotism. For example, the American national anthem is played at most professional sporting events, many professional teams wore special patches in support of the troops during the Gulf War, and logos for the National Football League, Major League Baseball, and the National Basketball Association are red, white, and blue. Sage argues that the relationship between professional team sports and US patriotism is a contradictory one because much of the licensed merchandise is made by foreign workers under exploitive working conditions.

Substantial support for consumerism exists in media representations of sport, and this provides obvious backing for capitalist ideology. No messages that oppose this viewpoint have been identified so far, but investigators do not appear to have searched carefully for them.

Winning and Success

Winning and success are dominant American values and are especially salient in discussions of the ideology of sport. Framed by the question "Who will win?," winning is a central focus of media narratives. Trujillo and Ekdom (1985) suggest that sportswriters have used winning as an "umbrella theme" under which to situate other themes in the journalistic narrative of sport.

Media emphasis on success in sport can be seen in the focus on game scores, team and individual victories, and championships. This emphasis on the "bottom line" of wins and losses reveals the business nature of sport. Wins, medals and championships are the products of sport, and individuals, teams, franchises and nations are ultimately judged by the number of victories accumulated.

Vande Berg and Trujillo (1989) found that winning and success were also defined as a process – the sense of bettering oneself in the act of competing. In their analysis of media coverage of the Dallas Cowboys NFL franchise, they found that journalists utilized this definition during periods in Cowboy history when the team was not winning very many games. During periods when the Cowboys were winning, success was redefined and articulated by the media to emphasize wins and losses.

The competitive structure of the sports valued most highly in Western capitalist nations suggests that they contribute to the reproduction of dominant values of achievement and success. Winning underscores the capitalist labor process, and central to discussions of winning and success are the sub-themes of competitive individualism and teamwork (Kinkema & Harris, 1992; Lalvani, 1994). At first glance, teamwork and competitive individualism appear to be contradictory themes. However, both are important in capitalist societies, and therefore it is not surprising that both are prominent themes in media renderings of sport. In his analysis of the Texas Rangers professional baseball organization and its star pitcher Nolan Ryan, Trujillo (1994) found that media coverage of Nolan Ryan reinforced both teamwork and individualism.

Competitive Individualism

Focusing on the accomplishments of individual athletes, the media portrays competitive individualism by emphasizing the personal qualities thought to be important for victory. Competitive individualism appears to be a salient theme in media portrayals of sport regardless of whether or not the text focuses on individual or team sports (Lalvani, 1994; Williams, 1977). Duncan and Brummett (1987) found that television productions of sporting events focused heavily on individual athletes rather than on groups or teams. They argue that this established a "kind of intimacy between the audience and the player" (1987, p. 172). Visual material emphasized the actions of individuals, often showing close-ups of particular players, and the commentary tended to reinforce this personalized focus. Whannel (1982) points to three ways in which individual athletes are highlighted in media coverage: Teams are discussed by focusing on star players; the focus is on one or two star players in individual events; and star athletes are often used as commentators for sport coverage. Butler (1994) suggests that individual personalities are as important as athletic ability in television's presentation of sporting events. 1992 Olympic volleyball player Bob Samuelson became a media celebrity not so much for his volleyball ability, but because he overcame a childhood illness which left him bald and because of his arguments with officials. One such argument cost the US team a game, and subsequently all of his team mates shaved their heads as a show of support. This action brought the team even more television exposure.

In an analysis of print media stories about athletes in individual sports who trained for the 1984 Olympics, Chalip and Chalip (1989) found that victory was usually made to appear contingent on having the right personality qualities. Winning personalities were characterized by self-control, an obsessive focus on winning, and the personal fortitude to overcome physical and emotional problems or other hardships. Edwin Moses, for example, was portrayed as a "Grand Champion" whose unprecedented success as a hurdler can be attributed to tremendous self-control. Excessive media focus on personality as the major determiner of victory tended to trivialize athletic skills and the grueling training and practice needed to perfect them. Chalip and Chalip argue that making victory appear contingent on personality rather than athletic talents places the possibility of achieving victory "within the reach of any of us who would choose to exercise the appropriate aspects of our personality" (1989, p. 11–24). In other words, achievement is made to appear attainable by anyone. This is an especially potent message in a capitalist society dependent on a high-achieving labor force.

In his analysis of the media representations of the 1984 Sarajevo Winter Olympics, Farrell (1989) argues that prior to the Games the American media attempted to plant the idea of American success in the minds of the audience. Commercials couched in the rhetoric of American victory, flashbacks to prior American Olympic victories, and the use of past Olympic champions as color commentators (who add expert perspective to the descriptions of play action by primary announcers) all helped to accomplish this. Farrell goes on to point out that this build-up featuring American success was at odds with the actual events at the Games. Americans did not win in as great numbers as expected. This resulted in a breakdown of the media renderings of the Games. The "Olympic story" did not unfold according to the "script." The media response to this breakdown is pertinent to our discussion of competitive individualism.

Instead of assuming responsibility for contributing to the discrepancy between the anticipation of American victories and the reality of the American lackluster performance, the media in part attributed mediocre performances to character flaws of the athletes. This process of "blaming the victim" is a common way to explain failure in capitalist societies. Success is thought to be available to all who work hard enough, and those who fail have only themselves to blame. Focusing on individual flaws detracts attention away from problems in the broader sociocultural context that may be contributing to human hardships (Sage, 1990). Farrell (1989) points to an example in which the American media provided a quick re-interpretation of eloquent commentary by the United States hockey coach exploring the depths of his reactions to his team's early loss. The coach's comments suggested that losing can have dignity about it, and that losers should be offered compassion and sympathy. ABC network Olympic sportscasters chose to reinterpret this by raising questions about character qualities of the American hockey team. In this way, the American loss was placed squarely in a light that was congruent with competitive individualism and therefore supportive of capitalist ideology.

Teamwork

Teamwork in the sport setting is often defined in terms of obedience to authority, maintaining loyalty to the group and placing the good of the group above individual interests. Reporting on journalistic accounts of the Chicago Cubs' 1984 baseball season, Trujillo and Ekdom (1985) found that sports writers focused on teammates helping each other and sacrificing for the good of the team. Partially entwined with individualism, stories about star players often described them as "team players." It was implied that this integration of teamwork and individualism was important in the Cubs' quest for a championship season. In a more recent analysis of star pitcher Nolan Ryan and the Texas Rangers Major League Baseball franchise, Trujillo (1994) found that reporters often described Ryan as a team player, committed to helping his team win. He was also portrayed as a team leader in the clubhouse.

Teamwork, as presented in media renderings of sporting events, also extends to obedience towards authority, a central component of the capitalist labor process. Both Clarke and Clarke (1982) and Jhally (1989) suggest that media portrayals of coaches and managers as decision-makers exemplify some of the alienating features of the capitalist labor process, although they do not provide specific examples from media coverage of sport to illustrate their argument.

Winning and success comprise a prominent theme in media renderings of sport, often serving as an overarching framework within which to situate discussions of other themes, especially individualism and teamwork. Vande Berg and Trujillo's discussion of the changing definition of winning and success, and Farrell's reference to the reinterpretation of American Olympic losses are examples of instances where oppositional material was found. Other alternative messages may also be present in media sport texts, but as yet they have received little systematic research attention.

Drugs

Although drug use by athletes is certainly not new, only recently have scholars investigated media representations of this (Davis & Delano, 1992; Donohew, Helm, & Haas, 1989; Hilliard, 1994; Hills, 1992; Messner & Solomon, 1993; Wenner, 1994a). The widespread availability of performance-enhancing substances combined with athletes willing to do anything to improve their performances have led to persistent drug use over the past 40 to 50 years (Coakley, 1994). Coakley argues that the use of performance-enhancing substances by athletes fits in a model he terms "positive deviance." Users are not morally bankrupt, but are rather among the most dedicated and committed athletes in sports. They over-conform to the ethic of sport that suggests they must be willing to take risks, ignore pain and do anything in order to be successful and, ultimately, continue to perform. Ben Johnson, for example, is a "product of an élite sports culture in which the drive to win and to gain the extravagant material rewards offered by international sporting success over-rode seemingly naive and out-moded notions of fair play and bodily health" (Rowe, 1995, p. 116).

Hills (1992) investigated journalistic renderings of athlete drug use. She found that although there was a fairly even amount of coverage of both performance-enhancing drug use and recreational drug use, the nature of the articles differed. Articles focusing on performance-enhancing drug use framed the issue as primarily a problem for sport, and blamed individual athletes for creating the problem. Governing bodies of sport were often portrayed as reformers seeking to "clean up" sports by controlling the behavior of a few rogue athletes. Structural problems in sport that may be related to drug use by athletes were almost never mentioned. Recovery by athletes was rarely discussed, and athletes who used performance-enhancing drugs and did *not* achieve success were never portrayed.

On the other hand, recreational drug use by athletes was contextualized as an individual problem. Information about athletes' struggles to recover, penalties imposed, and the harmful nature of drug use were prevalent in the media renderings. Athletes who used recreational drugs were portrayed as undisciplined or immature. Hills argues that the differing accounts can be explained by the importance of performance-enhancing substances to success in sports. Individual success and performance-enhancing drug use are interdependent, and, for athletes, the rewards of athletic success may be worth the known health risks associated with the use of performance-enhancing substances. Wenner (1994a) and Hilliard (1994) also found that drug stories were framed in the context of individual failure.

Several analyses have found that the media often report rumors of purported performance-enhancing substance use (Hilliard, 1994; Hills, 1992; Wenner, 1994a). Hilliard (1994) found that media discussions of drug use by Olympic athletes tended to focus on performance-enhancing drug use in the context of individual choice, and not as a part of a larger sports problem. The exception was media discussion of the athletic training systems of the Chinese and the East Germans, seen as monolithic systems that exploit their athletes. The latter clearly has ties to American nationalism.

Analyzing anti-steroid media campaigns (e.g., posters), Davis and Delano (1992) found that the primary theme treated drugs as artificial substances that would disrupt the natural processes of the body, and subsequently the male/female gender dichotomy. For example, one of the posters selected for analysis portrays a muscular, flexed bicep with accompanying text, "No additives. No preservatives. No steroids. Nothing artificial." Another poster shows what appear to be a woman's breasts. The text states, "The obscene thing is, this is a man." An underlying assumption here is that bodies are dichotomous relative to gender and that this dichotomy can be disrupted by using artificial substances such as steroids. Davis and Delano argue that this portrayal denies the physical reality of many people who do not fit neatly into the gender dichotomy, conceals the social practice of engendering bodies, and produces consent for the present gender order.

Scholars have only recently begun studying media portrayals of drug use by athletes. More attention needs to be focused on fleshing out the nature of this theme and the extent to which it exists in media renderings of sport. Hills (1992) found a few oppositional messages in her analysis of media portrayals of athletes' drug use. For example, some of the coverage included claims that the health risks of steroid use have been sensationalized. Additional messages which oppose dominant views associated with drug use in sport may also be present in media sport texts, but they have received little systematic research attention.

Violence

Studies of media portrayals of violence in sport have been influenced by a long line of scholarship in mass communication aimed at uncovering cause–effect links between viewer exposure to violence in the media and greater violence in society at large. The results show modest ties between the two, and the debate continues about the extent to which, and the ways in which, these are causal. Careful efforts have been made in studies of violence in sport media texts to point out that cause–effect relationships have not been conclusively demonstrated. In a critique of the media effects literature on violence in sport, Coakley (1988–89) makes the following points:

1   we know very little about the relationship between the media coverage of sports and violent behavior;
2   we know very little about how people integrate mediated sports into their daily lives;
3   we have not looked at relationships between violence in media coverage of sports and violence in society;
4   we have not examined links between violence in sports coverage, definitions of masculinity, and gender relations;
5   we have not looked at the types of sports violence that are typically included or excluded in media coverage;
6   we have not adequately defined violence and aggression or distinguished between various types of violence and various sports;
7   we have failed to distinguish between long- and short-term effects of viewing violent acts;
8   we have failed to include women in research designs; and
9   we have failed to give audiences credit for being able to resist the messages.

Media portrayals of player violence and spectator violence have both received considerable scholarly attention. Player violence has been studied primarily by Americans, and spectator violence has been examined mainly by British scholars focusing on soccer hooligans. Textual analyses of several sporting events shown on American television indicate that player violence is a prominent feature of these texts. Bryant and Zillmann (1983b) point to a variety of ways in which the texts highlight this, including extended coverage during games of violent or excessively rough players and/or acts, and clips of especially violent acts from previous matches placed in promotional segments designed to attract viewers to upcoming matches. They argue that heavy media focus on player violence occurs in order to attract audiences.

A growing scholarly focus on hegemonic masculinity in media representations of sport centers on violence as acceptable male practice both on and off the playing field (Kane & Disch, 1993; Messner & Solomon, 1993; Theberge, 1989; Trujillo, 1995; Young, 1991a). In an analysis of media portrayals of *Monday Night Football,* Trujillo (1995) suggests that the football player's body is transformed into a weapon, and ultimately an instrument of violence and aggression. Broadcast commentary reinforces the "sport as war" metaphor, and especially violent acts are shown multiple times utilizing close-ups and slow-motion replay. The media portrays players' bodies as tools of work, or machines of war. Player violence with resultant injuries is legitimized as part of the job of a professional football player in the NFL. Theberge (1989) asserts that media portrayals suggesting the acceptability of player violence serve to naturalize and legitimate violence as appropriate masculine practice. This is pervasive in North America according to Theberge, and it continues to have serious ramifications for the prevalence of violent behavior in the region. She points out that although media accounts of the 1987 World Junior Hockey Championships were cast largely in line with dominant viewpoints which legitimated violent acts, alternative interpretations characterizing hockey violence as symptomatic of deeper problems in sport were also present. However, these alternative interpretations were overtaken by the more prevalent expressions of acceptance of the violence.

Soccer hooligans in Britain have been the primary focus of work dealing with sport spectator violence (Hall, 1978; Hargreaves, 1986; Murphy, Dunning & Williams, 1988; Murphy, Williams & Dunning, 1990; Whannel, 1979; Young, 1986, 1991b). This research is usually situated theoretically in a media amplification framework. The major concern is with the extent to which media portrayals of hooligan violence incite the hooligans to commit further violent acts and encourage sport and government officials to make unnecessarily harsh responses. Whannel (1979) found, for example, that the British press tended to characterize hooligans as mindless lunatics, trouble-makers, and sub-human species. He argues that frequent use of this stereotyped characterization of hooligans by the press has led to the hooligans becoming a new British "folk devil":

> The *football hooligan* begets the football hooliganism problem. The establishment of a new *folk devil* leads to the development of a *moral panic* . . . Future incidents then appear within the framework of this *moral panic* as evidence of a trend, which is increasingly newsworthy *in its own right.*
>
> (p. 333)

The source of the hooligans' problematic behavior was viewed by the press to be the hooligans themselves, their "natural" mindlessness, mental illness, and savageness. Young (1991b) argues that this places the blame for the hooligan "problem" squarely on the shoulders of the hooligans and diverts attention away from broader societal problems that may contribute to the situation. It also supports conservative "law and order" ideology with the hooligans cast as villains who must be controlled for the good of the game.

Whannel (1979) also points out that the British media have tended to give a large amount of coverage to a relatively small decline in overall spectator attendance, prominently linking the decline to the hooligan "problem." Despite limited evidence, the hooligans are blamed for driving away "respectable" (and more affluent) family-oriented people, and the implication is that if the hooligan problem is eliminated, more desirable fans will be attracted.

Violence on the part of both players and spectators has been a prominent theme in sport media texts. One media rendering was found to run counter to the portrayals outlined above. Whannel (1979) notes an instance where excessive police brutality toward hooligans was acknowledged. This may have occurred because prominent leaders in soccer organizations, along with government officials, legitimated it by framing some of their own observations of events in this manner. Furthermore, the incident took place in France and therefore it was the French police, not local British law enforcement officers, who were being cast in this light. Murphy, Dunning and Williams (1988) point out that dominant media renderings of soccer spectator violence have changed considerably between the turn of the century and the present, at times seeming to downplay the violence and at other times giving it excessive focus. This is a reminder of the "constructed" nature of mass media portrayals.

To summarize, the major themes found in the content of mediated sport include global, national, and local relations; race relations; gender relations; commercialization; winning and success; drug use; and violence. The themes that have been identified thus far provide an initial framework for examining future mediated sport texts. Future analyses should continue to focus on linking the content of the text with the processes of production and audience interpretation. Many textual studies include brief mention of the production techniques used to construct messages. There has been more limited exploration of how audiences interpret texts in ways that oppose the "preferred" meanings of the text (Davis, 1993; Duncan & Brummett, 1993; Wenner, 1994b). These kinds of studies will paint a more grounded picture of textual dynamics and reception.

AUDIENCE

Although mediated sport research is heavily dominated by textual analysis, scholarly attention to audience experiences is increasing. Early television sport audience research was grounded in the traditional social psychological models of audience reception, known as "effects" and "uses and gratifications" research. While current investigations sometimes use such traditional approaches, theoretical frameworks that focus on ideology have become more prevalent. In addition, several recent audience studies explore more complex processes of sports fanship and gender relations in the context of sports viewing.

Effects Research

The study of audience responses to television is certainly not new. Traditional audience research was guided primarily by social psychological theoretical models that focus on processes by which television messages influence audience members, commonly known as "effects research." Within this framework, the effects of televised sport violence on viewers has been a major line of investigation.

Bryant (1989) summarized findings concerning the extent to which audiences enjoy hostility and violence in televised sporting events. Results suggested that (a) viewers with tendencies toward aggressive behavior were generally more fond of sport violence; (b) enjoyment of sport violence was dependent upon whom the violence was directed against; (c) "hatred" of a team or player led to especially high levels of enjoyment of violence; (d) sanctioned violence, such as that found in the National Hockey League was preferred by viewers over unsanctioned violence; and (e) committed sport fans, given the above-mentioned factors, seemed to enjoy violence in mediated sport texts. Generally, he found that audiences enjoyed viewing sport violence.

Effects of sports commentary on viewers, perceptions of, and enjoyment of, violence in mediated sport have also been examined. Bryant, Comisky, and Zillmann

(1981) found that the enjoyment of professional football plays by male audience members increased as the roughness increased, and that males enjoyed highly violent plays more than female viewers. Sullivan (1991) found that the commentary manipulated viewer perception of overt player hostility in men's collegiate basketball games. Neutral commentary resulted in higher tolerance for violence compared with no commentary.

A recent study (Schweitzer, Zillmann, Weaver, & Luttrell, 1992) investigating the effects of postgame affect on the perception of the likelihood of a feared event occurring (e.g., likelihood of war in the Persian Gulf) found that fans upset about the defeat of their team were more likely to perceive that the feared event would in fact occur.

Uses and Gratifications Research

Media sport audience research which has come from a uses and gratifications perspective has generally focused on the factors that motivate audience consumption and enjoyment of mediated sports. The research findings can be organized into three areas: fans, narrative and social context of viewing.

Several studies have investigated spectator involvement in watching televised sports. Gantz & Wenner (1995) found that the audience experience with televised sport varied on the basis of fanship. Fans, both male and female, were more "active, involved, invested consumers of televised sports" (p. 71). In an earlier study they found that the strongest emotional involvement with a televised sporting event came in "feeling happy" when favorite athletes and teams performed well (Wenner & Gantz, 1989). Walker (1990) investigated the relationship between viewers' gratifications associated with televised NFL football and audience reactions to the 1987 NFL players' strike. Viewers possessing active gratifications, such as "to thrill in victory" or "to learn about the sport" tended to view the strike as more salient and have high expectations for post-strike viewing. Viewers with passive gratifications ("to pass time") did not see the strike as particularly important. Viewer gratifications were unrelated to attitudes about the principal opponents in the strike.

At least one study has attempted to investigate audience enjoyment in the context of the dramatic nature of television sports. Bryant, Rockwell, and Owens (1994), investigating the role of suspense in viewer enjoyment of mediated sport, found that viewing a more suspenseful version of a sporting event on television made the game more enjoyable and exciting, and less boring. Once again, viewers enjoyed the broadcast more when their favored team experienced a favorable outcome.

Acknowledging the importance of social context in the viewing of televised sport, Rothenbuhler (1988, 1989a, 1989b, 1995) investigated American audiences of the 1984 Los Angeles Olympic Games using a large-scale survey. Olympic viewers, as compared to regular television viewers, were more likely to view the games in a group of family and friends with whom they regularly shared other important social occasions. Men and women watched the Olympic Games in relatively equal numbers, and eating and drinking were found to be important social components of the viewing experience. Olympic viewers surveyed also tended to plan television watching times, often rearranging their schedules to accommodate their interest in the Games. Olympic viewing as a social event reinforced friendships and a sense of local community. Emerson and Perse (1995) explored the functions that the 1992 Olympic Games served for the audience. They suggest that the Olympic Games are a special "media event" different from other televised sporting contests and that this helps to frame the audience's viewing. Four major reasons for watching the 1992 Winter Olympics were identified by respondents: cultural learning/media events, interest in athletes, rooting for US, and social utility. Sharing the viewing experience with others (social utility) was the least salient motive for participants.

Ideological Models

Audience research utilizing frameworks that incorporate ideological aspects of mediated sport generally focus on how audiences interpret or make sense of texts which favor particular political, economic, and social relations. An on-going debate centers around the relative influence of audiences and texts in the construction of meaning. Some argue that media texts are not ideologically deterministic, but, rather, open to a variety of interpretations by audiences (Fiske, 1987). Others argue that audiences do not have free reign to construct infinite readings or interpretations, but are swayed toward certain interpretations privileged by the ideological nature of the text (Condit, 1989). Interrelationships of audiences with texts become sites of struggle where meanings and interpretations are constructed within broader ideological limits and possibilities (Duncan & Brummett, 1993; Morley, 1992; Whannel, 1992)

The concept of "subject position" is thought to be a useful way of understanding the complex relationship between audiences and texts. Subject position refers to the manner in which audiences are "positioned" to interpret a particular text. Texts, because of their ideological nature, invite preferred readings which in turn encourage the formation of particular subject positions rather than others. These are known as "preferred" or "ideal" subject positions. For example, one subject position that is frequently hailed by texts has to do with the role of the audience as consumer. Producers of mediated sport texts, along with corporations who sponsor sports programming, usually assume that their audiences possess a certain desirable identity or perspective (Davis, 1993; Haag, 1996; King, 1993). In a textual analysis of *Sports Illustrated*, Davis (1993) found that audiences hailed by the text of this popular publication are White, relatively affluent, Western, heterosexual, Christian men with conservative political values. According to Davis, this is the ideal subject position for *Sports Illustrated* because these are the consumers that *Sports Illustrated* and its advertisers would like to attract.

In addition to subject positions corresponding with producers' images of an ideal consumer, other sorts of subject positions are thought to be possible. Duncan and Brummett (1993) found that despite the apparent constraining ideological nature of NFL football, which reinforces traditional notions of masculinity, audiences can interpret texts in oppositional ways. According to Duncan and Brummett, audience members whose interpretations resist the sexist, patriarchal nature of professional football presented in the text have assumed oppositional subject positions. In their study of television audiences of the NFL, Duncan and Brummett (1993) found that viewers (both male and female) assumed a variety of subject positions (e.g., fan, group member, privileged observer, physically demonstrative viewer, knowledgeable viewer). They point out that some of the subject positions tended to affirm the institution of professional sport. On several occasions, however, female viewers abandoned these preferred readings in favor of more oppositional or "subversive" subject positions. Displays of sarcasm and irreverence toward the game, players, and broadcasters, and refusal to remain committed to the broadcast, exemplified this subversive subject position. This form of opposition, they suggest, may lead to radical empowerment for the women watching NFL football. Duncan and Brummett provide no evidence, however, to suggest that these radical forms of empowerment actually occur. They also do not provide evidence of male viewer resistance to preferred readings, although it is likely that they occur.

Duncan and Brummett (1993) argue that in the case of female viewers of broadcast sport, both preferred and subversive subject positions could be considered empowering. However, these different methods of interpretation represent different forms of empowerment. Women are not typically hailed by mediated sport texts, therefore watching sports in preferred ways could be thought of as empowering in that women have opportunities to participate in the highly valued institution of sport. However, Duncan and Brummett believe that preferred strategies lead to "liberal" forms of empowerment in that female fans support the current structure of NFL football, an institution which is oppressive to women. They argue further that liberal forms of empowerment, when viewed in the broader context of societal gender relations, remain constraining for women. In their study, most of the women who watched NFL football were very knowledgeable, but they tended to resist preferred strategies of interpretation in which viewers would publicly display this knowledge, opting instead to subvert them. Subversive strategies such as a lack of commitment to particular players or teams, and displays of sarcasm, are related to more "radical" forms of empowerment of female viewers because these strategies serve to dismiss the game as anything legitimate or serious. Empowering subject positions are especially important because they ultimately offer possibilities for social change.

Audience as Fan

In the case of those who watch televised sports, one of the most important subject positions appears to be that of the sports fan (Melnick, 1989). Characteristics of fans include: investment of time, money, and emotion; knowledge of performers, statistics, and strategies; an emotional involvement with particular athletes and/or teams during the contest; and using sport in conversation (McPherson, Curtis, & Loy, 1989). Recent investigations of audience activity have focused on viewers who are fans of the National Football League (Brummett & Duncan, 1990; Duncan & Brummett, 1993). In this work, the subject position of sports fan coheres around a set of unifying experiences, such as football knowledge and loyalty to a particular team, that are thought to be unavailable to casual or uninterested observers. These unifying experiences help to make the televised sporting event meaningful, even pleasurable, for fans.

Eastman and Riggs (1994), using observations and interviews, investigated the ritualized viewing of sports on television by fans. Grounded theoretically in current work on fan culture (Fiske, 1992; Grossberg, 1992; Lewis, 1992; Real & Mechikoff, 1992), their analysis identified five concepts which appear to be useful for explaining the social practices of fans watching sports on television: membership; connection; participation; reassurance; and influence. They used these five concepts to organize the television viewing activity of sports fans. Guided by these, they suggest that viewers actively experience television sports in order to gain social and cultural empowerment. For example, fans might wear team colors or hats (membership) while watching the game, watch with other fans of the same team (connection), vocally support their team during the game (participation), engage in security-seeking rituals, such as turning off the TV if the game becomes too stressful (reassurance), or engage in rituals designed to influence the game outcome, such as eating a particular food with games (influence). Further exploration of these concepts and the connection between fan activity and issues of empowerment is needed across a wide variety of television sport viewing experience.

Audience Gender Relations

Televised sport is a male-centered genre that celebrates traditional notions of masculinity and femininity, and although men generally like viewing sports more than women, there is evidence that large numbers of women watch and enjoy a wide range of television sports programming (Bogart, 1995; Bryant, Rockwell, & Owens, 1994; Burnett, Menon, & Smart, 1993; Cooper-Chen, 1994; Gantz & Wenner, 1991; Impoco, 1996; Whannel, 1992). Gantz and Wenner (1991, 1995) found gender differences in the audience experience with televised sport. However, when men and women were both identified as fans, the viewing experiences tended to be similar.

Recent work has focused on the role of televised sport in domestic relationships (Gantz, Wenner, Carrico, & Knorr, 1995a, 1995b). Men were more interested in sports viewing and spent more time watching sports on television than their wives. Men also readily watched when their wives watched a favorite sport, but women were less likely to watch with their husbands as they viewed a favorite sport. Conflicts associated with the scheduling of television viewing were infrequent and usually resolved in a friendly manner when they did arise. The "football widow" stereotype has been a long-standing part of our conventional sport wisdom, although results of these studies indicate that sports viewing is a shared activity among domestic partners and that television sports play only a minor role in marital relationships.

Although research on audiences has recently expanded, it still remains the least developed domain of mass mediated sport research. Audience research is extremely important because it is through processes of audience interpretation that mass media texts become meaningful. Researchers should attempt to integrate studies of production and content with viewers' interpretations, keeping in mind that viewers do not necessarily interpret texts in the same manner as scholars, critics, or one another, nor do they simply receive programs as presented from producers.

EMERGING ISSUES AND FUTURE DIRECTIONS

Although research focusing on sport and the mass media has exploded in the past 10 years, there are a number of areas that merit future consideration. Increasingly, investigators are exploring links between production, text, and audience. However, in the future we need more holistic research that addresses the nature of such links in more detail. An early example of this was the groundbreaking collection of studies of the British television broadcast of the 1974 World Cup soccer matches (Buscombe, 1975) in which production processes were linked with textual content. Duncan (1993) examined production processes that were important in creating sport media texts with patriarchal ideological content. In each of these research projects, the investigators linked two of the three major domains – production, text, and audience. In a recent research monograph, Davis (1997) combined analysis of the *Sports Illustrated* swimsuit issue with interviews of both producers and consumers to show how ideas about hegemonic masculinity are generated and reinforced. This appears to be the only study linking institutional, textual, and audience study in one inquiry.

History, biography, and ethnography are common holistic approaches to research in the social sciences. Links among production, text, and audience might be facilitated through use of these holistic research strategies. There are a few excellent ethnographies of the production of television sporting events (Gruneau, 1989; Larson & Park, 1993; MacNeill, 1995, 1996b; Stoddart, 1994) that link production to ideological content of the texts. Oriard (1993) provides an excellent historical study of newspaper interpretations of American football as it developed in the late nineteenth century. Holistic approaches have not yet been used to study mediated sport audiences. One topic that is ripe for holistic investigation is home viewing of televised sporting events. Most television viewing occurs in domestic settings, and this would be an excellent site for an ethnography focused on the mass mediated sport audience. Eastman and Riggs (1994) provide a useful start in this area with their study of sports fans.

We also need analyses of a wider variety of televised sports. The themes that have thus far been identified in textual analyses are limited to only a few sports. If investigators look farther afield, they may find other important concepts that are central in televised portrayals of sport. Analyses of non-traditional and regional sports such as beach volleyball, bowling, lacrosse, NASCAR racing, and rodeo might be fruitful. For example, Lawrence (1982) found that rodeo contests portray tension in the American West between the wild and the tame. Given this characterization of live rodeo events, it would be interesting to note if these tensions are present in media renderings as well.

In some cases scholars have identified textual content or audience interpretations that seem to oppose dominant ideologies. Remembering that oppositional textual material may encourage alternative audience interpretations, increased efforts should be made to define what constitutes oppositional content, and investigators should make more systematic efforts to look for them.

Turning specifically to production, text, and audience, there are additional issues. The majority of work on mass mediated sport has dealt with analyses of the content of the texts. More research on production and audience is needed. Most of the production literature informs us about technical aspects of the process. Greater attention should be given to political and economic dimensions at local, national, and global levels.

In the area of textual analysis, more investigations are needed concerning sport advertising and the commercial nature of sport, and drug use by athletes. These themes are clearly embedded in today's sport, therefore relevant media portrayals are important to study. In the context of winning and success, the theme of teamwork and cooperation needs more elaboration. Most of the focus thus far has been on competitive individualism. This may not be surprising, given the individualistic nature of American society (Bellah, Madsen, Sullivan, Swidler, & Tipton, 1985) – scholars may be led to focus more on competitive individualism, and broadcasters may be led to highlight this more heavily as well. Nevertheless, more systematic efforts should be made to examine variations in themes of teamwork shown in televised sport.

There is scant research on audiences of mediated sport compared with work on production and text. Many scholars have commented that audiences are free to interpret texts in a variety of ways, some of which may run counter to the "preferred" reading. However, there is very little actual data. Harris (1995) suggests that the concept of identity would be useful for analyzing variations in audience interpretations of mass mediated sport. People's conceptions of themselves are an important backdrop for making sense of the world around them, including televised sport. Condit (1989) provides a useful model for demonstrating that audience interpretations can be influenced by viewer identities. More generally, there is a need to look systematically at conditions under which viewer interpretations may vary and change.

Moving in new directions, there is a need to study renditions of sport appearing in emerging electronic interactive technologies such as the World Wide Web and sports-talk radio (Haag, 1996). It will be important to investigate all three domains here – production, textual content, and audience. More broadly, scholars should make more concerted efforts to include in their research reports policy recommendations for changing sport media practices. Findings could lead to suggestions for policies in media organizations which would increase the numbers of women and minorities on production staffs. Findings could also lead to policies aimed toward reducing or eliminating organizational constraints that encourage gender and racial biases, like those found by Theberge and Cronk (1986). Some of this research could also lead to policies in media organizations to make production staffs more aware of the practices that lead to gender bias, racial bias, and nationalistic bias. For example, in their study of gender stereotyping in televised sport texts, Duncan et al. (1994) provide recommendations for reducing the trivialization of women in future broadcasts. With media sport casting an increasingly large shadow on social life, researchers have a responsibility to set the stage for policy that can help remedy inequitable cultural sensibilities that come out of the media and sport relationship.

NOTE

1   This is an expanded and greatly revised version of Kinkema, K.M., & Harris, J.C. (1992). Sport and the mass media. *Exercise and Sport Sciences Reviews, 20*, 127–159.

Part two

MediaSport

Institutions

Circuits of Promotion: Media, Marketing and the Globalization of Sport

David Whitson

This chapter sets out to explore some important aspects of the production and consumption of sport in the late twentieth century. In the 1990s, the North American based "major leagues" (in basketball, American football, ice hockey, and baseball) are all developing strategies to market their products – telecast packages, typically, and licensed merchandise – to audiences around the globe. Over a slightly longer time period, events like Formula One racing, the Americas' Cup, the Tour de France, and Wimbledon have become international media and commercial events, as well as sports events. The FIFA World Cup and Olympic Games, in particular, have succeeded in constructing themselves as global extravaganzas (Whannel, 1992; Gillen, 1994/5). They are watched by global audiences, and as a result have become highly attractive marketing vehicles for the promoters of a variety of global products, as well as offering promotional opportunities to the host city (Whitson & Macintosh, 1996). The common factor in these phenomena, beyond the construction of communities of sporting interests that transcend national boundaries, is that boundaries between what used to be related but separable activities – the promotion of sports, and the use of sports events and personalities to promote other products – are also being dissolved.

The discussion will begin by identifying some important features of the early commodification of sport in North America. It was observed some years ago by Bourdieu (1978) that the professionalization of popular sports, like that of "folk" music, simply returns to ordinary people, as paying spectators, commodified versions of practices with which they had once entertained themselves. Early professional sport was not yet commodified in all the ways we know today, if by commodification we mean production for the primary purpose of making a profit (Lee, 1993, p. xi). However, the production and staging of sport as commercial entertainment led to the emergence of entrepreneurial structures and practices that would slowly transform the relationships between sporting teams and the communities they ostensibly "represent." Among the most important early developments were the ownership of teams by private entrepreneurs, the movement of both teams and players to larger cities where there were higher profits and salaries to be made, and the formation of combines of team operators (i.e. leagues) who achieved national market domination (and labor market domination) within their particular sports.

It is important to recognize that professional sport has developed in historically specific ways in different countries. The traditional German practice in which even famous professional soccer teams were typically part of non-profit, multi-sport "clubs," managed by boards composed of local business people, offers an example of a more civically rooted, less entrepreneurial structure. So, too, does the Australian norm – now under threat – in which community-based Football and Rugby League clubs have been run by boards answerable to a local membership, on whom the club also depended for financial support. In North America, in contrast, professional sport developed from the outset along more business-like lines; and the entrepreneurial ownership structures, team movements, and league mergers that gave shape to American professional sports in the interwar years all prefigure later developments associated with expansion (in the 1960s and 1970s) and, today, globalization. It is not my intention, in this last remark, to equate globalization with the diffusion of American popular culture. Most sophisticated discussions today recognize that the economic and cultural dynamics involved in globalization are more complex than the terms of older debates about American "cultural imperialism" allowed for.[1]

However, I will propose that what may be more far-reaching in its effects on the sporting cultures of other countries than the spread of basketball, for example, is the adoption of "American" business practices and marketing strategies by their own sports (the 1995–6 struggle between the Australian Rugby League and "Super League" is a contemporary example). This more business-like approach to sport need not involve Americans in any way, however; indeed, the business norms alluded to here have long been standard practice in other businesses around the Western world. The significant development is that longstanding structures of professional sport in Europe and Australia are under pressure from the same combination of commercial challenges and opportunities that are transforming many other consumer oriented businesses. Until recently, the force of "tradition," coupled with a sense that these leagues were national institutions, had effectively insulated them against pressures for change. What the challenge to these traditional structures represents is the erosion of the idea that sport is somehow "different" from more ordinary businesses, and the ascendancy of the longstanding premise of the American entertainment industries: that cultural products are commodities, that audiences have a right to the latest and the "best," and that restrictions on consumer choice in the name of protecting national cultures are unwarranted restraints of trade.

An important aspect in the commodification of North American sport will involve tracing the relationships that developed between professional sports and the news media, and the role of the print media and radio in building audiences for "major league" sport, ultimately making the major professional leagues into national institutions. It is not only that the news media gave free publicity to the professional leagues simply by reporting their games as news. Equally important was that the popularity of sports coverage demonstrated the potential of sport to attract large and predictable audiences for advertisers. The relationships between professional sports and the media would change over the years, as business and cultural environments changed and as the media business, in particular, was affected by technological developments and changes in marketing practices; the details of this evolution are beyond the scope of this paper.[2]

In this chapter, I will argue that an important feature of the transformations in professional sport today is a new kind of corporate integration in the media and entertainment industries. At one level this means transnational investments and partnerships, and attempts to promote sports and associated products on a global basis. However, even more important is vertical integration between owners of distribution media, especially in cable and satellite television, and owners of those popular entertainment "properties" (in movies and animation, as well as professional sports) that can provide staple programming for burgeoning home entertainment markets. This shift towards integrated corporate ownership of both content *and* distribution is exemplified in the recent initiatives of News Ltd. and Disney, both of whom moved into professional sports ownership in the mid-1990s. Such moves signal the incorporation of sports into a global "promotional culture" and the inclusion of corporate teams and events in "circuits of promotion" (Wernick, 1991), in which different products in a large media empire are used to promote each other, as well as giving wider cultural presence to the corporate brand name.

One important result of this increasing integration of sport into commodity culture, it will be suggested, is to refashion the kinds of identifications that fans are encouraged to make with teams and players. In the early days of spectator sport, teams were largely composed of local men, and operated under the auspices of "clubs" that acted as organizers of ethnic, class, or town affiliations. Together, these phenomena contributed to a popular sense that teams were community institutions, and that their performance reflected the character of the communities they represented. Sporting contests between rival communities were full of social symbolism, and local "derbies" served as occasions for public rehearsals of the class, ethnic and religious identities that structured life in these rapidly industrializing societies. In these circumstances, cheering for one's 'home' team was taken for granted, and most fans identified with the fortunes of their local team. However, as the potential for making money from the staging of sporting entertainment became clearer, and as cities themselves grew and changed, these community associations and meanings would be abraded and transformed by the logic of the marketplace (Rowe et al., 1994). By the late twentieth century, although professional sports operators routinely appeal to civic (and national) sentiments when it suits their commercial purposes, the languages of communal traditions and loyalties are increasingly supplanted by corporate images and by the discourse of consumer choice.

MEDIA, FANS, AND PUBLICS: THE MAKING OF MAJOR LEAGUE SPORTS

The most immediate outcome of commercial sport was the development of labor markets in athletic talent, in which wealthy teams offered "traveling players" financial inducements to come and play for them. It was this, of course, that created the phenomenon of the professional athlete, even though labor market mobility (and hence salaries) would quickly be contained by the emergence of cartels in all the major sports. In the early 1900s, teams and leagues competed freely for player talent, and in this context, the meanings of sporting representation began to change. Civic teams were soon comprised of the best "representatives" local money could buy, and successful teams became products and signs of civic wealth, rather than the talents or character of local players. Sports teams had become popular symbols in the competitive discourses of civic identity that circulated in late nineteenth-century America (Gorn & Goldstein, 1993), and this helped to naturalize a politically trivial, "boosterist" version of civic pride. Predictably, moreover, teams based in provincial cities could not compete financially with teams in New York, Chicago, and Detroit; and talent quickly gravitated to the metropolitan-based teams. This led to the consolidation of one "major league" in each sport (in baseball, two, with a common championship). It was the achievement of Major League Baseball and, on a smaller scale, the National Hockey League, to establish loyal civic followings in the major commercial and manufacturing centres of the period, in the American northeast and midwest (in ice hockey, this would include the Canadian metropolitan centres of Montreal and Toronto). This contributed over time to a popular sense that teams like the New York Yankees, Detroit Tigers, Boston Bruins, and Toronto Maple Leafs were civic institutions, part of the culture of their respective cities.[3]

However, this didn't mean that Americans and Canadians in other regions were not active fans. Baseball had established a reputation as America's "national pastime" in the late 1800s, not least because the metropolitan newspapers of that era had already created communities of interest that reached as far as the influence of these famous papers. Wire service reports of major league games and personalities were also familiar fare in many small town and regional newspapers, and from the 1920s onwards radio broadcasts took "live" games into homes across North America. Radio, in particular, gave people in small town America the experience of being "present" at newsworthy events, and powerful stations in centers like St. Louis and Chicago were soon pulling in audiences for major league baseball across the west and the south. Baseball players were national heroes, the pennant races and the World Series were becoming an autumn ritual of American life, and the game and its affairs were objects of national interest and conversation (McChesney, 1989).

In Canada, there were also eager audiences for baseball especially at World Series time, but ice hockey remained the national winter pastime. After the appropriation of the best professional hockey by the big-city east in the 1920s, small town and western Canadians continued to follow the fortunes of Canadian teams (and favorite sons on US-based teams) in the sports press and on the radio. In 1933, "Hockey Night in Canada" broadcasts, sponsored by General Motors, became the first regular programs to reach audiences from coast to coast, and by the following season, the Saturday night broadcasts were drawing regular audiences of more than a million Canadians in every region of the country (Gruneau & Whitson, 1993). It is an important dimension of this story that the early successes of professional sports broadcasts in attracting listeners far from their "home" cities also attracted the attention of major manufacturers of mass consumer products. Companies like GM, Gillette, and Imperial Oil were looking, in the interwar years, for effective ways of advertising to national audiences, and their initiatives in sponsoring networked broadcasts of professional sports contributed in no small way to establishing the status of the "major leagues" as national institutions, as well as themselves as national brand names (Rutherford, 1978).

A key factor in building interest in professional sports was simply the normalization of the practice of reporting sports results as news. With the development of the sports sections and sportscasts that became regular features of the daily news, sport would stay "in the news" all week, even when there was no action on the field. Trade gossip, injury reports, pregame hype and postgame analysis all sustained interest in professional sports between events, and helped to establish the serial sagas of the sporting seasons as a familiar feature of North American popular life. Wernick's discussion of how serialized popular entertainments like sitcoms and comic strips create communities "of continuous gossip to which identifying audiences become addicted" (1991, p.105) offers an obvious comparison with the ways that fans become involved with professional sport, as well as insight into why the serial and series have become such ubiquitous cultural commodities. Wernick proposes that each installment promotes interest in its successors, and adds to the overall presence of the master narrative and its characters in popular culture. In the series comprised of self-contained episodes (e.g., the mystery), the closest parallel in format to the sporting season, nothing important is lost if an episode or game is missed. What matters in building audience interest is the continuity of the main characters, and the appeal of the dramatic situations that they repeat within a predictable range of variations. The professional sporting season conforms to these criteria perfectly. Each game is a self-contained episode, a competition and a communal rivalry that can be enjoyed on its own. Yet audience interest is dramatically increased as identifications are developed with teams and players, and as the serial dramas of playoff races and individual competitions for scoring or batting titles move towards their annual climaxes.

> The effect is to create ... a body of actual fans who serve, as that term suggests, to amplify the promotional effect ... Fans are linked to the patented cultural model, and to its imaged set of variants, by ties of loyalty which are only a more excited version of those which tie regular customers to any commodity brand.
>
> (Wernick, 1991, p.105)

One of the most effective forms of sports coverage for building audiences was human interest stories that invited identifications with the participants (favorite players, managers, rookies, etc.). Games were prefigured as contests between individuals, and readers were invited to identify with their hopes and plans – and afterwards, to share in the joys of victory and agonies of defeat. For those players who acquired reputations for producing the goods in decisive situations – whether home runs, goals, or touchdowns – their feats became legendary, and the men themselves were constructed as larger than life characters (Gorn & Goldstein, 1993). Such attention has turned figures from Babe Ruth to Wayne Gretzky into household names, and along with similar "star-making" publicity in the film and music industries, it has helped create the phenomenon of the celebrity entertainer. Famous names were shown to promote interest in the sports events or films they were part of, and also to help sell the products they endorsed. Thus, it was not long before the media and entertainment industries recognized their common stake in the manufacture of "names" for a public demonstrably fascinated by stardom. As Wernick would later observe, a star, for these purposes, is someone "whose name and fame have been built up to the point where reference to them . . . can serve as a promotional booster in itself" (1991, p. 106).

By the late 1930s it was possible to see in outline what would become the ubiquitous place of professional sport in North American popular culture. It is important to recognize that it was the development of newspaper chains and radio networks that became, in effect, national information systems, that facilitated the development of common knowledge and interests among geographically dispersed regions. Yet the fact that the emergence of national media in America was driven by the interests of advertisers in reaching national audiences also meant that the lines between news, entertainment, and advertising would be constantly blurred. This would help to make the place of both professional sport and its sponsors in the fun-oriented consumer culture that was part of the promise of "America" in the interwar period, and would become even more so after the war (Rutherford, 1993). At the same time, though, the cumulative effect of media coverage that brought America – and Canada, too – together for events like the World Series and Stanley Cup was to establish connections between professional sports and national identities, especially among those many ordinary people who did not share the interests of political and intellectual élites.

THE POSTWAR YEARS: EXPANSION AND TELEVISION

In the postwar years, the geography and economics of professional sport would start to change in ways that would both expand and change the character of audiences for professional sports. Economic growth was creating booming new concentrations of population and wealth in California and across the "sunbelt" states, and it was generating unprecedented spending on leisure and entertainment. The development of air travel had also made continent-wide competitions feasible, and major league owners began receiving overtures from potential operators in the west and south. There was also the specter, and for a brief time the reality, of competitor leagues. In these circumstances, all the major sports leagues came to see expansion through franchising as a preemptive move against potential competitors, and a reliable wealth creation strategy. It is noteworthy that franchising in professional sport involves the same kind of transaction as in other businesses: rights are sold to promote a nationally marketed product in a new market area. A familiar result of franchising is greater market penetration by national brand names, and the erosion of independent alternatives and regional differences. This is achieved, moreover, without further investment by the existing partners. Since the 1960s, franchise fees have provided sports owners with regular infusions of capital, and increases in franchise values have provided some owners with windfall profits even when operating profits have been weak.

However, the success of major league expansion and the dramatic rise in the values of sports franchises cannot be understood without reference to the impact of television. While franchising brought in important new revenues, the strategic objective for all professional sports from the 1960s onwards became to get, and increase the value of, national network television contracts (Bellamy, 1989). From the earliest days of sports television, it quickly became clear that television could augment sport's core audiences of already committed fans, both by taking "live" sport into new geographic regions and by presenting sports in ways designed to make them entertaining to new viewers. Replays and camera work helped television audiences to see things that stadium audiences often missed, while commentary sought to sustain excitement and to make viewers feel part of an important event. The latter was also true of radio, of course, but television's pictures were often worth a thousand words. In particular, television could bring athletes' faces into the living room, and this helped to "personalize" stars like Mickey Mantle, Joe Namath, and O.J. Simpson, adding to their celebrity status and hence the value of their images in endorsements. Televised sport was thus reworked according to the codes of the entertainment industry, and those who were successful at this (e.g., ABC's Monday Night NFL football telecasts, and in Canada CBC's "Hockey Night in Canada") built the biggest regular audiences in their respective countries.

This, not surprisingly, translated into lucrative advertising revenues, which in turn fueled spectacular increases in the monies the networks were willing to spend for exclusive rights to popular sports. The major sports would each develop their own methods of selling their product to television, with football, and later basketball, operating more collectively and sharing revenues more equally than either baseball or hockey – a difference that would produce important consequences that we shall return to shortly. In the 1960s, however, the most visible consequences of television money were increased profits, and players fighting for a share of these. With the successful establishment of player unions, all sports saw dramatic increases in player remuneration, culminating in the multi-million dollar contracts that are commonplace today. This would have the effect of making owners dependent on steadily increasing the value of their television contracts and this, in turn, would influence the strategic objectives and geographic directions of future expansions.

All claimants to "major league" status need a strong presence in the major metropolitan markets, but they also need to position themselves in places seen as growing and affluent markets. Most importantly, in the 1960s, major leagues needed to be able to offer the networks the prospect of "national" audiences. This would mean that all of the established "major leagues" would expand into cities and regions where their sports were not historically major, and it would favor growing and underrepresented television markets – in California, Florida, Colorado, the

Pacific northwest, and later the Carolinas – over cities, like Buffalo, whose television radius overlapped with the markets of established teams. It also led to the phenomenon of teams being promoted as state or regional representatives, even when (as in the case of the Denver Broncos or Portland Trailblazers) they still bore a civic name. Ultimately these dynamics (i.e., television and expansion) would promote interest in a variety of sports in cities and regions where one sport had traditionally dominated.

Here it is germane to return to the different ways that sports have sold themselves to (and through) television, and some of the consequences of these differences. It was arguably the NFL in the early 1960s that led the way in taking advantage of the opportunities afforded by network television (Bellamy, 1989; Klatell & Marcus, 1988). Under the leadership of commissioner Rozelle, the league assumed control of the sale of televised football, and pioneered the idea of a single, nationally-televised game. Revenues from the first network contract (with CBS) in 1962 were divided equally among member teams, who were no longer able to telecast their own games locally. The model of a single national telecast would be extended in 1964 to the popular double header (a game in the east followed by one in the west), and later to Monday Night Football on ABC. However, the fact that all of these broadcasts were exclusive, and didn't have to compete with locally-televised games, built enormous and reliable *national* audiences, who in turn pulled in enormous dollars for the networks from national advertisers. Culturally, Leifer proposes that the national exposure of carefully selected games also helped build general identifications with the league, the sport, and with teams like the Dallas Cowboys. "What had previously been presumed to exist only for championships – interest not rooted in locale – was here extended into the regular season. Fans were being lured into following not just … 'their' … team but other teams as well" (1995, p. 132).

This contrasts with the practice of baseball, which also sold the networks broadcast rights to a "Game of the Week," but the sport's commissioners could never secure the agreement of large market owners, in particular, to forego the sale of local television rights. This meant that national telecasts had to compete with a patchwork of locally and regionally televised games, and ratings suggested that local loyalties typically prevailed. Thus, although baseball attracted huge national audiences for the World Series, it has never succeeded in the way that football did in building them for regular season matches (Leifer, 1995). The economic consequences are that the value of baseball advertising to the networks declined well below that of football, and the networks became resistant to paying the increases that owners now needed to fund their exploding payrolls. This, in turn, has sustained the importance of the revenues that owners get separately for local and regional rights. Yet this entrenches the economic divide between large market baseball teams (and, now, teams owned by superstations or regional sports networks), and their small market competitors. Through the late 1980s, the networks continued to pay significant sums for rights to major league baseball, because they wanted the World Series. However they increasingly didn't televise mid-season games that they had rights to, and the signs were clear that the constantly rising revenues of the past were over. The contract signed in 1993 marked an end to guaranteed revenues, and the beginning of a very different relationship between television and major league baseball.[4]

The National Hockey League and National Basketball Association each have their own peculiar histories that differentiate them from the above "prototypes" (i.e., of a genuinely national audience versus the sum total of local audiences, following Leifer, 1995). The NHL has a long history as a national institution in Canada, and as noted above, CBC's hockey broadcasts have attracted Canada's first, and consistently largest, national audiences (Gruneau & Whitson, 1993). However although the NHL had a short-lived contract with CBS in the early 1970s, it attracted abysmal American ratings and was not renewed. In this context, US teams have had to develop the revenue opportunities afforded by local and regional television. Some teams have done well by this, especially since the advent of regional sports networks (e.g., in New York, Boston). However the absence of a US network contract has had consequences not dissimilar to baseball, both economically (a growing divide between large and small market teams), and in the regional nature of audience interest. Even the Stanley Cup playoffs are not a national event in the United States.

The NBA, in contrast, has moved from a problem-plagued position in the late 1970s when only the playoffs attracted national interest, to a status in American popular culture that now rivals that of the NFL (Leifer, 1995). Football's television revenues remain greater, but basketball's have risen dramatically to easily surpass those of baseball and hockey. From the time David Stern took over as commissioner, the league would follow the NFL model of centralizing control of broadcast rights and significantly reducing the competing product on the screen. The exclusive national exposure of the NFL's Sunday and Monday night broadcasts is harder to achieve in a sport that plays an eighty-two game season and schedules games throughout the week. However, the league has successfully imposed limits on local broadcasting (though not without opposition, notably from the Chicago Bulls), and the size and market value of the national audiences have risen sharply. There are other important factors in the NBA's remarkable ascendancy in the 1990s; and some of these, in particular merchandising and corporate marketing, will be addressed in the next section.

However, before concluding this discussion of the postwar period, I want to propose that ultimately, the most far-reaching consequence of television and expansion in major league sports has been the gradual "delocalization" of sporting tastes and loyalties. At first, in the 1950s and 1960s, this simply meant the further popularization of major league sport, and a corresponding decline (that would later be partially reversed) in the fortunes of the minors. Through the 1970s and 1980s, "delocalization" would refer to the increasing incidence of franchise movements, and to the rupture of traditionally understood relationships between teams and cities that the phenomenon of the moveable franchise represents (Euchner, 1992). Most generally, though, national television would encourage, and gradually normalize, the practice of fans identifying with teams based elsewhere, in contrast to older loyalties based in geography. Thus it was that the Dallas Cowboys became, for a time, "America's Team," while in later years national followings would develop for teams like the LA Raiders and Chicago Bulls. "Walk down any street in America and observe the diversity of team logos on caps, T-shirts, and bumper stickers. Fans for any team can turn up anywhere," and they register support of "their" teams not just by purchasing insignia clothing but by constituting large and geographically distributed television audiences (Leifer, 1995, p. 134). The significance of this tendency, which would become even more visible by the 1990s, is that it marks the gradual detachment of professional sports from loyalties and meanings based in place, and a normalization of the discourses of personal and consumer choice.

CORPORATE SYNERGIES: THE NEW ECONOMY OF PROFESSIONAL SPORT

We can illustrate this general proposition by examining some of the new "revenue streams" that have become important in professional sport: merchandising, corporate public relations, and cross-marketing. All of these trade on the symbolic meanings that can be attached to particular sports and sports celebrities, and their value rises as signifiers like the Chicago Bulls for example, or Wayne Gretzky, become meaningful to wider consumer audiences. Among the most visible symbolic commodities, of course, are the team caps and other merchandise that sport "official" major league logos. Baseball caps and hockey sweaters were historically a small revenue source for famous teams like the New York Yankees or Montreal Canadiens. However, the market for these items was tied to the team's historic prowess, and was typically confined to local boys for whom wearing a rival city's sweater was inconceivable.[5] In the 1980s, the NFL and the NBA, in particular, showed that merchandise associated with nationally-followed teams – and individuals – could be promoted anywhere. They also showed that a coordinated approach to the promotion of licensed merchandise could make team gear fashionable in the adolescent and young adult "sportswear" markets. Insignia sportswear is, arguably, simply a variant on the promotion of wearable advertising, modelled so successfully by the makers of sport shoes (e.g., Nike, Adidas) and other casual wear (e.g., Gap, Tommy Hilfiger). However, it opened up enormous new potential revenues, as well as reinforcing the place of sports logos and colours in the symbolic language and landscape of North American youth culture. The irony is that it is now team colors and logos (and names), rather than a team's competitive prowess, that sell merchandise. This is demonstrated in the merchandising successes of expansion teams like the San Jose Sharks and Toronto Raptors, and it has normalized the selection of names and design of uniforms by marketing departments.

A related aspect of the economy of contemporary professional sports involves the marketing of stars. This is not a new phenomenon in show business, as we have observed, but it takes on new dimensions in the television era. Television has made sports stars more recognizable, and added to the overall presence of sport in contemporary popular culture. The National Basketball Association has taken particular advantage of television since the 1980s to associate the game with the skills and personalities of a series of stars: Magic Johnson and Larry Bird, Michael Jordan and Charles Barkley, Shaquille O'Neal and Grant Hill. Televised basketball's "visible heads" mean that viewers get vivid individual images, both of the extravagant skills of a Jordan, and the emotions and "attitude" out of which imaged personae have been constructed around men like Barkley and Rodman. The NBA has built on these advantages with spectacular success, as have the shoe companies Nike and Reebok. The effect has been to create an unprecedented series of black American celebrities, whose celebrity has in turn augmented the visibility of the league and the game in American (and now global) popular culture.[6] What this illustrates is that "the aims and results of star-making are part and parcel of the brand-imaging of the cultural products, and companies, with which stars are creatively associated." (Wernick, 1991, p. 107)

It is important here to appreciate that the iconic status of a Jordan is not the result of skill alone, though skill is a necessary foundation. The construction of imaged celebrities is a promotional practice in itself and, when successful, it confers benefits on all partners in the exercise. Nike, in particular, attached its corporate persona to images of Michael Jordan, but when Jordan appeared in Nike advertisements in the early 1990s, he was adding to the global visibility of the Chicago Bulls, the NBA, and the game of basketball, as well as promoting Nike shoes (Barber, 1995). He was also, not incidentally, promoting himself and adding to his value as a promotional icon. Whether Nike and Jordan have helped to promote the NBA or vice versa is neither clear nor important (Williams, 1994). What this illustrates is that in "circuits of promotion" there are no obvious starting points and endpoints, but rather recursive and mutually reinforcing public texts that generate more visibility and more business for all concerned. It also illustrates that cultural commodities, including celebrities, can become vehicles for the promotion of more than one producer's product at once (Wernick, 1991, pp.105–9).

The most important developments in the sports business, however, follow from the rapid deployment of pay-tv technologies (i.e., cable and satellite services), and from technological and corporate developments that point towards tighter vertical integration in the communications and "infotainment" industries. Subscription television achieved near complete market penetration across the US and Canada by the early 1980s, not least because there was widespread consumer interest in the multiplicity of specialty channels that the new technologies could offer. Yet it was access to sports and movies that attracted the keenest interest and appeared decisive in persuading customers to subscribe to cable or to choose one service provider over another. In addition, specialty sports channels attracted the male audiences that many advertisers wanted to target (Sparks, 1992), and they did so more cost-effectively than the national networks. In this context, regional sports channels carrying the games of local teams provided more visibility for sports on television, and they provided an important revenue stream for the teams whose games they carried. However, in baseball and hockey where there was less central (i.e., league) control over broadcast rights, this would further sharpen the revenue gap between larger and small market teams, while also weakening the value of national network contracts (Bellamy & Walker, 1995, Leifer, 1995).

For our purposes, though, the other important consequences of the development of specialty channels and subscription television have to do with the corporate synergies that can be achieved by cross-ownership and cross-marketing. In the era of cable and satellite television, an important and far-reaching synergy is found in the ownership of sports franchises (increasingly, several in a city) by the owners of regional cable or satellite networks. Cable and satellite have vastly increased channel capacity and hence the need for programming, so that ownership of popular content can afford significant competitive advantages. In such mergers of distribution with content, television provides important revenues and publicity for the teams, while exclusive coverage of popular sports events helps to sell cable or satellite subscriptions. The latter has become especially important in Europe and Australia, where cable and satellite have achieved acceptance only in the 1990s. Exclusive rights to English soccer are widely seen as decisive in the success of the News Ltd/BSkyB satellite venture in Europe (Williams, 1994), while sports rights continue to be an important battleground in the competition between the two major cable providers in Australia. In the near future, competition for exclusive control of popular sports "properties" only stands to increase, as digital televisions are introduced and as technological and regulatory developments permit new kinds of telecommunications competitors (phone companies, Internet providers) to supply information and entertainment products to homes. Vertically integrated infotainment corporations have already bankrolled teams (in Europe and Japan), new events (rugby and cricket World Cups), and even new leagues (Australian rugby league's "Super League") as ways of promoting their own services – and it may not be far-fetched to imagine that leagues, or global sports bodies (like FIFA) will consider establishing their own pay television systems.[7]

Cross-ownership also makes possible promotional synergies at the conceptual stage, when different products in a corporate empire are designed and marketed so as to enhance each other's presence and fashionability. The promotion of toys and children's accessories (e.g., lunch pails, pajamas) in association with television shows and video games is a familiar and now controversial example of cross-marketing (Kline, 1993). However, the strategic use of intertextual promotion to build brand recognition in popular culture is modelled most effectively by Disney, most recently in their promotion of the (NHL) Mighty Ducks of Anaheim, along with the serialized Mighty Ducks films (in 1996, "Mighty Ducks III") and a corresponding range of insignia merchandise. Their 1995 purchase of Capital Cities/ABC may presage new circuits of promotion involving hockey, films, videos and television shows, themed environments, and other products aimed at children. Other major corporations engaging in innovative cross-marketing of a variety of leisure products include Blockbuster Video (now incorporating Viacom, along with several Florida sports franchises and a theme park) and, of course, Nike, whose themed Nike Town "shopping environments" now promote a full range of Nike products and images (Barber, 1995, pp. 132–3, 67–68).

All of these developments, it can be suggested, represent a new stage in the commodification of sport, and point to the further incorporation of mediated sport, in particular, into a postmodern "economy of signs" (Lash & Urry, 1994). In this economy, the market value of televised sport is increased exponentially by communications technologies that multiply distributive capacity while allowing distributors to charge. In this economy, the construction of symbolic meanings is crucial to adding value to many kinds of branded products, whether these are experiential products like NBA basketball or the Olympics, or material products like sneakers and sweaters and colas. In either case, it is the product name and the symbolic associations it carries that attract new consumers, and establish its value as a commodity-sign. In this economy, "innovative virtual industries . . . advertising agencies, corporate public relations and communications divisions" promote new ways of satisfying old needs, and associate the consumption of branded products with imaged identities and pleasures (Barber, 1995, pp. 68–69). In this economy, finally, where images and logos can be readily transmitted across thousands of miles and across cultural borders, the ultimate audience is global, combining the affluent markets of Europe and North America and mining the huge potential of the "emerging" markets of Latin America and Asia. "In Planet Reebok," as their advertising puts it, "there are no boundaries."

Thus in sport, even though the initial efforts of the National Football League to expand into Europe in the late 1980s met with only limited success, as have efforts to establish professional soccer in America, it is clear in the late 1990s that most of the major professional sports and the television conglomerates that now have investments in them are exploring how to reach global audiences (Bellamy, 1993). All the major professional sports seek to demonstrate to transnational advertisers that they can attract global audiences – in the manner of the Olympics. For those that succeed in demonstrating their marketing potential in what are now global circuits of promotion, the stakes are almost unlimited, in terms of merchandising and television revenues and the allied promotional revenues outlined above. For television companies, meanwhile, "their optimum economic strategy is to exploit the original material they make or own (rights to) to the maximum, by selling it in as many markets as possible" and using it to promote trademarked ancillary products (Murdock, 1992, p. 36). Indeed Fox's huge contract with the NFL only makes sense to the broadcaster (a part of the transnational Murdoch communications empire, which includes satellite broadcast networks in Europe, Asia and Australia) if Fox can develop global audiences for football broadcasts. Other major American distributors of televised sports product – including NBC and ESPN – are likewise forming international partnerships with distributors in Europe and Australia, not least because sport appears to appeal across cultural boundaries more successfully than other kinds of television programming, such as drama and current affairs (Bellamy, 1993; Williams, 1994).

MEDIASPORT AND TOMORROW'S GLOBAL CONSUMER

Many observations could be made about the developments outlined above. As far as the major North American professional sports are concerned, we can observe new stages and opportunities in the expansion and search for new publics (and new commodity forms) that have been characteristic of the American entertainment industries since early in the twentieth century. What is new for the major leagues in the 1990s is that North American markets are approaching maturity, and thus further significant growth depends upon globalization. What is unclear as we approach the next century is whether globalization will largely be limited to television packages and merchandising, or whether the North American leagues will seek to establish teams (or linked leagues) in European or Asian cities. The potential value of the global markets in ancillary products is enormous, as the NFL and NBA in particular, have begun to demonstrate; but efforts to attract live audiences for North American sports (the World League of American Football, and exhibition games by NFL and NHL teams) have met with modest success at best. The NBA, despite its aggressive international promotion of NBA "properties," disclaims any interest in overseas expansion (Jackson & Andrews, 1995). Indeed Leifer (1995) argues that the North American sports will encounter limits in the extent to which they can build sustained audiences (i.e., beyond interest in televised playoffs and championships, like the Super Bowl), for sports whose "representative" significance remains limited to their US heartlands. Despite global enthusiasms for Americana, he predicts that European and Asian audiences will not stay interested (once the novelty wears off) in regular season matches between Los Angeles and Kansas City, any more than Americans would stay interested in teams representing Nagoya and Okinawa, or Munich and Milan.

In Europe and Australia, meanwhile, even though the dominance of their traditional spectator sports (soccer, and in a few countries, rugby) has been to some extent shaken by the popularity of basketball among the young, the principal effect of the developments outlined above – especially those related to television – has been to push those sports towards business structures and marketing methods that will allow them to capitalize more widely on their product(s). In English soccer, the structure that traditionally allowed quite a number of small city clubs and London (neighborhood) clubs in their "major league" is being reshaped to suit the interests of television and of the major metropolitan clubs. Both want to concentrate on competitive matches that can maximize audiences and advertising values, and this means a smaller league comprised of big city, corporate sponsored teams (who, in contrast to American practice to date, already wear the names of their corporate sponsors on their jerseys). There is also talk of a European "Super League," and although this has not yet happened, the European Champions' Cup has adopted a new playoff-style format that produces more games between the top European teams for continent-wide television audiences. "Down Under" meanwhile, the traditionally Sydney-based Australian Rugby League has been shaken up by entrepreneurial ownerships in Canberra and Brisbane, and it was threatened in 1995 with competition from a "Super League" bankrolled by Fox and News Ltd. This initiative was derailed temporarily by a court decision that upheld the validity of AFL player contracts. However some more entrepreneurial structure will likely emerge out of this, and the Fox/News Ltd group is also promoting transnational professional competition in rugby union.

It is noteworthy that in all of these examples it is television revenues and especially the potential of cable and satellite revenues that are driving the transformation of the traditional structures of these sports. We noted above how a traditional tournament like soccer's European Champions' Cup was revamped to produce more television "product", and the same agenda has led to the initiation of new "World Cup" competitions in rugby union and cricket, both of which proved enormously popular with television audiences in the countries where those games are played. It is also worth noting that major national and world competitions, most of which continue to be available on broadcast (i.e., "free") television in North America, have moved much more quickly to a pay-tv environment in Europe, resulting in "two tier" access to events of wide popular interest (Williams, 1994; Rowe, 1996). What is manifest in these developments is that European (and former Commonwealth) sports are quickly becoming intensively commodified, aggressively pursuing revenue streams that developed over a longer period in America.

I return here to an idea introduced early in this essay, namely that the ultimate outcome of globalization is less likely to be the hegemony of American sports than the intensive commodification of any sport that will retain a place in a mediated global culture. I have traced the progressive transformation of American sport by the logic of business and the imagination of marketers, but outside North America professional sports remained tradition-bound for much longer, comfortably secure in their traditional national markets. There are certainly those who lament what they call the "Americanization" of their own games: the marginalization of smaller clubs, the moving of games "upmarket" (away from the price range and tastes of working-class male audiences, and towards family and corporate entertainment), the marketing of stars and merchandise, the adoption of American style team names and logos, and the general subordination of sporting traditions to the needs of "good television"[8] Yet, what they are really objecting to is the commodification and marketing that are building renewed (and new) audiences for these games, nationally and globally. This is a very different situation from the specter of a global monoculture, in which European and Commonwealth sports are supplanted by North American ones.

It is worth noting here Leifer's proposal (1995) that if any of the American team games is to constitute itself as a truly global sport, it will have to make a radical break with the traditional fiction that sports teams represent geographic communities. Leifer suggests that while this symbolic linkage of teams with cities was essential to the early development of local loyalties, and was not inconsistent with building national audiences in the era of national broadcast television, it now serves as a barrier to the development of global audiences. There are simply too many major cities, leaving important markets "unrepresented"; while fans do not remain interested in teams representing foreign cities. For Leifer, the solution is leagues comprised of teams sponsored by global corporations – the Toyota Tigers, for example, or the Nike Panthers – competing on world circuits not unlike those that tennis and auto racing have today. Cities would bid to host one or more games whose primary function, from the perspective of sponsors and the media, would be to increase interest in the televised games that would continue throughout the season. Teams representing global corporations would not have "home" locations – indeed Leifer suggests their lack of place identity becomes a virtue – while fans would develop positive associations with the corporate sponsors of their favorite athletic standard-bearers. "Were major league teams to attach directly to multinationals" (p. 298), this could confer popular identities on often faceless corporations, making them more fully than ever a part of popular life.

However realistic or fanciful this scenario might be, I want to close by raising three reservations about the promotion of "world class" sport, whether American or European in its origins. The first of these is simply that "global promo" costs lots of money, and one effect of all the dynamics I have described here is to privilege the highly professional and the slickly-packaged, and to privilege those sports that are large enough to be of interest to global infotainment corporations and their global advertisers. It is also to make games that were once parts of genuinely popular cultures increasingly expensive, and out of reach of "ordinary" fans. Second, the cumulative cultural effect of media/sport's determination to fully exploit the potential of once ancillary revenue streams from marketing and merchandising is to further colonize public space and discourse with the language and imagery of consumerism (Murdock, 1992). Sport is not alone here, of course, but when playing surfaces are surrounded with advertising, when the names of arenas are sold to corporate sponsors (like the names of competitions have been for a longer time), and when athletes routinely wear corporate logos, the effect is surely to naturalize and even make beneficent the role of these corporations in our lives. Much of this is so "natural," or at least so familiar by now, that it is tempting to dismiss it as harmless. Yet in the late twentieth century economy of signs, it is hard to deny that "the cultural capital of corporations has replaced many human forms of cultural capital. As we buy, wear, and eat logos, we become the . . . admen of the corporations, defining ourselves with respect to (their) social standing" and currency (Willis, 1993, pp. 132–133).

This leads to a final comment on the naturalization of consumer identities that is implicit in the promotion of sports signifiers as consumer choices, rather than signs of place identity. Lee (1993) has observed that the national brand advertising of earlier eras sought explicitly to break down loyalties to local products and producers, in part by inviting Americans (and others) to belong to America through their consumption of national brands (e.g., Coke, Ford, and Levi's). Likewise, today, the makers and purveyors of "world class" sports products seek to reshape identities beyond the national stage, and to equate membership in global culture with the consumption – even on television – of global events and celebrities. It can be granted that for the inner-city youth and other youth around the world who express their identifications through the wearing of NBA merchandise, their aspirations may have less to do with global citizenship than simply breaking with the constraints of age, class, and neighborhood (Jackson & Andrews, 1995). Yet in our naturalization of consumer identities, and the celebration of trivial affinities and differences that so frequently accompanies it, we render it harder to recognize the differences between market choices and social choices, and between elective affinities and more enduring kinds of common interests.

NOTES

1   For nuanced discussions of the globalization/Americanization debate, see Rowe et al. (1994), McKay et al. (1993), Maguire (1993b), Rutherford (1993).

2   See Jhally (1984), Klatell & Marcus (1988), Wenner (1989a), and for a British perspective, Whannel (1992).

3   For fuller discussions of these dynamics, see Gruneau and Whitson (1993, Ch. 3, 4) and Whitson (1995) on Canada; Reiss (1989), Euchner (1992), and Leifer (1995) on America.

4   See Bellamy & Walker (1995) for a fuller discussion of baseball on television, and the implications of the new "partnership" between ABC, NBC, and Major League Baseball in "The Baseball Channel."

5   Canadian author Roch Carrier's famous short story "The Sweater" captures the horror and shame of a young Quebec boy who was given, in error, the sweater of the rival Toronto Maple Leafs.

6   See Jackson & Andrews (1995), Cole & Andrews (1996), Andrews (1996a) for fuller treatments of the NBA creation of celebrities, and in particular, black American celebrities for "crossover" (mostly white) buyers.

7   "Sport and television: swifter, higher, stronger, dearer," *The Economist* 20 July, 1996, pp. 17–19.

8   See McKay et al. (1993), Maguire (1993b) and Williams (1994) for discussions of some of these phenomena and responses to them. See Lee (1993) for a discussion of "intensive commodification."

The Evolving Television Sports Marketplace

Robert V. Bellamy, Jr.

Surveying the relationship of US sports and television entities at the end of the 1980s, Eastman and Meyer (1989) predicted that sports programming "will change ... radically in the next decade" (p. 97) and become "the crucible for programming research in the 1990s" (p. 118). In the same volume, Bellamy (1989) characterized the relationship of sports and television entities as a "partnership of oligopolies ... not likely to be altered in the near future" (p. 132).

To a large degree, these relatively modest and somewhat contradictory predictions have come to pass. With a seemingly endless proliferation of television channels, sport is seen as the programming that can best break through the clutter of channels and advertising and consistently produce a desirable audience for sale to advertisers. In economic terms, the telecasting of sports provides a television entity with a level of product differentiation that distinguishes it from its rivals. This often takes the form of "branding"– whereby sports coverage becomes identified with a specific television provider, such as the "NBA on NBC" or ABC's *NFL Monday Night Football*. Brand identification is regarded as a key in leveraging corporate assets and in building audience loyalty at a time when viewers are now regarded as "restless" and likely to use a remote control device (RCD) to choose among many viewing options (Bellamy & Walker, 1996). Sports also are seen as a critical component of the international expansion plans of the US television industry. To Fox Sports' President David Hill, "sport is the last frontier of reality on television ... about the only thing that can guarantee an audience" because of its ability to offer viewers around the globe "a shared communication experience" (Lafayette, 1996, p. 145).

While the sports and television partnership maintains many of its traditional structural features, the combination of a rapidly developing multichannel and international television industry and the increasing marketing-driven nature of sports has caused some disruptions in the once predictable relationship (Cox, 1995). To a substantial degree, this volatility can be linked to the overwhelming economic success of the relationship. The US sports industry is a *media-made* phenomenon. Television through its power to manufacture "stars," sell products, alter lifestyles, and most importantly, commodify audiences made spectator sports an element of mainstream culture (Jhally, 1984; Maguire, 1993; McChesney, 1989; Real, 1989; Whannel, 1992). However, technological diffusion and regulatory change have altered the traditional economic structure and concomitant behavior of the television industry. The result is that sports entities are now able to exert more autonomy within the relationship.

The purpose of this chapter is to present an analytic overview of the present status of the big sports and big television partnership. Here, "Big sports" will primarily be defined by the Big 4 professional sports leagues operating in the US – Major League Baseball (MLB), National Football League (NFL), National Basketball Association (NBA), National Hockey League (NHL) – and such periodic mega-events as the Olympics. "Big television" will refer to the Big Four broadcast networks (ABC, CBS, NBC, Fox); such major television program suppliers and distributors as ESPN; and, where relevant, the Regional Sports Networks (RSNs) that have had such rapid growth in the last decade. While the primary emphasis will be on US sports and television entities, there will be some discussion of international deals that increasingly are important to the partnership. Ultimately, what follows is an analysis of the efficacy and attractiveness of sports product to television in a changing media environment. Underlying the analysis is a recognition that sport is one, and arguably the most, important exemplar of the programming critical to the success of the emerging "new" oligopolies in television.

A CHANGING TELEVISION INDUSTRY

The most salient point in any analysis of the US television industry is the reconfiguration of its traditional oligopoly structure. Prior to the 1980s, the history of the industry is tied directly to a scarcity paradigm. Basing the regulation of broadcasting on the technical limitations of spectrum and an ill-defined "public interest" concept, the US government instituted a spectrum allocation and licensing system that nurtured the establishment of the Big 3 oligopoly (ABC, CBS, NBC) that would come to dominate the television industry. The combination of technological diffusion (i.e. satellite transmission, cable television, computers) and a decided move toward deregulation as *the* major operational model of government and business relations in the US and most all capitalist nations led to the ascendancy of a marketplace paradigm that attempts to equate audience "share" with the public "interest."

A Premature "Demise"

The US broadcast television industry's argument that it needed relief from "onerous" governmental regulation was persuasive in a political climate predisposed to economic deregulation. Ironically, this was the impetus for the rise of alternative distribution outlets like cable which led to a new level of competition for the attention of the television viewer. By the late 1980s, the Big Three networks were consistently losing audience to cable services and the new Fox network. It was not uncommon at this time to hear arguments that the Big Three were "dinosaurs" unable and unequipped to compete in the new multichannel environment (Reith, 1991). One of the reasons these arguments were given credence was the increased amount of desirable programming cable was able to acquire.

Sports product provided one of the better examples of this as the upscale demographics of cable subscribers were seen as a more efficient match for the desired demographics of sports entities and advertisers (Hofmeister, 1995; "Regional," 1994). Although little sports programming was actually diverted from broadcast to cable ("Sports programming," 1993), there is no question that cable provided an amenable outlet for the proliferation of sports product that previously would have been confined to local stations or, in most cases, not telecast at all. The cable industry's dual revenue stream of advertising and subscriber fees enabled it to develop services that concentrated solely on sports product (i.e., ESPN, RSNs). By 1990, cable was a major or even essential revenue source for sports entities.

The increased presence of sports on cable can also be attributed to changes within the sports industry. With the ability to effectively control the salaries of players constrained by the advent of free agency, professional sports leagues and franchise owners sought new ways to generate revenues to pay for the now increasingly expensive players. Enhanced television exposure was a primary means of doing so, a strategy that would have been problematic in the pre-cable limited channel environment.

The combination of what many believed was a declining broadcast industry, the rise of alternative television outlets, and the perceived need of sports entities to maximize television revenues led to a fissure in the traditional big television/big sports partnership that seemingly reached its apex in the early 1990s. The Big Three networks vowed that they would not pay any more for sports rights due to the losses they were taking on their current contracts. They adopted a position that all programming was subject to the cost scrutiny and cutbacks then being implemented in all other areas of their operations as part of corporate "restructuring." The major results of this posture occurred in 1994 with the dramatic reduction in national television money for MLB and the end of the NFL's 30-plus year contractual relationship with CBS.

With CBS claiming at least a $500 million loss on its 1990–93 nearly $1.1 billion contract with MLB, the baseball owners entered into an agreement with ABC and NBC that generated almost $8 million less per team per year in 1994–95. Even that amount was not guaranteed as the new arrangement established "The Baseball Network" (TBN), an explicit partnership of MLB, NBC, and ABC with no minimum rights fee guarantee (Bellamy & Walker, 1995). TBN sold advertising time and was fully responsible for revenue generation. Ultimately, the MLB players' strike of 1994–95 prevented TBN from reaching its revenue projections. This led to its abandonment in favor of traditional rights fee contracts with Fox, NBC, and ESPN after the 1995 season. The huge value of this deal ($1.7 billion over five years) can be attributed to the mid-1990s sellers market for all sports and, more specifically, to the value that Fox places on the acquisition of sports product to expand its power in both domestic and international television markets (Wendel, 1996).

Fox previously had acquired a major portion of NFL television rights when CBS declined to pay a major increase for its traditional share of the rights. Although CBS's refusal to enter into another potential "loss leader" contract could be seen as fiscally prudent in the short run, it turned out to have serious public relations and financial consequences for the network. By losing the NFL, CBS not only lost the football audience and football advertisers but a substantial portion of its market-place legitimacy. Fox's acquisition of NFL rights for approximately $1.6 billion over four years, a figure reported to be more than $100 million a year more than the CBS bid, was a clear indication of its growing power as a major television force to the financial and advertising communities, and was the proximate cause of the loss of several key CBS affiliates to Fox which in turn severely affected CBS's overall ratings (Halonen, 1994; Jensen, E., 1994; Tyrer, 1994).

A key point here is that the value of sports product to television is different from that of most other program forms. Its value is directly tied to a program suppliers' market reputation and legitimacy. The supply of major live sports product is limited in comparison to series-based entertainment programming. But unlike most other major television events such as the "Academy Awards" or certain mini-series that can attract large audiences, major sports programming provides predictable, consistent, and demographically desirable audiences that culminate in "mega-events" such as the Super Bowl or World Series. For CBS, there was no appropriate substitute for NFL football. The best evidence of this was the network's 1998 reacquisition of an NFL package for $4.0 billion over eight years, or $500 million per year. This figure is 150 percent higher than the amount NBC had been paying for the same package (Lafayette, 1998).

Despite CBS's problems, talk of the demise of network television had for the most part ceased by the mid-1990s. A resurgent advertising market helped the networks recover from previous financial losses, while network television was subject to a re-evaluation by the advertising industry. It was seen as having no equal in generating the large heterogeneous audience that remained highly-desired by major advertisers (Bellamy & Walker, 1996). Most importantly, the networks increasingly were seen as valuable for their well-established "brand identities." The NBC brand name, for example, is used by General Electric for both domestic and international cable operations (CNBC, NBC Europe), Internet/World Wide Web ventures (NBC and Microsoft's MSNBC), and local stations owned and operated by the network, such as "NBC5" (WMAQ-TV) in Chicago.

A New Oligopoly

The re-evaluation of network advantage as an advertising and brand name vehicle has rejuvenated the US broadcast television industry. In fact, the Big Four oligopoly now operates on two levels. Level One or the "Old Oligopoly" is the continuing power of the networks to attract about 60 percent of the prime time viewing audience even with the many other viewing options available to the majority of US television households. Level Two or the "New Oligopoly" is the continuing vertical and horizontal integration of the ownership of the existing networks with other once disparate media companies (e.g., Disney/ABC, Fox/Prime Liberty, CBS/Westinghouse) and the extension of operations and influence across international boundaries. Although Level Two has yet to reach a stable structure, there is little doubt that the dual trends of media industry consolidation and convergence on both the economic and technological levels are continuing. The ongoing consolidation of firms is an indicator that high barriers to entry to the new order will exist. A limited number of companies within the industry will use these barriers to re-exert influence over the audience and program suppliers on an international scale.

Sports are essential to the developing structure. Although all the major US-based media firms are increasing their global investments (e.g., NBC Europe, Viacom's MTV Asia), ABC's ESPN subsidiary and Rupert Murdoch's News Corporation presently have the most elaborate sports operations. ESPN International, for example, now reaches in excess of 127 million households in 150 countries outside the US through its three international networks (in Latin America, Asia and the Pacific Rim, and the Middle East/Northern Africa) and investments in Eurosport, Sky Broadcasting, and the Japan Sports Channel (Burgi, 1994; "ESPN International," 1995). In fact, the worldwide value of the ESPN brand name was a key reason for Disney's recent acquisition of Capital Cities/ABC (Hofmeister, 1995). An important element of the new oligopoly is the increased emphasis on the development and brand exploitation of niche and sub-niche channels including many that focus on sports. ESPN, having grown into the largest US basic cable service, has spun off ESPN2 which targets younger more active viewers with a mix of the NHL and "extreme" sports, ESPNews with 24-hour a day sports highlights and scores, as well as Internet services, and a mix of licensed merchandise.

News Corp.'s international presence extends to the two-thirds of the world's television households the company now has access to through a variety of services such as BSkyB in Britain and Star in southeast Asia (Roberts, 1993). Murdoch has called sports the "cornerstone of our worldwide broadcasting" plans (Knisley, 1995, p. S-2). Elaborating on this theme, Fox executive Chase Carey stated that, "in a world with more and more clutter, sports are going to be an increasingly significant platform with which to distinguish and promote ourselves" (Lafayette, 1995, p. 23). Fox intends to use its acquisition of major domestic sports rights (NFL, MLB, and NHL) as a way to gain viewers and advertisers throughout the world (Dwyer, et al., 1994). This extends from the exploitation of television rights to the partnership with the NFL in the 1995 revival of the European-based World League of American Football (Mandese, 1994a), to the joint venture with Prime Liberty, the dominant owner of RSNs, that develops domestic and international services under the Fox Sports name (Lafayette, 1996; Sanger, 1995).

The sports industry is well aware of the recent and continuing trends in the television industry and its importance within the partnership. In fact, many of the elements that are considered of primary importance to the emerging new television oligopoly (brand identity, "lifestyle" marketing, globalization) are the very same elements considered crucial to the sports industry.

AN EVOLVING SPORTS INDUSTRY

Ozanian writes that, "sports is not simply another big business. It is one of the fastest-growing industries in the US, and it is intertwined with virtually every aspect of the economy" (Ozanian, 1995, p. 2). According to data reported by Helitzer (1996), sports is the twenty-second largest industry in the US with annual revenues in excess of $100 billion. As for professional team sports, the value of the 107 [now 113] franchises in the Big Four leagues was estimated to be $11.4 billion in 1994, a value estimated to increase to "unimaginable levels" in the next few years (Worsnop, 1995, p. 123).

The television industry obviously contributes a substantial portion of the value of professional teams. In the NFL, for example, media revenues (with the vast majority coming from television) constitute approximately two-thirds of total team revenues. Although the other leagues are not as yet so television-reliant, MLB and NBA teams derive over one-third of their revenues from media (Schaaf, 1995, pp. 103–05).

In addition to direct financial impact, the telecasting of sports events has provided leagues with the wide exposure essential to the merchandising of team names and logos, one of the fastest growing revenue streams in sports. Team and league licensed merchandising is now a $13 billion a year business in sales as compared to the approximately $10 billion a year spent on television sports rights (Helitzer, 1996, p. 5). The importance of merchandising is such that teams consistently modify the style and colors of their logos and uniforms in order to enhance sales (Lans, 1995). The success of merchandising is one reflection of the continuing and growing popularity and power of sports. This revenue stream not only supplements television money, but is built off it. In addition to merchandising, sports entities are increasingly adept at increasing their revenues through playing facilities and integrated marketing schemes.

Facility and Location Games

An indicator of sports influence is the relationship that teams have with cities which typically subsidize team operations with favorable rental fees in municipally-owned facilities, infrastructure (e.g., access roads, parking lots), tax breaks, low interest loans, and "sweetheart" deals on advertising signage and parking revenues. Local governments do this in order to have the prestige, publicity, and possible economic benefit of being a "big league" city (Osterland, 1995).

The perceived value of sports franchises to cities can best be seen in the large number of sports facilities that have recently opened or are under construction. In the 1990s, about half of the major professional teams have moved or will move into new or renovated facilities (Klein, 1995). By 2000, US cities are expected to have spent approximately $7 billion on new playing facilities (Helitzer, 1996). These numbers likely will increase as more teams threaten to relocate if they are not given new facilities that will make them competitive with other league teams (Halvonik, 1996).

Such threats have become the reality in the NFL where franchise "roulette" is a major trend. In 1995–97, four of the league's thirty franchises relocated with other moves seen as likely (Torry, 1995). This compares to three relocations in the 1980s and none in the 1970s. In each case, the primary reason given for the move was the inadequacy of playing facilities in the former market. The fact that a lack of attendance was either minimized or not given as a rationale is indicative of the changing economics of professional sports. There is little doubt that the fans most valued by professional sports teams are those that will purchase luxury boxes and accompanying amenities. The availability of such seating is considered a necessity in all new facilities (Osterland, 1995; Starr, with Heath, 1995). Of course, the price of such seating typically is a government subsidized tax deduction primarily used by corporations.

Local governments increasingly must provide the facilities and eliminate a team's financial risk. For example, St. Louis guarantees the former Los Angeles Rams at least $16 million per year in gross ticket sales, an amount approximately $2.5 million above the league average, and all the proceeds from 40,000 Permanent Seat Licenses (PSLs), a fee for the "right" to buy season tickets (Schaaf, 1995).

The new playing facilities are designed for television with excellent sight-lines for camera positioning, production facilities, and signage availability designed to appeal to the viewer and the advertiser. However, the movement of franchises can serve to work against the interests of the television industry. For example, the move of the Rams from Los Angeles (the second largest television market) to St. Louis (the eighteenth largest) dropped the television universe in NFL cities from 58 million to 52.5 million households (Goldberg, 1995). Although the league promises to return a team to Los Angeles (and Cleveland) by the turn of the century, the move is a demonstration of the NFL's clout in its partnership with television. With the league convinced that television money will continue to grow, it is willing to allow franchise movement to smaller television markets. Even if such movement is a short-term phenomenon, it is unprecedented and would have been considered unimaginable in past years. New playing facilities are an integral component of the fast-growing business of sports marketing and, more generally, the increased emphasis on integrated marketing which attempts to directly tie product to commercial sponsors.

Integrated Marketing

The new autonomy of sports entities is a function of their redefinition and evolution from spectator sports provider to television program supplier to integrated marketing product or "software" (Bellamy & Walker, 1995; Ozanian, 1995). Integrated marketing (IM) is the process by which the once disparate media activities of advertising, public relations, and promotion are collectively and systematically used to market a product or service (Duncan, 1993). IM is a way for sports teams and leagues to use their product "to build revenues indirectly – through [specialized] cable television, merchandise, advertising, and the like" (Ozanian, 1995, p. 1).

One reason for the increased emphasis on IM is that sports entities now see themselves as media companies actively involved in the development of new sources of revenue (Jensen, 1995). This is a changed perspective from the traditional situation where sports leagues and teams accepted money from television, opened their gates, and did little else beyond the sale or giveaway of souvenirs and occasional joint promotions with advertisers. Today the relationship between sports entities, advertisers, and television is such that Nielsen Media Research has a division that provides audience information specifically for the professional sports leagues (Jensen, 1995). As explained by NBA Properties' Rick Welts, the NBA has "1,100 new episodes every season with no repeats" (Jensen, J., 1994, p. 4).

In addition to this new perspective on television, most of the new playing facilities (e.g., Coors Field, Fleet Center, GM Centre, Molson Center, Pepsi Center) generate substantial revenue from major corporations (i.e., advertisers) who pay to have their names on the facility. These sponsors get not only name identification in every mention of the facility but signage that appears on telecasts, special seating, specifically-designed promotions, and other amenities. Corporations believe they get positive brand identification at a bargain price by linking their names to sports facilities or, at minimum, by purchasing venue signage and other forms of promotional identification with a team or league (Duncan, 1993; Finkelthal, 1994; Helitzer, 1996; Shanklin, 1992). Signage which appears in televised games is regarded as much less expensive than traditional spot advertising (Horovitz, 1992), and has the added benefit of being "zap-proof," integrated into the telecast so the RCD-armed viewer can not avoid exposure without also missing event coverage.

On the national and international levels, IM examples include the NBA's partnership with ESPN and Lifetime in promoting women's Olympic basketball (Hiestand, 1995), Coca-Cola's international partnership with the NBA (Boseman, 1994), and the numerous "official sponsors" of the Olympics ("Olympic," 1996). Advertisers now expect "value added" IM elements in sports. For example, the now defunct The Baseball Network was severely criticized as not understanding the IM concept because it did not offer stadium signage and more promotional events to sponsors (Mandese, 1994b).

Even as sports entities place increased emphasis on new revenue sources to supplement television revenue, they and their corporate benefactors remain dependent on television to create and enhance the value of signage, facilities, merchandising, and brand names. A review of the recent ways that the Big Four professional sports leagues and the Olympic movement have leveraged the television marketplace will make this explicit.

VIDEO CLIPS: RECENT DEALS BETWEEN BIG SPORTS AND BIG TELEVISION

In the following sections, the implications of present and recent television rights agreements will be examined. Trends affecting sports' relationship with television will be assessed in the context of other marketing initiatives.

National Football League

The NFL has long been regarded as the preeminent television sport, a position attributed to the limited number of games that enhances the value of each contest and the league's position as the pioneer in using national television as an instrument of growth and influence (Patton, 1984). Key to the success of this approach was the league's successful lobbying for the passage of the Sports Broadcasting Act of 1961 (P.L. 87–331) that allowed franchise owners in all professional sports leagues to equally share national television revenues.

The NFL's present national television contracts, which cover the 1998–2005 seasons, will generate at least $17.6 billion over eight years from Fox, CBS, and jointly owned ABC/ESPN. This more than doubles the annual amount the league collects from slightly below $1.1 billion to at least $2.2 billion, with the league having the right to renegotiate after five years (Lafayette, 1998). The NFL's success in leveraging its product can be further demonstrated by its ability to increase national television money by a factor in excess of 4.5 in the last decade ("Pass the money," 1998) – a time of network television viewer erosion and generally flat or even decreasings ratings for league games. NFL football clearly is seen as essential programming by the major television providers in limiting future viewer erosion. As explained by Fox President David Hill, "the NFL represents the only firm ground in the increasingly scary swamp of the TV industry" (Layfayette, 1998, p. 1).

Although the NFL has long tried to export its product outside the US through the international telecasting of games, the sale of team merchandise, "American Bowl" pre-season games, and NFL Europe (the newly named WLAF), the results have been decidedly mixed. Both television ratings and attendance at the American bowls have declined and the NFL Europe has yet to establish itself as anything other than a minor league (Greising, 1994). The NFL seems to be having problems in translating a game specific to the US to other nations, a serious impediment to long-term growth. Of course, with the Murdoch media companies just beginning to aggressively promote the game abroad the international audience certainly has the potential to expand. In addition to the NFL Europe, the NFL now partially subsidizes the Canadian Football League ("CFL's future," 1997), and telecasts games and highlights to approximately 190 nations ("International TV," 1997).

Domestically, the NFL continues to thrive in developing new revenue sources. The league leads all other professional sports leagues in generating over $3.5 billion per year in gross licensed merchandise sales (Schaaf, 1995, p. 234). The league has also developed a new source of revenue through its "NFL Sunday Ticket" pay-per-view service which provides feeds of out of town games to satellite dish owners (Helyar, 1994).

The NFL's main problems are internal and primarily related to franchise roulette rather than to television. The main concern of the league is that franchise relocations will lead to judicial and legislative challenges to the highly lucrative operational patterns of the league. In fact, the league has told Congress that they would stop the franchise movement if given another anti-trust exemption (Griffith, 1996). Of course, expansion from the present thirty franchises (an increase of only four since 1970) would minimize franchise movement. However, the league, like all other professional leagues, sees great benefit in keeping the number of teams artificially small. Scarcity enhances the revenue of existing teams and is the tool used to extract new facilities and other municipal subsidies.

National Basketball Association

The NBA is now regarded as the most television- and marketing-savvy of all the major sports leagues (Heisler, 1996). A key event in obtaining this status was the league's 1983 agreement with the NBA Players Association that instituted a salary cap while guaranteeing players a substantial portion of league revenues. This led to labor peace unprecedented in other major professional sports and encouraged the players and league to work jointly for the growth of the league. This agreement has been labeled the beginning of the "entertainment marketing revolution" (Jensen, J., 1994, p. 4). From this point, the league started to take advantage of some of the game's inherent characteristics such as the confined (i.e., television-friendly) playing space, the small number of players that contributes to an emphasis on "stars," and the international popularity of the game.

The success of the NBA's approach was such that league revenues grew from $140 million to $1.1 billion from 1983 to 1993 (Schaaf, 1995, p. 30). National television money grew from approximately $27 million per year in 1982–86 to at least $660 million per year in the present 1998–2002 contracts with NBC, TBS, and TNT ("TV pays," 1994). Even before the latest contract, the average NBA team media revenue of $14.9 million per year was close to the gate revenue of approximately $16.5 million per year (Schaaf, 1995, p. 218).

The NBA has been adept at extending its global influence. League games are now seen in over seventy countries, the league has expanded to Canada (Toronto, Vancouver), exhibition and even regular season games have been played in Japan and Mexico, and teams compete in the international McDonald's Open tournament ("Global NBA," 1997).

One of the primary means of the NBA's entry into the international market was its takeover of the operation and marketing of USA Basketball which oversees US involvement in international competition. This, of course, is the instrument through which NBA stars now compete in the Olympics and other events. USA Basketball is now marketing US women's Olympic basketball, and the NBA has established the US-based Women's NBA (Hiestand, 1995; "Inception of," 1996).

The NBA has been a pioneer and innovator in both domestic and international sports marketing. These efforts have placed the league in a position to be one of the largest contributors to and beneficiaries of the increasing globalization of the television and advertising industries.

Major League Baseball

MLB continues to have a problematic relationship with television. In fact, all of its recent economic problems can be linked to its television "problem." The refusal of MLB owners to more equitably share television revenue has led to considerable economic imbalance among teams. Baseball has long been considered a poor television sport due to the large amount of product (2,430 regular season games), the pace of the game, and a large playing field that is not "television friendly." Finally, MLB is generally regarded as having done a poor job in marketing its product (Berkowitz & Zipay, 1996). The problems of baseball culminated in the players strike of 1994–95 that led to the cancellation of the 1994 post-season, a shortened 1995 regular season, and the end of The Baseball Network partnership with ABC and NBC (Koenig, 1996).

Despite MLB's ongoing labor and television problems, it offers one of the better examples of the ability of sports entities to maximize revenues in a changing television environment. Beginning with the 1996 season, MLB receives approximately $1.7 billion over five years from Fox, NBC, ESPN, and Prime Liberty (i.e., Fox Sports). This is an increase of almost $4 million per team per year from the previous TBN and ESPN deals (Koenig, 1996; Wendel, 1996). Of particular importance is the presence of Fox as a television partner. Fox's willingness to pay a premium price for MLB is related to its continuing emphasis on sports product as the key element in its domestic and international growth.

MLB officials are increasingly committed to enhanced marketing and increased globalization as key elements in the game's revival. Although not as well positioned as the NBA in developing an international audience, MLB is regarded as having good opportunities in Asia and Latin America (Helitzer, 1996; Sands & Gammons, 1993). In order to create more saleable product, MLB has instituted a new round of playoff games and instituted interleague play (Williams, 1996). Although MLB has yet to overcome its television "problem," it clearly is working hard to do so and to figure out the best blend of international, national, regional, and local television coverage. The presence of such major media powers as Disney, Time Warner Turner, and the Tribune Company as team owners is another example of baseball's perceived value as television product (Lait & Hernandez, 1995).

National Hockey League

Historically, the NHL has been the most marginal of the major professional sports leagues. Confined primarily to Canadian and northern US cities, the league was without a broadcast network contract throughout the 1980s and early 1990s. Since that time, the NHL has secured a contract with Fox and attempted to increase its appeal by hiring Gary Bettman from the hugely successful NBA as Commissioner, placing expansion and relocated franchises in major "Sun Belt" markets (e.g., Dallas, Miami, San Jose), and devoting much more attention to the marketing of the game and individual players ("Gary Bettman," 1996; Taub, 1995).

Although the league continues to lag far behind the other major leagues in national television (approximately $47 million per year combined from Fox and ESPN and close to $30 million from Canadian television) and merchandising (over $1 million in 1993) revenue, the league has recently made major advances in both areas (Taub, 1995). For example, the money from Fox and ESPN is more than four times the amount of the previous ESPN contract ("TV pays," 1994). Although household ratings remain low, the NHL has been good investment for Fox. As

Fox's first major sports deal, it provided legitimacy in the sports marketplace. In addition, the demographics of the hockey audience (young, urban, male) are highly-desirable to advertisers (Cooper, 1994; Taub, 1995).

With no network ties in the 1980s, the NHL aggressively exploited cable delivery and became a key component of RSN programming. In fact, the RSNs provided a "lifeline" to the league during the lean television years that, in some cases, extended well beyond rights fees. For example, the Prime Sports/KBL (now Fox Sports Pittsburgh) RSN advanced money to the Pittsburgh Penguins so the team could remain competitive. In exchange, the RSN received all local and regional television (including cable, broadcast, and pay-per-view) and radio rights for twelve years, complete control of team merchandising, a seat on the NHL's Board of Broadcasters (its very existence an indicator of the strength of the sports and television relationship), and a winning team that would attract viewers. In a very real sense, the RSN and the team are explicit business partners (Brugnone, 1995).

The NHL has been called a "natural" for global expansion (Helitzer, 1996, p. 34). Hockey is played in many parts of the world and there has been an increasing amount of player movement from Europe to the US and Canada and vice versa. The league has been active in distributing its games abroad through ESPN International and international television outlets, and participates in the Winter Olympics ("Gary Bettman," 1996).

Although the NHL is unlikely to ever be as popular or as influential as the other three major leagues across the entire US, the development of new television outlets has enabled it to finally become a major sport in much of the nation. Indicators of this are the purchase of franchises by such major media firms as Disney (Mighty Ducks of Anaheim) and Viacom/Blockbuster (Florida Panthers), and the replacement of small Canadian cities (Quebec City, Winnipeg) with growing US business headquarters markets (Denver, Phoenix). The prognosis is for continued growth as a mix of a national, regional, and international sport.

The Olympics

The Olympic Games have been called "the largest media event ever" (Helitzer, 1996, p. 44). The economic value of the event increases every Olympiad as the International Olympic Committee (IOC) and the organizing committees continue to seek maximum exposure and revenue. One of the means of doing this was the end of the IOC's policy prohibiting the participation of professional athletes. The NBA "Dream Team," the most prominent result of the policy change, has bene-fited both the Olympics and the NBA. In addition, the IOC changed the Olympic cycle to every two years (alternating Winter and Summer games) to enhance the consistency of media attention and to allow rights bidders to better budget by not having to pay for two Games in one year.

The Olympics are a primary beneficiary of the present sellers market for television sport as existing rights holders "fight like hell to keep what they have," while newer sports media powers such as News Corp. (Fox) attempt to build world-wide market legitimacy (Zipay, 1995, p. 1). NBC Sports President Dick Ebersol explained that the prime value of the Olympics is in being "the only thing in all of television guaranteed to put the whole family in front of the TV set" (Harvey, 1995, p. 1).

A recent trend in the Olympic/television partnership has been the granting of telecasting rights so far in advance. In the summer of 1995 NBC acquired the rights to the 2000 Summer and 2002 Winter games with a "one time take it or leave it" secret offer of $1.27 billion (Lafayette, 1995, p. 1). The deal was seen as a preemptive strike to prevent Fox from adding another major event to its schedule. By the end of 1995, NBC paid another $2.3 billion for the 2004 Summer, 2006 Winter, and 2008 Summer games (Wilson, 1995), a deal reported as the "richest contract ever in television sports" (Harvey, 1995, p. 1). The IOC also negotiated a "revenue sharing" clause with NBC which will provide it with more money if NBC reaches certain revenue targets with its coverage. NBC's rationale for making the deal goes beyond the hoped for profits. By branding itself as the "Network of the Olympics," NBC reinforces its status as a leader in television sports, strengthens the loyalty of its affiliate stations at a time when affiliate switching is common, and helps to ensure the carriage of its cable services (CNBC, MSNBC) by using them as an outlet for Olympic events and related programming (Harvey, 1995).

The worldwide trend of television privatization and commercialization also has been of enormous financial benefit to the Olympic movement. While US television money will equal nearly $5 billion for the seven Olympiads of 1996–2008, the IOC expects to at least double that amount by selling rights to non-US television providers (Wilson, 1995). This is a major change from the situation of the mid-1980s when US television rights contributed approximately 80 percent of total Olympic revenues ("Olympic," 1996).

While television rights fees for the Olympics continue to set new records, the IOC has been adept at exploiting such IM trends as sponsorships. The success of the corporate-sponsored 1984 Los Angeles Summer Games prompted the IOC to establish The Olympic Programme (TOP) in 1985 "to offer worldwide sponsorships to multinational corporations and to develop an ongoing program for commercial business relationships with the IOC" ("Olympic," 1996, p. 1). The success of TOP is such that in the 1993–96 cycle, the IOC collected 34 percent of its revenues from sponsorships versus 48 percent from all broadcast rights and 10 percent from ticket sales ("Olympic," 1996).

The Olympics stand at the apex of global sports and provide a model for other sports providers. The combination of increasing television rights, sponsorship fees, and other marketing initiatives that are so critical to success are inspiring similar efforts in other international sports events such as the World Cup, figure skating, and gymnastics (McClellan, 1994; Rather, 1994).

PROSPECTS AND CONCLUSIONS

Ongoing changes in the television and advertising industries have exponentially increased the already considerable value of sports as programming. Sports is the best exemplar of the television programming that is most valued in the rapidly globalizing television industry. As has been the case since the development of the industry, sports attracts a desirable audience difficult, if not impossible to reach, with other programming. The live event nature of sports creates an exciting atmosphere that is difficult to replicate with other programming. On the international level, certain sports events have long demonstrated their ability to cut across boundaries of language and culture. This is of vital importance to a television industry that is evolving into a "new" oligopoly that will operate globally.

These attributes are enhanced at a time when the television industry is having to cope with an audience that has more power in its relationship with the medium. The diffusion of satellites, cable, VCRs, and RCDs has given the audience that can afford such technologies the means to choose from a large number of program offerings. Sports programming is regarded as having the ability to stop or at least arrest the channel changing inclination of the restless viewer. Sports also provide television with opportunities to produce both mass *and* niche audiences. For every Olympiad or Super Bowl, there are many once-fringe sports that can produce small but demographically-valuable audiences for advertisers.

Sports entities also benefit from the increasing trend of advertisers to spend money on integrated marketing schemes as a reaction to the clutter of spots and services on television and the increased power of the viewer to avoid conventional advertising. The sports marketing branch of IM is almost a $3.0 billion business in the United States and Canada and growing much more rapidly than traditional advertising ("Reality check," 1996). Of course, television coverage of sports creates much of the value of such schemes by showcasing the RCD-proof signage, the new television-friendly playing facilities, personalities, merchandise, and, in general, serving as primary promotional tool for spectator sports.

Sports entities clearly have benefitted and gained more power in the partnership from television industry flux. More than ever, the relationship is symbiotic with both partners needing each other to maintain and extend influence. The immediate prospect is for more joint ventures and further economic and operational integration of the sports and media industries to the point where it will make less and less intuitive sense to distinguish between the industries.

The evolving global sports media industry offers a rich research site, as the public policy and political economic issues discussed in this brief overview need more attention. The following are some of the issues deserving of ongoing scholarly focus:

1   **The limits of globalization**. Can US sports product be exported via television in anything other than the present relatively limited fashion? Can a lucrative market consisting of divergent nations and people be created and sustained over the long term? What impact will such a market have on indigenous sport and media systems (Bellamy, 1993; Maguire, 1993b; Wildman & Siwek, 1987)?

2   **The changing definition of fans**. Will the increasing linkage of sport to corporate benefactors manifest in new facilities, franchise relocations, and premium ticket prices and seating endanger the connection of sports to their traditional fan base (Gorman & Calhoun, 1994)? Will the mass popularity of sport be sustainable solely through television and other media coverage? Or, has the ascendancy of television and corporate sponsorship already made such considerations irrelevant?

3   **Internal problems of sports entities**. The present sellers market for sports has exacerbated internal tensions within sports leagues. In the NFL, for example, the Dallas Cowboys and the league sued each other over marketing deals made by the team that allegedly conflict with league deals (Jensen, 1996). The leagues' seeming inability to prevent franchise movement is another problem with policy implications for sports and the individuals and public entities that support and subsidize them.

4   **The new television oligopoly**. The recent changes in the television industry that have increased the power of the viewer and the suppliers of desirable programming have been called a transitional stage and prelude to a re-exertion of the industry's traditional power in these relationships (Bellamy & Walker, 1996). If this analysis is correct, what are the implications for sport's long-term value as television product and level of autonomy within the partnership?

This list is by no means exhaustive as the study of the relationship of television and sports ultimately is about the continuing influence of MediaSport on our culture and imagination. Further research on the many dimensions of this increasingly powerful partnership of global oligopolies is a necessity in tracking, understanding, and perhaps influencing the structure, behavior, and impact of global media on everyday life.

GENERAL REFERENCE

Women, Sport, and Media Institutions: Issues in Sports Journalism and Marketing

Pamela J. Creedon

They don't dunk. They don't talk trash. There isn't a 7-footer among them. So why on earth has women's basketball been ordained as the Next Hot Sport? Could it be because, well, they don't dunk, talk trash or stand 7-feet tall? [1]

The mass media depict life within our society. Their role is unique among institutions. They set the public agenda by providing us with information about all other societal institutions including the military, education, medicine, law and sport. "The mass media, in short, portray the life of society to society" (Turow, 1992). They provide us with entertainment and they report the news. Defining news or newsworthiness, however, often leads one around in circles. One approach is to define news as if it were the cultural equivalent to a natural law. If gravity can be defined simply as that which goes up must come down, then news can be simply that which is newsworthy. In the routinized and personified version of this definition, news becomes "whatever the editor says it is."

Not satisfied with this humanistic approach to defining news, communication researchers have taken great pains to quantify a definition of news. After decades of news media content studies, four general dimensions of newsworthiness have been identified: deviance (novelty, oddity or unusualness); sensationalism;

conflict or controversy; and prominence (Shoemaker, Danielian & Brendlinger, 1992).

Recently, social scientists even have begun to explore the nexus of cultural and biological bases for human communication and news reporting (Capella, 1996; Malamuth, 1996; Detenber & Reeves, 1996; Shoemaker, 1996). According to this account, it all began when one of our ancestors reported the "bad news" about a tiger or other predator lurking outside the family cave. This antediluvian news anchor "allowed our ancestors to avoid injury or death, and . . . survivors of environmental threats were more likely to pass on their genes to future generations" (Shoemaker, 1996, p. 35).

As simple, complex and far-reaching as these various approaches to defining news may appear to be, they do not address the role of the marketplace – directly or indirectly – in defining news or mass media content. The marketplace is ignored, in part, because it confounds libertarian arguments about the role of a free press in society. Journalists will steadfastly avoid any suggestion that market factors affect news judgment. Yet, both newsroom executives and communication researchers readily acknowledge that the mass media are economic institutions competing in the marketplace for audiences and advertisers.

Whatever the truth, the relationship between marketplace considerations and mass media content is particularly obvious in sport. Sports sell newspapers. According to Nancy Cooney, executive sports editor of the *Philadelphia Inquirer*, when the Philadelphia Phillies won the World Series, "it was good for up to 20,000 papers daily" (Giobbe, 1996). And it has been so since the newspaper sports page made its debut in the 1890s as a circulation builder, which in turn boosted advertising rates and revenue. Over the years, sports news has been viewed as "soft" or entertainment news by other reporters and the sports department often derided as the Toy Department or Toyland. However, the power of the sports page to attract readers and advertisers can not be denied.

The dynamics involving audience, advertisers and sports news lead us to some key questions that should be analyzed as we evaluate media coverage of sport played by women. An overarching question for women's sports has been: which comes first – marketplace viability or media coverage? If we reduce the question into its several dimensions, we may be closer to an understanding of what it will take to increase coverage of women's sports:

Question: How do advertisers decide when a sport event or activity is worthy of commercial media sponsorship?
Answer: When its audience has the desired demographics.
Question: What influence, if any, does audience size or potential audience appeal have on decisions about which sports or events are deemed newsworthy?
Answer: Everything. Readership and ratings rule.
Question: What influence, if any, do advertisers have in determining when a product or commodity becomes news?
Answer: More than either side (reporters or advertisers) will admit.

However, before we draw the simple and obvious conclusion that more coverage of women's sport will come when the audience is attractive enough to advertisers, we need to add another critical dimension to our study of the institutions of media and sport.

In the US and around the globe, sport is a gendered cultural institution. Equally so, the media system that spans the globe is a gendered cultural institution. Psychologists have defined gender "as a principle of social organization that structures relations between men and women" (Crawford & Marecek, 1989, p. 147). Both sport and the media are cultural institutions because they embody a value system that I have referred to in earlier work as an "infrasystem" or "foundation of institutional values and norms that determine an organization's response to changes in its environment" (Creedon, 1993a, p. 160). Ultimately then, the answers to the questions posed above pertain only to male sport. The decision as to when a women's sport event or activity that has not previously been on the media agenda, such as women's basketball, has sufficient audience appeal to be covered on a routine basis, is not as simple.

In essence, the mass media can serve as a platform for us to examine the cultural debate over the definition and legitimacy of women's sport. This chapter starts by examining the role of the institutions of sport and mass media in this debate. It also examines how the marketplace influences the debate.

SPORT AS A GENDERED INSTITUTION

The quote from an article in the *Wall Street Journal* about the American Basketball League that opens this chapter gives us both the "bad" and the "good" news. First, the "bad" news: female professional basketball players don't dunk, don't swear and they aren't 7-feet tall (i.e., they aren't male professional basketball players).

The reporter has identified a central theme in sport: the concept of male superiority and female inferiority. By using traditional definitions of "female" and "femininity" as the antithesis of "athlete" and "athletic," the *de facto* norm or standard against which performance is measured becomes maleness or "masculinity." Others would add that the norm is both sexist and heterosexist (Cahn, 1994; Griffin, 1992; Bryson, 1987; Lenskyj, 1986). The National Collegiate Athletic Association, which has controlled women's intercollegiate athletics for more than a decade, has openly stated its position about male superiority and female inferiority in college sport. A 1990 NCAA publication about women's sports was titled, "Continuing the Ascent" (Smale, 1990). According to the brochure: "As women become more competitive, the game gets better and it will breed (sic) more competitive female athletes."

The *Wall Street Journal* reporter also suggests that things might be changing. His "good" news: it might not matter that these women can't dunk, don't swear and aren't 7-feet tall. He goes on to depict female professional basketball as pure, innocent and team-oriented "[L]ike the men's game of yore" (Fatsis, 1996, p. B6). He appears to be suggesting that women's sport offers the audience a throw back to the "good old days" when athletes enjoyed playing the game and sports were just plain fun for fans to watch.

Nostalgia aside, let's follow the money to the core of institutionalized values, i.e., the infrasystem of values that determine why the media portrayal of women's sports uses a male norm. At the top of the sport system hierarchy is football – still almost an exclusive male preserve – where the top prizes of money and fame are found. In a marketplace economy, the pursuit of money and power is not an anathema. Arguably, American professional sport is a testament to the strength of these values.

Some might argue, however, that money and power don't dominate the institution of sport when it operates in the context of the institution of education. Walter Byers, first full-time director of the NCAA, provided an insider's view of the organization's values in his book *Unsportsmanlike Conduct* (1995). According to his analysis of college sport, the move to allow more control of NCAA policy by college presidents in the 1980s, ostensibly to reduce athletic recruiting and other violations, actually resulted in a greater concentration of wealth and power. Combining the Associated Press poll for ranking college football, attendance (ticket income) and qualification for a big bowl game to arrive at a "Power Index," he reports that twenty to twenty-five teams from six conferences dominated collegiate sport from 1990–1994 (Byers, 1995, p. 353).[2] He reports a similar finding for college basketball.

However, NCAA football attendance has been declining and television ratings are slipping. The 1994 Rose Bowl, for example, had an 11.3 Nielson rating, where one Nielson rating point equals 942,000 TV households (Byers, 1995, p. 358). This is a dramatic decline from 1955–1984 era when the Nielson rating for the Rose Bowl had been above 25.0 except for four years. Certainly, it's a cause for concern when television revenue accounts for more than three-quarters of the NCAA's income (Byers, 1995, p. 395).

Enter women's sports and fans. Attendance has tripled in women's college basketball since 1985 and television ratings and contracts are on the rise (Stockman, 1996). The 1996 NCAA women's championship game between the University of Connecticut and the University of Tennessee had a 5.7 Nielson rating while the men's title game (UCLA versus Arkansas) had a 19.3 rating (Gustkey, 1996). The women's title game earned triple the rating of Fox's debut of National Hockey League coverage, which ran during the same time slot, and had a higher rating than three regional NBA games on NBC (Lapchick, 1995, p. 8). Following its 1996 35–0 season, projected revenue for Connecticut's women's basketball team in 1996–1997 is $1.18 million, twenty-five times as much as five years ago (Fatsis, 1996, p. B6).

In three Pacific 10 Conference Schools – Oregon State, Stanford and Washington – women's basketball outdraws men's (Fatsis, 1996). Fifteen schools sold at least 4,500 tickets per game during the 1995–1996 women's basketball season (Gustkey, 1996). ESPN and ESPN2 are planning to televise sixty-four women's games this season (Fatsis, 1996).

After two unsuccessful attempts to start a women's professional basketball league in the 1970s and early 1990s, fans are supporting the fledgling American Basketball League. With a break-even goal for its first season of 3,000 fans a game, the eight teams in league are averaging 3,420 (Fans support, p. D6).[3]

What about money? Although Division I women's coaches reportedly earn about one-third of their male counterparts' salaries, University of Tennessee Head Basketball Coach Pat Head Summitt has a higher salary ($125,000) than the men's basketball or football coach (Fatsis, 1996). The ABL was hoping to pay an average player salary of $70,000, with stars such as former Stanford standout Jennifer Azzi earning in the neighborhood of $125,000 (Stockman, 1996). Clearly, there's money to be made. CBS purchased the broadcast rights to the NCAA basketball tournament (men's and women's) through to the year 2002 for a reported $1.725 billion dollars (TV sports, 1996). As the women's game "breeds more competitive athletes" and presumably attracts larger, and even more importantly new, audiences, the price tag can only go up.

These indicators suggest that the cream of the crop in women's basketball are starting to earn a living in the institution of sport.[4] Television contracts are increasingly lucrative and promise to bring in additional revenue. In this context, the chicken and egg debate appears to be answered: If you bring them (i.e., fans and/or television audience), we will pay you.

From the standpoint of power, however, control of women's sports remains vested in patriarchal, male-led sport institutions. The male-led NCAA, dominated by the presidents of the football power universities, controls women's collegiate sport. The ABL now faces competition from the NBA for a piece – maybe all – of the action. The NBA launched its eight-team league in 1997 to play during the men's off-season, i.e., a summer schedule. It seems inevitable that only one of the leagues will survive. Stanford Head Coach Tara VanDerveer, who led the US women's team to an Olympic gold medal, sums it up: "If the NBA ran a league on Mars, I think women would go there to play" (Stockman, 1996).[5]

According to the *Wall Street Journal*, the women's game, "emphasizes shot selection, crisp passing and close defense" (Fatsis, 1996, p. B6). But if women "continue the ascent" described by the NCAA, will the game change too? Most of the teams in the women's Top 25 have rosters with more height than the average for a men's high school or NCAA Division III team. Seven of the twelve members of the 1996–1997 Ohio State University women's basketball team, for example, were within an inch of 6-feet or taller.

MASS MEDIA AS A GENDERED INSTITUTION

Equality has been the focus of many critics of mass media coverage of women's sports. They want more coverage – equal coverage – of women's sports. Content studies have argued that female athletes are invisible, ignored and denigrated in the media and the dearth of women's sports coverage functions to symbolically annihilate their existence (Daddario, 1994; Kane & Greendorfer, 1994; Duncan & Hasbrook, 1988).

The number of women enrolled in journalism and mass communication programs has outnumbered men for over twenty years since 1977 (Beasley, 1993). A 1992 study of the journalistic workforce showed that women make up 33.9 percent of the daily newspaper labor force, 44.1 percent of weeklies, 24.8 percent of television and 29 percent of radio (Lafky, 1993). Formed in 1986, members of the Association for Women in the Sports Media, who pronounce their organization's acronym "awesome", are estimated to number five hundred (Cramer, 1994). However, women aren't expected to attain equality in newspaper editorships until 2055 (Beasley, 1993).[6] Radical feminist communication scholars have cautioned, however, that even if equality in terms of numbers and titles are achieved in the news business, presumably little will change about how we define or gather news. Why?

Sociologists tell us that entry-level employees adapt to workplace norms. Reporters are trained to use "official" sources that have institutional relationships for statements of "fact." Deadlines and space limitations affect what is presented as news. Work routines (e.g., beat reporting assignments) privilege certain types of news, i.e., the football beat versus the women's field hockey beat.

Feminist scholarship has shown that these journalistic norms privilege a patriarchal world view (Creedon, 1993b; Strutt & Hissey, 1992; Theberge & Cronk, 1986; Tuchman, 1978). Moreover, the practical result of the sport coverage hierarchy is that the women's sports beat is generally considered to be at the bottom of the food chain in the sports department (Cramer, 1994). Pay, prestige and professional advancement accrue to those who have the professional football, baseball or basketball beat, or the NCAA Division I football beat. While the salaries of several of the most senior female sports journalists/broadcasters reportedly have eclipsed $150,000, success does not necessarily equate with a desire to change the way women's sports are covered. CBS sport's Lesley Visser, a twenty-year sports reporting veteran who reportedly was 22 years old when she first entered a male locker room (professional tennis) as a *Boston Globe* sportswriter, has been quoted as saying: "Women who get into sports journalism don't want to cover women's sports. They want to cover sports that lead to success" (Cramer, 1994, p. 169).

The comment reflects a simple reality: the hegemony of the gendered media system. Hegemony refers to an infrasystem of values that overshadows our awareness and helps dominant groups maintain their power. The sports coverage hierarchy model is a manifestation of it.

Nearly two decades have passed since *Sports Illustrated* reporter Melissa Ludke sought access to the New York Yankees locker room through a sex discrimination lawsuit (Boutilier & SanGiovanni, 1983).[7] Personal accounts written by pioneer female sportswriters who were among the first to break the male-only barrier of the locker room are a rich – but terribly scarce – narrative source about the nature of the gendered mass media system in sport.

The first was *Toronto Star* reporter Alison Gordon's (1984) book recounting her experiences as the first female baseball beat reporter in the American League. Gordon describes herself as a 36-year-old feminist who naively jumped at the chance in 1979 to share the *Star's* baseball beat with a male sportswriting veteran of more than thirty years. She was the "beneficiary" of the court ruling that all Major League Baseball teams must open their locker room doors to women reporters. But access did not mean acceptance. During her first spring training she was presented with a pink T-shirt that read: "Token Broad Beat Writer" by a team official, publicly propositioned by a drunk player in a hotel restaurant, and bet $1,000 by another sportswriter that she would have a nervous breakdown before the end of the season (Gordon, 1984, p. 121–123). Whenever she entered the team's locker room, she was greeted with a shout of "Meat" or "Pecker Checker."

While Gordon went out of her way to avoid even eye contact with naked players in the locker room, *Washington Post* sportswriter Jane Leavy's 1990 fictional account of a female baseball reporter's experiences did just the opposite. Her novel fed the penis-envy Freudians enough fodder to catch the attention of the TV talk show circuit. Even former President George Bush sent Leavy a handwritten note promising to read her book (Leavy, 1990a). Much of this attention focused on book's first sentence: "You see a lot of penises in my line of work" (Leavy, 1990b, p. 3). Leavy fanned the Freudian flame even more when she acknowledged that the line between fact and fiction in the book was fuzzy at times (Leavy, 1990a).

Sacramento Bee sports reporter Susan Fornoff (1993), who covered the Oakland As for five seasons, describes herself as "a living lab experiment on what would happen to a child raised to dress, think, and act like a woman but sent to live in a world of men . . . of muscle and machismo" (p. xv, xvi). As the only female assigned to a traveling baseball beat during the 1993 season, Fornoff decided she had two options. The first, which she argues many female sportswriters choose, was to "Wear a nun's habit and drink milk and hide in my room" (Fornoff, 1993, p. 4). The second, which she chose, was to "Dress fashionably and drink beer and socialize with the people I covered, with the aim of having a good time getting paid doing something most people would pay to do" (p. 4). Fornoff, a self-described "token" female sportswriter who started her career aged 21 with the Baltimore *News American* in the early 1970s and was hired by *USA Today* one month before it was launched in 1982, fought for equality in the "locker room in the newsroom" (p. 55). At the *News American*, she would occasionally insert a sentence in her post game story asserting that player so-and-so was "unavailable for comment to women sportswriters" (p. 68) to get her editor's attention. At *USA Today*, she protested the fact that women only covered tennis, amateur and women's sports (p. 65). At the *Sacramento Bee*, she outlasted the harassment of slugger Dave Kingman and was rewarded by being the first woman asked to serve on the Board of Directors of the Baseball Writer's Association of America (p. 97). When she left her baseball beat in 1990, her concluding sentiments reveal that while she fought for equality, it was the gendered media system that wore her down: "It wasn't those little locker rooms that drove me away from sportswriting. It was that big locker room" (Fornoff, 1993, p. 227).[8]

A complete case-study analysis of the "big locker room" by Mary Jo Kane and Lisa J. Disch (1993) explores how male athletes sexualize the locker room environment to reinforce the power struggle between men and women. In their analysis of the 1990 Lisa Olson "incident," in which the then *Boston Herald* sportswriter was sexually harassed in the New England Patriots' locker room, the authors detail how media reports constructed Olson as either a classic rape victim (i.e., she asked for it by being there) or a classic hypersensitive female (i.e., she can't take a joke).

The battle continues to rage. Before the start of Game 3 of the 1995 World Series, NBC's Hannah Storm, who has been in the business long enough to be recognized and respected, was verbally harassed. Storm was in the corner of the Cleveland Indians dugout – not the locker room – with a camera crew waiting to conduct an interview. Indians outfielder, Albert Belle, who mistook her for CBS's Lesley Visser, started shouting obscenities at her. As one sportswriter put it, "Apparently, all those women sportscasters look alike to Belle" (Pluto, 1996, March 1, p. A1). Belle ended up with a $50,000 fine, the largest fine in baseball history.

The core issue is the infrasystem of values that construct physicality-as-power in the sports arena, i.e., male power over females. Female reporters seeking access to the locker room enter contested turf, a dangerous intersection between media and sport where gender values still privilege male power.[9]

Outside of the locker room, the survival strategy some female sports reporters have adopted is not to challenge the sports coverage hierarchy. Instead, they worship it. One example is Nanci Donnellan, the only female to have a full-time radio sports talk show, who is hyped as "The Fantastic Sports Babe" and who calls herself "an equal opportunity offender" (Creedon, 1994b). However, the contested turf for Donnellan, whose call-in radio show is also shown on ESPN2, is sports knowledge. In this arena, she has been able to throw the mask of femininity to the wind by successfully matching wits with sports trivia fanatics, primarily on the subjects of professional football, baseball and basketball.

Overall, it appears that some female reporters have reached a point where they are allowed to function within the sports system *if* they stay within the bounds of the sports coverage hierarchy. In liberal feminist terms, they have achieved equality. In radical or transformational feminist terms, nothing has changed. They are simply functioning to preserve – consciously or unconsciously – the hegemonic stasis of a gendered media system.

MARKETING, SPORT AND THE MASS MEDIA

When women's sports hits the marketplace, the bottom line is what sells. Conflict and controversy sell. The night that Tonya Harding and Nancy Kerrigan skated in 1994 Norway Olympics was the sixth highest-rated television program of all time (Brennan, 1996, p. 24). In the MediaSport world only two Super Bowls had ever produced higher ratings. Market research has shown that figure skating is the second most popular sport in America, and the most popular sport among US women (Brennan, 1996).

The attention and audience that the Harding–Kerrigan affair brought to figure skating certainly helped the United States Figure Skating Association land a $25 million contract with ABC to televise its events through to 1999 (Brennan, 1996, p. 127). In an interesting move, CBS, which lost its NFL rights to Fox, replaced the slots with ten made for TV figure skating events. Sponsorship dollars in the sport rose from an estimated $2.5 million in 1994 to $6.8 million in 1995 (Brennan, 1996, p. 127).

Little girls and sweethearts sell. Sports correspondent for the *Sunday Times* of London, Adrianne Blue (1987), explored how marketing the LPGA and women's professional tennis involves pressures to be slim, look sexy and act "feminine." *San Francisco Chronicle* sports columnist Joan Ryan (1994) wrote an exposé of the destructive power of feminine ideals of beauty, thinness and youth in figure skating and gymnastics.

Heroines sell. The supreme badge of courage in the hegemonic world of sport is to play through pain. *People Weekly, Newsweek* and *Time* headlined the effort of Olympic gymnast Kerri Strug as a "leap of faith." Overnight the 18-year-old unknown, who successfully completed her second vault with a severely strained ankle to help the US team win the gold medal, became an American hero (sic).

Of course, heroes make money, but heroines are tarnished by money. Strug signed separate contracts with Magic Productions, Inc. and with the Ice Capades reportedly worth $4–6 million (Starr, 1996). Her six teammates honored a contract signed before the Olympics for a thirty-four-performance tour sponsored by John Hancock, Jefferson-Pilot Corp. and Bill Graham Presents for about $200,000 per athlete (McCallum & Kennedy, 1996). Strug's decision to cash in on her fame brought new headlines: "Cash and Kerri" in *Newsweek* (September 30, 1996) and "A Team Torn Apart" in *Sports Illustrated* (September 9, 1996).

Reportedly, NBC sports programming strategy for the 1996 Atlanta Olympics was to target women viewers with stories that would "touch their hearts" (Gunther, 1996, p.62). The strategy worked, according to *Media Report to Women*, allowing NBC to boast a significant increase in prime-time viewership among women (1996 Summer, p. 16). Overall, prime-time ratings among women aged 18–34 were 13.1, up 30 percent from the Barcelona Olympics; among women aged 18–49 ratings were 14.1 percent, up 25 percent from Barcelona; and among women aged 24–54, ratings rose to 15.3 percent, up 25 percent (Rice, 1996, p. 45). The network expected to make a record $70 million in profits from the games and sold $685 million in advertising for the games (Rice, 1996, p. 45).

Homosexuality doesn't sell. *New York Times* reporter Grace Lichtenstein (1974) provided one of the first examinations of marketability, sexuality and politics in women's sport. Her first hand account of the controversy surrounding the start-up of the short-lived Virginia Slims Tennis Tour in 1970 documents the problems faced by Billie Jean King in maintaining the feminine image of women's tennis when she moved it from the country club scene to the first women's professional tennis league in pursuit of pay and prize equality. The total purse of the first-ever Virginia Slims tournament was $7,500, but by 1973 there were 22 tournaments and purses totaling $775,000 (Shelton, 1993). Despite their successes, King, who acknowledged her lesbian affair at a press conference in the early 1980s (Guttmann, 1991) and Martina Navratilova, an outspoken advocate for gay rights who also publicly acknowledged her lesbianism, have reportedly lost millions in endorsement money (Cahn, 1994).

Figure skating, a sport where female and male athletes wear heavy make-up, sequins, velvet and plunging necklines has tiptoed around the devastation of AIDS among the ranks of male figure skaters (Brennan, 1996). When USFSA officials fielded questions at a press conference about AIDS for the first time ever in 1993, they did so only after the representative from L'eggs, the corporate sponsor, had left the room (Brennan, 1996, p. 62).

However, homosexuality can be overshadowed – figuratively. "Lipstick" lesbians, the opposite of the stereotypical "butchy" lesbian, can, and undoubtedly have, passed as straight to save sponsorships. The LPGA has a fashion consultant who travels on the tour (Berkow, 1995) and public relations counselors who work hard to convince players to attend to "image" issues. The LPGA's prize money is up more than 40 percent over the past four years from $18.7 million to $25 million (Berkow, 1995). Event and television sponsors are as main street as mom and apple pie, ranging from McDonalds to General Motors. Yet, former CBS golf commentator Ben Wright still made headlines in 1995 with his charge lesbians in women's golf are "going to a butch game that furthers the bad image of the game" (Berkow, 1995, p. 25). Although the media criticized Wright and LPGA officials reportedly were outraged, his remarks reminded everyone that corporate sponsors want femininity. And homosexuals have become an attractive target market for certain advertisers. A study of Gay Games IV, held in New York City in 1994, suggested that sponsorships were expected to raise $1.2 million. Among the corporate donors, sponsors or suppliers were: AT&T, Miller Brewing Company, Naya Water, Hiram Walker, Visa USA., and Continental Airlines (Cramer, 1996).

Interestingly, the results are mixed on the most obvious marketing ploy of all – sex. Blatant sexy, heterosexual sex appeal has had mixed results at the women's sports marketing cash register. Women's Professional Beach Volleyball, where bronzed women, albeit gracefully muscular, in mini bikinis, jump, dive and roll around in the sand, has not seen increased sponsorship revenue despite increased television exposure (Baker, 1995).

However, heterosexual sex appeal, when presented in terms of fitness sells very, very well. A study of the transformation of *womenSports* magazine to *Women's Sports and Fitness* magazine examines the interaction gender, advertising and marketing in the magazine industry (Creedon, 1995). A new magazine, *womenSports* introduced itself to potential advertisers in January 1974 as "a women's magazine focusing on sports, not a women's sports magazine" (Creedon, 1995, p. 459). As its advertising manager, the former national sales manager at *Ladies' Home Journal* saw it, "If they [potential advertisers] opened it up and found all volleyballs and hockey pucks, I'd never get cosmetics" (Bateman, 1977, p. 99). Publisher, tennis star Billie Jean King and her editorial staff saw it differently, *womenSports* was intended to become the equivalent of *Sports Illustrated for Women*. The magazine struggled with the difference between hockey pucks and cosmetics for years. In the 1980s when aerobics and jazzercise became popular, the magazine officially changed its name to *Women's Sports and Fitness*, positioning itself to attract a niche market of fashion, beauty and shoe manufacturers. Emphasis on organized, competitive women's sports news declined, and advertising revenue increased substantially. What did the change in editorial philosophy say about gender values and sports marketing?

> The use of fashion models coupled with the title and logo changes substantially silenced the previous political agenda, promoted women's pursuit of improvement practices, and constructed women's bodies as passive, sexual objects.
>
> (Endel, 1991, p. 184).

Women are also an attractive target market. According to statistics compiled by the Women's Sports Foundation, since 1991 women have spent $21 billion per year in the purchase of athletic shoes and apparel (Lopiano, 1996). Lifestyle sports are increasingly popular with magazines and their advertisers. *Sports Traveler*, a magazine started in mid-1996, has brought in more than $1 million in advertising revenue in its first four issues aimed at upscale, active women (Kelly, 1996). Recently, Weider Publications earmarked $10 million for a teen girls lifestyle magazine they plan to launch with the title, *Jump*. (Kelly, 1996) The magazine, which will focus on fitness, beauty and sports, plans to use a $1 million television advertising campaign to bring it to market in February 1997 under the editorial direction of former *Sassy* editor Lori Berger. Not surprisingly, Weider executives expect advertisers to include: personal care, beauty, apparel, music, electronic and shoe manufacturers (Kelly, 1996). A third magazine, *Condé Nast Sports for Women* began publication in fall 1997.[10]

Where sport intersects with gender, the history lesson from the marketplace has been that female physicality and male femininity don't equate to advertising revenue. However, the marketplace appears to be in transition as media outlets multiply and audiences are more carefully defined.

Overall, in an era of shrinking state and federal government support for education, the influence of commercial interest in sport is growing. Commercial sponsors are paying the NCAA's Division I football powers "megabucks" these days for Bowl appearances. The Tostitos Fiesta Bowl, sponsored by Frito-Lay, tops the list, paying each team approximately $8.5 million to appear in 1996 (Wieberg, 1995). The Sugar, Orange and Rose Bowls also have payoffs of more than $8 million a team. What financially strapped college president these days can thumb his (sic) nose at such a bucket of gold at the end of the "Totes Rain Bowl?"

Marketing women's sport as a product is obviously a multifaceted task. The examples in this section have only scratched the surface. Equating marketing with product sales is simplistic, but it does allow us to see that marketers and advertisers appear to be poised to push a sport or pull their products into the market using women's sports as a vehicle. In this rapidly changing media environment, successful marketing revolves around matching the interest of a sport audience segment with a product or service. However, it can just as easily mean creating a sense of interest on the part of the audience in a sport to suit the needs of the marketplace.

CONCLUSIONS AND IMPLICATIONS

Power control theory teaches us that those who have power in an institution or organization determine its ideology. This chapter argues that the ideology supporting the institutions of media and sport, i.e., the infrasystem of values, seeks to preserve a gendered social structure so that these organizations can maintain stasis or control in their environment. One need only look at the evidence from advertising research to understand the hegemonic power associated with promoting gendered values in how we look, what we eat and what we wear (Lazier & Kendick, 1993; Kilbourne, 1987; Fox, 1984; Goffman, 1979).

We have argued that power and money drive decisions in the institution of sport. We have also explored how sport is a gendered cultural institution. What will control of women's sports by institutions such as the NCAA and NBA which value masculinity, heterosexuality and money mean in the long run? Are we missing the political implications of power relationships, i.e., the hegemonic system, that undergird the institution of sport by arguing for equality?

Many sports fans, including liberal feminists, generally accept media representations of sport and believe the battle to be fought is over coverage – equal space and air time. Others, particularly radical or transformational feminists, see these mass mediated representations as crucial political battlegrounds in determining our culture's self-definition (Turow, 1992). From the perspective of this chapter, it appears that in the cultural debate over content and values of women's sport, the ultimate arbiter will be the marketplace.

The core issue is, will marketing serve the interest of women's sport without changing the nature of the sport itself? In particular, in a market-driven system in which media, sponsors, advertisers and the like have an increasing presence, how much control will they desire in exchange for their financial support?

Equality does not mean sameness; difference does not mean inferior. The NCAA's stated goal is for women's sport to be "bred" in the image of male sport (Smale, 1990). Should the desired outcome of gender equality in sport be the modeling of the other gender's behavior? As women's sport becomes more commercially viable, will we be watching women playing women's sport or will we increasingly see women playing men's sport?

NOTES

1 Fatsis, S. (1996, Feb. 16). Women's hoops takes a long-range shot. *Wall Street Journal*, p. B6.

2 Conferences, in order of football 'power' rankings, are: Southeastern Conference, Big Twelve, Big Ten, Pac-10, Atlantic Coast Conference and Big East (Byers, 1995, p. 354).

3 The eight cities in the league are: Atlanta, Columbus, OH, Hartford/Springfield, MA, Richmond, VA, Denver, Portland, OR, San Jose, CA, and Seattle. Ironically, the Columbus Quest, the league's most winning team, were averaging only 2,223 fans a game, the league low (Fans support, 1996, p. D6).

4 It should be noted that top women performers in individual sports considered sex-appropriate such as tennis and golf have made a living for several decades.

5 The WNBA had a successful first season and announced expansion franchises in Detroit and Washington D.C. in October 1997.

6 Cathy Henkle, sports editor of the *Seattle Times* and former president of AWSM, is an exception. When she joined the *Times* staff in 1988, the University of Washington's women's basketball team was outdrawing men so they made women's basketball the official sports 'beat' and covered men's basketball with stringers, who are essentially freelance writers (Fornoff, 1993, p. 170).

7 Ludke no longer covers sports.

8 Fornoff left the baseball beat after 5 years to become a freelance columnist and official scorer.

9 For a detailed, chronological listing of 15 years of locker room harassment and access issues faced by women reporters from 1975 to 1992 see Creedon, 1994a.

10 *Sports Illustrated* printed two issues of *womenSport* (spring and fall 1997), but told subscribers that the magazine was still in a planning stage and ceased publication.

Sports Journalism, Ethics, and Olympic Athletes' Rights[1]

Margaret MacNeill

The Olympic sports media possess significant freedom to pursue their work in comparison to the athletes, who remain tightly hamstrung by rules and regulations. On the one hand, athletes must achieve clear-cut levels of sporting eligibility and abide by strict regulations during competition while, on the other hand, sport media are relatively unfettered because the *Olympic Charter,* press and broadcast guides do not stipulate codes of media ethics. In the attempt to reach the widest possible audience, the International Olympic Committee (IOC) accredit a wide range of media, who do not all work as news journalists but, since the 1980s, have officially been adopted into the Olympic "family". In the preamble to the IOC's *Media Guide,* President J.A. Samaranch writes:

> In all their forms, the media, in other words the written and photographic press, radio and television broadcasters, form an integral part of the Olympic movement and belong, in the fullest sense of the term, to the Olympic Family. Aware of the primordial role played by the media in the world today, the International Olympic Committee accords them the important position which they merit, in order to ensure that one of the fundamental principles of the *Olympic Charter* is respected: *The widest possible promotion of the Olympic Movement and its ideals.*
>
> (1990, p. 39)

This chapter will explore the slippery issues of journalistic ethics, Olympic athlete–media relationships and a case-study of athletes' rights within Canada's high performance sport system. At the Olympic Games, news journalists vie with enter-tainment media (print, broadcast and interactive) to be granted access to athletes for interviews. Journalists also jockey for access to event venues with entertain-ment media, public relations and marketing personnel, and privileged exclusive broadcasters. Each media genre produce different commodities for different audiences thereby making a single Olympic media code impossible. Nonetheless, the various Olympic media struggle to retain full autonomy over their work by hiding behind the cloak of press freedoms historically negotiated by news journal-ists whose work is mediated by codes of ethics. In the absence of formal Olympic media standards, the confusion élite athletes harbor about basic constitutional rights to free speech and about how they can effectively interact with the media has been ignored.

ATHLETES' RIGHTS AND JOURNALISTIC CODES OF CONDUCT

Sports Journalism Codes

> Sports journalism is anything but standardized. It is a conglomerate of multiple forms of expression, styles and methods and people, that, as in sports, for reasons of simplification, is given a common denominator. A certain unifor-mity has grown up in sports news and reports, but differences still remain. The alloys and combinations differ, with the result that personal accents are given prominence and different profiles are created. Sports journalism has many different faces, each of which satisfies the expectations of different tastes.
>
> (Claeys & Van Pelt, 1986, p. 95).

The lack of standardization in sports journalism fosters a vibrant field of stories and exciting images, but this context also disempowers many Olympic athletes. John Merrill calls journalistic ethics a "swampland of philosophic specu-lation where eerie mists of judgment hang low over a boggy terrain" (1974, p. 163). While ethical standards are the touchstones of professions such as medicine and law, they have become thorny issues among the media because many feel codes contradict the "rights" of the free press. Sports media generally refuse to discuss the topic of media ethics, which leaves rule-bound athletes confused about the roles and standards of the wide range of information gatherers, investigative reporters and entertainment sports media they come into contact with at international sporting events (Peel, 1993). Within the sports media profession there exist a wide range of understandings concerning ethical codes, including: ethical codes being institu-tionalized modes of censorship, or formal written codes of responsibility and decla-rations of integrity, and/or loose working guidelines for professional practice.

Historically, journalistic ethics have emerged from a liberal arts tradition that scrutinizes media conduct in reference to determinative principles such as freedom of speech (Christians, Rozoll & Fackler, 1987, p. xvii). Research about media ethics has tended to focus on questions of "right action" or journalistic conduct during reporting, decision making and moral deliberation while gathering news within institutionalized settings (Birkhead, 1991; Christians et al., 1987; Goldman, 1980; Ziff, 1986). By assuming ethics to be measurements of performance or "styles of behavior", researchers often treat journalists as moral agents using ethical frameworks to guide or justify actions rather than assuming journalists to be professionals capable of discerning value within their culture (Birkhead, 1991). Ziff argues that journalistic settings are so diverse around the world that uniformity in ethical standards cannot and ought not to exist (1986). In fact, the majority of sports media departments in print and broadcast media organizations across North America do not follow a specific code, although the trend to formalize guidelines is increasing.

Sports departments who have institutionalized a code of ethics, such as those within the Canadian Broadcasting Corporation (CBC Radio and Television) and members of the Canadian Press (CP), have heavily borrowed from the codes of general news journalism. CP, for example, strives to deliver comprehensive, objective, impartial, accurate, balanced and fair news (1989). Sport journalists are assigned to events to inform their audiences. The primary responsibilities of all CP reporters include:

1   Full investigation before transmitting any story or identifying any individual in a story where there is the slightest reason for doubt.
2   Citation of competent authorities and sources as the origin of any information open to question.
3   Impartiality in consideration of all news affecting parties or matters in controversy, with fair representation in the report to the sides at issue.
4   Limitation of subject matter of facts, without editorial opinion or comment and with proof available for publication in the event of a denial.
5   Prompt and frank admission of error.

(CP, 1989, p. 2).

Some sports writing associations, such as the College Sports Information Directors Association and Associated Press Sports Editors (APSE) now offer sport-specific codes. Since the 1970s, APSE has promoted professionalism and principles of print journalism to enhance the credibility of sports journalism (Garrison, 1989). Some of the key ethical guidelines of the APSE include (cited in Helitzer, 1996, pp. 429–430):

1   a "pay-your-own-way standard" for travel, meals and accommodation;
2   declining all gifts and gratuities of significant value;
3   avoiding conflicts of interest between journalist activities and "moonlighting" activities within sport such as serving as score keepers for teams.

While these are basic rules that news journalists abide by unquestionably, not all sports writers and sports broadcasters follow such guidelines (Jollimore, 1992) and not all media covering the Olympic Games are there to simply inform audiences. Generally, the nature of the relationship between the media and athletes and the topic of sports journalism standards have received scant attention prior to the 1980s.

Athletes' Rights

The broad issue of athletes' rights emerged in the 1970s as political and academic questions. Kidd and Eberts (1982) present the notion of athletes' rights as referring to "those benefits and protections the legislators and the courts have recognized as belonging to individuals who are members of athletic organizations and recipients of government sport services, or to individuals in similar positions" (1982, p. 17). The athletes' rights movement adopts a foundation of civil liberties, common law and the requirements for natural justice or fairness.

General studies of the rights of amateur athletes have examined three levels of issues. Early research first brought to the foregrounded issues of status and the protection of athletes' rights around topics such as team selection, the awarding of benefits and discipline, and the rights to free speech on the public agenda (Kidd & Eberts, 1982). Second, the social-economic status of national team members and their treatment by sporting associations became the focus as Canada prepared to become a host nation for the 1988 Winter Games (Beamish & Borowy, 1988). Third, questions about the degrees of institutionalized discrimination within national sport governing bodies targeted issues of gender in the 1980s and early 1990s (Hall, Cullen & Slack, 1990; Hall & Richardson, 1982; Macintosh & Whitson, 1990). Despite the emergence of research into athletes' rights and the formation of athlete associations, such as the IOC's Athletes' Advisory Commission and Athletes Can (formerly the Canadian Athletes' Association), athlete–media relationships have not been systematically explored.

Socio-Cultural Studies of Sports Journalism

The ethics of sports journalism is an emerging issue in the sociology of sports literature (Emig, 1986; Garrison & Sabljak, 1985; McPherson, Curtis & Loy, 1989; Petrovic & Zvan, 1986; Smith & Valeriote, 1983; Telander, 1984). Comparisons between sports and political journalism have led to a number of critical research projects. For example, daily newspaper coverage of sport has been found to perpetuate information journalism rather than investigative journalism by focusing on scores and background information (Emig, 1986). Yet, growing concerns about the ethical conduct of sports media have transformed the nature of relationships between athletes, journalists, and sporting organizations over the past half a century according to Rick Telander (1984). In the pre-television era, Telander has observed, sports writers and radio broadcasters served as team promoters who travelled with the athletes and easily constructed athletic heroes by simply ignoring their private lives.

In recent decades, print and broadcast journalists have evolved from being public relation and cheerleading arms of home teams to becoming serious journalists due to changes in both sport and society (Garrison, 1989). With the proliferation of televised sports coverage in the 1970s, fans have been offered growing opportunities to spectate athletic events, which has shifted the work of some print journalists from describing game action and reporting scores to investigating sport from behind the scenes and providing an "insider's" glimpse. Recent investigative ventures by print journalists that report on athletes' private lives, indiscretions, team exploits and sporting business have resulted in a greater reluctance by athletes and some sporting officials to be interviewed by the media (Telander, 1984). To redress these concerns and adjust to changes in the sport–media relationship, McPherson et al. suggest that sport journalists have a number of responsibilities to uphold, including: making sound decisions as gatekeepers of information, to present appropriate news rather than "smut" and "irrelevant" information; to avoid muckraking in order to increase sales; to report fairly and accurately; and to offer hard evidence for criticisms about sport (1989, p.163).

Petrovic and Zvan (1986) suggest the sports press and mass media have significantly influenced both athletes and sporting events by politicizing information for political-economic prestige during international event coverage and by promoting "victory fetishism." Their survey of world class Yugoslavian athletes found some athletes were affected by the media's pursuit of sensational stories. Sensationalism was found to exaggerate scandals out of proportion, to unduly increase performance pressure for 15 percent of world class athletes, and to foster an unfavorable team climate between athletes. This resulted in some coaches banning athletes from being interviewed by the sports media during training. A significant number of world class athletes (35 percent) were, however, motivated to excel by statistical coverage of sporting events found in the media. The researchers concluded that the demanding work of sports journalism requires both journalistic skill, knowledge of the sport being covered, and a respect for athletes who "co-produce" knowledge for the media.

Attention to the role and treatment of the athlete by the sports media is absent in other lines of research. Studies of the Canadian media have either examined institutional power, the effects of media coverage upon audiences, or have presented ethnographies of media work that all ignore the athlete's role in the sport–media complex. In 1988, John Barnes presented a fairly comprehensive critique of the legal aspects of the sports media. His case-studies were limited to analyses of American anti-trust laws governing broadcasting rights ownership and their role in the governance of international sporting leagues; specific attention to the consequences of these agreements for athletes was not pursued. Likewise, Smith and Blackburn (1978) and Nattrass (1988) have examined the historical development of the symbiotic relationship between media organizations, advertisers and sporting organizations. In this research athletes were considered to be the raw material of the sporting spectacle, but were not considered to be social actors within the broader sets of human relations that constitute the media nexus. Another traditional line of media research has scrutinized the "effects" of portrayals of sporting violence on the audience (Smith, 1983; Young & Smith, 1989). While this line of research has provided some valuable insights about the influence of the media on audiences, it has ignored the physical, psychological and social consequences of the glorification of violence on athletes. Finally, production ethnographies of media crews have focused on the political-economic relationships between media corporations, media work routines, gendered and commercial gatekeeping decisions, and/or the processes of making of meaning (see, for example, Cavanagh, 1989; Gruneau, 1989; MacNeill, 1992, 1996; Theberge & Cronk, 1986). These lines of research have contributed to a broader understanding of institutionalized corporate relations and media labour struggles, however, the treatment of the athletes during interviews and broadcast coverage has not been fully investigated as part of these projects.

PRESS FREEDOMS, ETHICS AND JOURNALISTIC PRINCIPLES

Media ethics and the principles of the free press are founded in wider concerns for personal liberty, democratic social responsibility, concerns for organizational structures and processes of moral reasoning (Christians et al., 1987; Russell, 1994). Sports media journalists and entertainment personalities make a wide variety of judgments during the production of sporting events. Judgments are steeped in a variety of discourses emerging from personal moral values, aesthetic values assigned to sport, professional values and through a sense of craft. To evaluate the processes of reasoning, Christians et al. suggest that the circumstances of media labor must be identified, values motivating media decisions be carefully evaluated, appeals to particular ethical principles be clarified (such as norms of "truthtelling", norms of protecting sources, norms of protecting the innocent), and loyalties be articulated (1987, p. 3). Within formal news departments, pragmatic decisions are made by journalists on a daily basis using standards that have been negotiated historically. These standards have emerged from:

1   the official missions of their organization to serve the public stakeholders or private stockholders;
2   the established mandates of their departments to investigate, entertain and/or educate;
3   restricted access to the sporting event and athletes due to exclusive media rights agreements and security and;
4   other limits and pressures of their work such as meeting deadlines or gaining access to phone lines (Christie, 1996).

On a practical level, therefore, journalistic ethics are "socially informed pragmatism" (Toulmin, 1986, p. xvi). No one set of ethical rules can be adopted by or imposed upon the world's sports media at the Olympic Games because not all media personnel covering athletic events act as news journalists. Sport is packaged in a variety of ways to attract different audiences during the Olympics. As competition for audiences intensifies in the North American private sector and public media, boundaries between media that inform or entertain are shifting and in some cases dissolving. Journalists are aware of the wide range of working rules, ethical standards and corporate imperatives affecting their colleagues at major sporting events (Christie,1996, Telander, 1984). Ethical codes do not, therefore, stand alone as the yardsticks of integrity (Mackie, 1987) because they are historically conventionalized within each culture and are value-laden.

World-class athletes exist within a restricted rule-bound social setting at the Olympic Games yet interact with the media without a formal framework of expectation. Athletes are expected to display media savvy and respect the work of the world's media at competition venues. The IOC's Athletes' Commission is now striving to strengthen media contact with athletes by appealing to the media's sense of responsibility and understanding the plight of athletes at major events (IOC *Media Guide,* 1990, p. 54). However, except for a few superstar Olympic athletes who regularly interact with the world media, most high-performance athletes are not keenly aware of the daily pressures acting upon the media during their labor to communicate. Athletes are also rarely fully cognizant of their basic human rights when dealing with the media and sporting officials as the last section in this chapter will discuss.

From Freedoms of Expression, to Press, to Commercial Speech

Press freedoms are historical extensions of individual rights to expression in liberal democracies. The freedom of expression has long been part of the democratic traditions of nation-states such as Britain, Canada and the United States. In Canada, the *Charter of Rights and Freedoms* (1982) provides all Canadians with constitutional guarantees of freedom of expression and, by extension, it guarantees freedom of the press to the media. Section 2(b) of the Charter states, "freedom of thought, belief, opinion and expression, including freedom of the press and other media of communication" are fundamental freedoms structuring Canadian society.

Freedom of expression includes both the right of the citizenry to know, the right to speak or communicate through other modes of expression without acquiring the permission to do so from authorities, and the right to express opinions without the risk of the law forbidding citizens to do so (Martin & Adam, 1991). Accredited sports media members exercise the democratic right of a free press on behalf of fans' "right to know" when fans cannot attend games or lack access to the decision makers in the sporting world. However, the right to know is not the same as the right to express. There are legal limitations upon the right to expression (for media and athletes alike) including libel, creating danger to human lives by inciting riots, and expressing prejudicial ideas before a trial that may prevent an accused person from receiving a fair trial. In addition, there are other legal statutes that circumscribe the work of journalists and sports entertainment media. The sports media are subject to specific restraints set out within provincial laws such as breach of confidentiality, privacy, defamation, property rights and contract.

Longstanding concerns about the political curtailment of basic freedoms of expression and of the press by governments broadened in the 1960s to include concerns about concentrated economic power in media monopolies. The principal concern has been that concentration of ownership of media organizations reduces the number of observations and opinions about the news of the day. Over thirty years ago A.J. Liebling critically observed that the function of the press in North America "is to inform, but . . . its role is to make money" (1961, p. 7). In 1981 The Kent Commission (A Royal Commission on Newspapers in Canada), warned the growing concentration of media ownership was a serious threat to journalistic freedoms. "Freedom of the press," the Commission stated, "is a right of the people, not a property right of owners" (1981).

Private sector players in the North American media industry, including the marketing sector, have recently parlayed press freedoms and individual rights to expression into the "freedom of commercial speech." Commercial media outlets have extended press freedoms to packaging non-news formats, such as sports entertainment shows, without posting responsible journalistic codes of coverage to justify qualifying for press freedoms. Commercial speech rights have been assumed by the advertising industry to promote all legal products and services. However, exclusive rights-holding media, exclusive sponsors of the Olympic movement and sponsors of the media programming claim the right to benefit from privileged vantage points at sporting events that block competitors' access. The freedom of commercial speech is thus pursued within an uncompetitive environment of exclusive monopoly.

Press freedoms cannot be democratically distributed to media working in environments of unequal access. As sporting events are packaged as "properties" that can be purchased in the marketplace, the freedom of commercial speech by exclusive broadcast rights holders and by sponsors is at odds with traditional journalistic press freedoms to cover the event. Today, exclusive agreements further strengthen the monopolistic power of a few broadcast organizations over print media and non-rights holding broadcasters. Non-rights holding broadcasters are limited to 3 reports (each a maximum of two minutes long) separated by three hour periods during the Olympic Games (IOC *Media Guide,* 1990, p. 178). "Balance," a central principle of news journalism, is difficult for print journalists to achieve at the Olympic Games when they are regularly forced to wait until after rights-holding broadcasters have completed post-game interviews with coaches and athletes. Non-rights paying print journalists have difficulty gathering the breadth and depth of information they require before meeting editorial deadlines (Christie, 1996). The media contribute to the democratic political process and have significantly increased the popularity of sport in North America, yet the sports media rarely investigate the political issues of sport and have not sought to protect the basic human rights of athletes to the same degree that freedom of the press and of commercial expression are now being protected.

Richard Pound, the IOC member who negotiates television rights for the Olympic movement, rejects the interest among political business reporters covering the Olympics in establishing ethical codes for Olympic media (1992). The IOC is willing to stipulate minimum technical requirements in broadcast media agreements and employment history criteria for gaining journalist credentials agreements. Written ethical codes and standards of behavior are argued to be outside of the technical jurisdiction of the IOC and are considered to be censorship by Olympic officials. By reproducing standard libertarian ideologies about a free press the context of a commercialized sport–media event, the issues of fair treatment and ethical journalistic pursuit are ignored.

There are debates between members of the sports media about what constitutes a journalist and what constitutes a member of the entertainment media. Radio, for example, did not negotiate separate broadcast rights to the Olympic Games until 1984. Since radio media worked as both live broadcasters and reporters, they were simply admitted to the games by both IOC Press and Television Commissions (Young, 1989). George Young, a former reporter for CBC Radio Sports, argues that radio broadcasts do not seek to produce entertainment as do television broadcasters and therefore should not have to pay media rights:

> a price tag should not be attached for the right to broadcast news, any more than it should be imposed on the thousands of newspaper and magazine journalists that cover the Games. People have a right to hear the news, and that shouldn't be dependent on the ability of the networks or stations to pay.
>
> (Young, 1989, pp. 3,16)

Globe and Mail reporter James Christie also criticizes the unequal treatment of print media access:

> There is a lack of access I find most disagreeable, however. It is imposed by "rights holding" broadcasters, who have paid substantial amounts to televise the Games, are given priority interviews with athletes while written press facing deadlines, languishes outside. No one should be allowed to "buy the news." The IOC, to maximize its take of TV dollars, sold not only the event, but control of the people [athletes] in it.
>
> (1996)

The journalistic responsibility to comprehensively cover an event or interview athletes about an issue is hampered by other entertainment media who possess exclusive media rights to broadcast the Games. Broadcast media producing live event programming see themselves as story tellers, cheerleaders, part of the home team at the Olympic Games, and producers of live media events argue that they do not "owe" access to colleagues in other media because of their exclusive payments (MacNeill 1992, 1996). Audiences attracted to Olympic coverage are rarely well informed about athletes because the media package the professional sport properties and ignore élite amateur sport between the Olympic Games (Fisher, 1989).

In response to the concerns of journalists about access, IOC press advisor Fékrou Kidane, has drafted a number of resolutions to be submitted to the 105th Session of the IOC in July 1996. Resolution Number Two guarantees that media coverage will be accessible to the world by assigning a quota to each country with a national Olympic committee. This resolution also stipulates that adequate working conditions and moderate rates for accommodation and press center space rental, and access to telecommunications be established; that the media be guaranteed the right to information and free access to sites for all accredited journalists (1996, p. 215). However, the various forms of Olympic media will continue to be assigned hierarchical access to athletes. The descending interview order at competition venues will be as follows: the host broadcaster, television crews with live unilateral coverage (national broadcasters with exclusive rights), television crews from the nation of the athlete, international media agencies, national agencies from the country of the athlete, then other media (IOC *Media Guide,* 1990, p. 58). The inequities of information gathering and production will continue to mediate media–athlete relationships and media labor in this context of exclusive rights agreements.

The Olympic movement does not impose a formal set of ethical guidelines on the sports media as a condition of accreditation to the Games (Pound, 1992). Official discourses of Olympism promote issues of fair play and humanitarism yet ironically ignore the issue of media-athlete relationships and the ethics of mediated pursuit. In a broader discussion of commercialism and the Olympic movement, Richard Pound discusses ethical values:

> The IOC is committed to the principle that sport organizations must retain the full autonomy of decision in matters of sport. This includes the nature and frequency of competitions, the rules of play, decisions affecting sport competition, concerns for the health and safety of athletes and the ethical values inherent in the concept of Fair Play. No agreement with any organization will compromise these responsibilities.
>
> (1994, p. 11)

However, journalists attending these global events are expected to follow the standards of the media outlet they represent, although the IOC claims it upholds one set of ethical values. The emergence of ethical debate surrounding media conduct and content is due to questions regarding media responsibility when balancing the public's right to know, the public's appetite for information and sporting entertainment, and questions of power derived from exclusive commercial media rights.

A CASE-STUDY OF HIGH PERFORMANCE ATHLETES' RIGHTS AND RELATIONSHIPS WITH THE MEDIA IN CANADA

Olympic and national team athletes are expected to perform for media cameras and journalist microphones with scant understanding of their rights and obligations in doing so, and with minimum preparation by their coaches and sporting associations. This section investigates the present state of the media–high-performance athlete relationship from the perspective of Canadian high-performance athletes. The *Media Ethics and Sports Journalism Project* (1994) surveyed 1,200 national team members and recently retired élite amateur athletes belonging to the Canadian Athletes' Association. This project explored (1) the relationships of social and legal power between the Canadian sports media and national team members by identifying the rights of athletes and the degree to which these rights are protected, and (2) Olympic athletes' understanding of their legal rights when dealing with members of the media.

Many high-performance athletes could not answer the questions about media relationships because they had never received formal attention from the media. Of the 155 respondents who completed all questions regarding media ethics and relationships (12.9 percent of the association's membership and the sample that will be the focus of this section), 76 respondents were female athletes and 79 were male athletes. The majority of this sample (86 percent) were currently members of national teams; another 14 percent had retired within the last six years.

The average age was 26 and the average number of years on the national team was 5.7 years.

The survey revealed that the majority of national team athletes (64 percent) acknowledge they are ignorant of their legal rights when dealing with the media and sporting officials. While the Canadian Charter protects both athletes' rights to expression and press freedoms, 10.3 percent of athletes were forbidden by coaches to talk to media, 2.6 percent were forbidden by their sporting association, and 0.65 percent of the respondents were forbidden by their sponsor(s). In addition to explicit prohibitions regarding granting media interviews, the frequency of media–athlete interviews and the quality of media coverage were all hampered by athletes' fears of negative media treatment. A significant group of national team members indicated that they withhold information from reporters during media interviews out of fear of punishment from coaches (17.4 percent) or retribution from their sporting association (7.1 percent). Whether or not legitimate grounds for trepidation exist, athletes' reservations indicate a significant margin of non-confidence that the sports system and the media will treat them fairly. This also suggests the range and depth of media coverage has been limited by a poor exchange of information and opinions between athletes and media. Issues of media accuracy, comprehensiveness, and respect for basic athlete/human rights to privacy emerged from the survey and will be addressed separately.

Journalistic Principles of Accuracy and Comprehensiveness

To "keep faith" with the public, news should be presented "comprehensively, accurately and fairly, and by acknowledging mistakes promptly." This statement of principles, by the Canadian Daily Newspapers Association was released in 1977 to post the ethical code of responsibility the press upholds to retain its freedom. It acknowledges that healthy diversity of journalistic rules and standards should exist between media organizations but that press freedoms are a public trust. In the survey, athletes expressed significant anger about a disregard for this trust. Many mistrust the media because they have been misquoted in the past. 64.5 percent of athletes reported being misquoted by the sports media (21 percent attempted to correct the errors). Many news agencies and media outlets have guidelines addressing balance and accuracy in coverage. According to CP, for example, "accuracy is fundamental ... the discovery of a mistake calls for immediate correction ... being reliable is more important than being fast" (1989, p. 1). Fairness requires a balanced presentation of the relevant facts in a news report, a balanced portrayal of all "substantial opinions" in "issues of controversy," and that conflicts of interest must be avoided (Desbarats, 1990, p. 177).

Yet, athletes naively assume that fairness in media coverage means that the media should equally cover all athletes and sports in terms of time and space. The ideology of the level playing field in high performance sport has been transposed by athletes onto their expectations about how the media field operates. Members of the sports media are assumed to be unknowledgeable about amateur sport and national team athletes outside of the Olympic Games period according to respondents. Athletes expressed disappointment:

1   about the lack of attention they received in comparison to professional athletes;
2   that many sports receive scant attention at the Olympic Games; and
3   that good Olympic athletes are also ignored in shadow of sponsored super-
     stars.

During an Olympic year, athletes provide an average number of interviews each year at the rate of 4.9 interviews to the print sports media, 2.7 to television crews, and 2.1 to radio reporters. During non-Olympic years, national team athletes provide an average of 4.3 print media interviews, 2.0 to television crews, and 1.7 to radio reporters. 65 percent of the athletes claimed the sports media have never attended practices at tournament sites or during the regular training year. Over a typical training year, Canadian media attended at least one practice of 35 percent of the respondents.

On a human rights level of respect for human difference and accuracy of representing different communities of people, it is an infringement of the Criminal Code of Canada for the media to willfully promote hatred of an identifiable group, such as an ethnic group, a religious sect or creed. No athletes responding to the survey indicated they had been victims of defamatory comments or of hate propaganda by the media. Less than 1 percent of the sample claimed they had been explicitly treated in a racist manner by the media. 23.7 percent of all females claimed they had been treated in an explicitly sexist manner by the Olympic media.

Athletes' wide range of misunderstanding of informal rules of sportscasting and taken-for-granted slogans could endanger the reputations of journalists and sports officials. For example, athletes have differing views on what the statement "off the record" means. Journalists are not liable for publishing/broadcasting "off-the-record" statements unless it is a breach of confidence or defamatory. Athletes wrongly assume that communicating "off-the-record" statements to sports media will protect either their anonymity and/or the privacy of the person or organization they are commenting about. Most athletes assume this phrase will guarantee that journalists will neither reveal the information publicly nor reveal the source of the information (68 percent). Another 13 percent assume "off the record" means that the information will be released to the public in sports coverage regardless of whether or not it is true, but the source (the athlete's name) will not be revealed. Six percent believe the statement is meaningless because it is not legally binding. Four percent believe the statement means the journalist–athlete interview is concluded and both parties can continue to communicate privately as friends. Nine percent of athletes could not define the statement. Some athletes are, therefore, not aware that the media are held legally accountable for all statements published/broadcast. Professional sports media claim that leaving "off-the-record" statements out of the public domain to be "good will" or a professional "courtesy"; they warn, however, that athletes should adopt a working rule to not say anything to the media they do not want communicated to the public (Christie, 1992, 1996; Young, 1992).

Athletes generally mistrust the media yet paradoxically feel confident in their exchanges with the Canadian media. Most do not get nervous when being interviewed and thrive on the attention (53.5 percent): some athletes become a little nervous (37.4 percent), while approximately 9 percent became somewhat or very nervous when interacting with the media which affects their training and competitive performance.

Privacy and Trespass to Property

According to S.M. Robertson, invasion of privacy includes spying, eavesdropping, using letters or diaries without consent unless it is in the public's interest to know (1983). Journalists can call athletes to request information and interviews but not to harass. Athletes in some provinces can obtain a court order to stop the invasion of privacy or sue for damages when privacy has been violated. The 1994 survey revealed that a small contingent of athletes (6 percent) reported their privacy had been invaded by harassing telephone calls at home from reporters or by the interception of cellular phone calls at competition sites. Private conversations cannot be intercepted and used by the media without consent. Under the Canadian Criminal Code, the media cannot persistently follow an athlete from place to place if he or she does not want to be interviewed. Off the field, members of the media cannot enter the property of an athlete or of a private organization if they are told they are not welcome or after an invitation has been revoked. No athletes reported media trespassing on their property but they did raise a number of concerns regarding privacy of personal information.

Many athletes expressed deep concern about personal information being released to the media by their sport organizations and other athletes. Over half of all athletes closely guard their personal lives: 9.7 percent did not want any information released to the media by their sporting associations, 46.6 percent indicated that sport-related information (such as competitive histories, performance statistics, awards and records) could be released to the media if data excluded medical status. With permission, 39.4 percent of the athletes indicated they are willing to disclose personal information such as biographical details about school, occupational status, volunteer work, home life, etc. 4.3 percent were reluctant to have biographical information because they might change their minds about what information should enter the public domain.

In addition to concerns about sporting organizations inadvertently releasing private information, 45.8 percent of respondents were concerned about athletes working as journalists at the Olympic Games. Almost half of the athletes feared that personal "insider" information might be published or broadcast by athletes. IOC media accreditation rules now prohibit athletes being issued media credentials. Athletes, such as Carl Lewis at the 1992 Barcelona Olympics, have been able to circumvent the need for journalist credentials by simply carrying cellular phones to broadcast from venues or by using facsimile and e-mail technology to file stories to newspapers. Members of Canadian national teams were divided about IOC rules of media accreditation because the sports media is a future career option for many athletes. Half of the athletes (54.8 percent) believed that athletes should be allowed to formally work as media personnel at major competitions. Strategic interventions into media event policy, the promotion of responsible media work, and enhanced athlete education and event preparation are needed to improve athlete-media relationships.

STRATEGIC INTERVENTIONS TO BALANCE THE NEEDS OF THE SPORTS MEDIA AND ATHLETES' RIGHTS

The relationships between the sports media and athletes are conducted on slippery but negotiable terrain. National athletes tend to be ill-prepared to communicate effectively with the media and are not schooled in basic human rights. Moreover, the foggy boundaries existing between news and entertainment media allow sports media to focus on marquee athletes and events. This power to "make or break" an athlete's reputation and level of fame, discourages athletes from complaining about misquotes, and it promotes the withholding of information because of athletes' mistrust of the media and fear of sporting officials. Academies and athletes' rights organizations are perhaps the most promising forums for athletes to begin to redress prohibitions to free speech, communication barriers, and problems establishing mutually beneficial relationships with the sports media.

Journalists and press officers from sports organizations offer a number of suggestions to improve relationships between the sports media and national athletes that could be addressed by such sporting associations (Christie, 1992, 1996; Jollimore, 1992; Robertson, 1996, Young, 1992). First, the sports media should request honest and straight answers from athletes because every word the media print or broadcast puts their reputation on the line. Second, all athletes should possess historical knowledge about their sport to contextualize their stories. Third, athletes should create media "game-plans", that clearly indicate where and when they will be available to the media at events, and that strategically plan how they will cope with the media based on their competition needs and communication skills. Fourth, the sports media want athletes to understand the major pressures affecting media work at major games, including

1 pressures from time (meeting deadlines, coping with time zone differences when filing stories, travel time between venues, etc.);
2 pressures from technology (media compete for access to the tools of their trade in media venues, they also struggle to make their equipment compatible with different electrical and telecommunication systems);
3 the frustrations of tracking and gaining access to the athletes at major event sites.

Fifth, sports journalists do not want to be associated with the entertainment media in the minds of athletes. Athletes often harbor the misconception that all media at the Olympic Games should act as patriotic cheerleaders (Christie, 1996). Finally, the sports media want to debunk the myth that they lack professionalism. This myth is particularly disturbing to veteran Olympic journalists. Christie, for example, recently stated:

> Probably the worst misconception is that the media are not professionals, that we are hit-and-run mongers, cynical and ignorant of Olympic sport, out to enjoy the Games as a lark. I can only assure athletes that while some of the reporters they meet may be ill-prepared, the majority treat an Olympic assignment with as much importance as athletes. From one Games to the next, we

scan the wires for national and international stories. We study not only athletes, but the business of the Games, from IOC level, through National Olympic Committees, to local organizers and even individual venue management. We're responsible for knowing what gets broadcast and why; who broadcasts it; who advertises, how much is paid. We must stay abreast of sport technologies and rule changes and sport medicine.

(1996)

While organizations such as the IOC set out technical and economic agreements with the media, agreements do not usually include content regulations or rules of journalistic conduct. Most sports organizations are reluctant to introduce these kinds of agreements because they assume these rules would be a form of censorship. However, since the Olympic charter ensures humanitarian international exchanges at the Olympic Games and promotes a philosophy of fair play, media agreements and guidelines should ensure that basic human rights of athletes are respected by the entire Olympic family including the media.

The media have their own agenda and privileged codes of content for sport, however athletes could play a much greater role in promoting the way that sport could be covered, in expanding the range of narratives by regularly offering suggestions for story topics and angles. Professional journalists and entertainment media know that every athlete has a story to tell. A number of new opportunities in traditional sports media and new multimedia now provide avenues for athletes to communicate with audiences and to conduct regular exchanges with sports media. Examples of some of the new opportunities include: athletes being involved in Internet press conferences in which fans ask questions; athletes have the option to answer detailed questionnaires that are shared by both the broadcasters in an on-line data bank and in media handbooks provided by the national Olympic Association; athletes can e-mail journalists directly; athletes are writing guest articles to provide an "insider's view" for papers such as the *Toronto Star*; and journalists are now beginning to cover athletes for months prior to the Olympics so that audiences are familiar with national team members by the time the opening ceremonies begin.

Formal ethical codes and informal standards can be concerned about the "harmonious satisfaction of desires and interests" (Toulmin, 1986, p. 223) between media, athletes and sporting organizations. Because all genres of sports media demand the same freedom of press accorded to news journalists, it is appropriate to question the degree to which they all uphold the basic principles of responsible journalism. While the media readily admit that they possess formidable power and influence over the sports they cover (Young, 1989), journalists generally address codified ethical standards with a great deal of skepticism because codes seem prudish and do not apply easily in daily processes of decision making (Desbarats, 1990, p. 180). Furthermore, many sports media and event organizers consider codes to be institutionalized censorship rather than guidelines based on collective wisdom of their field regarding craft style, taste and responsible reporting.

Athletes generally do not know when sports media cross legal borders and ethical boundaries because the Olympic movement and the media fail to post minimum ethical standards as bench marks of responsible media–athlete relationships. The number and role of athlete representatives on IOC Press and Media

Commissions could be strengthened to facilitate stronger athlete–media relations and to ensure the basic human rights of athletes are respected. After consulting with athletes and media outlets worldwide, the media could negotiate a code of ethics at a pre-Olympic Media Congress. Ideally, codes of journalistic ethics can promote responsible and responsive media coverage to a changing social and political-economic world of sport. Collectively these efforts may enhance the quality of Olympic coverage, improve the working conditions for the Olympic sports media, and improve the competitive conditions for athletes.

Toward Understanding the Press–Athlete Relationship

To foster better relationships between high-performance athletes and the Olympic media, further inquiries into a number of pressing issues are required. For example, to what degree have high-performance athletes historically been denied the right to express themselves to the media by Olympic coaches, sporting federations, or agents? What specific prohibitions are placed upon athletes? Do athlete's jeopardize their national team selection chances when they speak to the media? How can athletes be better prepared to communicate effectively with the media and to learn about their basic rights? What is the range of formal ethical codes and/or informal working guidelines that world press and broadcast media currently employ at the Olympic Games? Should the International Olympic Committee establish a journalistic code of ethics and/or a broadcast media code of ethics? What is the current state of relationships between rights holding broadcast media at the Olympic Games and the written press? Are exclusive broadcast media rights agreements a threat to news journalists' access to athletes? Do struggles over access to venues and opportunities to interview athletes cause tension between the media? If so, what is the impact of intra-media relationships on athletes? How has the introduction of multimedia technology into the athletes' village affected athlete–media relationships and the content of coverage? How does sponsorship of athletes, media broadcast crews and events affect the quality and quantity of media coverage? Is there an imbalance between the individual athlete's right to freedom of expression, press freedoms, and the freedom of "commercial speech" by advertisers and media organizations? As the athlete has more and more become defined as a product in the eyes of the media and the public, answers to questions such as these will help define the contours of this commodification and the consequences it may have for athletes interested in competing at élite levels.

NOTE

1   Earlier versions of parts of this chapter were presented to the annual conference of the North American Society for the Sociology of Sport in Savannah, Georgia, USA in November 1994. The author would like to acknowledge the support of a Connaught Grant to conduct this research.

Part three

MediaSport Texts

Come Together: Sport, Nationalism, and the Media Image

David Rowe, Jim McKay, &
Toby Miller

During the [1990] Asian Games in Beijing, a giant helium-filled balloon advertising M&M candies bobbed up and down over Workers Stadium. In a match apparently between nationalism and commercialism, members of the Chinese balloon cadre repeatedly lowered the balloon to avoid its competing for attention with the Chinese flag, to which Mars candy representatives invariably responded by hoisting the balloon so that it would fall within range of the television cameras.

(Nafziger, 1992, p. 495)

It was not, said one smiling Scottish player yesterday, who thought it better not to be named, to do with rugby but nationhood. "Our soccer team have not done much lately" he said. "So I dare say we have been chosen in this match to right the ills of Thatcherism, the poll tax and Westminster government."

(quoted in Maguire, 1993, p. 293)

[Chinese women] were so rampant at world short-course [swimming] championships – with the acne, the body hair and the deep voices – that some of our girl place-getters wanted to sit down on the dais in protest ... Then, of course there were the Chinese women weightlifters in Melbourne. After seeing that bunch of King Kongs tossing weights around like confetti ... I won't bother watching the pixies in the Super Bowl this year.

(Wells, 1994, p. 25)

In contemporary social science the idea of the nation has become increasingly problematic. An intensified analytical, albeit contradictory, emphasis on global and local processes seems to bypass the nation altogether. First, there is the concept of globalization, which suggests, in general terms, that the differences between nation states have been substantially eroded and that global economic, political and cultural integration is, if not complete, then certainly well advanced (Waters, 1995). At a radically different level there is the concept of localization, which proposes that the nation state and any form of national culture is at best a hegemonic fiction, with "authentic" place- and community-based systems of meaning that are deeply marked by the cultures of the marginalized (for example, of women, subaltern ethnic minorities and so on), repudiating the confected communality of the patriarchal state. Where, then, can the contemporary nation be found?

The immediate answer is that the nation is conjured up at those moments when an affective unity can be posited against the grain of structural divisions and bureaucratic taxonomies. This is the cultural nation we experience through diverse feelings, policies, and practices, the parameters of which are inherently difficult to define. Perhaps it is an empirical group of people caught in the early morning light before the TV set, as when Australia "stood still" to watch the winning of the America's Cup off the Atlantic coast in 1983, or when Canadians erupted "spontaneously" after their ice hockey team's dramatic defeat of the USSR in their first "open" competition in 1972. This symbolic binding of the people of a country through culture is a concept derived from social and political theory and public policy, but popular culture – notably televised sport – is the site where populations are targeted by different forms of governmental and commercial knowledge/power. For instance, a major international sporting event, such as the Olympic Games or the soccer World Cup, without comprehensive media coverage, national flags flying, national anthems playing, politicians involved in the ceremonies, military displays, tables comparing national standings, athletes competing in national uniforms – and no men – is almost inconceivable. Such sporting spectacles, beamed across the globe to competing countries and many others, are almost impossible to decode without recognizing these nationalistic signs and interpretations (Larson & Park, 1993).

In this chapter we will interrogate the symbolic process of nation-making through sport and the key mythologizing role of the media. The media sporting nation is shown to be deeply gendered, tending to obscure and legitimize not only hegemonic gender divisions, but also those that apply to social class, to indigenous people and to non-Anglo/Celtic migrants. We also discuss, however, unpredictable fractures in the ideology of "mediatized" sporting nationalism along lines that present new possibilities for counter-hegemonic discourses. A brief, illustrative case study of soccer in Australia – the "world game" with a distinctly problematic articulation with the idea of an Australian nation – highlights the complexity and dynamism of sport, nation and media in combination. The sporting nation is, therefore, shown to be a profoundly ideological formation, whose artificiality – that is, its "constructedness" – is matched only by its drive to affirm its organic purity.

SPORT, MEDIA AND NATIONAL MYTHOLOGIES

Soccer in Brazil, cricket in the West Indies, and rugby union in Wales and New Zealand are examples of male-dominated sports which the media represent as embodying the character of a nation or region. Richard Gruneau and David Whitson (1993, p. 7), for example, remark that ice hockey has often been portrayed as having an "enduring link to the idea of 'Canadianness.'" This idea of hockey representing a unified Canadian identity is, they demonstrate, mythical in Roland Barthes' sense – stories we tell ourselves about ourselves. Myths are not total delusions or utter falsehoods, but partial truths that accentuate particular versions of reality and marginalize or omit others in a manner appealing to deep-seated emotions. Dominant myths depoliticize social relations by ignoring the vested interests surrounding whose stories become ascendant in a given culture. Critically, myths disavow or deny their own conditions of existence; they are forms of speech that derive from specific sites and power relations, but are passed off as natural and eternal verities. National sporting myths lend themselves particularly well to this apparent time-lessness fashioned out of the "invention of tradition" (Hobsbawm & Ranger, 1983).

As both Andrew Tudor (1992) and Hugh O'Donnell (1994) have comprehensively shown, national mythmaking through sport is common across continents. These stereotypes signify as ethical norms, mobilized to advocate, shape and generate new habits amongst the citizenry, encouraging active participation at both a physical and an ideological level. Many accounts of sport situate it as a central tenet of national culture in either a welcoming or critical way. This practice reifies the term "sport," denying the fissures – of gender, class, ethnicity, media coverage, public participation, and region – that it sometimes tries to reconcile. Increasingly, though, the tensions that these fault lines describe are finding expression, and in ways that are not restricted to intra-national sites. During the 1994 World Cup, for example, Iranian TV viewers were given a special form of montage. Whenever US cameras cut from the players in the scorching heat to shots of the crowd, programmers in Iran edited-in footage of people in winter garb from other matches in order to hide the decadence of Western attire. Meanwhile, US marketers continued to advertise the sport as more truly international than the World Series, Super Bowl, and so on, which looked so intramurally North American by contrast. What is a virtue at one site – difference and diaspora – is, it seems, a problem at another.

We are not suggesting that media audiences of sporting events are automatically "programmed" – as Hodge and Kress (1988, p. 12) argue, "Meaning is always negotiated in the semiotic process, never simply imposed inexorably from above by an omnipotent author through an absolute code." We are claiming that the homosocial media are deeply implicated in deciding "what the people get." King and Rowse (1983) maintain that popular media representations are best understood – both materially and symbolically – as part of a tripartite structure consisting of readers/viewers who are interpreting the world(s) represented or implied, and those who are doing the representing. They describe media professionals' influential representation of a diverse imagined community in a unified way as populist "plebiscitary rhetoric" .

There are indications across the history of nation, sport, and media, however, that powerful political issues can be put on the international public agenda at this uneasy, sports-sponsored meeting ground. The circulation of Leni Riefenstahl's documentary film *Olympia* (1936–38), for example, stimulated much public debate over the rise of Nazism. The entry of the USSR into the Olympics in 1952 produced a medal-table rivalry along Cold War lines that was constantly nourished and analysed by the media. The salutes by Tommie Smith and John Carlos after the 200 meters sprint in the 1968 Mexico Games captured the world spotlight for African-American politics. Later, coverage of the murders in Munich and political boycotts of sporting competitions by African nations, the US, and the USSR emphasized the deeply conflictual intersection of "domestic politics and international struggles" (Goldlust, 1987, p. 118). Much of that history is tragic, but it opens up a series of major ideological differences to the international public gaze, frequently by means of the protocols of international sports law (Nafziger, 1992). Attempts to buttress the British Commonwealth, for example, now center on international sporting exchange through a Working Party on Strengthening Commonwealth Sport, which was established in 1989 to reform the Commonwealth Games by increasing representation of women's sport and assisting underprivileged young sportspeople (McMurtry, 1993). This complex intrication of nation, state, ethnicity, and gender forms the grid within which an effective analysis of contemporary sport can take place. Before proceeding, however, it is necessary to look more closely at the historical and theoretical underpinnings of what we have come to know as the nation.

NATIONS AND SPORTS

At the same time as nations (or, more precisely, nation states) are said to be in decline (Held, 1989), paradoxically, they seem to be multiplying. We live in an age of inter-national proliferation. That very formulation presupposes the existence of an equally strong age of the national. The nation is a oneness of imagination that binds citizens to states without the everyday apparatus of repression. It is a means of identification with persons and places beyond the perceptual horizon. How can we render so slippery a term of belonging analytically useful? Why should it be that "everyone" wants to form nations, just as the more unreflective or dystopian/utopian amongst us continue to insist on the obsolescence of the "national" in a new era of global capital? Perhaps the answer to this question lies in Tom Nairn's (1993, p. 157) paradoxical remark about the renaissance of "medieval particularism" that "[s]mall is not only beautiful but has teeth too." Our contemporary moment registers both intra- and trans-nationalism through multifarious sporting organizations based on nations (the Olympic, Pan-American, World Student, European, and Commonwealth Games, the World Cups of soccer, rugby union, cricket, and so on). Diasporic movements and First-People dispositions, at the same time, gather momentum as sources of political and/or sporting power through protests at international sporting events and the global trade in players. The most concentrated and powerful intersections of media, nation and sport take place at these time- and space-compressed international competitions. It is worth pausing to historicize such occasions, as our case study uses a specific occasion where bicentennial celebrations of a nation produced just such a site.

Formal celebrations marking the appearance of sovereign states date from the decision by French Revolutionary republicans to evoke the classical Athenian and Roman models of citizenship by creating festivals to commemorate what was still in the process of being produced – a love of place, liberty, and history. Spontaneity needs organization, in a way that mirrors the processes of domestication that have marked the trajectory of organically-formed sporting pastimes into codified and governed activities (Elias & Dunning, 1986). One of the earliest international athletic competitions was organized alongside the British Exhibition of 1851, while the first three Olympic Games this century were timed to coincide with international expositions, providing opportunities for the press to celebrate national technology and manhood at the one site (Wilson, 1988, p. 156). In his comparison of three contemporary celebrations (the Australian and US Bicentenaries and the Canadian Centenary), John Hutchinson (1992) demonstrates that these Anglo-settled, cultural-capitalist, constitutionally federal, immigrant nations display markedly similar tensions at moments of public festivity. Their treatment of indigenous peoples, in particular, provoke outbursts of protest (such as at the Commonwealth Games of 1982 in Brisbane) at just such moments when national communality is advanced.

The continuing history of imperialism, colonialism and immigration problematizes foundational mythology and points to the contingent processes by which that mythology is formed, endorsed, and transmitted. As the market for players from around the world for "national" European soccer leagues demonstrates, such notions of natural patrimony are forever in question. This series of contradictions reveals tensions in the connection of tradition and custom. The former is a set of practices dedicated to inculcating and exemplifying values of historical unity that stress continuity and solidarity despite profound social change. Tradition is clearly imposed from above. Custom, by contrast, claims a variation over time but in a way that is more obviously tied to contemporary power relations that are found to connect with the past through precedent rather than rupture (Hobsbawm, 1983, pp. 1–3).

In the case of sport, the media clearly operate in the space between tradition and custom, doing so, as we argue below, with an almost exclusive concentration on men as the plenipoteniaries of national character. Hans Kohn (1945, pp. 8–9) argues that the only "homeland which a man 'naturally' loves is his native village or valley or city," whereas travel, teaching, the media, and sport produce an awareness of something wider to love, covet and police. Nationalism, he says, is "our identification with the life and aspirations of uncounted millions whom we shall never know, with a territory which we shall never visit in its entirety." Nations are, paradoxically, pronounced upon and manufactured at the same time as their authentic existence is already assumed (Guinchard, 1987), an ontological dilemma that induces Benedict Anderson (1993, pp. 13–16) to approach nations as "cultural artefacts" that draw on "a deep, horizontal comradeship" and an "image of [their] communion" when "the members of even the smallest nation will never know most of their fellow-members, meet them, or even hear of them."

This collective identity was historically achieved through the spread of the printed word using local forms of European language after the sixteenth century. The popular book opened up the prospect of simultaneity, of knowing that people like oneself could be reading similar books at another place but at the same moment. There was a similar iconographic change, as extensively reproduced images elided time and space. In the current age, our own sense of the simultaneous is of events occurring at the same moment in different places. Sporting events like the Super Bowl may physically occur on a field where it is a hot afternoon, but be watched by TV viewers in morning warmth and afternoon cold. At that moment, the men's bodies on display transcend such time zones to bring spectators together. This chronotropic logic was not available prior to the advent of the nation state and its communication technologies. Past, present, and future were essentially one. Now, we distinguish between them in order to delineate a shared national cultural history. "Live" coverage of such events as the Olympics and the World Cup are space-binding and time-splitting technologies of international sporting culture, recorded and read across the world through a complex prism of nation, region, race, class, sexual practice, and gender.

These are, however, participatory as well as celebratory and plebiscitary moments. On a global scale there is an increasing governmental obsession with rearing hearty youths, and a new corporate interest in recruiting and maintaining healthy employees. For this reason there has come to be a significant national component to sporting policy and also a trend towards national considerations in the coverage of global events, as research into successive soccer World Cup competitions indicates (Tudor, 1992). Compulsory education, public arts subventions, physical education, and media regulation logics of self-formation can be seen as training modes in constructing a language community. They are also technologies of affiliation to the sovereign state (Gellner, 1981, p. 757), creating the preconditions for what Anthony D. Smith (1990, pp. 9, 11) calls the "bureaucratic nationalisms" of countries that must accommodate a migrant world and form a new (if always partial) subjectivity. Yet this congenial space of self-expression, where recreation allows the citizen at rest either to watch sport as an entertained spectator or play it as an engaged amateur, is something more. As an audience, sports spectators are constantly subject to interpellation, especially as patriots, complete with a vast array of stereotypes to characterize both themselves and their "others." The motivation underpinning this administrative discourse is governmentality (as proposed by Foucault, 1979), with healthier, fitter populations designed to reduce the cost of public health, guarantee a functioning workforce, and help in the foreign and domestic circulation of tourist spaces (such as Australia and the Caribbean) known for their sporty, outdoor image.

This disciplinary motive becomes quite apparent when national governments seek justifications for involving themselves in sport. For example, a New Zealand Minister of Recreation and Sport, operating in an intensely neoclassical economic policy environment, has referred to his portfolio as a route to "social and economic prosperity" in promoting "active, physical lifestyles." On the more conservative social policy side, there is another benefit – that of disciplinary control – because "being into sport" ensures being "out of court" (quoted in Volkerling, 1994, p. 8). Even the former Jamaican Socialist Prime Minister, Michael Manley (also a distinguished historian of cricket), has adopted this rationale for sport (McMurtry, 1993, p. 422). Here, male violence is a category of danger that can be pacified and redirected into an appropriate sphere – literally, that of national fitness – and the singular category of the nation turned into several categories. In Philip Schlesinger's (1987, p. 219) terms:

> "cultural identity," "audiovisual space," "national culture" function as so many useful handles; they offer respectability and brand identification for a variety of contending politicoeconomic projects in the cultural domain.

In 1985, Australia's Minister for Sport outlined one such project in arguing that sport had a "dominant role in our development as a nation" because it "cuts across race, age, sex and class and is deeply ingrained in the fabric of our society" (Brown, 1985, p. v). It is instructive to compare that statement with an elaboration by a senior public bureaucrat appearing in the same publication:

> At present Australia has no national philosophy towards sport. Some nations use sport ideologically to show that their style of government and their style of life are superior to those of other nations; some use sport under the "bread and circuses" syndrome to keep the people's minds off other issues; some nations have used it to overcome the effects of war; some Third World countries use sport to show that they are catching up to the rest of the world; while other national sports philosophies have racial overtones. Australia has no such philosophy and hence, as a nation, we are not at all sure why we are so involved, except that sport is a good thing – we love it – and we have to win at it.
>
> (Dempster, 1985, p. 121)

The media and the state sometimes play a more overtly ideological game, as when the American networks intercut interviews of disappointed US athletes reacting to the decision to boycott the Moscow Olympics with scenes from the USSR invasion of Afghanistan, while the British media diminished planned coverage and articulated what remained against a highly political editorialism (Real, 1989, p. 197; Wilson, 1988, p. 159). During the 1991 Gulf War, government ministers attacked the Australian Broadcasting Corporation's coverage of it on various grounds, including a lack of patriotism and anti-Americanism. They happily acceded, however, to the Australian national broadcaster carrying images of hard-core Americana during its telecast of the Super Bowl, and to its decision to displace regional coverage of a cricket match between Australia and England on the Australia Day public holiday (McKay, 1991a). Here, the state appears to be responsible for national philosophy by enunciating or enforcing it. Televised sport works to connect people who have never met and do not expect to do so, yet industrial culture divides even as it rationalizes, enabling the creation of diffuse collective identities as well as the spread of officially endorsed ones (Schlesinger, 1991). This key role of the sports media in the simultaneous articulation of national unity and difference is worthy of fuller inspection, particularly in the light of one of the most pronounced structural divisions over which the state presides – gender inequality.

GENDERED NATION, GENDERED SPORT

The sporting nation is constructed by the media in a highly gender-specific manner that sees men arrogating to themselves the right to fight for the feminine virtue of the nation. For illustration of this point, we consider again the America's Cup and the following comments of Bruno Trouble, owner of a French marketing and advertising agency:

> With Australia's success in 83 many thought the America's Cup was going to die; it was as if the America's Cup was a virgin, untouched for 132 years – then when the Aussies took her, well she sort of lost her virginity, so they thought, "this girl is of no more interest."
>
> (quoted in Martin, 1987, p. 18)

Here we can see an intensely gendered, patriarchal deployment of metaphor that doubly delineates boat and nation as female, with each one's protection and control a matter of national and international pride among men. While women clearly are involved in international sporting competition – and, indeed, are often more competitively successful than their male counterparts (in Australia, for example, female competitors have proportionately gained many more Olympic medals than male athletes) – the discourses of media, sport, and nation remain unfavorable to them. The individual achievements of women athletes (such as Chris Evert and Billie Jean King) may be of great media significance, but at the level of team sports, where the source of pride is collectivized, women are denied the status of bearers of national qualities that the media and the apparatus of the state conventionally accord to men. This is usually the case even when women represent national teams, as is demonstrated by the contrasting coverage and fanfare concerning the male-only Davis and female-only Federation Cups in tennis. In short, heroines may enunciate desirable qualities of femininity, but that significatory power rarely extends to the domain of the team, the group of like-minded and -bodied representatives of national pride.

The nation as a group of readers has routinely been for the taking, but it is "taken" in distinctly partial ways. For when women are offered up as representatives of the nation, it is in a way that usually sexualizes performance, objectifying them for a male onlooker. The following snippet of sports journalism exemplifies this practice:

> She was a seductress on skates, with looks and moves that could melt the hearts and minds of any Cold War zealot. Katarina Witt is back in the Olympics, this time as a commentator. When audiences last saw her [at the 1988 Olympics] she was the skating Carmen in red, a glamour girl who received thousands of love letters and silenced all those cruel jokes about steroid pumped-up East German women. Since then, the Berlin Wall has fallen, Germany has reunited and Katarina Witt is fast becoming a lady of capitalism, promoting Danskin, DuPont and Diet Coke ... If Witt is discovering America, be sure that Hollywood has discovered her Vogue model's face and flawless smile.
>
> ("This time Katarina bears witness," 1992, p. 18)

It is because of such gendered conceptions of national representation that Iris Marion Young proposes a model of "differentiated citizenship." This model acknowledges the value of universalism in terms of "a general will and common life" but rejects the "demand for homogeneity" (1990, pp. 117–19, 126) that excludes so many groups from dialogue and political power. Sport, she argues, is an important vehicle of such exclusion:

> If there is a particular female person participating in sport, then, either she is not "really" a woman, or the sport she engages in is not "really" a sport. These two interpretations of the phenomenon frequently occur in our society, often together. Most of the sports played today have their origins in male experiences in sex segregated activities, such as hunting or warfare. None have arisen from the specific activities of women or from women's specific experience.
>
> (1980, p. 147)

Young's revised program for citizenship proposes that minorities should, first, organize to identify themselves and forge a critique of the social; second, make formal arrangements that allow the initiation and discussion of social policy proposals; and, finally, exercise the power of veto over policies with direct impact over them.

Already, we can see some additional openness to inclusive cultural policy in international organisations through innovations such as the 1976 European Sport for All Charter and its 1992 successor, the European Sports Charter, feeding into other liberal developments inside the state apparatus, such as the Canadian Sport Coalition (Hargreaves, 1994, pp. 183–84). For this reform to take place at the level of signification, of course, there would need to be an equivalent shift in media production protocols and their broader presentation of "national" sport and culture. The sports television production process, for example, has long been powerfully influenced by the ideologies and aesthetics of gender. The BBC's instructions to camera operators prior to the 1976 Olympic Games specified a gendered notion of the shot:

> straight lines . . . suggest strength, security, vitality and manliness and if overdone can imply harshness, whereas curved lines suggest grace and sweetness and if they're overdone then insecurity and weakness result.
>
> (quoted in Peters, 1976, p. 17)

Material effects flow from such instructions, as is shown, for example, by network television rarely covering the Olympic sport of women's synchronized swimming, or the London *Daily Mirror* marking the first English women's cricket match at Lord's with a photograph of the English captain staring into a baby carriage (Peters, 1976, p. 19). This process fashions a particular image of "sporting citizenship" in advanced capitalist societies, setting "real" sports and athletes apart from the "unreal" (sports gendered as female, sports in Third World countries, and disabled activities – McKay, 1991, pp. 92–93). The media, as key articulators of these hierarchies of sports and citizens, invite a close examination of their ideological role in the symbolic making of the nation.

THE NATIONAL SPORTS MEDIA

The media constitute an uneasy junction between the terms "audience" and "nation." The culture industries negotiate complex relations connecting these terms; audience and nation can only profitably meet, as far as the commercial sector is concerned, under the sign of pleasure. Herbert Schiller (1989, p. 130) has said of sport that "the audience is targeted in its most vulnerable condition, relaxed yet fully receptive to the physical action and the inserted sales pitch. It is the ideal ambience for the penetration of consciousness by a wide variety of ideological messages." It is no surprise, then, to find that the French firm Peugeot Talbot decided to underwrite British athletics in the 1980s because the company sought to connect its cars in the minds of UK consumers with health, success, and beauty, "a very necessary and important association," as one executive put it (British Film Institute, 1986).

Most forms of popular culture ask the public to reconsider their intra-national social allegiances, to play ambiguously with class, gender, or ethnic identification, and permit themselves to be entertained, sometimes even beyond the point where their nation encounters another (Hartley, 1992, pp. 111, 116). When viewers tune in to the Olympic Games, they are certainly addressed as biased observers. It is assumed that they wish to see representatives of their nation at work, but it is also believed that they wish to see a more transcendent excellence – that they want to watch the best. It is further assumed that they want to be present as part of an ethic, however fractured, of international spirit; it may even be that this spirit is most clearly present in its televisual reality, rather than amongst competitors and officials. A study of the 1984 Olympics analyzing viewers' reactions across seventeen nations and six countries indicates the broad basic appeal of the event, but also that it encourages a sense of disgruntlement. This anger was created out of the contrast between the forms of cultural imperialism, nationalism, and chauvinism on display and the notional Olympic ideal (Real, 1989, pp. 233–4).

Despite this spirit of internationalism, there is normally at least a residual referent in the (gendered) nation. For example, on February 8, 1993 Australian viewers of television coverage of the English Football League heard a commentator refer to an Australian goalkeeper as "calm and confident, like all sportsmen from his country." More spectacularly, the day before the 1966 World Cup Final between England and West Germany saw one British newspaper editorialize that if the Germans "beat us at our national game, let us take comfort that twice we have beaten them at theirs" (quoted in Maguire, 1993, p. 296). Here, national stereotypes become not just aspects of verbal description, but influences on the wider discourse of the nation, both internally and overseas. Because North Americans play team sports that are usually of minimal interest to the people of other nations, the televised Olympics are certainly a rare opportunity for national sporting identity to be claimed in opposition to an actual opponent – the "Americanness" of baseball is mostly achieved in a vacuum. Television anchor people achieve this neat fit between sporting success and media coverage by integrating success in a particular sport with a putative national way of life. For the BBC, yachting gold medals are interpreted as one more occasion of British naval conquest, an imperial historiographic reading that borrows from earlier triumphs to create a wistful nostalgia (Peters, 1976, p. 8).

The 1992 Winter Olympics were the first occasion after the collapse of state socialism in Europe for US TV to address international ideology in sporting commentary, and a major turnabout from the reaction to the failure of "Team USA" at Calgary in 1988, which saw George Steinbrenner retained by the US Olympic Committee to investigate how the communists had done so well (Kottak, 1988, p. 53). TNT and CBS described the Albertville Games as apolitical, but national stereotypes and politics suffused their televisual presentation. The huge investment in rights, at a time when recession was hitting the advertising industry hard, saw an immediate move towards capturing the audience through partisanship, if with a condescending thought that "the Unified Team will take its gold medals back to the gray streets of a struggling homeland and people who need real heroes now more than ever" (CBS host quoted in Riggs, Eastman & Golobic, 1993, p. 258).

The interplay of sport, media, and nation is frequently made manifest in capitalist shibboleths about rationality and meritocracy (Lawrence & Rowe, 1986b). Investing sport with highly adversarial forms of drama has long been integral to such commentary (Bryant, Comisky & Zillmann, 1977). Instructions to broadcasters such as the following are not uncommon:

> Create a feeling that the competitors don't like each other . . . Studies have shown that fans react better, and are more emotionally involved, if aggressive hostility is present . . . Work the audience at the emotional level and get them involved in the game.
>
> (Hitchcock, 1991, p. 75)

Although the derogation of opponents is not obvious in promotions for all sports, it is quite clear in games such as international cricket. Australian TV theme songs, for example, have contained lyrics such as "each game the stakes get higher, the white ball is on fire . . . We'll bring him to his knees, just watch him bend", "carve each other up in the World Series Cup", and "gentlemen, we'll tan your flamin' hide" to describe matches against England (quoted in Miller, 1989, p. 594).

Garry Whannel (1992, p. 191; also see Buscombe, 1975), however, proposes a more conflictual model of the intersection of sport, media, and nation. He argues that television, in particular, has been a critical force in the generation of a star system for sports that is in conflict with national values of togetherness, thrift, and identity. Television draws upon verbal myths of collectivity and unity through audio commentary emphasizing the nation as embodied in its team representatives and by means of visual coverage that concentrates on specific stars. In the process, contradictions may open up. Television commentators are trained to lay stress on the personal, gladiatorial aspects of sport. The operative theory is that sport is one of the few areas where people can construct and follow heroes. In place of the relatively "thick description" offered by radio, the thinness of TV commentary enhances the pictures and selectively produces narratives of individualization that seek out difference, "character", history, and conflict as momentary distractions from the excitement or boredom of the main play (Morris & Nydahl, 1985, p. 105). The various media that merge to describe a special event – newspapers, television, radio, guide books on how to follow the competition, video tapes, and genres (news versus highlights versus live coverage) – scramble the unity of such moments. Part of such mediated heroism is conflict, because the qualities of the hero are logo-centrically dependent on low, base, undesirable and, above all, different (non-heroic) behavior.

It would be misleading to assume that either a Left or Right functionalism can adequately describe the characteristics of TV sport. The careful development of character produced for the English soccer player Paul Gascoigne during BBC and ITV coverage of the 1990 World Cup of soccer, by turns tough and soft, insufferably arrogant and impossibly tender (Hamilton, 1993), suggests that the activity we are witnessing is far more complicated than any account of a TV sport beholden to masculine hegemony or capitalist rationality will allow. For when English soccer commentator Jimmy Hill observes "[t]hat is the danger with the developing countries, that they can't defend their own goal area against high crosses," or his colleague John Helm describes a shot of a T-shirt covered with the autographs of the Cameroon team with the breathtaking "well, they can all sign their names" (quoted in Tudor, 1992, pp. 400–01), we are not so much in the domain of Eurocentric domination as the space of thought disorder, recognized and mocked as such by many in the audience.

As production costs have traditionally been low, television and sport are "naturals" together, but with the move towards imported drama and tabloid programming, the price paid for major sporting events looks more prohibitive (Korporaal, 1995). For example, in 1994 a minute of TV sport cost on average US $7,000 in Germany, up from $1,800 just five years earlier. Free-to-air TV coverage of sport is down in many parts of Europe because of financial pressures (Sportel, 1994, p. 16). At the same time, those codes that are selected to represent the (male) nation continue to be popular with both audiences and TV executives. Clearly, the new international division of cultural labor, combined with media globalization, means that sports and athletes are now moving around the world both in person and as signs in ways that open up issues of race, gender, and nation in the interests of capitalist expansion, but in centralized ways that will transform local TV. Arrangements such as The Olympics Programs are essentially huge multi-national sponsorship infrastructures that coordinate services to corporations, negotiate media coverage, and license intellectual property rights across the globe (Jarvie & Maguire, 1994, pp. 230–63; Rowe et al., 1994; Nafziger, 1992, p. 502). The case-study below will examine an instance where some of these pressures have produced conflicts which highlight the fissured nature of both nation and sport.

SOCCER AND THE MEDIA IN AUSTRALIA: A CASE-STUDY

The case-study of soccer was selected because it combines our themes of masculinity, the state, media and celebrations of nationalism inside a sport that is the most truly international team activity. Soccer styles itself as "the world game" and is probably watched and played by more people than any other sport, yet it occupies a highly variable position in the structure of culture of different nations. In Australia, for example, soccer's status is problematic, as there are three other principal codes of men's football – rugby league, rugby union, and Australian rules. Very clear social divisions inform this split. Soccer, league, and rules are played professionally and semi-professionally as well as in their recreational modes. All strive to have viable national competitions and all experience divisions between the six States and two Territories of Australia's federal structure. Up to the 1990s, when it became officially semi- and then fully professional, rugby union was an amateur code. It continues to be dominated by private school boys and graduates living in New South Wales and Queensland. Rugby league is based in Roman Catholic and government schools and working-class and rural areas of New South Wales and Queensland. Australian rules is a cross-class indigenous code, strongest in Western Australia, Tasmania, South Australia, Victoria, and the Northern Territory. Soccer is played all over the country, but is very much the province of ethnically-differentiated clubs. Unlike league and union in particular, its organizational strength lies outside the Anglo-Celtic population, with clubs frequently known by titles of Macedonian, Serbian, Greek, Croatian or Italian origin.

Despite the incantation that more people, particularly young people, play soccer than any other footballing sport in Australia, the code has not achieved the pre-eminence as a spectatorial carrier of the health of the nation that it signifies in Europe and Latin America. Internal to the soccer world, debates proceed *ad nauseam* between polarities stressing, respectively, the need to maintain an existing base in ethnic identity, and the desirability of integration with the mainstream norms of sporting businesses. Soccer has a marked status as the only popular sport in Australia known by its association with a diffuse set of migrant cultures. The game is somehow transgressive because of this marking and because it stands in for a material human presence differentiated from the Anglo-Celt that problematizes the power of a transplanted English language as an expression and constitution of unity. The fragility of any concept of a unitary national cultural subject is nowhere clearer than in such fractures. It is insufficient to be numerically powerful as a participant sport in order to qualify as properly local. Rather, a structure of feeling must be invented that interpellates the game within the mythic universal Australian subject (and vice versa), so that it can be deployed as an agent of sport and nation-building. This task can only be achieved through a symbolic cleansing of the sport's self-misrecognition as a legitimate memory of or commitment to countries and cultures that are positioned as Other. The awkward invocation of the soma associated with the nation (for instance, "the body politic" or "the health of the nation") produces, as Jean Laponce (1984, pp. 977–78, 988) notes in his study of ethnically marked soccer in Canada, an enduring tendency to homologize, integrate, and confuse the body and cosmology. Deploying bodily images can conjure up questions of the internal articulation between "organs" and the dominance of some parts over others, now translated into the relationship between sectional interests, social institutions and the "life" of the nation.

Such anthropomorphism links the status of a sporting code such as soccer with a maturational ethos akin to the discursive conventions of nations and their architecture and management. Nationhood or personhood are most usefully conceived, outside romantic rhetoric, as a question of administration – the regularized policing of discursive and material norms of unity. The Australian National Soccer League's requirement to expunge all traces of origin from club names by removing references to Macedonia, Croatia, Greece, and so on sits oddly as a cultural nationalist imperative alongside the NSL's acceptance of sponsorship that saw it renamed the "Coca-Cola National Soccer League" and, later, the Ericsson-sponsored A-league. Presumably, American or Swedish internationalism is seen neither as ethnic nor as un-Australian by the game's national administrators. Yet, when Coca-Cola dropped its sponsorship of the League and adopted the national team instead, this move was seen by Anglo-Celtic commentators as an appropriate response to a wrongheaded form of public sphere:

> the national league represents a different type of democracy. It is the demo-cratic right of groups, not individuals. It represents the preservation, not the liquidation, of old enmities. It transports those deadly boundaries into this country.
>
> (Wells, 1994a, p. 70)

Such pronouncements rehearse debates over the merits and demerits of ethnically organized and identified clubs, which activists within the sport in search of increased media coverage, especially television, see as related to a "lack of professionalism and ability to address the Australian way of life." Paradoxically, soccer clubs that display principally neighborhood-based forms of affiliation associated with Australia's particular history of multiculturalism are faced with a strong newsprint critique for failing to be "local" enough. *The Australian Soccer Weekly* sums up the problem in condemning "nationalistic clubs" and demanding that "Nationalism must go" (Santina, 1988, p.17; Gilmour, 1988, p. 3). This is a nationalism not of Australia nor of the imaginary integrated local subject, but of the ethnic origin of club officials, players, and supporters, which is seen to signify a fractured subjec-tivity. The "soccer citizen" in Australia is split, divided both in terms of sporting affiliation and of the ideal, assimilated migrant subject. When the Croatian foot-ball team visited Australia in 1992, thousands of expatriates demonstrated during the tour about the war in Bosnia-Hercegovina. In the eyes of many journalists, this made the Australian national men's team (the Socceroos) "pawns in a situation which should not have been tolerated" (Gatt, 1992, p. 22). This puzzlement at "not letting go" is replicated elsewhere, for example in the similar accusations of insuf-ficient integration made by British Tory politicians (such as Norman Tebbit) during the early 1990s over support from Asian migrants for visiting cricket teams. Tests of political loyalty are founded, then, on cultural (in this case sporting) chauvinism (Maguire, 1993, p. 298–99). Nationality has become a problem here, not a teleo-logical solution to the issue of local and global disorder (Jalai & Lipset, 1992/3), and sport is inescapably bound to it.

In 1988, the Australian Bicentennial Gold Cup of Soccer competition was staged between Australia, Brazil, Argentina, and Saudi Arabia as a key event in the celebration of two hundred years of white invasion. Australian coach Frank Arok and team captain Charlie Yankos provided metonymic accounts of the rela-tionships pertaining to the sport, the national team, and the public:

> They've got a mission. They have to do something about the sport in this country and they are doing it – Coach, speaking of team.

The Australian people understand what we're doing and they are supporting us and lifting us when we need it – Captain, speaking of public.

(quoted in Hurst, 1988, p. 67)

Small wonder, then, that (Australian-turned-American citizen) Rupert Murdoch's newspaper *The Australian* should headline the defeat of Argentina in the Gold Cup with "Socceroos meet their Gallipoli" (Warren, 1988, p. 11), the intertext being the First World War battle that is popularly credited with the birth of a white male cultural identity for the newly federated nation. By contrast, the notion of the Australian women's soccer team "meeting their Gallipoli" is a spectacular *non sequitur.* Again we see shifts of register that describe a complex connection between elements of the soccer subject and its adjacency to Australia, a restless set of movements grasping at an authentic location from which "Australian soccer" can be made to interpellate a national subject, the white, male citizen, in a sovereign, non-sectarian way. The terpsichories required to unify sports in this way and represent them as national signifiers, however, involve improbable moves that serve to emphasize conflict and difference as much as genuine unity, even within traditional masculinist notions. These cracks in the edifice may lead to a more open, genuinely pluralistic and international model of the sporting citizen, even if the reactionary foundations of sporting nationalism are formidably entrenched.

CONCLUSION

In this chapter we have argued that the sport-nationalism-media troika is no passing fad. Even if we accept (with, for example, Lash & Urry, 1994) that nation states are in decline after only a brief flowering, there is no reason to believe that nationalism as an ideological and cultural force is also on the road to oblivion (Turner, 1994, p. 121). In fact, the reverse is the case – the more that national-political, economic, and military sovereignty is undermined, the greater the need for states to construct a semiotically potent cultural nation. There is surely no cultural force more equal to the task of creating an imaginary national unity than the international sports-media complex. It is for this reason that when the peace-time world is at its most self-consciously global – the periodic media sporting spectacles of the Olympics or the soccer World Cup – nationalist identification is probably at its most intense.

This is not to argue that a seamless national unity endures through sport that always and everywhere effaces internal and highlights external divisions. Instead, as we have argued, because nationalist ideology is deeply contradictory – not least because its inclusivist rhetoric cannot match its exclusivist practice – it is also necessarily unstable, offering also the possibility of generating new alignments and throwing into stark relief older but partially obscured hierarchical structures. The sports media are charged with the daily task of rendering nations to themselves by weighing and classifying citizens and their actions. The task ahead is not to tell the sports media to desist from speaking of the nation – which would be futile – but to encourage the cultural brokers of the sports media to re-cast their regimented images of sporting citizens and represent them in all their chaotic, hybridic diversity.

The Sports Hero Meets Mediated Celebrityhood

Leah R. Vande Berg

Our word "hero" is derived from the Greek word *heroes*, meaning a person distinguished for exceptional courage, fortitude, enterprise, superior qualities or deeds – the "embodiment of composite ideals" (McGinniss, 1990, p. 16). However, the ideals that embody heroism are not consistent. As Drucker and Cathcart (1994) have put it, "all cultures have heroes, but the hero and the heroic vary from culture to culture and from time to time" (pp. 1–2). The purpose of this chapter is to examine the changing nature of heroism as featured in contemporary American sports media. I begin with a brief review of the nature of heroes as cultural phenomena, then focus attention on traditional and postmodern sports heroes in American culture. I conclude by considering issues for the future study of the sports hero in society.

HEROES AS CULTURAL PHENOMENA

In ancient times, the hero, usually a warrior, was a legendary figure who performed brave and noble deeds of great significance, who possessed attributes of great stature such as bravery, strength, and steadfastness, and who was thought to be favored by the gods. According to Curtius (1963), the first printed appearance of the word hero was in Homer's *Iliad*. There, as Arendt (1958) reminds us, hero was a descriptor attached to each free man who had fought in the war and whose deeds could be recounted in a story.

Campbell (1968, p. 30) argues that the hero is an archetype and that heroic narratives have common elements which span time and cultures:

The standard path of the mythological adventure of the hero is a magnification of the formula represented in the rite of passage: separation-initiation-return: which might be named the nuclear unit of the monomyth. A hero ventures forth from the world of common day into a region of supernatural wonder: fabulous forces are there encountered and a decisive victory is won: the hero comes back from this mysterious adventure with the power to bestow boons on his fellow man.

According to Klapp (1962, 1964), heroes and heroic narratives serve a variety of social functions: as role models embodying public values and ideals, as unifying social forces which "transport an audience vicariously out of everyday roles into a new kind of reality that has laws and patterns different from the ordinary social structure" (1964, p. 24), and as compensatory symbols who console people for their "recognized lack of what a hero represents . . . [and] for what people think they ought to be but aren't" (1962, p. 139).

Mediated heroes in contemporary times perform acts of far less significance and possess attributes of far less stature than did mythological heroes of ancient times. Nonetheless, the contemporary hero generally is still understood to be "a human figure . . . who has shown greatness in some achievements" and whose greatness "has stood the test of time" (Boorstin, 1978, p. 49).

The Social and Mediated Construction of Heroes

Without denying that heroes are persons of great deeds, we should recognize also that heroes are constructed in an interactive process. As Fairlie (1978) argues: "We choose the hero [and] he [or she] is fit to be chosen" (pp. 36–37). Similarly, Strate (1994) notes that

> as a general rule, members of a society are separated from their heroes by time, space, and social class and therefore know their heroes only through stories, images, and other forms of information. In this sense, there are no such things as heroes, only communication about heroes. Without communication, there would be no hero.
>
> (p. 16)

Consequently, the term "unsung hero" is an oxymoron.

Orrin Klapp (1956, 1962) identified three social types, or shared role models in American society – heroes, villains, and fools. Based on further analysis, Klapp developed a typology of five types of heroes: winners, splendid performers, independent spirits, heroes of social acceptability, and group servants (1962, pp. 27–28).

While Klapp's focus was on heroes as an abstract social type of role model, other scholars have theorized and explored the creation of such social types. Ong (1981) and Strate (1985, 1994) have argued that the dominant mode of communication of a culture also shapes a culture's concept of the hero and the heroic. For instance, in oral cultures, heroes were known through poems and songs that were often performed in public spaces. As a result of the ephemerality of the spoken word, and the fact that relatively little information can be stored in oral poetry and song, early heroic narratives tended to focus on memorable, larger-than-life deeds of a limited number of individuals. As Ong (1981) explains, oral heroes were "heavy figures":

> When the dominant cultural medium is orality there is an emphasis on the immediate and concrete. The figures around whom knowledge is made to cluster, those about whom stories are told or sung, must be made into conspicuous personages . . . In other words, the figures around whom knowledge is made to cluster must be heroes, culturally "large" or "heavy" figures like Odysseus, or Achilles or Oedipus . . . These figures, moreover, cannot be too numerous or attention will be dissipated and focus blurred. The familiar practice sets in of attributing actions which historically were accomplished by various individuals to a number of major ones . . . Thus the epic hero, from one point of view, appears as an answer to the problem of knowledge storage and communication in oral-aural cultures (where indeed storage and communication are virtually the same thing).
>
> (pp. 204–205)

In this way, oral cultures created economical, memorable narratives about the actions of archetypal heroes in dramatic contests, conflicts, and combat (Strate, 1994).

With the advent of the print medium, however, the nature of heroes changed. The limitations of human memory were overcome with print because information can be stored. Strate (1994) explains that heroes became more individualized and more realistic as a result:

> With the presence of a means to store information outside of collective memory, the heavy figures of myth and legend were no longer necessary, and greater numbers of lighter heroes were made possible. As oral poetry and song were replaced by written history, the hero was brought down to earth, and as more information could be stored about any given individual, heroes became individualized. The heroes of literature cultures are realistic, mortal figures, objects not of worship, but of admiration.
>
> (p. 18)

With the advent of television, the distinction between fact and fiction once again became meaningless. The electronic media have turned heroic acts into what Boorstin (1978) has labeled "human pseudo-events"; they have constructed a proliferation of heroes which, Boorstin and Strate argue, trivializes the notion of the hero and ultimately replaces the hero with the celebrity. According to Boorstin (1978),

> The hero was distinguished by his [sic] achievement; the celebrity by his image or trademark. The hero created himself; the celebrity is created by the media. The hero was a big man; the celebrity is a big name.
>
> (p. 61)

Boorstin argues that individuals who perform legitimately heroic deeds are ultimately transformed into celebrities. As he writes, "inevitably, most of our few remaining heroes hold our attention by being recast in the celebrity mold. We try to become chummy, gossipy, and friendly with our heroes" (p. 74) Similarly, Klapp (1962) notes that heroes – including athletic heroes – have degenerated into mere celebrities in whom surface qualities of attractive physical appearance, physical strength and prowess, and ability to perform and entertain hide the absence of intellectual and moral strength. Barney and Barney (1989) concur, arguing that there are many celebrities – individuals acclaimed for particular performances – but few heroes. They argue that heroes can be recognized not only for long-term, consistently outstanding performance and success in achieving excellence but also for their exceptional morality, social responsibility, and intellectual capabilities.

Joshua Gamson (1992) cautions that the characteristics of contemporary celebrity are not solely the result of mass culture. He argues that contrasting notions of fame existed long before mass-mediated technologies. He points to the contrast between the ancient Roman notion of fame as a celebration of public action "for the good or the ostensible good of the state" and the alternative notion of fame celebrated by the early Christian tradition – a fame "of the spirit," a fame of being rather than action (pp. 16–18). Likewise, Nixon (1984) argues that at some level heroes and celebrities become interchangeable because both types "sell the ideologies of the American Dream and consumption to a broad cross-section" of American society (p. 225)

Invisible Heroes and their Heroic Narratives

Missing from most mainstream discussions of heroes are *female* heroes or heroic narratives featuring women as anything other than victim or trophy. Although in his discussion Browne (1983) notes that female as well as male heroes have appeared in Western mythologies (e.g., the story of Amor and Psyche) and histories (e.g., Boadicea, Joan of Arc, Israeli Queen Esther), he adds that

> Through the centuries men have treated women heroes as invisible. They have kept women stored away, like explosives in a warehouse, priding themselves on the treasures they possess, yet afraid to unleash that power lest it tend to overpower its possessor.
>
> (p. 1)

In short, most books on heroes portray women either as prizes or victims; the hero takes a journey, passes a series of tests /defeats the enemy/saves the woman in distress, and then "marries the daughter, or widow, of his predecessor" (Raglan, 1975). The biased recognition of male heroes and the symbolic annihilation of female heroes typifies most books about heroes (see Campbell, 1968; Klapp, 1962; McGinniss, 1976; Raglan, 1975; Sabatini, 1934; Wecter, 1941), and exceptions, such as Frasier's (1988) *The Warrior Queens*, are still rare.

In his discussions of various types of heroes Klapp (1962) found only "one specifically feminine for every three masculine hero types." And among the contemporary types of female roles ("the faithful, submissive Penelope-mother-sufferer helper" and the "erotic queen") that he discussed were "beauty contest winner, prima donna, glamour girl, best dressed woman, Lady Bountiful, and self-sacrificing nurses" (p. 97).

As Fayer (1994) explains, there are several reasons for the invisibility of female heroes. First, most histories have been written by men, have emphasized the activities of men, and have defined heroes in terms of "male characteristics." A second, but related reason, is that definitions of heroes reflect cultural values. Thus, since women, activities of women, and characteristics of women have not typically been valued or viewed as appropriate public role models, it should not be surprising that female heroes have generally remained largely "invisible" (p. 34).

Lumpkin and Williams (1991) analyzed the covers of *Sports Illustrated* from 1954 to 1989 and found that women were shown on about 6 percent (114) of the 1,835 covers they examined. Moreover, sportswomen of color appeared on only five of the 114 covers, and four of these appearances highlighted Jackie Joyner-Kersee and Florence Griffith-Joyner's world Olympic trials and successes in 1987–1989. Their study indicates the extent to which female sports heroes have remained largely invisible in mainstream sports media. In the next section I examine the most commonly constructed mediated sports hero, the modern male sports hero.

THE MODERN SPORTS HERO

As Harris (1994) notes, "part of the reason for the prominence of spectator sports in many societies – including American society – is that they are cultural performances . . . that provide opportunities for people to engage reflexively with salient societal values and social relationships" (p. ix). Trujillo and Ekdom (1985) for example, have demonstrated how mediated coverage of the American cultural institution of baseball reflects and affirms many American values as well as the apparent tensions between them, including the juxtaposed values of work and play, tradition and change, teamwork and individualism, youth and experience, logic and luck, and the power of winning versus the character-building lessons of losing.

Athletes become heroes, Barney and Barney (1989) argue, because of long-term, consistently outstanding performance as well as their morality, social responsibility, and intellectual capabilities. Loy and Hesketh (1984) concur, asserting that sports heroes are classic agons: individuals who gain honor by publicly displaying their personal prowess, moral character, and social worth in competition evaluated by their peers and the broader society. Smith (1973) explains that modern sports heroes have outstanding physical abilities, sustain excellence year after year, over-come adversities, and display individual flair or charisma. Modern sports heroes, then, are models of athletic competence and of social values who are admired for their outstanding and skillful athletic performance, their courage, expertise, perse-verance, assertiveness, generosity, social ideals, dependability, honesty, and char-acter (see Csikszentmihalyi & Lyons, 1982; Miller Brewing Company, 1983). For example, Harris's (1994) study of hero characterizations by youths in Greensboro,

North Carolina, found that the most valued quality in well-known athletes was personal competence (athletic skills, ability to win, endurance of hardships – e.g., long years of hard practice, the pain and violence of intense competition). Far less important, though still mentioned, was social supportiveness.

As a result of contemporary media, today's heroes inevitably become celebrities as well as heroes, and what the media celebrate is the dominant form of masculinity. Bryson (1987) explains that "sport celebrates the dominant form of masculinity . . . which excludes women from the terrain completely, or effectively minimizes their achievements" (p. 349). Media representations of sports heroes reproduce and instantiate hegemonic masculinity so that, as Messner (1996) explains, in sport "men's power over women becomes naturalized and linked to the social distribution of violence. Sports as a practice suppresses natural (sex) similarities, constructs differences, and then largely through the media weaves a structure of symbol and interpretation around these differences that naturalizes them" (p. 78).

Nolan Ryan: Traditional Hero & Celebrity

Trujillo's (1991) study of baseball pitcher Nolan Ryan demonstrated how media representations of Ryan reinforced hegemonic masculinity by reaffirming the "power" of the male body in narratives describing Ryan's pitching ability, depicting Ryan as a "successful male worker in an industrial capitalist society," portraying Ryan as a family patriarch and as a rural cowboy symbol of the American frontier, and stressing Ryan's physical attractiveness and heterosexuality.

Media coverage of Ryan over his twenty-seven years as a professional athlete demonstrated that he passed the traditional tests of the hero – namely, that he performed great deeds. He was the oldest pitcher to win an All-Star game (1989) and at age 42 he was the oldest of the twenty pitchers ever to get 300 strikeouts. He was the only pitcher to ever throw 5,000 strikeouts and seven no-hitters. When he finally retired at the age of 45 he was the oldest pitcher in baseball (Trujillo & Vande Berg, 1994).

Despite relentless media coverage, however, nothing emerged to challenge Ryan's passage of the second test of traditional heroes – untarnished embodiment of mainstream cultural values. As Klapp (1962) explained, "Heroes state major themes of an ethos, the kinds of things people approve" (pp. 27–28). Throughout Ryan's career reporters focused on his hard-work ethic, his commitment to home and family, his wholesomeness (he drank orange juice not champagne when he broke Sandy Koufax's record for pitching the most no-hit games; his humble lifestyle and respect for tradition was embodied by living in the same small town he grew up in). In fact, according to Dallas Morning *News* columnist Skip Bayless, who developed a reputation for shredding the reputations of revered sports heroes with his investigative inquiries, the only indiscretion about Nolan Ryan he ever discovered was that once Ryan "was accused of scuffing the ball on his change-up in the National League" (Trujillo & Vande Berg, 1994, p. 237). Bayless (1989) told his readers that he dug deeply into Ryan's background, assuming that "no wealthy baseball star can be as humble and clean-living as Ryan's supposed to be" only to discover that Nolan is Nolan – a cowboy rancher who embodied frontier values on and off the mound, a cowboy rancher who really raised cattle on his Texas ranch in the off-season.

Media representations of Ryan also illustrate the inevitable combination of hero and celebrity in contemporary culture. Ryan received much publicity throughout his career and this garnered him many commercial endorsements which used his heroic status as a tool to sell various products. His identity as a commercial spokesperson – for Advil, Bic Shavers, BizMart office supplies, Whataburger, and Wrangler jeans – itself became the focus of front page news stories (see Baldwin, 1990). These ads all functioned to turn this athlete of exceptional perseverance, accomplishment, and longevity into a celebrity. For example, in several ads for Wrangler jeans, Ryan was portrayed on the pitchers mound at Arlington Stadium wearing his baseball uniform and also a cowboy hat, a western style shirt, and Wrangler jeans. The same set of Western images has been used by reporters to characterize Ryan as western hero and by advertisers to cash in on Ryan's identity as both hero and celebrity to sell their products and services. Ryan illustrates that traditional heroes can still be found in contemporary sports, but that today's heroes must also be celebrities. However, Ryan also illustrates that in becoming celebrities, heroes who perform great deeds over time do not necessarily diminish their status as heroes.

Joe Montana: Modern Hero and Icon of Hegemonic Masculinity

A number of sportswriters have argued that Joe Montana is the best quarterback American football has ever seen (Dickey, 1989; Miller, 1991). Montana stepped into the national limelight in 1979 when he led Notre Dame from a 22-point deficit to a Cotton Bowl victory in the last seven minutes of the fourth quarter. From 1979 to 1993 Montana led the San Francisco 49ers to four Super Bowl victories, was named Most Valuable Player in 1982, 1985, 1990, and set numerous NFL records (e.g., all the major career playoff records for most touchdowns, completions, yards).

Muller (1994, 1995) has demonstrated how the media repeatedly stressed Montana's humble origins, his exceptional talent on the field, his ability to overcome adversity (e.g., his 1986 back injury and charges of ageism in 1988), his ability to remain calm and unflappable in high pressure situations, his modesty despite his extraordinary athletic success on the field, his happy family life, and his financial success. *San Francisco Chronicle* sportswriter Lowell Cohn wrote about him, "Montana's gift, aside from his ability to find receivers, is an eerie ability to reduce larger-than-life moments to manageable unglamorous, routine segments. He has made himself like a machine capable of functioning flawlessly despite the pressure" (1990a, p. D1). Another sports journalist noted that "Montana is an ordinary man. He is someone who has been lifted up by some special gift of grace to heights far above those reached by others in his field, but he wears his greatness lightly. And this makes us treasure him all the more" (Kamiya, 1990, p. 21).

Montana, too, illustrates the modern hero's inevitable integration of the heroic and the celebrity. One place this can most clearly be seen is in the ways in which ads for Hanes underwear, athletic shoes, L. A. Gear, and Nuprin pain reliever use Montana to commodify traditional heterosexual masculinity. In many of the Hanes underwear ads Montana is shown driving a rugged 4 x 4 vehicle and playing with blonde-haired blue-eyed children at a beach (the new dad who can play a violent game one day and nurture children the next). In another Hanes ad he is shown sitting on the floor with his crotch at the center of the ad whose caption reads "Nothing else feels so right." As Muller (1994, p. 102) has explained, "commodified in this manner, Montana functions as a hegemonic device which perpetuates a gender hierarchy and valorizes the dominant masculine qualities that Montana the athlete represents" – a strong, rugged, seductively heterosexual yet clean-cut family man. Clearly, the media represented Montana as a "culturally idealized form of masculine character" (Connell, 1987, p. 83). *Sports Illustrated* writer Montville (1990) summarized the characteristics of this hegemonic masculine modern sports hero Joe Montana:

> You look at his life and it has been a series of challenges that he has met and mastered ... The football coach benched him as junior, he came back the same season and was the best. He went to Notre Dame. He was listed seventh on the depth chart, and rose to the top. He was the best. The Pros neglected him, the Niners drafting him in the third round, and he met the challenge again. He was the best. He even had back surgery – the doctors doubted he would play again – he overcame that, too. He is the best.
>
> (p. 105)

Clearly Ryan and Montana are quintessential modern heroes. Only the vaguest rumors of a scuffed ball ever shadowed Ryan's heroism (Trujillo, 1994), and vague rumors about NFL quarterback cocaine use which surfaced days before the 49ers fourth Super Bowl appearance never explicitly mentioned Montana's name (Muller, 1994). In short, nothing marred the mediated portrayal of these paragons of hegemonic masculinity. One reason may be, as Chalip and Chalip (1989) suggest, that "the individual athletes themselves are substantially less important than are the paths to achievement which athletes generically represent" (p. 11/22).

THE HEROIC ANTIHERO

One contrasting persona that has existed side-by-side with the modern sports hero is the sports antihero. While there are many ways to define the antihero, most would fit within Smith's (1973) broad definition of an antihero is someone who "eschews traditional heroic qualities" (Smith, 1973, p. 67). According to Smith, the characteristics of antiheroes are "disillusionment with and alienation or withdrawal from societal problems; opposition to or rebellion against those problems; or mockery and derision of heroes themselves" (Smith, 1994, p. 18).

Reisling (1971) argued that in the 1960s and 1970s, "antiheroes, not heroes, are enjoying a primacy hitherto not according them" (p. 4). Disillusioned with

American society's racism, sexism, and government scandals like the Pentagon Papers and Watergate, social and political antiheroes organized protest marches, took over college campuses, and leaked secret government documents revealing the lies told to and by presidents. In sports, several antiheroes at the 1968 Olympic Games raised clenched fists in support of black Power, and 18-year-old Cassius Marcellus Clay, Jr. won the light heavyweight gold medal in the Rome Olympics for a country which had restaurants that refused him service simply because of the color of his skin.

A few years later, a New York Jets quarterback named Joe Willie Namath wore white spikes and long hair, Billie Jean King beat 55-year-old self-proclaimed male chauvinist pig Bobby Riggs in front of 48 million television spectators, and Muhammed Ali, a recent convert to the religion of Islam, refused induction into the US Army because, as he explained, he had no quarrel with the Viet Cong (Kindred, 1996).

According to Smith (1994), "some antiheroes are rebels with causes, while others are dropouts convinced that society and human relationships are worthless" (p. 18). In some cases, an athlete may be regarded as a hero by some and an antihero by others. This was the case for both Ali and King. Hank Aaron said about Muhammed Ali, "When no other black athletes dared say anything, he said it for us" (Kindred, 1996, p.6).

Some of these antiheroes helped bring about social change because their sports fame gave them a position of leadership from which to express disillusionment with the status quo – in society and in sport. Such, for example, was the case with Muhammed Ali and anti-war protests. Likewise, in 1970 Billie Jean King became the first female professional tennis player to win over $100,000 a year, though Rod Laver, the top male winner in 1970, won three times as much for playing in one-third as many tournaments. Her disillusionment with the inequities of professional sports impelled her to lead a boycott in protest, to launch a separate women's pro tennis circuit sponsored by Virginia Slims, and to organize the Women's Tennis Association to represent women professional players on the tour. As a result of the boycott she led, the USTA was pressured into equalizing the prize money in tournaments like the US Open (Cahn, 1994).

Today the links among sports, sex, and race are still rife with contradictions. While black male athletes are highly visible in many sports, few of them are coaches or managers of professional teams (Sabo & Jansen, 1992). As Messner (1996, p. 71) explains:

> It is now widely accepted in sport sociology that social institutions such as the media, education, the economy, and (a more recent and controversial addition to the list) the black family itself all serve to systematically channel disproportionately large numbers of young black men into football, basketball, boxing, and baseball, where they are subsequently "stacked" into low-prestige and high-risk positions, exploited for their skills, and finally, when their bodies are used up, excreted from organized athletics at a young age with no transferable skills with which to compete in the labor market.
>
> (see Edwards, 1984, Eitzen & Purdy, 1986; Eitzen & Yetman, 1977)

THE POSTMODERN HERO

"Heroism," Drucker & Cathcart (1994) argue, "is not dead, but it has been changed by the pace and form of contemporary media" (p. 10). Indeed, as Smith (1973) noted nearly a quarter of a century ago, "Whether the traditional hero is simply undergoing a metamorphosis, to later emerge in a new and vital role, [or] has reached the end of his usefulness and is doomed to extinction, only the unwinding of the century can reveal" (p. 70).

If the antihero is one metamorphosis the sports hero has taken during the latter part of the twentieth century, another is the postmodern hero. No single definition of postmodern sports heroes (or even postmodernism) exists; however, one starting place is with the extension of definitions of postmodernism generally to sports. Postmodernism can be described as a reaction to modernism which features "a semiotics of excess"; a pastiche style which juxtaposes unlikely combinations; a breakdown of grand narratives; a loss of social consensus about belief in science and progress; a blurring of the real and the simulated; an ethic of conspicuous consumption; a fragmented sensibility in which knowledge is discontinuous and impermanent; and a culture dominated by the pleasure principle, relativism, privatism, and schizophrenia of styles (Real, 1996, pp. 238–239). Best and Kellner (1991) explain that "against modernist values of seriousness, purity, and individuality," postmodernism is characterized by "a new insouciance, a new playfulness, and a new eclecticism" (p. 11). Two features associated with postmodernism are the excessive extension of modernism's

1   adoption of the role of self-exiled hero (see Barthes, 1984) – that is, "willful self-marginalization"; and
2   focus on technique and language as the real content – the end not the means to larger ends (Collins, 1995, pp. 328–329).

Real (1996) uses the modern Olympics as a pre-eminent example of how sport today reflects the postmodern "culture of excess" which "rewards extremes of size, flamboyance, self-promotion, consumption, fame and extravagance" (p. 257). Two individual examples of mediated postmodern sports heroes I look at in the next section are Michael Jordan and Dennis Rodman.

Michael Jordan: Hero as Commodity

Michael Jordan, forward for the Chicago Bulls professional basketball team, has appeared on the cover of *Sports Illustrated* more times than anyone else in the magazine's 42-year history – thirty-four times, thereby adding a new twist to the classic American commercial phrase, "Be like Mike."

According to *USA Today*, "Michael Jordan's bigger than basketball; he's a pop icon" (Snider, 1996, p. 3D). Participants in a 1995 *Newsweek* poll identified Chicago Bulls basketball player Michael Jordan as the person who most represented "American ideals" (see Snider, 1996). So did polls conducted by Sponsorship Research International (*USA Today*, 1995, p. 26) and *Men's Journal Buying Guide*

(*Chicago Tribune*, 1995, November 16). Jordan's agent, David Falk, describes Jordan's image as that of an "All-American . . . Norman Rockwell values, but [with] a contemporary flair" (Castle, 1991, p. 30).

Jordan *is* an international mediated sports icon. A recent international communications study concluded that Jordan was the most recognized American figure on the planet (*Chicago Tribune*, 1995, March 24). Beijing's star basketball player Huang Gang characterized Michael Jordan as "the most popular sportsperson in China" (*Chicago Tribune*, 1995, March 20, sec. 1, p. 1). Sports columnist Bernie Lincicome commented, after seeing a life-sized model of Jordan in a sporting goods store window in Weimar, Germany, "I do not credit Jordan for the fall of communism, but they were wearing Air Jordans on top of the Berlin Wall" (*Chicago Tribune*, 1994, November 1, sec. 1, p. 12).

Clearly, Michael Jordan embodies many of the characteristics of the traditional modern sports hero. His strength, endurance, and athletic prowess place him head and shoulders above all other basketball players in memory. As 68-year-old Chicago Bulls assistant Johnny Bach reminds everyone, "The main thing to remember about Michael is that God only made the one" (McCallum, 1993, p. 20.). Jordan has been the National Basketball Association's leading scorer for seven seasons. He has led the Chicago Bulls to a record fifth NBA championship and the 1992 "Dream Team" to the Olympic Gold Medal. In 1983–84, before Jordan joined the team, the Bulls averaged 6,365 fans a game. They now average 17,273 fans a game and they have sold out over 500 consecutive games at home – since November 1987. *Sports Illustrated's* Rick Telander put it this way: "As any sports fan knows, the Chicago Bulls were born in October 1984, when 21-year-old Michael Jordan got off a plane at O'Hare Airport" (Telander, *SI OnLine*, 1996).

Devotion to family is another characteristic of the traditional American hero Jordan possesses. After his father, James, was murdered in May 1993 while napping along a North Carolina road in his Lexus, Jordan retired from basketball; he decided to try to fulfill a dream his father had had of Jordan playing professional baseball. He joined the Birmingham Barons minor league team, and worked hard all season to achieve a mere .202 batting average. This, however, did not deter Jordan, who said,

> Believe in what you believe in and make an attempt at it; don't give up before you even try. If you don't succeed, then at least you know by giving it an opportunity. For all the criticism I've received for doing what I'm doing, it's only an opportunity that I've taken advantage of. If you're given an opportunity to take advantage of something you truly love and dream about, do it.
>
> (Hersch, 1996, *SI OnLine*)

The next season he played for the Scottsdale Scorpions of the Arizona Fall League, hitting a .252, and labeled himself his team's "worst player." Still he stuck with it, working as hard as any of his teammates for his $850 a month plus meal money baseball salary[1] until March 1994, when the White Sox management began to pressure minor league players to play as replacements for the striking major league players. Jordan walked out of spring training, quit baseball, and announced "I'm back." At the end of March, in his second game back in the NBA after 21 months away, Jordan scored a record 55 points against the Knicks at Madison Square Garden. His teammate John Paxson commented, after Game 6 of the 1993 NBA Championship, "Night after night, year after year, he just carries this team. He never avoids it, never shirks it" (McCallum, 1993b, p. 21). And as a result, in 1996, after he and the Chicago Bulls won their fourth NBA Championship on Fathers' Day, a crying Jordan told the world on television that "I won for Daddy" (Araton, 1996, p. B-13).

Michael Jordan also embodies other qualities of traditional sports heroes. He is a ferociously hard-working competitor, but he never forgets that it is a game, not life or death. "I tell my wife that what I do for a living is a game," Jordan says. "I love to compete and it isn't for the money. I like the challenge. I could play you for a dollar. But . . . if I'm going to play then I'm going to win. That's enjoyable to me. That's fun . . . We can play for pride. That's enough. But I am going to beat you" (Vancil, 1995, pp. 49, 76). However, Jordan is quick to smile and add, "My mother would say, 'I think you should get more money, son. I think you should hold out and get what you're worth.' That's the business side of my mother. And I have some of that, too" (p. 85).

He certainly does. In 1995 Jordan's yearly salary was $3.9 million, but his endorsements earned him over $40 million that year (*USA Today*, 1995, December 4). In 1996, Jordan signed a 1-year deal to play another season for the Bulls for an NBA record $30 million (Urschel & Hiestand, 1996). Three recent separate polls found that MJ is the most popular marketing commodity in the world; he is the sports figure most able to persuade consumers to buy products (Armstrong, 1996). One day after Jordan started for the Chicago Bulls wearing a new number (UN 45) on his Jersey, the company licensed to sell NBA uniforms to the public reported receiving orders for 180,000 Bulls UN 45 jerseys (*New York Times*, 1995, March 21, p. B14).

Jordan, however, is far from perfect. Unlike traditional sports heroes Nolan Ryan and Joe Montana, Jordan has been dogged by rumors and questions about his character. For example, before Game 2 of the 1993 Eastern NBA final against the New York Knicks, news media reported on his late-night activities in an Atlantic City casino. Rumors about Jordan's six-figure gambling debts escalated before Game 6 when his golfing partner Richard Esquinas's book, *Michael & Me: Our Gambling Addiction . . . My Cry for Help!* was published and Esquinas alleged that Jordan had run up seven-figure gambling debts with him. NBA commissioner David Stern investigated and concluded that while Jordan had gambled, he was not a compulsive gambler (McCallum, 1993a, p. 24). Ever the consummate professional, Jordan did not let the rumors prevent him from averaging 41 points, 8.5 rebounds, and 6.3 assists a game during the finals.

Michael Jordan's sporting ethos and his accomplishments place him in a sports hero category by himself. However, so have his mediated depictions. "Postmodern society transforms everything into saleable commodities" (Armstrong, 1996, p. 340). Media depictions of Jordan's athletic talent and happy family life, as well as Jordan's successful marketing campaigns for Nike, the NBA, Wheaties, Hanes underwear, Coca-Cola, Gatorade, Chevrolet and McDonald's have framed Jordan's incredible physicality as a non-threatening, black masculinity. McDonald (1996) has observed,

Michael Jordan as a spectacular athlete and willing corporate apologist stands in stark contrast to another powerful vision of yesteryear: that of African American athletes as political activists and outspoken critics of the establishment ... Michael Jordan is popular precisely because his commodified persona negotiates historically specific and complex gendered, racialized and sexualized meanings in ways that are socially accepted and culturally envied by mainstream audiences"

(pp. 347–348, 361).

Through media discourses like the 1985 Nike ad that displayed Michael Jordan leaping through the air, wearing Nike athletic shoes, as the voice-over asked "Who said man was not meant to fly" (Murphy, 1985, p. 34), he has added "a distinctive style, an elan that only a few players in NBA history could have matched" (McCallum, 1993b, p.21). "Michael the Marketed" has arguably become a postmodern sports commodity of truly heroic proportions.

Dennis Rodman: Postmodern Pastiche of Excess

Dennis Rodman is a postmodern sports hero commodity of a different sort. Currently Jordan's teammate, this 6' 8" member of the Chicago Bulls basketball team who specializes in rebounding, is "a postmodern pastiche of disparate styles." Rodman is insouciantly playful and excessively flamboyant. He also, by his own admission, is consumed by self-doubt (Rodman, 1996). Rodman's self-promoting, arrogant, emotional, cross-dressing panache offers a sharp contrast to Jordan's calm, conservative, family persona. However, for both of these postmodern sports heroes, image – as André Agassi says – is everything. *Sports Illustrated* described Rodman as

> A guy who flouts more convention in a day than [mystical new-age Bulls coach Phil] Jackson has subverted in a lifetime: Airing his dogs in a playoff game? Head-butting a referee? Appearing in drag at his booksigning session? Rodman, the human pincushion, takes the potential for disaster wherever he goes. His entertainment value is high, but not too many coaches got into this game to be ringmasters.
>
> (Hoffer, 27 May 1996, p. 81)

Flamboyance is one common postmodern characteristic regularly used by the sports and news media to describe Rodman. According to *SI* writer Phil Taylor (1996, June 17): "Some athletes put on their game faces; Rodman does his game hair. The new 'do' he unveiled before Game 1 [of the 1995–96 season] was a multicolored jumble of symbols and designs that made him look as though graffiti artists had mistaken his head for an abandoned building" (p. 46).

While the "clean-cut, all-American" public look and persona may have retired with such traditional sports heroes as Nolan Ryan and Joe Montana, few athletes – male or female – have flaunted their sexuality as outrageously or as ambiguously as Dennis Rodman. As Rodman himself explains:

I've learned something through all the years of diving for loose balls and coming down with the flamboyant rebound: People want excitement, enjoyment, and a winning team. They also want something different. I walked out onto the court in San Antonio with bleach-blond hair, and right away I saw how much those people loved what Dennis Rodman was giving them. The excitement was right there, right now.

(1996, p. 59)

Apparently, the Carl's Jr. fast-food restaurant chain agreed, for during 1994–95 they aired a commercial featuring Dennis Rodman, replete with a Carl's Jr. "Happy Star" dyed into his hair, as a spokesperson for this national family fast-food franchise.[2] Furthermore, according to Rodman, the May 1995 "female" flesh-laden *Sports Illustrated* issue whose cover story featured Rodman wearing leather and an exotic bird on his shoulder was the second best-selling issue of the year – the first was the swimsuit issue (Rodman, 1996, p. 94).

Another indication of Rodman's status as postmodern sports hero was John Edgar Wideman's *New Yorker* article devoted soley to Dennis Rodman. Wideman's essay began with a quote from postmodern theorist Baudrillard: "An attraction that has all the characteristics of breaking and entering and of the violation of a sanctuary" (1996, p. 94).

According to former Detroit Pistons coach Chuck Daley, Rodman is "'the most unique player in the history of the N.B.A.'" (Wideman, 1996, p. 94). Rodman subverts traditional basketball:

Not exactly a forward, guard, or center, Rodman invented a role for himself which subverts the logic of traditional positions. His helter-skelter, full-court, full-time intensity blurs the line between defense and offense. He "scores" without scoring, keeping the ball in play until one of his teammates drops it through the hoop . . . On the playgrounds of Pittsburgh, where I learned the game . . . the best we could say about a guy like that was "cockstrong": "the brother's cockstrong."

(Wideman, 1996, p. 94)

Wideman uses the phrase to characterize the unique urban street-version of black male sexuality Rodman has brought to professional sports. In contrast to Jordan's non-threatening black sexuality, Rodman explicitly sets out to commodify uncontrollable sexuality. He wears pink feather boas to his book signings and a sequined women's halter top to the MTV Music awards. He poses nude on his Harley for his book's cover, has his nails painted once a week, wears earrings and nose rings, and promises to play a basketball game in the nude before he retires (Rodman, 1996, p. 176). This "cockstrong" athlete has not behaved like a traditional sports hero – or even a traditional celebrity or rebel. He has broken many of basketball's on-court rules: going AWOL from his team, head-butting referees and other players, challenging NBA commissioner David Stern to suspend him, and most recently, deliberately kicking a photographer in the groin. For the latter, Rodman was suspended for eleven games (which cost him roughly $1 million in salary) and fined $25,000 (Armour, 1997, pp. F-1, F-4).

Equally important, he has broken many off-court cultural rules and challenged hegemonic masculinity, the patriarchal sports order, and the neo-colonialist society in which he lives and works. As Rodman explains,

> I paint my fingernails. I color my hair. I sometimes wear women's clothes. I want to challenge people's image of what an athlete is supposed to be like ... I'm always looking for new ways to test myself, whether it's on the court or off. There are no rules, no boundaries ... Nobody's going to tell me it's not manly to drive a pink truck or wear pink nails. I'll be the judge of my own manliness ... People are threatened by me. Rich whites, rich blacks, it doesn't matter. Both sides are going to think I'm a threat because of the way I look. If I wasn't who I am, I wouldn't be allowed into nice restaurants – or even movie theatres – because they would automatically think I was a gang-banger. One look at me with my tattoos, my hair and my jewelry, and that's all they would consider. People accept me now only because I have money and some fame.
>
> (Rodman, 1996, pp. 166, 168, 141)

Wideman (1996) argues that Rodman's cross-dressing and cross-naming (he sometimes calls himself Denise), his hair painting, and his frequenting of gay night clubs may have played as much or more of a role in his failure to be voted onto the 1996 All-Star team as his on-court peccadilloes. Rodman, however, doesn't seem to mind. He revels in challenging the images of the traditional, heterosexual sports hero, and "in an age of hype, a world where simulation and appearance count as much as substance and authenticity, where appropriation and replication are viable substitutes for creativity, where show biz is the only business, the storm of publicity Rodman's bad-boy act generates is worth a fortune" (Wideman, 1996, p. 95).

When the NBA handed out its harshest punishment in 20 years to Rodman on January 17, 1997, Dennis's agent, Dwight Manley, acknowledged that Rodman agreed that his actions warranted some kind of punishment. However, Manley argued that the punishment was harsher simply because Dennis Rodman and not someone else was the perpetrator – "Dennis is willing to accept the punishment, but it seems the punishment is also for past occurrences. To punish him ... for just being Dennis is not right" (Armour, 1997, p. F-4).

Unlike traditional sports heroes, Dennis Rodman doesn't provide sports fans with a "nourishing set of rituals" (Oriard, 1992, p. 64). Instead, like other postmodern celebrities, and like rebel-with-a-cause sports antiheroes and scholars, he constantly interrogates social conventions, dominant gender attitudes, the importance of sport, and the notion of heroism itself. The fact that "Dennis Rodman is the guy laughing at the NBA ... He laughs at his teammates. He laughs at the referees," as Seattle Supersonic's coach, George Karl, explained during the 1996 NBA playoffs, makes many people very uncomfortable (Taylor, 17 June 1996, p.46).

According to Wideman (1996, p. 95), this is because Rodman refuses to act like a traditional, heterosexual male sports hero:

> Why does Rodman's refusal to allow his identity to be totally subsumed by a game offend people? Is our sense of who we are so fragile, our defense

against chaos so easily breached, that we can't bear to look when a sports celebrity reminds us that the games we play and worship are only games?

I would argue that the answer is yes; Rodman's challenge to American culture's hegemonic masculine notions of sport, power, and patriarchy is deeply threatening to the predominantly male media/sport establishment. Interestingly, some evidence suggests that Rodman makes adults (and especially adult male sports journalists) far more uncomfortable than he does children. Take, for example, the 1996 Bulls' charity "FestaBulls" extravaganza where fans mingled with players. When this event occurred in 1996, Rodman was just coming off of his fourth day of a six-game suspension for head-butting a referee. Despite this, and his recent appearances at a book signing in a dress and that infamous pink boa, there were just as many people crowding around Dennis Rodman as there were around Michael Jordan – and many of them were kids with green and orange hair, earrings, and fake tattoos all over their bodies (Armour, 1996, p. 4). Their behavior confirms Harris's (1994) findings that children and adolescents think of athletic heroes as neither totally vacuous and shallow nor as totally pure, brave, clean, thrifty, and reverent.

Rodman is a pastiche, and pastiche is "THE style of postmodernism" (Real, 1996, p. 239). Like such other postmodern mediated sports heroes as André Agassi ("Image is Everything"), "Sir Charles" Barkley ("I am NOT a hero"), and Michael Jordan, Rodman combines aspects of the celebrity, the commodity, and the sports hero. The characteristics Real (1996) argues typify postmodern media culture also typify Rodman: "a sense of irony, bald commercialism, a playful ambiguity, nostalgic blend of past and present, disparate art styles, a lack of absolutes, and more" (p. 238). Rodman, Jordan, Agassi, Barkley, and other postmodern sports heroes, "convey a liberal spirit of great freedom at the same time as they serve the conservative economic needs" (p. 241) of sports and media organizations; they have created and are constantly recreating their identities.

"Postmodern culture" Real notes, "is marked by a depthlessness in which appearance is all." In it "the individual too becomes a postmodern pastiche of disparate styles . . . [and] depthlessness and fragmentation are not failings but goals, to create a different order of meaning and purpose" (p. 254). Far more than such postmodern models of commodified sports herodom as Jordan or Agassi, Dennis Rodman has interrogated traditional notions of sports heroes. He has done so by combining extraordinary success on the sports playing floor with extraordinarily public challenges to hegemonic masculinity. Arguably, however, in doing so he has simply further marginalized the black athlete from mainstream culture – African-American as well as EuroAmerican, AsianAmerican, HispanicAmerican.

Until Tiger Woods.

THE NEXT GENERATION: TIGER WOODS, NOSTALGIA, AND THE NEW AGE SPORTS HERO

In December 1996, 21-year-old golfing phenomenon Tiger Woods was chosen 1996 "Sportsman of the Year" by *Sports Illustrated*. *SI* columnist Gary Smith's cover article on Woods begins by explaining that "Tiger Woods was raised to believe that

his destiny is not only to be the greatest golfer ever but also to change the world."
Smith argues that Tiger Woods may indeed signal the next generation of "real
heroes." *Sports Illustrated*'s Rick Reilly agrees. He notes that "Golf used to be four
white guys sitting around a pinochle table talking about their shaft flexes and
deciding whether to have the lettuce soup." To understand what golf is now, he
explains, you have to look at who is out on the golf courses watching Tiger Woods:

> Young black women in tight jeans and heels. Tour caddies, back out on the
> course after hauling a bag 18 holes. White arbitrageurs with cell phones, giant
> groups of fourth-graders, mimicking their first golf swings. Pasty golf writers
> who haven't left the press tent since the days of Fat Jack. Hispanic teens in
> Dallas Cowboys jerseys trying to find their way around a golf course for the
> first time in their lives. Bus drivers and CEOs and mothers with strollers
> catching the wheels in the bunkers as they go.
>
> (Reilly, 1996, p. 47).

Woods, America's outstanding college golfer of 1996, turned pro in 1996 after
winning a third straight US Amateur Tournament. He went on to win two PGA
tour events. As a result this young man become not only a celebrity, not only
Michael Jordan's hero, but the hero of millions of Americans:

> Letterman and Leno want him as a guest, *GQ* calls about a cover; Cosby,
> along with almost every other sitcom you can think of, offers to write an
> episode revolving around Tiger, if only he'll appear. Kids dress up as
> Tiger for Halloween – did anyone ever dress up as Arnie [Palmer] or Jack
> [Nicholas]? – and Michael Jordan declares that his only hero on earth is Tiger
> Woods. Pepsi is dying to have him cut a commercial for one of its soft drinks
> aimed at Generation Xers; Nike and Titelist call in chits for the $40 million
> and $20 million dollar contracts he signed . . . women walk onto the course
> during a practice round and ask for his hand in marriage; kids stampede over
> and under ropes and chase him from the 18th hole to the clubhouse.
>
> (Smith, 1996, December 23, p. 38)

"Why do so many people want a piece of me?" Tiger Woods asks. The answer
is that people are starved for real heroes. According to cynical *SI* writer Gary Smith
"It's a communal craving, a public aching for a superstar free of anger and arrogance and obsession with self" (1996, p. 38). Baudrillard (1983) has observed that
"when the real is no longer what it used to be, nostalgia assumes its full meaning"
(p. 12). Thus, one could argue that sports fans celebrate Dennis Rodman as the
deconsecrated hero with a tragic flaw – not unlike Robert Musil's "man without
qualities" – while they celebrate Tiger Woods as the newly resurrected, newly consecrated hero in a restored grand heroic narrative. Tiger Woods provides a "source
of renewal against postmodern negations" (Real, 1996, pp. 259–263), for he literally embodies those truly utopian ideals of multi-culturalism, inner peace, confidence without arrogance. He satisfies the nostalgic turn of the late 1990s: 'Look
at us, the audience, standing in anticipation of something different, something pure'
(Smith, 1996, p. 31).

According to the October 28, 1996, cover of *Sports Illustrated*, "In two months as a pro, he has transformed an entire sport." However, Tiger Woods' father Earl explained at the Fred Haskins Award dinner to honor Tiger Woods as the outstanding college golfer of 1996, that he and Tiger's mother had raised Tiger not only to transform the sport of golf, but to transform the world:

> He will transcend this game ... and bring to the world ... a humanitarianism ... which has never been known before ... I know that I was personally selected by God himself to nurture this young man ... and bring him to the point where he can make his contribution to humanity ... This is my treasure ... Please accept it ... and use it wisely ... Thank you.
>
> (Smith, 1996, p. 31)

Tiger Woods is a quiet young man who was raised in a happy family of three: himself and two still-married parents who love him deeply and supportively in their very diverse ways. His 64-year-old African-American father is a retired Lieutenant Colonel in the army, a former Green Beret, who has taught Tiger self-discipline and perseverance. His 52-year-old Thai mother, Tida, raised Tiger as Buddhist, as she explains, so that he would have inner peace and the best of both worlds, "Tiger has Thai, African, Chinese, American Indian, and European blood," Tida says. "He is the universal child" (Smith, 1996, p. 38). The universal child with a cause and a message.

Tiger Woods is a non-violent, thinking young idealist. He is also a celebrity who uses the commercialized media sports complex as fully as it uses him. Woods' first Nike ad featured images of Tiger over which these words were superimposed: "There are still courses in the United States I am not allowed to play because of the color of my skin. I've heard that I'm not ready for you. Are you ready for me?"

Woods certainly both illustrates the problems and the possibilities of sports. As a 3-year-old child, Tiger's playing privileges were revoked twice at the Navy Golf Course in Cypress, California, at which the only blacks were cooks and servers – despite the fact that the 3-year-old beat the golf pro after spotting him a stroke a hole, playing off the same tees (Smith, 1996). Tiger Woods knows that racism is still alive and well in sports and in American society. As he explains,

> What I realized is that even though I'm mathematically Asian – if anything – if you have one drop of black blood in the United States, you're black. And how important it is for this country to talk about this subject. It's not me to blow my horn, the way I come across in that Nike ad, or to say things quite that way. But I felt it was worth it because the message needed to be said. You can't say something like that in a polite way. Golf has shied away from this for too long. Some clubs have brought in tokens, but nothing has really changed. I hope what I'm doing can change that.
>
> (Smith, 1996, p. 52)

However, Tiger Woods also illustrates the power of sport to continue to eradicate this social evil. The only question is "Will the pressures of celebrity grind him down first?" (Smith, 1996, p. 29).

> Maybe, every now and then, a man gets swallowed by the [celebrity] machine, but the machine is changed more than he is. For when we swallow Tiger Woods, the yellow-black-red-white man, we swallow something much more significant than Jordan or Charles Barkley. We swallow hope in the American experiment, in the pell-mell jumble of genes. We swallow the belief that the face of the future is not necessarily a bitter or bewildered face; that it might even, one day, be something like Tiger Wood's face: handsome and smiling and ready to kick all comers' asses. We see a woman, 50-ish and Caucasian, well-coifed and tailored – the woman we see at every country club – walk up to Tiger Woods before he receives the Haskins Award and say, "When I watch you taking on all those other players, Tiger, I feel like I'm watching my own son" ... and we feel the quivering of the cosmic compass that occurs when human beings look into the eyes of someone of another color and see their own flesh and blood.
>
> (Smith, 1996, p. 52)

For the time being, Tiger Woods is a hero – on the face of it, he has done some real great deeds.

CONCLUSION

In contemporary society, the mass media serve as the primary vehicles through which we learn of the extraordinary accomplishments, courage, and deeds of cultural heroes and the faults and ignominious deeds of villains and fools. There are, as Boorstin and others have noted, few heroes left. The days in which American politics provided profiles in courage seem to have disappeared. Hollywood's celebrities are rarely seen portraying themselves, and few of them embody or seriously interrogate dominant institutions and practices. One of the few places where heroes can still be found is sports.

Sports heroes embody, articulate, and interrogate abstract ideals and cultural values; they highlight social problems, and they proffer hopeful solutions. Mediated heroes, Drucker and Cathcart explain, "speak of who we were, who we are, and who we would be" (1994, p. vii). This essay has provided several mini-case studies supporting Daniel Boorstin's observation that "in the last half century the old heroic human mold has been broken" (1978, p. 48). It has argued, in contradiction to Boorstin's claim that there is a single new mold of heroes – empty celebritydom – that there are now several heroic molds.

Nolan Ryan, Joe Montana, Michael Jordan, Dennis Rodman, and Tiger Woods all illustrate the impossibility of separating the hero from the celebrity, but they also demonstrate that important differences remain among contemporary sports heroes. All five are extremely gifted athletes whose athletic achievements have been transformed into saleable commodities by themselves, the sports organizations for which they work(ed), the professional associations which govern professional sport, and the media. All exemplify the postmodern era's concern with image. They differ, however, in the extent to which they reflect the fragmentation of contemporary life.

Modern and neomodern heroes articulate and enact utopian social values. Postmodern heroes like Rodman, and to a lesser extent Michael Jordan, interrogate those values. However, even postmodern, fragmented celebrity-heroes like Dennis Rodman, are a force for social renewal. Postmodern heroes like Rodman not only accomplish great feats, they also interrogate modernist assumptions about sport, masculinity, and race. For feminist and neocolonialist critics, this is indeed an important function.

On the other hand, neomodernist heroes like Tiger Woods reinvigorate traditional, modernist assumptions and cultural values. In a time when we decry the lack of common social ground and values, when we avoid discussing our social problems with racism and sexism, Tiger Woods illustrates the promise Deleuze and Guattari (1983, 1986, 1987) argue postmodernism provides. From this perspective, Woods constitutes the physical embodiment of utopian ideals of cultural diversity and tolerance, excellence, and humaneness. As Real (1996) explains, "these twin emphases on the body and on utopian values are important because they provide standards of measurement for actions and ideals. If media products serve real needs of the body or inspire true utopian ideals, they have value because of that. The body and utopianism suggest such positive measures within postmodernism, belying the negativism associated with much postmodernism" (p. 263).

Being an icon of postmodernism clearly isn't Tiger Woods' job. "Athletes aren't as gentlemanly as they used to be," Tiger Woods says. "I don't like that change. I like the idea of being a role model. It's an honor." (Smith, 1996, p. 44).

NOTES

1   However, Jordan was also still being paid his $4 million salary from the Bulls as well as earning $31 million in endorsements. The latter explains how he was able to purchase a $337,000 luxury bus with thirty-five reclining seats, six television sets, and a wet bar for the Birmingham Barons 10-hour bus rides to their games (Hersch, 1996, *SI OnLine*).

2   However, Rodman's January 1997 fiasco – kicking a sports photographer in the crotch when he got in Rodman's way under a basket – not only earned Dennis an eleven-game suspension, it also cost him the Carl's Junior commercial endorsement: they have quit running the ad – at least temporarily.

Race and Ethnicity in US Sports Media

Laurel R. Davis & Othello Harris

In his discussion of resistance to the sports establishment by African-American athletes in the 1960s, Edwards (1969) suggested that (white) sports reporters fail to give African-American athletes credit for their accomplishments. Subsequently, other scholars who are concerned about the topic of racial relations and sport have started to study media coverage. In this chapter, we review research on racial/ethnic meaning in sports media texts. We focus mainly on the United States. It is worth noting that most studies focus on African-American male athletes. While there has been some recent attention to media treatment of African-American female athletes, only a few studies examine coverage of Native-American, Latino/a(-American) or Asian(-American) athletes. The extensive media coverage of African-American male athletes and limited coverage of other athletes of color partly explains this research trend. We begin by looking at the extent of coverage and stereotyped treatment of athletes of color in the media. We assess whether racism in the coverage has declined and examine the use of African-American athletes as evidence of the American Dream. We consider the causes and consequences of racially-biased sports coverage, and then conclude with suggestions for scholarship.

EXTENT OF COVERAGE

Magazines

Studies of magazines have compared the amount of coverage received by African-American and European-American athletes. A number examine coverage in *Sports Illustrated* (*SI*), the nation's leading sports magazine. Condor and Anderson (1984) found limited coverage of African-American (male) athletes in *SI* until 1974, when increased coverage began.[1] In examining *SI* stories about men's Division I college basketball between 1954 and 1986, Francis (1990) concluded that coverage of African-Americans sharply increased as the number of African-American basketball players had grown, but that "[i]n proportion to their population and their performances on the court, black basketball athletes received far fewer articles than their contribution to the sport seems to warrant" (p. 60). Similarly, Lumpkin and Williams (1991) concluded that *SI* feature coverage of African-American male athletes was not proportional with their participation in many sports, and that there was an overall lack of coverage of African-American female athletes. *SI* had a thirty year gap between its first and second cover featuring an African-American female; over a 35-year period African-American women appeared on only five of 1,835 covers (Williams, 1994). Davis (1993a) found an absence of people of color in *SI* advertisements until the late 1960s/early 1970s, and treatment since has represented African-American men in a tokenistic manner while rarely including other people of color.

Studies of other magazines reveal similar trends. Corbett (1988) found African-American women athletes underrepresented in 14 different magazines.[2] *Women's Sports and Fitness* magazine features an underrepresentation of African-American women, and coverage actually decreased in the late 1980s (Leath & Lumpkin, 1992; Rintala & Kane, 1991). Perhaps the decrease is due to producers targeting more "desirable" consumers, such as women in the upper-income brackets who are interested in fitness rather than women athletes.

Television

Some scholars have examined coverage of athletes of color on television. In examining NBC's coverage of the 1992 Summer Olympics, Hilliard (1995) found no features on Native-American or Asian-American athletes and only two on Latino-American athletes.[3] He found NBC feature stories about African-American men were shorter than those about European-American men, although feature stories about African-American women were longer than those about European-American women. In a more extensive study of several televised international sports events, Sabo et al. (1996) found that race/ethnicity did not influence the length of stories about athletes. They conclude that the amount of coverage of various racial categories seems fair, and that racial and cultural diversity was emphasized throughout the coverage. In a study of television coverage of African-American athletes competing in the NCAA men's basketball playoff, Wonsek (1992) argues for placing such findings into context:

> although the sporting event itself is dominated by black players, these images are mitigated and undercut by the overwhelming predominance of white images, some of which represent individuals in positions of authority (coaches and sportscasters). Not only does this place the black players in a secondary and entertainment role, but it may also serve to reassure the white majority that its dominance is not really being threatened.
>
> (p. 454)

In examining the advertising environment for the coverage, Wonsek (1992) found African-Americans appeared in only 19 percent of the commercials, were featured in only 9 percent, and did not appear in many types of advertisements (e.g., personal hygiene, home improvement, automobiles). When they do appear, Wonsek suggests that stereotyping may reassure European-American viewers of European-American importance to basketball. In comparing African-American athletes to European-American athletes of equal ability, several scholars link African-Americans' receipt of fewer product endorsements to less frequent appearances in advertising (Corbett, 1988; Corbett & Johnson, 1993; Green, 1993; Hoose, 1989).

Other Points of Comparison

In addition to studying television coverage of athletes of color, the amount of coverage received by predominantly African-American colleges has been examined. Braddock (1978a) found that coverage by the *Washington Post* of a predominantly European-American college, University of Maryland, was characterized by more and longer articles, and more frequent placement on the front page, than coverage of a predominantly African-American college, Howard University. In a similar study, Pearman (1978) found a predominantly European-American college received more coverage, but also that a winning record diminished "black invisibility." In contrast, when Braddock (1978b) compared the professional career statistics of players from predominantly African-American to predominantly European-American colleges he found that the greater coverage of predominantly European-American colleges was not due to superiority of sport performance.

The relationship between type of sport and the amount of coverage by race has been considered. Much coverage of African-American athletes is concentrated in particular sports. Coverage of African-Americans is much more common in boxing, baseball, and football (Condor & Anderson, 1984). Achievements in basketball and track and field receive the heaviest coverage (Condor & Anderson, 1984; Corbett, 1988; Leath & Lumpkin, 1992; Lumpkin & Williams, 1991). In Olympic coverage, Hilliard (1995) found European-American men represented in more sports (eleven) than European-American women (eight), African-American men (four), and African-American women (two). Rintala and Kane (1991) found African-American women featured in *Women's Sports and Fitness* more likely to be team sport athletes, while other women were likely to be individual sport athletes. Concentrating the coverage of African-American athletes in particular sports reflects the bias of media producers, but is also linked to social constraints that limit African-American participation in many sports (Corbett, 1988; Corbett & Johnson, 1993; Lumpkin & Williams, 1991). Stories that address these concerns and other problems facing African-American athletes are rarely seen (Francis, 1990; MacDonald, 1983; Thomas, 1996; Wonsek, 1992).

In short, African-Americans athletes are receiving increased media coverage, although not at levels comparable to their European-American peers. Media coverage of African-American athletes concentrates on a few sports; and predominantly African-American colleges are relatively invisible. Other athletes of color are even more invisible in the sports media.

STEREOTYPING IN COVERAGE

A stereotype is a generalization about a category of people that is negative and/or misleading. Stereotypes are used to predict and explain the behavior of a social category; in doing so they obscure the variability within such categories. For much of the history of the United States, people openly articulated the stereotypes that African descendants are ignorant, lazy, happy-go-lucky, savage and animal-like. However, much of this blatant racial stereotyping has been replaced by stereotyping which is more subtle, elusive and abstract in rhetoric. Many argue that the sport media play a role in disseminating and maintaining racial stereotypes. Most contemporary sports media stereotyping is covert, with media commentary rarely overtly discussing race or ethnicity (Sabo et al., 1996; Wonsek, 1992).

Classic Stereotypes of African-American Athletes

Studies of stereotyping of African-American athletes have focused primarily on male athletes. In a classic study, Rainville and McCormick (1977) found that European-American players received more praise and less criticism than African-American players in NFL commentary:

> In his description of play, the announcer is building a positive reputation for the white player by more frequently praising him during play, more often depicting him as the aggressor and granting him more positive special focus. The announcer is, at the same time, building a negative reputation for the black player by negatively comparing him to other players, making negative references to his past achievements, and depicting him as the recipient of aggression.
>
> (p. 24–25)

Braddock (1978a) found more positive story headlines in coverage of a predominantly European-American college compared to a predominantly African-American college. Furthermore, individual European-American athletes received more favorable treatment. J. F. Harris (1991) found television commentary on African-American women college basketball and volleyball players more negative than for European-American players. Her findings seem to suggest a "conscious attempt to cast white players in a positive light, for even when they made mistakes, a qualifier was attached to the comment" (p. 160).

In a study with a small sample Francis (1990) found feature articles about male African-American college basketball players in *Sports Illustrated* generally positive in tone, although no comparison was made to stories about European-American players.[4] More recently, Sabo et al. (1996) found black athletes less likely than white athletes to receive negative television coverage in international competition. This treatment might be better explained by the nationality, rather than race, of the athletes. If there is a higher percentage of black athletes from the United States, nationalistic bias may lead to positive treatment for a United States audience.

Media coverage implies that there is a relationship between race and ability to control one's own sport performance. Rainville and McCormick (1977) suggest that the NFL announcers they studied believe African-American performances are due to uncontrollable external forces while European-American performances are due to controllable internal forces.[5] In a study of magazine coverage, Murrell and Curtis (1994) found the performances of both African-American and European-American quarterbacks attributed to internal forces. However, the internal force for European-Americans was controllable "hard work" while the internal force for African-Americans was uncontrollable "natural ability."

Media often reinforce the stereotype that African-Americans are "natural athletes." This stereotype poses white athletes as clearly disadvantaged relative to black athletes, who are seen as having superior physiology (e.g., Edwards, 1969; Harris,1993; Staples & Jones, 1985). Many in the media echo commentator Billy Packer's observation, "There just aren't many [whites], to be honest, in terms of pure athletic ability" (Hoose, 1989, p. 15). Most often African-Americans are portrayed as naturally quick and good at jumping (Jackson,1987). This is sometimes "scientized" (Davis, 1990; Mathisen & Mathisen, 1991). Perhaps nowhere was the stereotype of African-Americans as natural athletes more shamefully displayed than in NBC's 1989 program *Black Athletes – Fact and Fiction*. The framing of this program made this stereotype seem legitimate. For example, invalid interpretations were drawn from data, alternative explanations for African-American athletic success were neglected (Mathisen & Mathisen, 1991), and African-Americans were portrayed in a monolithic manner (Davis, 1990). A recent *Sports Illustrated* article about sport in Soweto, South Africa reinforces the stereotype of blacks as natural athletes. The author predicts that with apartheid's demise, Soweto would "become a world giant in sports" because "Soweto's children are so talented and hungry" (Reilly, 1996, p. 125). The author then quotes a white South African who says that he sees "kids dribbling like they were born with a ball in their hands" (Reilly, 1996, p. 128).

Studies have found the "natural athlete" stereotype is common in the media. For example, D. Z. Jackson (1989) found that the performances of African-American players were more often attributed to "brawn," while European-American players received a disproportional percentage of negative comments about their physicality. Another study (Harris, 1991) concludes that ". . . a combination of subtle implications and innuendos . . . suggest that black female athletes rely almost exclusively on their physical capabilities for athletic success" (p. 4). Andrews (1996b) remarks that entire teams, such as Georgetown's men's basketball squad, can be characterized in ways that reflect this stereotype. McDonald (1995) argues that media producers often use media technologies, such as slow-motion, in ways that embellish and reinforce this stereotype. Contrarily, two studies found the sport performance of European-Americans more likely to be associated with physicality than the performance of African-Americans (Rainville & McCormick, 1977; Sabo et al., 1996).

The "natural athletes" stereotype is often supported by media labeling of European-American athletes as more hard working than African-American athletes (e.g., Edwards, 1969; Sabo & Jansen, 1994; Staples & Jones, 1985). Media highlight the efforts of African-American athletes less often than the efforts of

European-American athletes (Cole & Andrews, 1996; Harris, 1991; Hoose, 1989; Jackson, 1987; Murrell & Curtis, 1994; Wonsek, 1992). D. Z. Jackson (1987) comments that, "The automatic effect is the subtle devaluation of the efforts of black players" (p. 4). Teams associated with European-American players, like the Boston Celtics, are sometimes characterized by their hard work (McDonald, 1995). This type of coverage reinforces the stereotype that African-Americans are lazy (Davis, 1990). Several scholars link the popularity of Magic Johnson and Michael Jordan to media coverage of them as hard working, in contrast to the portrayal of the majority of African-American athletes (Cole & Andrews, 1996; Andrews, 1994; 1996b; Cole & Denny, 1994; McDonald, 1995).

Media treatment is more likely to give European-American athletes credit for being mentally astute, whereas African-American athletes are seldom credited for their intellect. For example, D. Z. Jackson (1989) found that comments about European-American male athletes more often focused on their "brains," while African-American athletes were more apt to receive "dunce" comments. The message about African-American women athletes is equally clear: "Blacks run like horses and jump out of the gym, but they rarely think it all through" (Harris, 1991, p. 160). The success of an entire team can be attributed to the intellect of an European-American coach (Andrews, 1996b). Messner, Duncan & Jensen (1993) place even good efforts by the media in context:

> We observed what appeared to be a conscious effort on the part of commen-
> tators to cite both physical ability and intelligence when discussing successful
> Black and White male and female players. However, this often appeared to
> be an afterthought.
>
> (p. 131)

Related to the stereotype about intelligence is the notion that African-Americans do not make good team leaders, coaches or administrators because they lack requisite knowledge possessed by European-Americans. While European-American athletes are sometimes labeled as leaders, African-American athletes are often portrayed as lacking leadership skills (Edwards, 1969; Hoose 1989; Jackson, D.Z. 1987, 1989; Staples & Jones, 1985).

Some have examined whether race influences whether athletes are portrayed as solely athletes or as "whole people" with lives beyond athletics. While some (Francis, 1990; Hilliard, 1995) have found African-American athletes more often treated as solely athletes, J. F. Harris (1991) found African-American female athletes treated in more complete ways than European-American female athletes. The latter finding may be an exception, as African-Americans were more likely to be covered in *Women's Sports and Fitness* magazine because of their competitive attributes while European-Americans were more likely covered for other reasons (Rintala & Kane, 1991).

Another media stereotype paints African-American athletes as self-centered, selfish and arrogant, while depicting European-American athletes as team players. For example, African-American athletes are portrayed as whining about money (Cole & Andrews, 1996) and intent on displaying personal talent at the expense of team performance (Rosenbaum, 1995). *Sports Illustrated's* cover story about

"Petulant Prima Donnas" features whining "petulant" NBA players who are all African-American (Rosenbaum, 1995). Creating mediated images associated with humility and charity can enhance the popularity of some African-American players (Andrews, 1996b; Cady, 1979; McDonald, 1995). Media portrayal of some African-American NBA superstars as unselfish and modest may have helped the NBA to draw European-American fans (Cole & Andrews, 1996; Rowe, 1994).

Stereotyping Male African-American Athletes as Deviant

Worse than media portrayals as selfish and arrogant, African-American athletes, like African-Americans in general, have been stereotyped as deviant and linked to a threatening "urban black masculinity" (Cole & Denny, 1994, p. 129). McDonald (1995) maintains the NBA was able to shed much of its image of "deviant urban blackness" (p. 92) by creating "wholesome" atmospheres in arenas, media person-alities for players, elevating the slam dunk as a signature of the league, and becoming active in anti-drug activism. Much of Michael Jordan's popularity was achieved by contrasting his image to the deviant image of other African-Americans in the media (Andrews, 1994; McDonald, 1995).

The deviant stereotype sees African-American male athletes as uncontrolled, excessive and addictive (Cole & Andrews, 1996; Cole & Denny, 1994; Cole & Orlie, 1995; Lule, 1995; McDonald, 1995; Wonsek, 1992). This stereotype is often linked to drug-addiction, but also connected to an uncontrolled style of play, sexu-ality and gambling. For example, the drug-related death of Len Bias and Michael Jordan's gambling were shown through the lens of this stereotype (Cole & Andrews, 1996; Cole & Denny, 1994). Cole and Andrews (1996) argue that this stereotype was associated with more than the NBA during the 1970s and 1980s:

> according to the racist rhetoric of an increasingly influential American New Right, the NBA was *too drug infested* simply because it was *too black*. The mainstream media used the specter of drug abuse within the league as evidence of the pathological depravity of the African American males who dominated and thus threatened the existence of the NBA and, by extension, the nation as a whole.
>
> (p. 145)

The stereotype of African-American men as oversexed and unable to control their sexual desires influences the media portrayal of African-American male athletes. Magic Johnson's contraction of HIV and Mike Tyson's rape conviction have been depicted using this stereotype (Cole & Andrews, 1996; Cole & Denny, 1994; Lule, 1995). About Tyson, Lule (1995) observes:

> Just two portraits of Tyson emerged. He was either a crude, sex-obsessed violent savage who could barely control his animal instincts or he was a victim of terrible social circumstances, almost saved from the streets by a kindly overseer, but who finally faltered and fell to the connivance of others. Both these portraits demean and debase Tyson, depicting him as a creature

helpless either to basic instincts or the machinations of others. Both portraits depict a man without self control or determination.

(p. 181)

About the Johnson HIV story, Cole and Andrews (1996) argue:

the media's turn to the professional world of sport is steeped in racially-organized fears of black masculinity, sexuality, and miscegenation . . . [M]ale athletes are positioned through racial codes of the street: they are compulsive, reckless, and absent inseminating black males that were repopularized through Reagan's familial politics and the war on drugs.

(p. 162)

Sometimes the media distance particular African-Americans from these stereotypes. Rowe (1994) observes that the media distanced Magic Johnson from this stereotype by blaming the women who were his sexual partners. Michael Jordan has also been protected from association with this media stereotype. In Hanes underwear commercials, Jordan is shown fully clothed, "shy," less interested in sex than his wife, and as a happy [nuclear] family man who talks to his father about responsible sex (McDonald, 1995).

Portraying African-Americans as naturally athletic and oversexed suggests that they are "closer to nature" than European-Americans and thus "animal-like." So, it is not surprising some media treatment of African-American male athletes implies that they resemble animals (Andrews, 1996b; Jackson, D. Z., 1989; Jackson, S. J., 1992; Lule, 1995). J. F. Harris (1991) found that television commentators often compared African-American women athletes to animals, something not done in discussing European-American women athletes.

Male African-American athletes have also been stereotyped in the media as violent. Cole and Andrews (1996) note portrayals of African-American NBA players as criminally violent "thugs." The mediated image of Charles Barkley as aggressive and violent is so well known that Nike can have Barkley jokingly say " 'Pardon me, I'm sorry, excuse me' as opposing players fly by the wayside" (MacDonald, 1995, p. 101). Contrary to this stereotype, Rainville and McCormick (1977) found European-American football players were more likely to be shown as aggressors, while African-American players were often shown as recipients of aggression. The violence stereotype is often related to criminality. D. Z. Jackson (1989) contends that many African-American athletes ". . . leave the game with a verbal resume more worthy of a mugger than a coach" (p. A28). McDonald (1995) suggests that the NBA constructs positive media images of Michael Jordan and others to counter this stereotype.

Depictions of African-American athletes as deviant often imply that African-American culture and communities are to blame, suggesting that this culture is deviant (Cole & Andrews, 1996; Cole & Denny, 1994; Lule, 1995; McDonald, 1995). Media often link the (portrayed) deviance of African-American athletes to stereotypes of dysfunctional single-parent families, welfare dependency (Cole & Andrews, 1996; Cole & Denny, 1994), and drug-infestation associated with African-American communities (Wenner, 1994d). The media can enhance the image of someone like Michael Jordan by showing his life in contrast to the stereotypes of welfare dependency and shattered nuclear families (Andrews, 1994; McDonald, 1995). Others (Cole & Denny, 1994; Rowe, 1994) note that after the announcement of his HIV status, Magic Johnson's tarnished media image was partly redeemed through association with the ideology of nuclear families.

Stereotypes of African-American Athletes that Appeal to Many European-Americans

The media portrayal of African-American athletes depends not only on negative stereotypes, but also on stereotypes that appeal to an European-American audience. Much here relies on stereotypes of African-American athletes as hip and cool. Seiter (1995), who studied commercials that feature children, puts it this way:

> Most commercials which use African-American children today feature a rap theme and/or some reference to sports. The presence of African-American children in a commercial is used to define the product as "cool," modern, up-to-the-minute. They are set up as more lively, more cool, more fashionable, more with-it than whites. Thus, their presence verifies the product's fashionability.
>
> (p. 104)

McDonald (1995) argues that the NBA lauds African-American athletes for their "apparent chic expressiveness and overall hipness" (p. 110). While some European-Americans find such portrayals as attractive, others see them as evidence of a bad attitude and distasteful racial/cultural difference (Cole & Andrews, 1996b; Rosenbaum, 1995; Seiter, 1995). Some have suggested that mediated treatment of African-American athletes allows (some) European-Americans to fulfill voyeuristic desires to look at black bodies (Cole & Denny, 1994; Dyson, 1993; McDonald, 1995; Morse, 1983). Sabo et al. (1996) note that similar voyeuristic desires may influence the coverage of Asian athletes:

> The greater use of slow-motion replay [of Asian athletes] may be a visual extension of the tendencies among commentators to focus on the physical characteristics of Asian Athletes, to exoticize them, or perhaps to prolong or intensify "gazing" on their otherness.
>
> (p. 15)

Media coverage of African-American athletes may also appeal to racist sympathies by featuring accommodating, docile or non-threatening images of African-American athletes. Cole and Andrews (1996), in describing the mediated image of Magic Johnson, put it this way:

> Johnson's black identity drew from racialized narratives that represented African American men as docile, childlike, and unthreatening. Tracing his representational lineage back to Uncle Tom, Amos and Andy, Rochester, and

> Nat King Cole, Magic Johnson was heralded as the latest, and, at the time, the most visible manifestation of the acceptable image of black masculinity.
>
> (p. 149)

Rowe (1994) sees Johnson's media treatment in a similar way, relying on a big smile and "consoling affability" (p. 15). Michael Jordan is portrayed as a congenial "corporate apologist" (McDonald, 1995, p. 6). Such representations allow African-American athletes to become mediated symbols of nationalism (Andrews, 1994; 1996b; Jackson, 1992; 1993; Jackson & Andrews, 1995; McDonald, 1995; Wenner, 1989a).

The "accommodating" stereotype of African-American athletes sometimes relies on constructions of childlike character. This stereotype is reinforced when commentators make more frequent use of the first names of African-American male athletes than they do in describing European-American male athletes. This "infantization" diminishes the adult status of African-American athletes (Duncan, Messner, Williams & Jensen, 1990; Messner, Duncan & Jensen, 1993). However, the relationship between the race of the athlete and the use of first names by commentators may be weakening (Bruce, 1995). Media producers also create immature images of African-American athletes by portraying them as clown-like (Francis, 1990; Rowe, 1994; Wenner, 1994a), mirroring a long history of such imagery of African-Americans.

Representing African-American athletes as "colorless," race-transcendent, "white replica" heroes also makes them less threatening to European-Americans. Again, Michael Jordan's media image provides an example:

> Through the mutually reinforcing narrative strategies employed by Nike, the N.B.A. and a multitude of other corporate interests (e.g., Coca-Cola, McDonalds) Jordan was constructed as a racially neutered (hence non-threatening) black version of a white cultural model . . . Jordan's racially transcendent image was All-American . . . Jordan became a commodity-sign devoid of racial integrity which effectively ensured the subversion of racial Otherness, but which also – because of his media pervasiveness . . . further ensured the celebration of the N.B.A. as a racially acceptable social and cultural space.
>
> (Jackson & Andrews, 1995, p. 4)

Andrews (1996b) argues that such images do not actually transcend race but set these particular athletes apart from other African-Americans. McDonald (1995) contends that such images do not strip away all vestiges of race but reduce race to style.

Despite the accommodating image that the media can construct for some African-American athletes, these athletes can easily lose their "privileged status" as national heroes and be "re-raced" when associated with deviance. For example, the media linked O.J. Simpson to stereotypes of African-American criminality after he was accused of murder (McDonald, 1995). While winning for Canada the media portrayed Ben Johnson as a Canadian hero, then after he was caught using performance-enhancing drugs the media re-labeled Johnson Jamaican (Jackson, 1992; 1993). The media racialized Magic Johnson after he contracted HIV (Cole & Denny,

1994), and Michael Jordan was temporarily racialized when the media publicized several of his "deviant" acts such as gambling and refusing to wear the Reebok symbol at the Olympics (Andrews, 1996b; Cole & Andrews, 1996).

A final way media texts please European-American audiences is by portraying athletics as a multi-cultural world of racial harmony (McDonald, 1995; Rosenbaum, 1995; Sabo et al., 1996; Seiter, 1995; Wenner, 1989b; 1994a). Rosenbaum (1995) suggests that European-American liberals' dream of "colorblind" racial integration has given way to "virtual integration" (p. 104), where European-American media consumers see élite African-American basketball players as "the imaginary black playmates white sports guys poignantly want but rarely actually have" (p. 104). The virtual integration dream is threatened when the sports are seen as the exclusive domain of African-Americans, as was the case with the NBA in the late 1970s and 1980s (Cady, 1979; Cole & Andrews, 1996; McDonald, 1995).

Because European-American athletes are underrepresented and less stylish in some sports, many European-American sports fans search for "white hopes" (Rosenbaum, 1995). The talent and style of Larry Bird and Nolan Ryan revived European-American spectator interest (Cole & Andrews, 1996; Trujillo, 1994). More recently, the predominantly European-American 1995 NCAA women's basketball champion University of Connecticut received much attention in comparison to former championship teams with high percentages of African-American players. We suspect that many European-American basketball fans are attracted to women's basketball because it is seen as less dominated by African-Americans and less deviant than the men's game.

Additional Racial/Ethnic Stereotyping

Research on racial/ethnic stereotyping in the sports media has focused on the portrayal of African-American athletes to the relative exclusion of other racial/ethnic categories. Still, there is a small amount of research on coverage of athletes from other racial/ethnic categories. For example, Sabo et al. (1996) found that while television commentators avoided making negative comments about Latino/a athletes in international events, they were more likely to focus on the physical characteristics of these athletes. Hoose (1989) observed that media often portray Latino-American athletes as hot tempered. Rintala and Kane (1991) found Latina-Americans more likely to be shown as athletically skilled and covered because of their competitive success than European-American women athletes.

Coverage of Asian-American women athletes also seems more likely to highlight competitive success (Rintala & Kane, 1991). Sabo et al. (1996) found that Asian athletes are stereotyped as obsessive conformers, rigorously self-disciplined and "excessively hard workers" (p. 13), feeding into a larger stereotype of Asians. Asian athletes were also portrayed as unemotional and machine-like, which dehumanized them and "diminished their achievements" (p. 15). Much in this portrayal suggests that Asian athletes are being typed as "exotic" foreign enemies, replacing the Soviets of the Cold War period (Sabo et al., 1996).

Media coverage of Native-American women athletes also seems more likely to accentuate their competitive success (Rintala & Kane, 1991). Native-American sport mascots (Banks, 1993; Davis, 1993a; 1993b; Hribar, 1992) have been the subject of more research than media treatment of Native-American athletes. Stereotypes of Native-Americans are reinforced by media coverage of teams that have Native-American mascots (Banks, 1993; Davis, 1993a; 1993b).

Finally, foreign athletes are often subject to ethnocentric stereotyping (Kinkema & Harris, 1992; McGuire & Wozniak, 1987; Sabo et al., 1996). United States television coverage of international events devotes much more attention to athletes from the United States, and portrays them more positively and less stereotypically than foreign competitors. Foreign athletes, especially those from communist or post-communist countries, are often cast as dishonest, unfeeling or robotic (Sabo et al., 1996). Professional wrestling and its coverage characterize foreigners as threats to United States' citizens and their way of life. For example, when Sergeant Slaughter (a former US Marine drill sergeant) and his troops met the Iron Sheik and Nikolai Volkoff (allegedly Iranian and Russian fighters), Slaughter and his crew were draped in patriotism (they entered the ring waving the United States flag and kissing babies), while the Sheik and Volkoff were described as dirty (illegal) fighters who harbor anti-United States sentiments (McGuire & Wozniak, 1987).

REDUCTION OF RACISM IN MEDIA COVERAGE?

Some see a reduction of racism in the coverage of African-American athletes (Condor & Anderson, 1984; Francis, 1990; Messner & Sabo, 1994; Sabo & Jansen, 1994; Sabo et al., 1996). Sabo et al. (1996) find that

> the disparity between our findings and those of previous researchers suggests that media professionals have responded to past criticisms of prejudicial treatment of Blacks in sport media . . . The lower use of physical descriptors and negative evaluations with reference to Black athletes suggests a heightened sensitivity, maybe even a guardedness among commentators, concerning negative representations of Black athletes.
>
> (p. 13)

Responding to pressure groups, some media producers initiated "sensitivity training" for their sport commentators (Sabo et al., 1996; Sabo & Jansen, 1994; Thomas, 1996). According to Messner and Sabo (1994), Arthur Ashe

> said "word came down from the top" – from executives at the TV network for which he was doing sports commentary – that "we should stop attributing black athletes' successes to 'brawn' and white athletes' successes to 'brains and hard work'".
>
> (p. 128)

While these recent changes offer some hope, the bulk of research findings show evidence of racism in sports coverage. Although overt racism has largely disappeared, covert racism, while perhaps less malignant than in earlier periods, can still be seen. New forms of racism may be evolving with the times.

The "accommodating" stereotype of some African-American athletes and using their success as evidence of the American Dream is problematic. Portrayal of this accommodation and success appear just as the vast majority of African-Americans are sinking even deeper into economic quicksand.

AFRICAN-AMERICAN ATHLETES AS EVIDENCE OF THE AMERICAN DREAM

The American Dream posits that if individuals just work hard enough they can achieve financial and other successes. For the American Dream myth to persist, it needs success stories. Here, the current media treatment of African-American sports stars helps. Media portrayals of Michael Jordan's determinism symbolize "the continued efficacy of the rags-to-riches parable of the American dream ..." (Andrews, 1994, p. 20). Images of African-American success in athletics provide powerful evidence of the American Dream, because those who challenge its validity often point to the experiences of African-Americans as evidence that the Dream is myth. Media show African-American sports stars overcoming formidable barriers, and sport is portrayed as the ideal avenue for African-American upward mobility (Andrews, 1996b; Bierman, 1990; Dyson, 1993; McDonald, 1995; Sabo & Jansen, 1994; Wenner, 1994d; Wonsek, 1992). The association between athletics and African-American success is not surprising, given that sports is just about the only type of mainstream, (non-fictional) media coverage where one can see images of many successful African-Americans (e.g., Bierman, 1990; Jackson, 1987; Seiter, 1995; Wonsek, 1992). If African-American athletes are increasingly being portrayed as evidence of the American Dream, then it is logical that sports coverage would highlight the hard work that has led to success and downplay the "natural athlete" stereotype. Perhaps this is why some scholars detect a reduction of classic stereotyping in the coverage of African-American athletes. Such "improvement" is most likely to appear in international coverage where African-American athletes can be used as nationalistic symbols of the American Dream.

Two major problems arise from using African-American athletes as symbols of the American Dream. First, these images may foster the belief that African-Americans regularly make it in the economy (McDonald, 1995; Sabo & Jansen, 1994). Second, undue focus on African-American athletes who "make it" can foster the belief that African-Americans who do not make it are simply morally inferior (e.g., are lazy) (Andrews, 1994; 1996b; Hilliard, 1995; McDonald, 1995). This view reinforces the notion that sport is the ideal way to "save" African-Americans from their natural/cultural immorality (Andrews, 1996b; Cole & Hribar, 1995; McDonald, 1995; Wenner, 1994d). Wenner (1994d) argues that Nike advertisements where Michael Jordan and Jackie Joyner Kersee ask "Who would I be without sports?" suggest that sport saves African-Americans from drug use. Others contend that media show sports participation, with the guidance of European-American coaches, as helping African-American athletes to find salvation from themselves and thus from (their tendency toward) deviance (Andrews, 1996b; McDonald, 1995). Such themes are easily exported; a recent story implies that white led sport helps to save poor black residents of Soweto, South Africa (Reilly, 1996).

The reinforcement of the American Dream in sports coverage of African-American athletes contributes to contemporary problems. It helps to mask racism, conceal structural economic problems and oppressive political policies, and fuel beliefs that most African-Americans have made it in the economy and that those who have not are morally inferior.

DISCUSSION

Reasons for the Biased Coverage

The main reason most scholars offer for the racial bias in sports coverage is the prejudice of European-America. As there are few people of color who make decisions about mediated sport, covert prejudice can too often slip into sports coverage without repercussions. Rainville, Roberts and Sweet (1978) have suggested that the "practice of assigning white announcers exclusively to give the play-by-play in games which involve black and white players leads to a prejudicial treatment of the black players" (p. 259). Some have argued that European-American announcers have little basis to understand African-American athletes (Harris, 1991; Hoose, 1989).

Market forces rather than prejudice may explain some media practices. Media producers profit by attracting large audiences with desirable demographic characteristics. Thus, sports coverage caters to a largely upscale European-American audience (e.g., Davis, 1993a; Edwards, 1969; Lumpkin & Williams, 1991).

Some predict sports coverage will gradually become less racist as media producers target consumers of color (Sabo & Jansen, 1994; Sabo et al., 1996). Still there are dangers that coverage of African-American athletes is designed to entertain European-Americans. As Davis (1993a) remarks:

> Perhaps the fact that contemporary African-American men athletes receive significant coverage in *Sports Illustrated* indicates that the producers now assume African-American men are a significant part of the audience, or that the producers are attempting to attract more African-American men readers. On the other hand, other aspects of the coverage and advertisements ignore African-American consumers, suggesting that the primary reason for featuring African-American men athletes may be to entertain whites.
>
> (p. 177)

The sports media appear to be catering to the new version of conservative ideology prevalent in the (European-American) market. The new conservatism conceals the devastating consequences the contemporary period has produced for most African-Americans.

Probable Consequences of the Biased Coverage

Many scholars conjecture on race/ethnic-related consequences of sports coverage, even though data have not been collected on the perceptions of actual audience members. Some argue that some aspects of the coverage deny African-American athletes the prestige they deserve and limit future opportunities and rewards (Braddock, 1978a; 1978b; Edwards, 1969; Green, 1993). This coverage may influence the self-image of African-American athletes (Gaston, 1986; Murrell & Curtis, 1994). Barrow (1991) sees limited television coverage of predominantly African-American colleges stifling their revenue generation and attractiveness to "blue chip" athletes. Stereotyped coverage of African-Americans as natural athletes may limit endorsements because the African-American athletes may not be seen as "deserving" (Corbett, 1988; Corbett & Johnson, 1993). Racially-biased coverage may also limit African-American opportunities to play particular positions and to become sport leaders (Jackson, 1987). Deviant imagery of African-American athletes may encourage undue attention and constraints on the athletes' personal lives (Cole & Andrews, 1996; Cole & Denny, 1994; Cole & Orlie, 1995). The heightened celebration of successful African-American athletes may stimulate unrealistic interest in professional athletics, while working to stifle interest in education and other career options, for young African-American men (Bierman, 1990; Dyson, 1993; Gaston, 1986; Hoose, 1989; Sabo & Jansen, 1994). The coverage may compound racial prejudice by encouraging the belief that African-Americans are not fit for occupations that require intellectual skills (Davis, 1990; McDonald, 1995; Sabo & Jansen, 1994). The portrayal of African-Americans as natural athletes encourages biological determinist explanations, obscuring human agency of African-Americans and sociopolitical forces that limit opportunities (Davis, 1990).

Sports media coverage that reinforces the American Dream has effects on all African-Americans. Suggestions that most African-Americans have achieved economic success or that African-Americans who have not achieved economic success have moral failings only reinforce European-Americans' image of themselves and their country's social structures and culture as free of racism. Such messages discourage the pursuit of changes that would benefit people of color and thus help to perpetuate racial inequality.

Thinking About the Future

Scholarship on race/ethnicity and the sports media needs to expand and move beyond the topics we address in this review. As old forms of racial prejudice become increasingly unacceptable new forms of subtle prejudice, such as "symbolic racism," emerge. Here, people of color are not seen as inherently inferior to European-Americans, yet it is believed that racism is no longer a serious problem, people of color compete on equal footing, the culture of people of color is the source of many social problems, and people of color want unfair advantages (Jaret, 1995). Scholars need to link any new forms of racial prejudice they discover in sports media coverage to social structures, especially the larger political economy.

It is important to move beyond speculating about media effects and begin real audience study. We need to understand what audience members from different social categories bring to their readings of sport media texts, and how varied social contexts shape meaning.

Scholarship that focuses on race/ethnicity in the context of sports media production would add an important element to what we know. How do media producers think about race, ethnicity and sport? How do these views shape sports media production practices and become encoded into sports media texts? How does the socio-political and economic context of sports media shape production decisions and practices in ways that affect treatment of race?

Finally, it is critical that scholarship focus on people of color other than African-American men. Current coverage virtually ignores Native-Americans, Latino/a-Americans and Asian-Americans. We need to interpret this omission and consider its consequence. In doing this, we should be careful not to "reduce race to a variable" (Birrell, 1989, p. 214). Given that race is culturally produced and contested in the context of power relationships, it is important to examine how the sports media play a part in these processes. Recent scholarship on moral deviance, accommodating images, and the American Dream in mediated sport is moving in some fruitful ways to consider this broader social context.

NOTES

1   Condor and Anderson (1984) neglected to compare the coverage to the percentage of African-American athletes participating in the sports *SI* features and to coverage of European-American athletes in *SI*.
2   Like the Condor and Anderson (1984) study, the Corbett (1988) study lacks a proper point of comparison.
3   Here, proportionality to the athlete population was not assessed.
4   The categorization system/criteria the author used is also of questionable validity.
5   Rainville and McCormick (1977) articulated this notion in an attempt to explain their finding that NFL announcers were more likely to speculate about the future performances of African-American athletes.

Chapter 11

The Media Image of Sport and Gender

Margaret Carlisle Duncan &
Michael A. Messner

Sport in the twentieth century has given men an arena in which to create and reinforce an ideology of male superiority (Bryson, 1987; Hall, 1996; Kidd, 1987; Messner, 1988; Theberge, 1981). By excluding women from this arena and by making athleticism virtually synonymous with masculinity, sport provides opportunities for men to assert their dominance at a time when male hegemony is continually challenged and opposed in everyday life. Connell (1987) asserts that ideals of masculinity are "constructed and promoted most systematically through competitive sport" (p. 84). For this reason, women's and girls' entry in the sporting world has been regarded as an incursion into a sphere that is most properly men's. Although the 1972 passage of Title IX resulted in a striking increase of female sport participation with greater numbers of female athletes, more and better sport programs, and the closing of the "muscle gap," sports media have been slow to register these changes, perhaps because athletic women and girls symbolically threaten masculine hegemony (Messner, Duncan, & Jensen, 1993; Sabo & Jansen, 1992).

This overview of sports media compares the construction of men's sport and male athletes with the construction of women's sport and female athletes, examining four significant areas:

1   production,
2   athletic attributions,
3   formulae of exclusion, and
4   symbolic dominance.

Although these are overlapping categories, for analytical purposes we review them separately. In each category we use our research findings from our 1990 and 1994 studies sponsored by the Amateur Athletic Foundation of Los Angeles as a benchmark for discussion. We have chosen this approach because this is the research with which we are most intimately familiar and which covers each of the areas we address here. We supplement the AAF findings with other relevant research in order to present the most comprehensive picture.

THE AMATEUR ATHLETIC FOUNDATION STUDIES

The 1990 AAF study examined both quantitative and qualitative aspects of televised women's and men's sports. The data included six weeks of televised sports news coverage (KNBC, Los Angeles) during 1989; the "Final Four" of the women's and men's 1989 NCAA basketball tournaments; and the women's and men's singles, women's and men's doubles, and the mixed doubles matches of the 1989 US Open Tennis Tournament.

Conceived as a replication of the 1990 study, the 1994 AAF study again investigated both quantitative and qualitative aspects of women's and men's televised sport. The data included three two-week segments (a total of six weeks) of late-night televised sports news coverage on three Los Angeles networks during 1993; the "Final Four" of the women's and men's 1993 NCAA basketball tournaments; and the women's and men's singles, women's and men's doubles, and mixed doubles matches of the 1993 US Open Tennis Tournament.

PRODUCTION

In this section we discuss three aspects of production: amount of coverage, technical quality, and intentional audience building. Each aspect shapes the way men's and women's sports are portrayed and suggests preferred or dominant meanings to audiences. We assume that whether a viewer interprets a mediated sporting event according to these preferred meanings depends upon many factors. These factors have been analyzed by reader-response and audience studies (Ang, 1996; Lull, 1990; Moores, 1993; Morley, 1992; Radway, 1991) and will not be addressed here.

Amount of Coverage

The 1990 AAF television study demonstrated "symbolic annihilation" (Gerbner & Signorelli, 1979) of female athletes in the dearth of women's sport coverage: in six weeks of television sport news, men's sports received 92 percent of the air time, women's sports, 5 percent, and gender neutral topics, 3 percent. The follow-up study in 1994 revealed no significant change, with men again receiving far greater coverage (93.8 percent), despite the fact that this more recent sample included three different networks. Furthermore, during evening and Sunday sportscasts, we found that stories on female athletes were much less likely than stories on male athletes to be accompanied by interviews with the players or coaches. Since such interviews give the coverage of sport more viewing appeal and build audience interest in the players and their competitions, the minimal coverage that *was* given to women tended to lack pizzazz.

The AAF newspaper study (1991) also showed disproportionate space given to men's sports: "Stories focusing exclusively on men's sports outnumbered stories addressing only women's sports by a ratio of 23 to 1" (p. 3) and "Front page stories covering only women's sports were even more scarce, comprising 3.2 percent of page one articles, compared to 85.3 percent devoted exclusively to men's coverage" (p. 3). Finally, "92.3 percent of all photographs were pictures of men" (p. 3).

The skewing of these percentages has been documented in other media studies. For example, in an analysis of *Sports Illustrated* from 1954 to 1987, Lumpkin and Williams found that 90.8 percent of all articles featured the sporting achievements of male athletes. Not only was the number of stories on female athletes limited, articles featuring sportswomen were shorter than those featuring men (1991, p. 16). Rintala and Birrell (1984) documented striking quantitative differences in portrayals of females and males in the magazine *Young Athlete*. In every category – cover photographs, text, and inside photographs – there was far less representation of female athletes than male athletes. Even a review of selected issues of the *NCAA News*, a publication that serves those associated with both men's and women's sports, found that women were underrepresented in articles and photographs; in some cases issues devoted less than 10 percent of the written coverage to female athletes and women's sports (Shifflett & Revelle, 1994).

The underrepresentation of female athletes and the overrepresentation of male athletes occurs in media outside the US as well. The sports section in one of Canada's national newspapers, The *Toronto Globe and Mail*, from July 1988 to June 1989, devoted 82 percent of the total space for articles, editorials and photographs to males and 6.3 percent of the total space to females (Crossman et al., 1994, p. 128,). A survey of media coverage in Australia revealed that in 1980 only 2 percent of sports reporting in major city newspapers was devoted to women's sport. In 1984 that figure decreased to 1.3 percent. In 1980, Australian television devoted 200 hours of coverage to sport during the survey period. Of this total, only five minutes were given to women's sport (Bryson, 1994, p. 54).

Technical Quality

The 1990 AAF television study reported that production values for men's sports were far superior to those for women's sports: "Significant differences in the quality of technical production tended to trivialize the women's games, while framing men's games as dramatic spectacles of historic significance" (p. 2). Camera work, editing, and sound were decidedly better in men's games than women's games. More slow-motion replays and more onscreen statistics enhanced the viewing of the men's game. One example of the lack of technical resources devoted to the women's game was the clumsy camera framing of the women's free throws.

Although the 1994 AAF television study found "notable improvements in the quality of production, camera work, editing, and sound in the 1993 women's games, compared with the 1990 study" (p. 2) – for example more slow-motion replays and better quality technical coverage of women's free throws – the production quality of the women's games tended to be haphazard and inferior to that of men's games. Furthermore, men's games featured several "extras" that heightened viewing appeal: graphics that showed the player's name, position, year in school, height, and weight; frequent slow-motion replays and displays of statistics, liberal use of the game clock and telestrator. Women's games lacked these touches.

Intentional Audience Building

As numerous authors have argued, the media do not simply report news; they actively construct it by *framing* it, that is, by offering a context for viewing or understanding an event (Fiske, 1989; Duncan & Brummett, 1987; Messner & Soloman, 1993; Tannen, 1993; Wenner, 1989b). In televised sports, framing may start weeks before the competition begins in the form of television commercials hyping the event. For example, in both AAF television studies, we observed that men's televised NCAA basketball was framed as heroic, significant, and news-worthy. A significant portion of that framing took place during the pregame, half-time, and postgame analysis of the men's competition, but also, during *the women's competition*. Much of the commentary in the 1993 half-time show of the women's NCAA championship game dealt with the upcoming men's game, how exciting it would be, who the important players were, and so on. No comparable hyping of the women's game occurred during any of the men's Final Four. Given this kind of disparity, it is not surprising that the women's basketball competition seemed less dramatic and less important than the men's competition. In particular, we observed that the women's pregame, half-time, and postgame shows were much shorter and of lower quality than the men's games.

One typical justification for showing less coverage of women's sports and lower quality production relates to "supply and demand." Television producers have sometimes argued that the sports audience is composed mostly of men who aren't interested in women's sports; therefore, producers are simply giving viewers what they want by devoting more resources to the men's games. Yet, the increasing participation rates of girls and women in sport do not support the notion that women don't care about watching women's sports. Instead, it may argued that women are discerning viewers who find, as we did, that women's televised sports are less inter-esting because of the inferior production qualities and lackadaisical framing (Kane & Greendorfer, 1994; Messner, Duncan, & Wachs, 1996).

In actuality, television producers are not merely giving audiences what they want to see. Producers, in association with athletic organizations, actively build audiences for major sporting events like the NCAA Final Four, the Super Bowl, and the World Series. As noted in Messner, Duncan, & Wachs (1996) and the 1994 AAF television study, successful audience building for a sporting event such as the men's NCAA tournament involves at least six strategies:

1   airing many regular season games to build audience familiarity with the teams, players, and announcers before the tournament even takes place;

2   transforming particular athletes into stars, who become media "personalities," and draw the attention of fans;

3   drumming up interest in upcoming competitions with numerous television and print ads as the games approach;

4   creating compelling pregame shows that spark audience anticipation and interest;

5   hyping approaching games and airing live or prerecorded interviews during half-times and dead times;

6   depending upon network news shows to enhance viewer anticipation by covering games and providing interviews with players and coaches.

These strategies insure that audiences will be primed and eager to watch championship games, such as the men's NCAA Final Four.

While producers systematically created an audience for the men's 1993 NCAA games by employing all of the above strategies, they failed to use any one of them to build an audience for the women's 1993 NCAA games. This failure, coupled with the inferior production values, virtually guaranteed less audience interest in the women's competitions. These types of media "neglect" are probably not conscious strategies used by producers to discriminate against women. Rather, they are simply part of the routine, day-to-day workings of the institutions of sports media (Jhally, 1984; Theberge & Cronk, 1986).

ATTRIBUTIONS

In this section we examine three categories of attributions that encompass the most commonly used descriptions of athletes. We call these: a) larger than life, b) strength versus weakness, and c) agency. Each category exaggerates the differences and inequalities of male and female athletes. The use of these categories also naturalizes inequality by making it appear to be biologically essential that men and women differ in these characteristic ways.

Male Athletes: Larger than Life/Symbolic Superiority

Both AAF television studies described how commentators rendered male athletes "larger than life," by labeling the stars and their performances as "big." The 1990 study reported that tennis players were described as "'big' guys with 'big' forehands, who played 'big' games" (p. 19). In 1993 commentators continued to use the imagery of "big" in their descriptions of men; one announcer opened the men's basketball championship by declaring, "We have the two most talented teams in the country, maybe the two *biggest* from one through eight in depth. Although this place is the Superdome, and real *big*, that court's going to look real small with all the *big* bodies out there tonight" (Duncan et al. 1994, 1994, p. 21).

It is interesting that the descriptor "big" seems to symbolically defuse the threat that female athletes pose to male athletes. As Kane (1995), Davis and Delano (1992), Birrell and Cole (1990) and others argue, the social positioning of males and females as unambiguous binary opposites (e.g., men as "big" and "strong," women as "small" and "weak") obscures the existence of a continuum of performance (rather than categorical gender differences) in sport. In fact some females are better athletes than some men, and some females are bigger and more powerful than some men.

Because it is so important ideologically for male athletes to maintain this image of strength and power, media characterizations tend to play up images of strong men. Trujillo (1995) found media portrayals of football players as iron men, whose bodies were invincible weapons and hardworking tools. Jansen and Sabo's (1994) study of sport metaphors in the media rhetoric of the Gulf War pointed to the sport/war tropes that link masculinity to highly valued skills and to the "positively sanctioned use of aggression, force, and violence" (p. 10). White & Gillett's (1994) study of body-building ads identified three themes relating to the hypermuscular male body as a symbolic enactment of power and control. The authors concluded that "the advertisements in *Flex* . . . naturalize the desirability of male muscularity thus producing meanings about the significance of physical gender differences – that the larger, more muscular male body is biologically superior to that of the lesser female body" (p. 33).

Strength and Weakness

Clearly size and strength are related, yet for the purposes of our discussion we wish to draw a distinction: whereas size is often used in commentary as a metaphor for the magnitude of the sporting event itself (or the personalities as reflecting the importance of that event), strength and weakness refer more particularly to specific individuals and their abilities. The 1990 AAF television study identified dramatic differences in the descriptions of strength/weakness of male athletes and female athletes. In both men's and women's competitions, commentators used attributions that suggested strength ("powerful, confident, gutsy, dominant") and weakness ("weary, frustrated, panicked, dejected"). Commentators describing men's tennis used almost four times the number of strength attributions as weakness attributions. By contrast, however, commentators describing women's tennis employed nearly equal numbers of strength and weakness attributions.

Similarly, in men's basketball attributions of strength to weakness were roughly 6 to 1, while in women's basketball, they were closer to 2 to 1. This disparity left the viewer with the impression that while men, overall, were extremely powerful, women were only moderately so. In addition, when power descriptors were used to characterize female athletes, they were often neutralized by their pairing with weakness descriptors (e.g. "she's tiny, she's small, but so effective under the boards"). This practice of undermining sportswomen's accomplishments by coupling suggestions of strength with suggestions of weakness has been called "ambivalence" and has been noted in numerous media studies (Duncan, 1986; Duncan & Hasbrook 1988; Hilliard, 1994; 1995; Halbert & Latimer, 1994; Kane, 1989; Kane & Parks, 1992; Higgs & Weiller, 1994).

Strength and weakness are conveyed not only verbally, but also visually. Duncan, in her two sports photograph studies, noted differences in the ways that male and female athletes are visually depicted (1990; Duncan & Sayaovong, 1990). Meanings connoting strength and weakness are suggested by the athlete's physical appearance, poses, body positions, facial expressions, emotional displays, and camera angles; captions function to anchor those meanings.

In these studies, some female athletes were photographed in poses (the "come-on" with slightly parted lips and angled glance) that bore a striking resemblance to soft-core pornography. This pose symbolically framed women as vulnerable and sub-missive. Males, on the other hand, were almost never photographed in beefcake poses. Body parts that signaled female sexual difference – thighs, breasts, buttocks, and crotches – were sometimes highlighted in photos of sportswomen, diverting attention from women as strong and competent athletes and reducing them to sexual objects.

Sportswomen were more likely to be photographed in postures connoting deference (lower physical positions, smaller size, head and body canting) than men, while men were more likely portrayed in postures connoting dominance (higher physical elevation, larger size, positions of protectiveness and distance) than women. If men and women were shown together, men would often be placed in the center (the power position) with women on the periphery (the subordinate position). Active poses (which highlighted athleticism) were more characteristic of the way male athletes were photographed; passive poses (in which the athletes were obviously positioned for the camera or were motionless) were more typical of the way female athletes were photographed.

Female athletes were more often shown in tears or being consoled by others after a defeat than were male athletes. Even camera angles functioned to suggest strength and weakness; more women were photographed in below-eye-level angles (connoting vulnerability in relation to the viewer); more men were photographed in above-eye-level angles (connoting strength in relation to the viewer).

Consistent with this emphasis on male strength is the symbolic suppression of weakness; attributions that might call the power or competence of a male athlete into question tend to be minimized. A telling confirmation of this symbolic suppres-sion is found in the sport pain and injury literature. As Nixon (1993) points out, sport has fostered a "culture of risk," whereby male athletes are encouraged to ignore or deny injuries and pain incurred in practices and competition. To admit injury or suffering is seen as tantamount to admitting weakness. Recent research conducted on female élite gymnasts and figure skaters (Ryan, 1995), who are coached mainly by men, suggests that to compete at this level women and girls are also, unfortunately, socialized into a culture of risk.

Poe (1976), Rintala & Birrell (1984), and Leath & Lumpkin (1992) have all documented the tendency of the sports media to feature female athletes passively posing, rather than actively engaged in their sport. In their study of the covers of *Women's Sports and Fitness*, Leath & Lumpkin (1992) noted that : "Non-athletes (female models) were shown on 44.7 percent of the covers. Almost all of the non-athletes and 58.3 percent of the athletes were shown in posed shots, rather than actively participating" (p. 123). By using models who are flawlessly beautiful but not necessarily athletic, and by placing them in static positions, the magazine is sending the message that what is valued about women is *not* their athleticism, but their appearance. Leath & Lumpkin also noted the dearth of black female athletes on covers.

Agency: Successes and Failures

In this context, we refer to "agency" in terms of how successes and failures are accounted for or explained by commentators, thus defining the competence of athletes as persons. A recurring trend in the AAF data was the framing of men as active agents, engineering their own successes and their opponents' failures. By contrast, women were framed as passive, reactive agents, succeeding sometimes because of their talent, but also because of forces outside their control (luck, family support). More significantly, women were framed as failing because of their own inability to take control. The 1990 study observed that commentators tended to attribute men's success to their raw talent, power, intelligence, size, quickness, discipline, and risk-taking. Commentators sometimes attributed women's success to talent, enterprise, hard work, and intelligence, but more often invoked emotion, luck, togetherness, and family to explain the positive outcomes of women's competitions than of men's.

When men failed, commentators tended not to mention the losing team's shortcomings, but instead focused on the great strength, power, or talent of the winners. In short, success was attributed to men's competence, and failure to their opponents' competence. In contrast, when women failed, commentators were likely to fall back on stereotyped attributions: female athletes were nervous, not aggressive enough, too emotional, or uncomfortable. Unlike men's failure, women's failure was thus almost always attributed to the women's incompetence, rather than to their opponents' skill.

Other studies have confirmed the use of stereotyped attributions such as emotional vulnerability to account for sportswomen's failures. Hilliard (1994) described how sports media focused on the mental health of top female tennis players and blamed losses on sportswomen's fragile emotional states. In their study of a televised tennis match between Martina Navratilova and Jimmy Connors, Halbert and Latimer (1994) pointed to commentators' preoccupation with Navratilova's feelings (mentioned seventeen times) compared to Connors' emotions (mentioned only a few times). In addition, commentators made much of Navratilova's reliance on her coach and her mentor for emotional support, while they never discussed Connors' reliance on his coach or friends.

Daddario (1994), discussing the 1992 Olympic media's compensatory rhetoric, identified numerous attributions relating to female athletes' mental problems, for example, Yelena Bechke, a Soviet figure skater, was labeled "anxious" and wanting to win "so badly she tries too hard and can't relax" (p. 280). In a study of sports newsgroup postings to the Internet, Duncan, Aycock, and Messner (1996) noted that posters tended to characterize female tennis players as lacking mental toughness (e.g., "They have no mental stamina. Every time I watch . . . I always expect them to have a mental breakdown or start crying after the first set" p. 16).

In the 1994 AAF study, we noted some changes in commentators' attributions. Descriptions of women athletes' abilities seemed less ambivalent and more positive, especially in the women's tennis commentary. Tennis commentators were more likely to attribute the failures of a woman to the power of her opponent, constructing female athletes as more actively controlling their own destinies.

In basketball, however, we continued to discern significant differences in the attributions of agency commentators used to describe male and female athletes. These differences were much less obvious than the strength/weakness differentials we detected in the 1990 study. Following Foucault, we call these differences "formulae of exclusion." We discuss formulae of exclusion in some detail below because they represent a fresh perspective on our understanding of attribution and agency, and may offer opportunities for important new research.

FORMULAE OF EXCLUSION

In televised sport, expert commentators have considerable power to define audiences' expectations about how athletes will perform. As commentators define these expectations, they render some attributes of the players socially visible by bringing those qualities to the audience's attention; simultaneously commentators make other characteristics of the athletes socially invisible. This social structure of visibility and invisibility must then constantly be defended; we refer to these defensive discursive practices as "formulae of exclusion" (Foucault, 1994, p. 115; 1970, p. 26). During our analysis of the 1993 NCAA men's and women's basketball games, we discovered two kinds of these social structures, or formulae of exclusion; one pertaining to athletes' actions; the other, to their status as agents. The first formula of exclusion involved actions, the way that expert commentators described errors, and in particular, misses, during play. We call this formula "missing in action." The second formula of exclusion had to do with agency, the way that expert commentators explained errors during play. We call the second formula "the secret agent." These two formulae are closely related, since the quality of social actions and the identities of those who perform them define one another.

Missing in Action

The first formula of exclusion related to the language of "misses" in women's basketball in contrast with the representation of success in men's. In commentary on women's games, the locution "so-and-so misses the shot" was common; in men's games, that locution rarely occurred. In the first women's game we examined, we noted that the commentators used the word "missed" or some variation twenty-four times. In the comparable men's game, none of the commentators used the locution "so-and-so misses the shot" until the second half, and then only five times. This relentless attention to "misses" in the women's game coupled with the relative absence of the locution "misses" in the men's game created contrasting impressions of women's failure, men's success.

In the men's games, commentary functioned to linguistically transform errors into successes. This linguistic alchemy was present in all of the men's Final Four Games, yet it was virtually absent in the women's games. In one men's game, a frequently recurring locution was "Too strong" (in other words the player threw the ball too hard and missed). This locution overrides suggestions of failure by pointing to the player's unbridled power. "Too strong" is a typical framing of a failed shot in the men's game, unmatched by a comparable locution in the women's game.

Other examples of failure turned into success in the men's games: "Webber tried to do too much on that possession" (the player is so strong and competent that his raw ability got in the way!) and "Sometimes when you get a little bit scared you really focus in, and that's been the case of Michigan so far in this game (here what might otherwise have been termed Michigan's "fearful" or "weak" performance was turned into excellent "focus.") Another comment covered up the fact that the player missed the shot on two crucial occasions: "That's the second time tonight he almost made a great play." After another player missed a shot and continued to try unsuccessfully to get it in, the announcer framed it as praiseworthy, saying, "Reece not giving up."

The Secret Agent

The second formula of exclusion was the way commentators accounted for errors during play. Commentators of the men's game softened or even neutralized suggestions of incompetence by alluding to mitigating circumstances, for example: "[The throw] was intended for Prickett, he thought maybe there was another team mate behind him," and "Montross is saying my fault, my fault; it was a very tough ball to catch, though, 'cause the backboard was causing some problem." In a frequently occurring accounting, errors were minimized by suggesting they didn't reflect the players' true skill; for instance: "He could not get off the ground, but you can't fault him, he's played some kind of game today," "Kind of unusual to see Jordan throw that one away, of course he had a great Final Four." About another player, "He has not had his usual excellent game," and "That's the kind of shot Juwan Howard usually makes, though it was way too strong." In the corresponding women's games, there were virtually no accounts that mitigated errors in women's play, simply bald statements such as "She missed." Thus, the accounts in the men's games created an impression that men's errors were unavoidable and caused by factors other than their incompetence ("the backboard was causing some problem"), or that errors did not reflect the athlete's true skill ("He has not had his usual excellent game"). Positioned against the game script, the absence of such accounts in the women's games constructed an impression that women's errors were due to their own unmitigated incompetence.

This impression was strengthened by the frequent subtraction of agency in commentary when a male player missed the basket or made another error, and the frequent emphasis on flawed agency in expert commentary when a female player missed the basket. When commentators mentioned misses by male players, they often stripped their language of pronouns so that the error was rendered peculiarly subjectless (hence, a "secret agent"), as though the action occurred in a vacuum. For instance "Hits high" (instead of "Jordan hits high"), "That's a big miss," "The ball hits the rim and bounces off." This agentless framing contrasted with the explicit attribution of errors to female athletes, "Kirkland misses a three-pointer," "Jarrard grabbed the shot away, but missed," "Swoopes missed her shot," "Kirkland misses from three," and so on.

SYMBOLIC DOMINANCE

Symbolic dominance emphasizes the difference between men and women, where men represent the standard and women represent the Other. It positions men as dominant, women as subordinate. Here we discuss three kinds of symbolic dominance: a) asymmetrical gender marking, b) infantilization/hierarchies of naming, and c) sexualization.

Asymmetrical Gender Marking

The 1990 AAF study documented the verbal and visual "marking" of female athletes. By referring to the "Women's National Championship," or the "Women's Final Four," rather than the "National Championship" for example, commentators cast female athletes in a derivative, secondary role. The men's game was virtually unmarked, typically referred to as the "National Championship," or the "Final Four" without gender markers, positioning it as the standard. The AAF 1994 study showed that verbal gender marking in the 1993 coverage of women's NCAA basketball occurred at about the same rate as in 1989, but graphic gender marking rose significantly. In 1993, another kind of visual gender marking occurred when the pictures of individual sportswomen were flashed on the screen; in these shots, female athletes appeared not in their uniforms, but in non-athletic clothing, with jewelry and styled hairdos. Pictures of sportsmen always showed them in their uniforms.

Other studies have confirmed this pattern of asymmetrical gender marking. An analysis of sports commentators' language during the "Battle of Champions," a match between Martina Navratilova and Jimmy Connors, revealed repeated gender marking when Navratilova was mentioned, e.g., "That's the thing that set her apart in *women's* tennis for so many years." When Connors was referred to, his skills were rarely gender-marked: "Jimmy Connors' return of serve was considered the best in the game" (p. 302, Halbert & Latimer, 1994, 11, 298–308). An investigation of the 1992 Summer Olympics turned up similar findings in the coverage of women's basketball and of the male "Dream Team," as well as in other same-sport events (Higgs & Weiller, 1994) Finally, a content analysis of sixteen televised basketball games from the 1988–90 seasons revealed asymmetrical gender marking in which the men's game was referred to as "basketball," while the women's game was repeatedly qualified as "women's basketball" (Blinde et al., 1991).

Infantilization/Hierarchies of Naming

The 1990 AAF study identified striking contrasts between how men athletes and women athletes were referred to by commentators. In both the tennis and basketball coverage, adult female athletes were frequently called 'girls,' 'young ladies,' and only occasionally 'women.' This commentators' practice symbolically "infantilized" mature women. Adult male athletes, on the other hand, were usually referred to as 'men,' 'young men,' or occasionally 'young fellas.' Consistent with this labeling of women as child-like and the contrasting labeling of men as adults, we also discovered "hierarchies of naming." For example, when commentators used only the first name ("Steffi") to identify an athlete, that athlete was more often female than male (52.7 percent to 7.8 percent). This trend was somewhat less evident in the 1993 coverage. One important change in 1993 was that the practice of calling women athletes "girls" had all but disappeared. In addition, in women's tennis first name only use dropped from 52.7 percent to 31.5 percent. However in the 1993 mixed doubles segment, women were called by only their first name 41.4 percent of the time, while men were never referred to at all by only their first name. These contrasts in the identification and labeling of athletes served to linguistically "infantilize" and subordinate women, while men were raised to full adult status. In our 1993 (Messner, Duncan, and Jensen) article on gendered language, we argued that dominants (either by social class, age, occupational position, race, or gender) are more typically referred to by their surnames (frequently preceded by titles such as "Mr."). Conversely, dominants usually refer to subordinates (lower-class people, younger people, employees, members of ethnic minorities, women, etc.) by their first names (Henley, 1977; Rubin, 1981; Wolfson & Manes, 1980). This asymmetrical practice of referring formally to dominants but informally to subordinates reflects and reconstructs social inequities, as Brannon (1978), Miller and Swift (1976) and Eitzen and Baca Zinn (1989) have demonstrated.

Other studies have observed infantilization of female athletes and hierarchies of naming in televised sport. In another investigation of televised tennis, Halbert and Latimer (1994) studied the "Battle of the Champions" match between Jimmy Connors and Martina Navratilova and found that the latter was frequently referred to as "Martina" although Connors was called "Jimmy Connors" or "Connors," but never "Jimmy." In addition, Navratilova was labeled a "girl" and a "lady," while Connors was never labeled a "boy" or "gentleman." Blinde et al. (1991) noted the repeated use of "lady" and "girl" in ten televised intercollegiate basketball games. In the comparison sample of men's basketball, men were rarely referred to as "gentlemen," and then only outside of the sport context. Duncan, in her discussion of *Sports Illustrated*, points to the infantilizing practice of referring to female swimsuit models by their first names ("Vendela," "Christy"). Higgs and Weiller (1994) discovered hierarchies of naming in televised Olympic volleyball coverage and infantilization in gymnastics coverage, where female gymnasts were called "girls" thirty-seven times, but male gymnasts never called "boys". In swimming coverage, Summer Sanders was continually labeled a "babe" and a "glamour girl." No such infantilization occurred in the men's swimming coverage. Finally, Daddario (1994) reported television coverage of the 1992 Winter Games in which female speed-skaters were linguistically reduced to juveniles. For example, Bonnie Blair was called "America's little sister" and "America's favorite girl next door" while Cathleen Turner was referred to as "a pixie, a 29-year-old Tinkerbell, who, on this night, had found the magic dust of youth and dreams" (p. 282).

Sexualization

We have placed this subcategory last because it epitomizes the sport media's treatment of female athletes and because this theme serves as a summary of all the arguments and illustrations that precede it. We describe several contexts for media sexualization here: appearance, humor, and sexual orientation.

Appearance

As in the other two subcategories, the sports media construct women and girls as Other; here difference is emphasized by focusing on women's appearance. Stereotyping female athletes as attractive and feminine shifts attention from their physical prowess to their looks and minimizes the symbolic threat sportswomen pose to male hegemony. Numerous media studies (Kane & Parks, 1992; Duncan, 1990; and many others) have observed that sports commentary on female athletes often contains references to their hairdos, faces, and bodies, while sports commentary focusing on men rarely does so. A recent study of postings to a sports newsgroup on the Internet (Duncan, Aycock, & Messner, 1996) identified a significant theme suggesting that women athletes' appearance – their personal beauty or clothing – was fundamental to fans' assessments of their performance (for example, "where would women's tennis be without those cute random butt shots when serving and their tennis skirt flips up just a bit?" (p. 17) and "As to G, she is not really ugly, as any of the small interview clips on HBO will attest to. H almost seems to 'uglify' herself, pulling, slicking her hair back, etc." (p. 17)).

Difference is also constructed by media *sex-typing*: when there is coverage of women, it tends to be in sex "appropriate" sports or physical activities: individual, aesthetically pleasing events such as figure-skating, gymnastics, tennis, swimming, diving – all sports thought to be consistent with conventional "femininity" (Kane, 1988; Kane & Snyder, 1989; Leath & Lumpkin, 1992; Rintala & Birrell, 1984). Or – in the case of *Sports Illustrated*, whose coverage of serious women's sports is minimal – the swimsuit issue featuring models and not athletes shows women sunbathing in the briefest of bikinis on tropical beaches. (Davis 1992; Duncan, 1993) When sexually objectified in this way, women are symbolically subordinated to the erotic desires of men.

When the sports media highlight men's sexuality, it is almost always within the context of heterosexual conquests. For example, in a *Sports Illustrated* article on tennis, the writer emphasized Boris Becker's sexual exploits with a female fashion model (Kane & Parks, 1992), thus portraying women as sexual objects, once again. Needless to say, the characterization of Becker as a stud enhanced rather than detracted from his portrayal as an athlete.

The Humorous Sexualization of Women

The 1990 AAF study noted that women were portrayed repeatedly in the sports media as humorous sex objects rather than as serious athletes. Throughout the six weeks of televised sports news, women made appearances mainly as bosomy spectators in the stands. Camera cutaways to women in bikinis or tank tops were often accompanied by sly commentary. When female athletes did appear in sports news, it was usually a gag feature, a golfer driving her ball straight into a water hazard, with a humorous remark made by the newscaster. Although the 1993 sample of television sports news contained no cheesecake shots of sexy female fans in the stands, a notable improvement, the coverage of women's sports continued to focus on the humorous, exotic, and weird, endowing stories on female athletes with a kind of freakshow aura: nuns in habits and bikini-clad women cavorting in a celebrity volleyball game, a female aerial freestylist performing a variety of gymnastic moves during freefall from a plane, a woman demonstrating trick billiard shots. Features such as these received significantly more air time than serious coverage of major women's sports such as basketball, tennis, golf, and distance running.

In the 1990 and 1994 AAF television studies, men were almost never depicted as sex objects, and although they occasionally appeared in gag features, the great preponderance of coverage cast men as strong, competent athletes. Men's status as athletes was never seriously compromised by the rare humorous portrayal.

Sexual Orientation

It has become all but a cliché to point out that much media commentary emphasizes sportswomen's sexuality, femininity, or status as wives and mothers, thereby effectively trivializing their athletic achievements. A telling example of this focus on sexuality occurred in Australia, where a women's cricket team became the subject of a titillating media controversy (Burroughs et al., 1995). A female cricketer dropped from the Australian team alleged that she had been discriminated against by lesbian team members because of her status as a married heterosexual. Overnight, the women's cricket team was raised from virtual invisibility to a media preoccupation. Unfortunately very little attention was paid to the team's excellent record of sport performances; rather, the press made lesbianism the issue by speculating on "gay plotting" (p. 278) and opining that lesbian participation in women's sport had a "stultifying effect" on women's cricket (p. 277). The attention directed to the specter of lesbianism completely eclipsed any interest in the team's accomplishments.

Similarly, Duncan, Aycock, and Messner (1996) discussed how postings to an Internet sports newsgroup speculated about female tennis players' sexual orientation, implying that women's sexuality takes precedence over their athletic accomplishments. References to players' possible lesbianism abounded, although the posters never clarified the connection between sexual orientation and tennis skills: "I read somewhere recently – somewhere online – that the AP reported in a story about gay athletes that X and Y are a couple and that their relationship is an 'open secret' on the tour," "Everyone knows about A. I can suspect a few others, so here is my list: B, C, D, E," and "I don't think B is lesbian. She is married, right?" (p. 19). Kane (1995) argues that labeling female athletes as lesbians is an "effective form of containment precisely because we live in a homophobic culture that views lesbians and gay men negatively" (p.211). Here Kane uses "containment" to mean defusing the symbolic threat excellent female athletes pose to male hegemony. Nelson (1994) argues that the lesbian label "names male fears of female empowerment" (p. 40). In short, an easy way to discredit female athletes is to cast aspersions on their sexuality so their accomplishments can be dismissed as abnormal, freakish, deviant. Other authors such as Cahn (1994), Griffin and Gebasci (1990), and Lenskyj (1992) have also noted the association of female sporting competence with lesbianism.

CONCLUSION

Throughout this review, we note the ways in which women's sports and men's sports are differentially constructed by the media. Using the 1990 and 1994 AAF studies as reference points, we identify contrasts in portrayals of women's versus men's sports in four major areas: production, attributions, formulae of exclusion and symbolic dominance. The first area, production, includes the amount of coverage, the technical quality of the coverage, and the degree of audience building. The second area, attributions, encompasses three categories of athletic descriptions: larger than life, strength versus weakness, and agency. The third area, formulae of exclusion, reveals two related structures of visibility and invisibility: missing in action and the secret agent. The fourth area, symbolic dominance, includes three categories of expression: asymmetrical gender marking, infantilization/hierarchies of naming, and sexualization. When we examine each of these areas, we find contrasts in the ways that female athletes and male athletes are depicted.

Although some of the more overt media stereotyping has decreased since the 1990 study, we still discern gender differences in the media accounting of successes and failures, in the media descriptions of female and male athletes, in the quantities of media coverage, in the technical production of sporting events, and in the gender marking and naming of athletes. Numerous other investigations confirm these differences and supplement our findings. We argue that these differences may have significant consequences in the ways audiences interpret mediated sporting events.

We offer three recommendations for future research on sport media portrayals of women's and men's sports. First, scholars need to go beyond the mere textual content to discover how the discourse itself is framed by a deeper "structure of expectation" (Tannen, 1993, p. 15; Duncan, 1993). Such a frame provides an audience with an easily understandable context for interpreting individual texts (Messner & Solomon, 1993). Identifying frames in sports media gives scholars a stronger feeling for the persuasive appeal of sexism and the power of masculine hegemony (Duncan, 1993). We have analyzed two examples of framing in this chapter: audience building and formulae of exclusion.

The first example concerns how producers frame their expectations about audiences for televised sport. As we mentioned earlier, a typical justification for investing more production time, money, and expertise in the men's games flows from the producers' expectation that the sport-viewing audience is composed of mainly males who want to watch only men's sports.

The second example involves how audiences frame their expectations of successful athletes and successful teams. We noted that commentators for the men's NCAA basketball games employed certain linguistic structures or frames that rendered men's failures largely invisible, and other frames that played up men's successes. In contrast, the commentators for the women's NCAA basketball games framed women's failures in ways that made them particularly visible and neglected to use frames that would call attention to women's successes. We need more research that examines the frames or structures of expectation invoked by the sports media.

Second, researchers must look at gender within the context of other power relationships; in media portrayals, how do gender, race, class, ability, sexuality, age, and ethnicity intersect? Examples of more complexly nuanced analyses include Linda Williams' (1994) discussion of the film, "Personal Best," which looks at gender and sexual orientation, and Christine Anne Holmlund's (1994) examination of gender, race and sexuality in the "Pumping Iron" films. In the 1989 NCAA basketball data, our discovery of a hierarchy of naming which encompassed race as well as gender suggests that the dynamics of power are multi-layered and that one power differential is not easily reduced to another.

Third, we need research on new trends in sport media such as global media, global fan culture, and sport mediated by the Internet and World Wide Web sites. Some current research suggests that instead of reducing gender hierarchies, media globalization may simply lead to the reinforcement of conventional patriarchal hierarchies on a worldwide scale (Duncan, Aycock, & Messner, 1996). Much investigation remains to be done; for example, the relationship of race and gender in global media sport cultures has been largely unexplored.

Chapter 12

Media Treatment of Female Athletes: Issues of Gender and Sexualities

Mary Jo Kane &
Helen Jefferson Lenskyj

> What accounts for the staying power of a stereotype that is so extreme it should be laughable except that so many people believe it to be accurate?
>
> (Pat Griffin 1992, p. 252)

In his analysis of cultural studies, politics and identity, Douglas Kellner (1995) argues that media culture has become the dominant cultural form which provides ideological and concrete materials for identity formation. He further argues that media culture shapes the prevalent views of the world by reflecting and reinforcing our most deeply held values. Finally, Kellner outlines the ways in which the media help to define a common culture, particularly as it relates to dimensions of power and control: "[M]edia stories and images provide the symbols, myths and resources which help constitute a common culture for the majority of individuals ... Media culture spectacles demonstrate who has power and who is powerless, who is allowed to exercise force ... and who is not" (pp. 1–2).

Scholarly critiques of cultural representations in sport media echo Kellner's claims. Over the last two decades sport sociologists have convincingly demonstrated that media representations of women's identities in sport link their athleticism to deeply held values regarding femininity and sexuality (Duncan, 1990; Hargreaves, 1994; Kane, 1996; Kane & Greendorfer, 1994; Lenskyj, 1986, 1992, 1994). In both print and broadcast journalism these representations create the prevalent world view that female athletes are, by definition, a less authentic version of their male counterparts. This is because sports media images and stories provide us with endless symbols, myths and spectacles that equate male athleticism with strength, courage and competence, while simultaneously equating female athleticism with sexual appeal, femininity and a so-called limited physical (biological) capacity (Kane, 1996; Willis, 1982). This stereotyped coverage constitutes a common sports culture in which men have power and women (by comparison) do not, in large measure because women's athletic accomplishments are trivialized by the media (Duncan & Hasbrook, 1988). But as we know, mass media representations of sportswomen do far more than trivialize them. According to Michael Messner (1988), asymmetrical patterns of portrayal both in terms of amount and type of coverage severely limit the post Title IX female athlete's ability to redefine herself in ways that fundamentally challenge men's ideological and institutional control of sport. While the 1972 Title IX law as enforced by the US Department of Education's Office of Civil Rights mandates parity of resources in athletic programs at educational institutions receiving federal funding, actual institutional practices and cultural changes have come slowly.

The notion of men's control over sport highlighted by Messner is an underlying theme of much of the sports media scholarship, particularly from a feminist perspective (Daddario, 1994; Duncan & Brummet, 1993; Duncan & Hasbrook, 1988; Kane & Disch, 1993; Lenskyj, 1991). The basic premise of this research is that because women's athletic efforts and achievements are systematically ignored, underreported or denigrated when covered, the media become an important technology for constructing dominant ideologies, practices and power structures related to gender: "Sports tend to be presented in the media as symbolic representations of a particular kind of social order, so that in effect they become modern morality plays, serving to justify and uphold dominant values and ideas" (Hargreaves, 1982, p. 127). Another body of knowledge which takes as its fundamental premise men's domination of sport is the emerging literature on homophobia in women's athletics. For example, Pat Griffin (1992) argues that homophobia, along with sexism, have been the cornerstones of fear, intolerance and oppression that have kept women out of sport or contained them once within it. In this sense, she joins numerous scholars (Bennett, Whitaker, Smith & Sablove, 1987; Nelson, 1991; Thorngren, 1990) who argue that the real or imagined presence of lesbians in sport threatens male domination. Citing the work of Bryson (1987) Griffin states that:

In a sexist and heterosexist society (in which heterosexuality is reified as the only normal, natural, and acceptable orientation), women who defy the accepted feminine role or reject a heterosexual identity threaten to upset the imbalance of power enjoyed by white heterosexual men in a patriarchal society.

(1992, p. 252)

A related feature of both bodies of knowledge is the claim that as women become increasingly visible and struggle for more opportunity and power, mechanisms of counter-resistance intensify to contain women's potential. For example, Messner (1988) argues that the influence of the women's movement on sport, reflected in the passage of Title IX and the on-going battles for gender equality, has created an environment in which women's quest for self-definition, equality and control over their own bodies is being resisted by defenders of the status quo. He further suggests that stereotyped media framings of the female athlete, and her body, increasingly undermine any potential threat to male power posed by sportswomen. Similarly, Kane and Greendorfer (1994) point out that the type of media coverage afforded the post Title IX female athlete represents a modern day attempt to impose traditional images of femininity and sexuality on sportswomen. These images in turn marginalize and trivialize women's sporting efforts and thus subvert their ability to gain a foothold in an institution of immense status, wealth and power. Similar themes run throughout much of the literature on homophobia. Griffin (1992) argues that as women's sport has become more visible and potentially marketable, there has been an intensified effort to purge the lesbian image. Mariah Burton Nelson (1991) observes that although homophobia is by no means a new phenomenon, it appears to be increasing in direct proportion to sportswomen's expanding opportunity and visibility in the post Title IX era. Nelson supports such observations by citing Don Sabo's analysis of the function of homophobia as a weapon of control and power that is used to maintain the status quo. He argues that the so-called concerns about a lesbian presence in sport aren't really about sexual preference but about fears related to gender equality because "homophobia doesn't pertain to genitals but to jobs" (cited in Nelson, 1991, p. 145). In effect, Sabo asserts that homophobia perpetuates male power in sport by maintaining men's monopoly on existing resources.

Even though both literatures have extensively examined the ideologies, structures and practices by which men control sport, few have addressed at any length how homophobic media representations also serve such ends. Sabo and Messner (1993) discuss how the liberating potential of sport to empower women's bodies and minds is being undermined by both the media and homophobia. Yet they offer no analysis on how these factors may link together to contain sportswomen. They are not alone in failing to make this link. Much of the sports media scholarship has examined the overabundance of media images and narratives that impose traditional notions of femininity and sexual appeal as normative expectations for female athletes. But few authors have explicitly outlined how these images and narratives are primarily about the "image problem" that pervades women's athletics. As Griffin (1992) points out, the insistence that sportswomen conform to traditional notions of femininity is really an insistence that they be, or appear to be, heterosexual: "The underlying fear is not that a female athlete or coach will appear too plain or out of style, the real fear is that she will look like a dyke or, even worse, is one" (p. 254). To counteract such fears, female athletes have gone to great lengths to assure themselves and others that sport can (and should) be highly consistent with what this culture deems to be womanhood (Griffin, 1992; Lenskyj, 1986). Part of this effort is to engage in practices which overtly reject the notion that the sport experience masculinizes young girls and women. According to Griffin, one important way this is accomplished is by encouraging, and in many cases requiring, sportswomen to "engage in the protective camouflage of feminine drag" (1992, p. 254). And there is no more consistent and effective means by which such "protective camouflage" is ensured than through media representations.

The media landscape is filled with both implicit and explicit manifestations of homophobic coverage. An example of implicit homophobic coverage is when visual and written texts emphasize a woman athlete's sex appeal and femininity in ways that tie her to traditional beliefs regarding heterosexuality. For example, in her analysis of press coverage of the 1984 and 1988 Olympic Games, Margaret Duncan (1990) discovered that Florence Griffith-Joyner (Flo-Jo) was frequently portrayed on magazine covers because she fit conventional standards of beauty: "It is no coincidence that Joyner's rapier-like, intricately painted fingernails are often visibly present in the photographs . . . Griffith-Joyner's nails are an external adornment that shouts femininity" (p. 28). A more explicit manifestation of homophobic coverage is one that directly links a well-known female athlete to a heterosexual role, typically as a wife or a mother. It seems safe to suggest, for example, that Chris Evert and Nancy Lopez enjoyed much of their popularity precisely because they occupied both roles. In fact, much of the media coverage surrounding their respective careers emphasized these facts. When Evert announced her retirement from professional tennis in the late 1980s, *Sports Illustrated* acknowledged its significance by putting her on its cover. However, the caption that accompanied her posed, non-athletic photograph was: "Now I'm Going To Be a Full-Time Wife." In the feature article which accompanied *SI*'s cover we are provided with a pictorial chronology of Evert's "career." We see a timetable of photographs beginning with a shot of Evert with her first boyfriend, Jimmy Conners, then with short-lived flame Burt Reynolds, followed by Steve Ford (son of former president Gerald Ford), then with first husband, John Lloyd, and, finally, with her current husband Andy Mill.

The continual bombardment of such implicit and explicit images results in what Griffin calls a "promotion of a heterosexy image" (p. 255) as a way to purge a lesbian presence, while simultaneously reassuring fans and corporate sponsors that the "image problem" in women's sports is under control.

WHY FEAR LESBIANS IN SPORT?

As previously stated, numerous authors have made the claim that a lesbian presence in sport is threatening because it challenges male hegemony by upsetting existing power structures based on gender and sexuality (Griffin, 1992; Lenskyj, 1991, 1992; Thorngren, 1990). The question is, why? Monique Wittig (1993) has argued that there is no such thing as a natural category of women; we are culturally imagined, not born. In a similar vein, Wittig asserts that lesbians too are socially constructed artifacts whose existence poses a direct threat to heterosexist assumptions regarding the so-called natural, and therefore immutable, connection between sexuality and gender. According to Wittig, refusing to become or remain a heterosexual is tantamount to refusing to become a man or a woman, whether this is conscious or not. This refusal has particular material consequences for lesbians that relate to men's control over women: "For a lesbian this [refusal] goes further than the refusal of the role 'woman.' It is the refusal of the economic, ideological, and political power of a man" (p. 105).

If one accepts Wittig's propositions, sport becomes a particularly troublesome area of concern because female athletes fit the profile of lesbians: They are frequently in groups without men; they are physically active in ways that do not have to do with being sexually appealing to men; and they are engaged in activities that do not enhance their abilities to be good mothers and wives (Griffin, 1992). Perhaps this is why the history of women's sport involvement has been identified with two inter-related concerns or fears regarding the presence of lesbians: 1) that there is an overabundance of women athletes who are gay; and 2) that sport participation causes females to become lesbian. By exploiting such popularly-held assumptions, those who oppose women's attempts to gain equal access to sporting opportunities and resources can (and do) call forth homophobic assertions about dangerous lesbians running rampant throughout sport. Griffin (1993) points out how this works. She argues that a particularly effective way to prevent any serious challenge to male domination is to label, and therefore stigmatize, female athletes as lesbians. This intimidation tactic often silences and marginalizes all women, regardless of any particular athlete's sexual orientation. In this way, the balance of power in men's favor is maintained.

On the whole, we do not disagree with the preceding analysis regarding the practices and consequences of homophobia in women's athletics. We are sensitive to the very real dangers posed by intolerance, hatred, and the verbal, physical and sexual assaults that are often engendered by a homophobic environment. We are concerned, however, with the approach scholars have typically taken when attempting to counteract homophobic assertions, particularly those assertions which suggest that many female athletes are lesbian and that involvement in sport makes girls gay. A common counter-argument has been to point out that such assertions are linked to myths and stereotypes; therefore, goes this argument, any fears related to the threat of a lesbian presence are simply unwarranted. For example, Mariah Burton Nelson cites sports psychologist Bruce Ogilvie who argues that popularly-held beliefs about connections between women's sport participation and lesbianism are phobias without foundation: "If a person's orientation is uniquely heterosexual, then the 'threat' of the sports environment changing that is no different than anywhere else in society" (cited in Nelson, 1991, p. 148). Griffin (1993) takes a similar approach when she argues that linking a person's sexual preference to involvement in sport, or any other activity, has more to do with gender role stereotypes than with accurate information regarding sexual orientation.

Although we certainly agree that involvement in sport does not cause someone to become a lesbian, and that myths and stereotypes about lesbians in sport abound, our concern is that the counter-offensive typically employed by scholars can lead to the conclusion that the presence of lesbians in sport need not be feared. We want to argue that lesbian existence *should* be feared and we will take up this position momentarily. But first we want to set the stage for why we have raised such reservations. The well-intentioned logic behind counter-arguments to fears regarding lesbians in sport goes something like this: On the whole, lesbians are no different from their heterosexual counterparts. Who is and who is not a lesbian is a private, individual matter. Lesbians certainly are present in sport, but this is the case in all walks of life. And, finally, lesbians have the same hopes and dreams as do heterosexuals – job and life satisfaction, successful interpersonal relationships, and personal fulfillment. In short, feminist scholars appear to be saying that because lesbians are "just like heterosexuals," they ought not to inspire fear.

Although we do not take issue with the sentiments underlying these arguments, we support the position advanced by Celia Kitzinger (1987) that such reasoning centers the analysis on "the extent to which lesbians conform with or can be assimilated into the existing social system" (p. 50). She argues that such a liberal humanistic approach, which takes as its premise that homosexuals are equally successful and valuable members of society, frames the issue as one of "we are all just people" and, as such, reduces the analysis to an individual, private matter. Kitzinger rejects such a personalized approach and argues instead for a radical feminist critique which sees heterosexuality and lesbianism as political institutions. Taking a radical feminist approach allows us to see that a lesbian existence is not simply about "personal choice" or "alternative lifestyles," but about a fundamental social, political and economic challenge to male-defined versions of reality. Kitzinger supports such claims through her analysis of the term homophobia. Although she acknowledges that the term has been useful in providing "both an explanation of and a weapon against hostility towards lesbianism" (p. 34), she nevertheless argues that homophobia should not be considered an irrational fear, nor an affliction of bigoted, intolerant individuals. Assessing and supporting Kitzinger's position, Claudia Card (1995) points out that hatred and hostility toward lesbians are not irrational or phobic but are instead "grounded in a valid apprehension of lesbians' political challenge to patriarchy" (p. 157). In this sense, homophobia, far from being based in irrationality, is in fact a very rational response by those who would oppose lesbian commitments to undermine and alter patriarchal conceptions of gender and power. How does such an analysis relate to the real and imagined presence of lesbians in sport? It is to this issue that we now turn.

SPORT AS FERTILE GROUND FOR LESBIAN EMPOWERMENT

Our starting point for this section is Mariah Burton Nelson's (1991) observation that myths and stereotypes about lesbians in sport often contain a grain of truth. Even though she states that sports do not create lesbians, she argues insightfully that, like many other liberating experiences, they can create opportunities for women to bond with each other: "A sporting experience, by developing a woman's body and mind, may give her the courage to act on feelings of attraction – sexual, emotional, intellectual – toward other women" (p. 148). This is the crux of the matter. This is the rational fear that provides the foundation for the hyperheterosexual overlay imposed on (and rigidly maintained in) women's athletics. An extension of this rational fear is that sport serves as fertile ground for women bonding passionately with and loving other women, whether this love and passion become sexual or not. We say this because central to many sport experiences is the development of trust, admiration and respect for one's opponents and teammates, as well as passion, joy and commitment to one's self. When these feelings take place in a physically intimate setting, and, in many cases, within a sex-segregated environment, homoerotic love between women becomes a distinct possibility. Taken within this context, and borrowing from Claudia Card (1995), we argue that the lesbian possibility in sport should be frightening. At the very least, such fears reflect how much is at stake in controlling women's power. How ironic that those who use homophobic tactics to silence and purge the possibilities of women loving other women have, although unwittingly, gauged the stakes in the contest far more shrewdly than have we.

In her groundbreaking article on compulsory heterosexuality, Adrienne Rich stated that the original intent of her analysis was to examine how "woman identi- fication" and bonding do not simply reflect a validation of personal life choices, but can also serve as a "politically activating impulse" (1993, p. 227). Following Rich's lead, we argue that sport is fertile ground for the empowerment of women, not only as a site which cultivates self-respect and self-possession of one's body (Mackinnon, 1987), or as an experience in which women feel their bodies free from male domination (Theberge, 1986), or as an important vehicle for gaining a sense of mastery and competence (Duquin, 1989). Sport can also be an important arena where women learn respect, love and passionate commitment *for each other*. Also borrowing from Rich, we want to emphasize that an enormous amount of cultural work goes into preventing sportswomen from identifying and bonding with each other in such ways. In fact, the vehemence of the prohibitions against women's commitment to one another suggests that this commitment forms a powerful counter force which must be systematically kept at bay.

Recent empirical and anecdotal evidence clearly establishes how the counter force of women loving other women in sport is harnessed. For example, Nelson (1991) points out that straight women often avoid lesbians because they are afraid they will be stigmatized by the lesbian label. It is also the case that lesbians avoid other lesbians, as when so-called straight-looking lesbians do not want to be iden- tified with those who look "too manly" according to heterosexist standards. Qualitative research studies indicate how the specter of lesbianism undermines and disrupts women's ability to bond with each other, not only physically but emotion- ally and politically. Vikki Krane (1997) interviewed twelve collegiate athletes who self-identified as lesbians and discovered that many of them hid their identity from their teammates because of the tensions that such revelations could bring about. For example, one lesbian athlete described a locker room incident with a teammate that conjures up notions of lesbian as sexual predator. The teammate first accuses her [the lesbian] of "looking at me when I'm naked," and then tells her in no uncer- tain terms: "Don't talk to me when I'm naked" (p. 155). Blinde (1990) also inter- viewed intercollegiate female athletes and found that many of them had internalized homophobic and sexist ideologies. Several of these athletes indicated that they resented the presence of lesbians on their team because of the negative image it created. They also argued for the importance of projecting a so-called feminine image to counter this lesbian presence. As one women stated:

> I don't fit the stereotype. I mean, the stereotype based around women that are very masculine and strong and athletic. I wouldn't say I'm pretty in pink, but I am feminine and I appear very feminine and I act that way.
>
> (p. 239)

In a follow-up publication, Blinde, Taub and Han (1994) pointed out that even though female athletes are well aware of gender inequality in sport, they frequently emphasize their lack of identification with feminism. This disassociation is expressed in ways that reflect negative feelings towards lesbianism. For example, feminists were often viewed as extremists or lesbians who were considered "counterproductive to women's advancement" (p. 56). Griffin (1992) points out how divisive such attitudes can be in terms of bonding between and among women: They can prevent or rupture friendships among teammates, undermine relationships with female coaches and severely limit identification with other women unless that identification conforms to rigid stereotypes of femininity and sexuality.

What is clear from the preceding analysis is that the potential for women bonding with and loving other women needs to be suppressed by "rendering invisible the lesbian possibility" (Rich, 1993, p. 238). One of the most effective techniques for erasing a lesbian possibility in sport is to render it invisible in the mass media. By doing so, any countervailing force posed by a lesbian existence becomes neutralized. In the next section of the chapter we outline the various ways in which a so-called lesbian image is systematically suppressed in media representations of female athleticism.

THE UBIQUITOUS BUT INVISIBLE LESBIAN IN SPORTS MEDIA

We have already discussed one consistent way the media subvert any notion of woman identification that may suggest a lesbian presence: Female athletes are portrayed in ways that emphasize conventional standards of femininity and/or they are explicitly linked to heterosexual roles. A second way that a lesbian image is rendered invisible is through a process called erasure. Erasure involves the symbolic annihilation of women who participate in sports such as ice hockey and rugby (Kane, 1995). Both sports are combative in nature and also require strength, speed and physical aggression; because of this they are considered "male" sports. Erasure thus occurs because of the commonly-held belief that women who engage in such activities must be too masculine and therefore lesbian.[1] Although most sportswomen receive token recognition at best, it is no coincidence that these particular athletes have been most ignored by the media: Evidence that thousands of women eagerly pursue this kind of physical activity offers a potential challenge to heterosexist assumptions and expectations regarding the physical characteristics, interests and capacities of females.

A third sport that is erased from the mainstream media landscape is softball. Though this is one of the most popular sports in the US with over eight million girls and women participating nationwide (NSGA, 1994), we suggest that it is rarely seen in media outlets because of its long association with a highly visible lesbian presence (Zipter, 1988). For example, Nelson (1991) points out that women's softball leagues often make up the backbone of the lesbian community in many cities and towns. To give public recognition to such an activity in the form of mass media exposure could obviously undermine attempts to construct female athleticism in a hyper heterosexual mold.

In addition to systematically ignoring certain so-called masculine sports, the media also neutralize a lesbian existence by severely underrepresenting images and narratives that reflect women's physical and emotional bonds with each other such as hugging and embracing. The homoerotic nature of men's sports has recently been identified (Pronger, 1990). There are countless media images and narratives of men's physical connections (e.g., patting each other on the buttocks, holding hands in the huddle) and emotional ties (e.g., the glorification of sports warriors who respect and love each other with great passion). Parallels in media coverage of women's athletics are rarely found. In fact, we would suggest that visual and written texts of women bonding in ways that express their physical and emotional passions for each other are even more invisible than those that highlight women's competence as skilled athletes.

MEDIA REPRESENTATIONS OF AN EXPLICIT LESBIAN PRESENCE: A CASE-STUDY APPROACH

We have just analyzed how the media symbolically annihilate any lesbian presence in sport that may undermine sexist and heterosexist assumptions regarding sport, gender and power. In this next section we employ a case-study approach to examine media constructions of recent incidents in sport that rose to the level of controversy or scandal and specifically involved a lesbian presence. The first two incidents concern sport in Australia, specifically cricket and track and field. In the first instance we explore how the media covered allegations by a heterosexual woman cricketer that she failed to make the national team because of reverse discrimination. The second incident involved the public controversy surrounding the publication of a fund-raising calendar which portrayed women track and field athletes in highly sexualized poses. The third incident occurred in the US where former CBS golf analyst Ben Wright accused a lesbian presence of hurting women's professional golf.

Through an in-depth analysis of these incidents we see how many of the issues raised throughout this chapter get played out in mass media accounts. We draw particular attention to the ways in which lesbianism, rather than homophobia as a social, political and economic institution, is constructed as the overriding problem in women's athletics. In a related vein, we explore how the media fail to analyze the presence of lesbians in sport as an issue related to structural dimensions of power and oppression. Instead, they use a liberal humanist approach that frames lesbianism and heterosexuality as individual matters. Finally, we analyze how mass media accounts give voice to those who would use lesbian-baiting as a tactic to undermine lesbian athletes, and how such baiting can disrupt potential bonds among sportswomen.

The three incidents under discussion demonstrated remarkable staying power in the mass media – over two weeks in the LPGA example – and the fact that they were frequently taken up as general news items and not simply relegated to the sport section is indicative of both public and media preoccupation with sexualizing female athletes. Moreover, it appears that the liberal tone of the media coverage resonated with the "common sense" convictions (in the neomarxist meaning of the term) held by many Australian and North American readers that sexual issues are private, and that sex, sport and politics should be kept firmly apart. And, in contrast to the outbursts of neoconservative critics of women's sport, liberal arguments took on a deceptive aura of reasonableness and fairness, as evident, for example, in the media's tendency to focus on the actions and merits of individual sportswomen. In doing so, however, they generally failed to contextualize or politicize the events surrounding these three stories.

In the context of women's sport, the problem of homophobia – erroneously labeled the "image problem" – has a long history (Lenskyj, 1986, 1991). Given the public focus on the sexuality and private lives of women who venture into non-traditional spheres of activity, such women experienced implicit or explicit pressure to present themselves in ways that were unequivocally heterosexual; "femininity" became the code word for this heterosexual image. Feminist commentaries of the 1970s referred to the "apologetic" in women's sport, a similar concept to Connell's "emphasized femininity" (Connell, 1987). Neither concept, however, gives sufficient salience to the pervasive problem of homophobia and the pressure on lesbians to remain invisible for the alleged "good" of women's sport. With the gains of the last two decades in terms of human rights legislation and more liberal societal attitudes about sexuality, there is somewhat less pressure on female athletes to proclaim their heterosexuality. Self-disclosure by increasing numbers of lesbians and gay men in public life has contributed to the changing climate.

However, as previously mentioned, many sport administrators, female as well as male, continue to express concern about the "image" of women's sport. Coaches and sponsors of women's teams often impose dress codes that include revealing uniforms, long hair, shaved legs and make-up. On some American university campuses, there are mandatory "makeover classes" for members of women's varsity sports teams and a beauty consultant began traveling with the LPGA tour long before the current controversy (Lipsyte, 1995). The homophobic message in these marketing strategies is clear: Sportswomen, already seen as non-conformists because of their sporting activities, should at least try to conform to prevailing standards of heterosexual attractiveness – that is, to "keep up appearances." This is not to suggest that there are no material benefits accruing to the individual credentialled heterosexual sportswoman, as a comparison of the sponsorships offered to Martina Navratilova and Chris Evert amply demonstrates. However, in the case of the NCAA and the LPGA, the corporate agenda and the profit motive override any consideration of fair treatment for individual athletes.

TWO AUSTRALIAN EXAMPLES

In January 1994, women's cricket captain Denise Annetts, after failing to be selected for the team's upcoming New Zealand tour, tried to lodge a complaint of sexual discrimination (on the basis of her heterosexuality) with the New South Wales Anti-Discrimination Board. She subsequently aired her complaints in numerous interviews in the mass media, where she claimed, among other things, that lesbians were running women's cricket.

In July of the same year, Australian sportswomen again made headlines for reasons largely unrelated to their sporting achievements, this time when female track and field athletes appeared in pin-up-style poses in a fundraising calendar. A second edition of the calendar was produced in 1995.

Coverage of Annetts' complaints in major Australian newspapers was overwhelmingly sympathetic, with some conservative journalists (e.g., Devine, 1994; Kavanagh, 1994) expressing outrage that anti-discrimination laws did not protect heterosexuals and blaming the "political correctness" movement for this alleged bias. In the words of one columnist, the rights of "the 98-plus [sic] percent heterosexual majority in Australia" were in jeopardy (Kavanagh, 1994).

The more moderate commentators who espoused the "other side of the coin" arguments avoided any analysis of the complex issues of power, equity and equality. They frequently grounded their rhetoric in unquestioned assumptions about rights and justice, for example, the belief that fair treatment means the same treatment. As Matt Ridley, executive director of the Australian Women's Cricket Council explained, the players' sexuality "is no issue. Whether you are heterosexual or homosexual or black or white, you get the same go. It doesn't matter" (cited in Harari, 1994).

Following up on Annetts' claim of a so-called lesbian takeover, some journalists saw fit to survey (presumably heterosexual) female cricketers for their views. Overall, their homophobic comments added fuel to the fire. (No openly lesbian Australian athlete was available for comment, although one report cited American lesbian sport scholar, Pat Griffin (Smith & Hudson, 1994).) The women's cricket team manager was reported as saying that she "feared" for her own reputation, and that the charges of lesbianism at the administrative level of women's cricket were "a terrible slight on sport generally, and particularly on women's sport" (Harari & Smellie, 1994). One team member was quoted as saying that she was "horrified at the inference she (Annetts) made and its reflection" on herself, and the reporter went on to say that team members and national administrators felt "cruelly tarnished and betrayed" (Wilson, 1994). A female softball player spoke of the sexual tension among lesbian players while on tour and labeled the social and sexual activities of these players "disgusting" (Smith & Hudson, 1994). This litany of negative epithets speaks for itself.

Presenting themselves as having the welfare of women's sport at heart, some sportswomen cited in newspaper reports expressed concern that allegations of lesbianism might deter aspiring young athletes or their parents; even the president of the Australian Women in Sport Foundation espoused this position (Harari, 1994). Other reports called for the strengthening of majority (heterosexual) rights and implied that human rights policies might not protect the very athletes who would promote a positive public image of women's sport – that is, white, conventionally attractive, credentialled heterosexual women (Harari, 1994; Harari & Smellie, 1994; Harris, 1994). A male netball coach claimed that lesbianism became a problem when senior players and coaches who were lesbian had "access to young people who look up to them as role models" (Smith & Hudson, 1994). And, in a statement that effectively robbed lesbians of the right to self-identification, an anonymous retired female cricketer claimed that élite female athletes "are spending more time with each other and they don't see enough outside perspective about the outside world" (Harari & Smellie, 1994).

A minority of newspaper reports identified the irony of the controversy: "Women's cricket has never received the attention it craved. Now the sport is reeling from sex bias allegations by one of its most decorated players" (Wilson, 1994; see also Smith & Hudson, 1994; Smith, 1994). Some of the more progressive voices agreed that there are lesbians in cricket but called the whole issue "a distraction" and "not relevant" (Harari & Smellie, 1994; Smith & Hudson, 1994).

Some similar patterns emerged in the newspaper debate over the Golden Girls calendar. Supporters presented themselves as allies of women's sport who simply wanted to correct negative stereotypes of female athletes, although, in fact, many of those quoted perpetuated these same negative images, along with some implicitly homophobic messages. According to a spokesman for the company that produced the calendar, the public image of female athletes is "masculine with hairy armpits" and the calendar presented women who appeared "feminine, soft and sexy" (Games girls' fund-raising, 1994). In an opportunistic follow-up in the Brisbane *Courier-Mail* – beauty makeovers and before-and-after photographs of four top female athletes – a swimmer was quoted as saying that it was "nice to feel like a woman because you just feel like a dog after training with your hair all wet" ("Stars back glamour for promotion," 1994). Similarly, one of the women in the 1995 calendar claimed that young girls are turned off sport because "they don't want to look muscle-bound and sweaty and grimy" and that the "glamorous" sportswomen in the calendar would encourage girls to participate (Wells, 1994, July 30–31).

Defenders of the calendar unabashedly supported using sex (meaning heterosex) to sell women's sport as simply a sensible marketing strategy (Harris, 1994), and referred to several male sports – for example, rugby, football, and Iron Man contests – that used images of men in provocative poses. According to the common refrain, "what was good enough for the boys of rugby was good enough for the girls of athletics" (Games girls' fund-raising, 1994). One newspaper editorial was titled "Different rules for female athletes?" (Green, 1994) while a female columnist pointed to the "blatant sexual overtones" of men's sports and asked, "Why are women's sports any different?" (Bates, 1994; see also Huxley, 1994; McNicoll, 1994).

In another twist on the liberal rationales, there was an implied rejection of a feminist position that has been inaccurately characterized as "victim feminism." Newspaper reports stressed that the women in the calendar were agents of their own destinies, and hence, to be applauded for their participation; the idea came from the women themselves, with no male input or pressure, and the photographs, while provocative, were well within the bounds of good taste. Disassociating themselves from the "bad girls," one sportswoman explained, "We are prepared to pose for the sport but if it meant pulling our cozies [swimsuits] half way up our bums then we wouldn't be in it. We are not those sorts of people" (Porter, 1994).

Such arguments need to be situated in the broader context in which coercion and exploitation invariably accompany sexualized images of women. Thus, while it is unlikely that the provocative poses of male rugby players will render them, or other men, (hetero)sexually vulnerable, this is a distinct possibility in the case of women. Men's and women's bodies are read very differently in a society where men as a gender group have greater power and privilege, and where violence against women is a widespread and chronic social problem. Indeed, the predictable verbal leer from *Australian* newspaper columnist Jeff Wells would certainly confirm feminists' fears that, no matter how "tasteful" the image, some male viewers will subvert the intention with the usual objectifying and commodifying of female body parts.

On the other hand, from the perspective of gay and lesbian viewers of these kinds of images, alternative readings are possible. The men's sports calendars are popular with gay men, and the women's calendars no doubt have their share of lesbian admirers. All of this complexity is overlooked in the simplistic explanations about individual freedom and the (apparently politically neutral) project of marketing women's sport.

It should be noted that one lone feminist voice was reported in the media debate. The response of Federal Cabinet Minister Dr. Carmen Lawrence, who called the Golden Girls calendar not "the best way to go about drawing attention to women in sport" but indicative of sportswomen's "desperation," was sympathetically reported in the *Australian* and elsewhere (McLean, 1994). However, the position taken up by the majority of newspapers was that such objections were prudish, outdated and impractical.

LESBIANS IN THE LPGA – ONCE AGAIN

In May 1995, CBS television's golf analyst Ben Wright, subsequently described in newspaper reports as a "veteran" of 25 years, was quoted in Valerie Helmbreck's *Wilmington News Journal* article as saying, "Let's face facts. Lesbians in the sport hurt women's golf. When it gets to the corporate level that's not going to fly. They're going to a butch game and that furthers the bad image of the game. . . . Lesbianism on the tour is not reticent. It's paraded. There's a defiance in them in the last decade" (Helmbreck, 1995, p. 3c).

CBS pulled Wright from his scheduled coverage of the next day's LPGA tour and summoned him to a meeting in New York with CBS officials. Wright convinced the network that he had not made these statements. The president of CBS Sport subsequently called the *News Journal* story "totally inaccurate and extremely distasteful," and stated that Wright "is a man of integrity" who "has been done a grave injustice" (Craig & Blaudschun, 1995, p. 94). CBS allowed Wright to resume his broadcasting responsibilities the next day, and to take air time early in the tele-cast to renounce the story (Phipers, 1995, p. D2).

Several journalists (e.g., Finney, 1995, p. C7; Phipers, 1995) drew parallels between Wright's sexist and homophobic comments and reporter Jimmy Snyder's on-air racist characterizations of black football players, several years before, that had resulted in CBS firing him. This is not to suggest that racism in men's football was necessarily taken more seriously than sexism and homophobia in women's golf, although it is probably fair to say that the second-class status of women's sport was a factor here. However, in Snyder's case, a video provided conclusive proof that he did make the comments, whereas in Wright's case, it was the word of an older male golf analyst who had CBSs backing, against that of a younger female features writer from a small-town newspaper. This power differ-ence was noted by two newspaper journalists (Finney, 1995; Sandomir, 1995), and it was suggested that Wright let down his guard precisely because Helmbreck was female, "small-town" and therefore non-threatening (Finney, 1995).

Indeed, while Wright became a household word for a few days, Helmbreck was rendered a nameless *News Journal* reporter in the majority of newspaper stories, although *USA Today* carried her follow-up *News Journal* story (Helmbreck, 1995). In it, she reiterated Wright's statements, reported on the supportive comments of LPGA commissioner Charles Mechem and matter-of-factly discussed lesbian fans' strong interest in the LPGA, especially the Dinah Shore Classic in Palm Springs which, according to another source (Reed, 1994), has become "a landmark of lesbian subculture."

Very few of the articles reviewed here revealed any sympathy for Wright, and many seized the opportunity to ridicule him and to lampoon the entire situation, gaining easy mileage from the infamous "boob" comments. Several reporters criticized CBS for its superficial investigation and hasty reinstatement of Wright. In a sidebar titled "Wright no stranger to controversy," the *Chicago Tribune* gave prominence to another blot on Wright's record that CBS apparently ignored: His 1991 on-air reference to Japanese golfer Jumbo Izaki as "the Jap Ozaki, who is striking a blow for the foreigners" ("Wright no stranger to controversy," 1995, Section 4, p. 10).

LPGA players and commissioners, cited at length in newspaper accounts, were the most likely source of liberal-humanist rationales that relegated sexual issues to the realm of the private and the individual. "What we do afterward is our own business," said Michelle McGann (cited in Ormsby, 1995; p. B8), while Amy Alcott claimed that "these people out here [fans] don't care what anyone does in the bedroom" (cited in Craig, 1995; p. 76). According to incoming LPGA commissioner Jim Ritts (cited in Sheeley, 1995; p. D8): "I think on the LPGA, as in every walk of life, there is homosexuality and heterosexuality, and I think to the fans ... neither of those things has any impact on why they're out there. I don't think they [care] about their lifestyle."

In "the best defense is offense" category, Nancy Lopez asked: "Why doesn't he [Wright] talk about all the men on the tour who fool around on their wives?" (cited in Rubenstein, 1995, p. A17). Echoing the Australian "other side of the coin" arguments, she went on to say, "I wonder why it is that men can room together and women can't?" (Hodges, 1995; p. C1). Thus, Lopez implied that lesbian relationships are in the same category as marital infidelity, not a particularly helpful way to confront homophobia. In a more constructive attempt to address the criticism directly, LPGA commissioner Charles Mechem was widely quoted in the media as saying, "In my five years, I have not had one phone call or one letter from a sponsor or a fan suggesting that lesbianism is a problem" (Reinmuth, 1995; Section 3, p.1).

Not too surprisingly, the *San Francisco Chronicle* was the source of the most lesbian-positive analysis (e.g., Carroll, 1995; Ostler, 1995; Ryan, 1995), although there were other newspaper reports that also gave voice to progressive points of view: The issue of lesbianism "is a way for men to keep women in their place" (Amy Alcott, golfer, cited in Craig, 1995, p. 76). In terms of the *Chronicle,* columnist Jon Carroll said: "I hope one day to live in a world in which the commissioner can say, 'Our lesbian golfers, and there are many of them, serve as a shining example for young women across the nation, and any implication that they are injuring the sport is not true'" (1995, p. E8). A final example of media accounts that were lesbian-positive was the following statement from *Golfweek* Editor Steve Ellis: "CEOs (of corporations sponsoring LPGA) know they have gay people working for them, and I'm sure they wouldn't want their companies defined by the sexual preference of their employees. So they're not about to define the women's tour in that narrow way, either" (cited in Markiewicz, 1995, p. 7B).

It should be noted that Wright was eventually fired, although not because Helmbreck was believed. In January, 1996, Wright's contract with CBS was terminated after it was widely reported in the press (with one particularly damaging story from *Sports Illustrated)* that others had come forward to say they had overheard Wright making such comments.

CONCLUSIONS AND IMPLICATIONS

In their analyses of sport media's treatment of women, critical sport scholars have consistently shown how stereotyped images of femininity and (hetero)sexuality serve to marginalize and trivialize women's sporting efforts. In addition, homophobic representations of female athletes, most notably the symbolic erasure of women who participate in sports traditionally considered a male preserve, play a central role in perpetuating male sporting hegemony.

In this chapter we paid particular attention to one specific manifestation of homophobic media coverage that helps to maintain the balance of power in sport – the protective camouflage of feminine drag through which female athletes, gay and straight, are presented (and present themselves) in a hyper heterosexual mold either in a particular role (wife/mother) or in a particular style (hyper feminine). Such media representations serve to create a female sport culture in which traditional notions of heterosexuality are rigidly enforced. As a result, they counteract any potential a sporting environment has to offer as a place where passionate bonds and commitments among women are forged and solidified.

We conclude this chapter by arguing that feminist sports scholars need to identify and challenge the ways in which media representations equate women's sporting experience with a lesbian presence, particularly as that equation is used to prevent women's empowerment. We suggest that one critical starting point in this regard is to take a radical feminist approach, both theoretically and politically, and move away from an analysis of homophobia as an irrational fear, to one that sees it as a very logical response to the power of sport – the power to, in Rich's terms, create a "politically activating impulse." Such an impulse must resist a liberal humanist position that sexual orientation is an individual, private matter and that lesbians in sport are no different from their heterosexual counterparts. The case-studies presented here illustrate why we make this claim.

Not surprisingly, in all three cases, the lesbian presence, and not homophobia, continued to be constructed by the print media as a major barrier to the advancement of women's sport. But just as important was the finding that coverage that was not explicitly homophobic often reflected popular liberal humanist rationales: Denial that there was a problem, "other side of the coin" arguments, and the privatization of issues related to sexual orientation. In this latter regard, the overwhelming majority of media accounts – even those in more progressive outlets – took the position that who was or was not a lesbian was "no one's business" because such issues are a private, individual matter. As a result, any serious discussion of homophobia in general, and lesbianism in particular, as structural issues related to power, gender and sexuality went unexamined.

In contrast to the virulent backlash to gains made by progressive social movements, including the women's movement and lesbian and gay rights movements, the liberal focus in sport media's treatment of women may appear "reasonable" or "balanced." On closer examination, however, it is clear that such coverage continues to ignore the thorny questions of sexuality, power and privilege as they play themselves out in women's sport, and thus perpetuates the barriers to women's bonding and empowerment through sporting participation.

NOTE

1   Griffin (1993) points out the oppressive nature of such beliefs. First is the assumption that lesbians look like men. Second, large, physically powerful women are more likely to be labeled masculine, therefore lesbian, simply for possessing the physical attributes necessary to perform their sports.

Chapter 13

Prometheus Unbound: Constructions of Masculinity in the Sports Media

Don Sabo & Sue Curry Jansen

From the ancient Olympiad to the present, sport has been a primary site for defining, cultivating and displaying Western ideals of masculinity. The athletic male body – its discipline, symmetry, strength, and performance – is synonymous with power. It is the prototype valorized in Western art throughout the ages from the friezes on the Parthenon to the neoclassicism of Michelangelo's David to Rodin's rendering of The Thinker. Its visual resonances cut across Euro-American history, cultures and ideologies. It can, for example, be found in the god-like figures that represent national identity on coins, in Leni Riefensthal's Aryan Olympians, in socialist realism's sinuous workers, in the stylized ornaments on the hoods of early auto-mobiles, in the highly stylized figure of Hermes used to represent early radio communications, and in the fanciful representations of the superheroes, the "men of steel," who capture the imaginations of children, especially boys.

The linguistic counterparts of these images are so pervasive and so deeply embedded in the English language that a few strokes on the keyboard of any computer equipped with a thesaurus will yield a word list that conflates courage, strength, and power with masculinity, virility, and potency. In short, since antiquity the sexual economy of symbols in the West has equated masculinity with physical performance: with feats of physical strength, dexterity, and sexual prowess.

Within this semiotic system, the athlete represents the peak performance of manly youth. He is Prometheus unbound. He transcends, at least for a time, the ordinary constraints of embodiment and mortality. He presses beyond the natural limits of time, space, duration, resistance, and embodiment. The qualities he represents are synonymous with high performance on the battlefield, in the political sphere, and in science, technology, and industry, not just on the playing field. The foundation metaphors that animate the language games that operate within these disparate arenas of power are nearly interchangeable (Jansen & Sabo, 1994).

The vocabulary and images of athletic perfection provide the invidious standards against which all men are measured. They also represent the categorical antithesis against which women are defined and "othered" as always sexed, embodied, and subject to nature's rhythms and limitations. The highly stylized, hyperbolic, and melodramatic language of contemporary sport is suffused with the ancient mythos of Greek tragedy and its patriarchal narrative structures. Malszecki (1995) has traced the role that sport has played in the maintenance and production of heroes and warrior values from the time of Homeric Greece to the present. He argues that war has been a central experience of Western patriarchy. Building on Bell's (1975) theories of political linguistics, he asserts that male privilege and supremacy have "depended on the powerful but invisible workings of male-dominated discourse" that combine sport and war metaphors (p. 273). Similarly, McBride (1995) has excavated some of the linguistic moorings of androcentrism and masculinist power in the multiple intersections of sportive and military cultures.

Within this sexual economy of symbols, iconic and metaphoric representations of the athlete play crucial roles in the denial of embodiment, the Promethean myth, that lies at the heart of Western dualism (Bordo, 1987; Romanyshyn, 1989). The athletic body defies the normal limits of embodiment, rises above it, even escapes from it by performing like a god. The great athlete is body transmogrified to mind. He is transported by his superlative performance to Mount Olympus where he communes with the gods and achieves immortality.

The Promethean myth is a cultural archetype, an origin story, that reflects and reproduces the binary categorical structures of Indo-European languages. These categories, in turn, reinforce exaggerated emphasis on sexual difference within Western "gender regimes" (Connell, 1987). According to the Promethean myth, Zeus created the first woman, Pandora, in revenge for Prometheus' act of defiance in going to heaven to light his torch and bring fire back to earth. Pandora, of course, opened the forbidden box, and unleashed all the calamities and miseries that have spread throughout the world to afflict man forevermore. The mythology of this Greek origin story continues to resonate in a highly stylized and abstract form within the narrative structures, rhetorics, semantic resources, and visual representations of athletic performance in contemporary sports media.

In this chapter we examine some of the ways the discourse and images of contemporary sports media draw upon the resonances of this faded mythology. That is, we look at how these ancient, but resilient, metaphors continue to influence mediated representations of athletic prowess. We examine the rhetorical work they do in constructing ideological firewalls that maintain male dominance in sport. More specifically, we explore how representations of men in sports media are implicated in the social reproduction of the cultural and structural dynamics of dominance systems within the changing gender order. Connell (1987) uses the term gender order to refer to the "historically constructed pattern of power relations between men and women and definitions of femininity and masculinity that emerges and is transformed within varying structural contexts" (pp. 98–99). We draw upon feminist theory and a concept of hegemony loosely derived from Gramsci in order to discuss some of the ways that sports media feed into the constructions of hegemonic and counter-hegemonic masculinities.

Our task is made difficult for two reasons, one practical and the other sublimely nuanced. First, while there has been a good deal of research on representations of female athletes in sports media during the last 5–10 years, analytical focus on men, qua men, has remained rare. Since the publication of our previous essay on images of masculinity in sports media in 1992, very little additional research on men has appeared. Second, we are only partially conscious of the superimpositions of patriarchal values and customs on to the ritual of sport. As Leach (1976) observes, "We engage in rituals in order to transmit messages to ourselves" (p. 45). The problem is that we are too immersed in the taken-for-granted meanings and representations affixed to sports ritual to fully unpack them, despite our critical commitments. Catholics, for example, ordinarily do not consciously reflect upon the dynamics of ritualized cannibalism while receiving the Holy Eucharist, even though primitive stirrings of blood sacrifice resonate in this devotion. And so it is with mediated representations of men in sport. We only apprehend fleeting glimpses of the forest through the trees; the deep structures of Promethean myth, patriarchal warfare, hierarchy, misogyny, and sexual dimorphism, continue to elude awareness and confound analysis. Indeed, the willingness and ability of researchers and scholars to study and theorize women in sports media may, in and of itself, reflect women's foregrounded position as athletic anomalies, invaders of male territory, and outsiders within the masculinist culture of sport. Conversely, in a Gestalt-like fashion, men have been naturalized and backgrounded by their historical omnipresence in sport. This has served both to expand and deepen the androcentricity of representations of athleticism in Western cultures while, at the same time, camouflaging them.

WHY MEN MATTER TO FEMINIST ANALYSIS OF SPORTS MEDIA

Within media research as a whole there has been a growing recognition that the meaning of images cannot be studied without reference to the semiotic systems in which they are embedded (Gerbner 1970, 1996; Jhally & Lewis, 1992). Studying representations of women or men athletes without reference to the larger sexual economy of images that gives these representations meaning leaves the systems of domination in which the images are embedded unexamined and unchallenged. We have argued that representations of men and masculinity in sports media contribute to the social reproduction of cultural values and multiple systems of domination within the gender order as a whole. More simply stated, we see sports media as an important primer for gender socialization in contemporary times.

"Watching" sports is one of the few transgenerational experiences that men and boys, fathers and sons, still share in the post-Fordian economy. Sports talk, which today usually means talk about mediated sports, is also one of the only remaining discursive spaces where men of all social classes and ethnic groups directly discuss such values as discipline, skill, courage, competition, loyalty, fairness, teamwork, hierarchy, and achievement. Sports and sports fandom are also sites of male bonding. The images of manly character that boys and men consume in sports media become embodied by star athletes who reflect and reinforce men's collective power over women. Trujillo's (1994) careful analysis of the meanings constructed by media around beloved and heroized pitcher Nolan Ryan revealed that "power itself is masculinized as strength, force, control, toughness, and domination" (p. 98). Ryan has been portrayed as a "power pitcher," "power personality," "strong father," "cowboy," and sex symbol. Trujillo concludes that:

The sports media reinforce a traditional sense of masculinity when they emphasize the power of the male athlete, the institution of familial patriarchy, and mythos of the frontiersman, and the symbolism of the phallus.
(1994, p. 109)

The content analysis based research on sports media that has been published since the early 1980s has focused primarily on women athletes, specifically on the ways female athleticism has been marginalized and devalued by sports discursive and production practices that take manly prowess as the norm. Feminist researchers have concluded that sports media trivialize, eroticize and objectify women athletes and, by implication, that boys and men who "watch" sports perceive women athletes primarily in sexual or stereotyped terms. In these ways sports media are said to contribute to the social reproduction of hegemonic masculinity (Duncan, 1990; Higgs & Weiller, 1994; Kane, 1996, Kane & Greendorfer, 1994; Messner, 1988).

While there is much theoretical accuracy in these formulations, a current problem facing sports media researchers is that so little research actually examines how media producers and audiences actually perceive and construct interpretations of female athleticism. Many researchers have simply assumed that viewers perceive representations of men and women athletes in binary heterosexual terms; that is, neatly dividing images and meanings into either "masculine" or "feminine" realms.

To some degree, this practice is an artifact of method; few researchers using content analysis problematize the concept of gender. Conversely, researchers who problematize gender are likely to regard content analysis as epistemologically contaminated and use other methods.[1] Standard content analysis protocols treat gender dichotomously as a demographic variable rather than as a social "construct" or mode of "performance." This, in turn, predisposes content analysis researchers to develop dichotomous coding categories or gradients ranging, for example, from strong to weak, active to passive, sexualized to neutered, and so on.[2] As a result, sociologists studying sports media tend to divide "men" and "women" viewers into separate epistemological and gender-political camps rather than attending to the multiplicity of sense-making devices and interpretive strategies that male subjects engage when they consume sports media. Such an approach precludes discovery of any conundrums or emerging fractures in male hegemony in sport, sports media, or sports fandom. Yet, such fractures may be occurring. For example, a recent Harvard Business School survey of fans (as cited in the Women's Sports Market Report, 1996) at ten of the top women's NCAA basketball programs found that males comprised 40 percent of the fans. What brings these men to the women's games? Is it plausible to assume that when these male fans of women's basketball devote several hours of their time to watching women's NCAA Final Four games on television, they are simply subjectively "feminizing," "trivializing," or "eroticizing" the women players on the screen? It is far more probable that a variety of subjective interpretations of the women's game, women athletes, and men's relationships to men's sport and women's sport inform their interpretations of the event.

Since the late 1970s self-criticism within the feminist movement and feminist theory has exploded the heterosexist, racist, and classist foundations of the easy essentialism of this kind of naive realism. As a result, contemporary feminist researchers are acutely aware of the epistemological problems posed by research that imports *a priori* demographic categories. They are also hyper-sensitive to the pluralities of "differences", standpoints, identities, and interpretive priorities and skills that media researchers as well as media practitioners and members of media audiences engage in making sense of mediated messages (Harding, 1991, Jansen, 1993; Radway, 1984).

As the unmarked category, masculinity has not been as fully interrogated, and most mainstream social research still investigates predominantly male behavioral domains such as war, politics, science, and sport, without reference to the gendered constituents of these domains. Sports sociology generally follows this convention. Even research undertaken in the interests of progressive social agendas (e.g., studies of gender discrimination in sport and sports media) have generally been methodologically conservative. As a result, much research in sport sociology conducted during the late 1970s and 1980s essentialized gender.

With the publication of Connell's *Gender and Power* in 1987, however, sports sociology gained access to epistemologically sophisticated and richly nuanced schemata for conceptualizing gender, especially male hierarchies. Connell enjoined theorists to think in relation to "masculinities" rather than "masculinity." A "new men's studies" began locating and studying diverse masculinities in myriad cultural sites and structural circumstances; e.g., men of multiple racial and ethnic identities, different income levels, occupational groups, physical abilities, and sexual identities (Brod, 1987; Kaufman, 1986; Messner & Sabo, 1990; Sabo & Gordon, 1995). As awareness of gender diversity grows, it is likely that conceptualization of research on gender in sport media will move beyond its binary moorings. Two recent studies demonstrate the need to move in these directions.

First, Chroni, Bunker and Sabo (1996) analyzed a sample of 779 children's perceptions of the official pictograms developed by the Atlanta Committee for the 1996 Olympic Games (ACOG). These black-on-white silhouettes of thirty-one athletic events, which were purported to represent "universal human form," appeared in a wide variety of electronic and print media surrounding the 1996 Games. When the pictograms were first released nearly one year before the 1996 Games, an initial survey of fifty-six adult, élite women athletes found that 98 percent felt the pictures were mostly male figures. The researchers hypothesized that, if the pictograms did indeed overrepresent male figures, then children would identify them as being pictures of men rather than women. The overall results showed that 53 percent of the children perceived the pictograms as "either a man or a woman," 33 percent as "definitely a man," and 14 percent as "definitely a woman." Since one-third of the children perceived the figures as men, the researchers concluded that evidence for gender bias was verified. And yet, a secondary finding was that children appeared to be much less likely to perceive the figures as mostly men than did their adult counterparts in the initial pilot survey. It may be that today children bring less stereotyped gender expectations with them when interpreting athletic imagery than previous generations of adult women. The implication of this latter finding in the present context is that, similar to the adult women in this study, sports media researchers who conceptualize gender relations within a bipolar framework when designing their projects and interpreting data may, in effect, not be aware of more nuanced differences in the behavior, experiences, and/or perceptions of persons under study.

Second, in a detailed analysis of the media production and consumer reception of the annual *Sports Illustrated* swimsuit issue, Davis (1997) concluded that:

> The problematic aspect of *Sports Illustrated's* strategy, of securing a large audience of men by creating a climate of hegemonic masculinity, is that it tramples over women, gays/lesbians, people of color, and people from the (post) colonized world on the way to the bank.
>
> (p. 184)

Davis's research on the construction of male hegemony in sports media takes existing theory several miles further down the road. She shows how the swimsuit issue is produced in order to feature beautiful models inside a predominantly men's sports magazine and not women athletes *per se*. In other words, she shows what is obvious to media researchers but perhaps less so to sports sociologists; that is, commercial imperatives drive the production of these images. *Sports Illustrated* is being responsive to its target market, advertising buyers and the customers who actually purchase the magazine, not feminists who voice political objections to the issue.[3] If the swimsuit issue did not deliver readers to advertisers, it would not be produced.

SPORTS MEDIA, HIERARCHY, AND MEN'S VIOLENCE

Critical feminist sports scholars examine how sports media are implicated in cultivating, legitimating, and reproducing social inequalities. Since power relations have always been linked to violence and coercion, critical feminists have been concerned about potential linkages among sports, masculinity, and men's violence (Messner & Sabo, 1990). Sabo, Gray and Moore (1997) conducted in-depth telephone interviews with eighteen women who reported that they were regularly beaten by male partners during and/or shortly after televised athletic events. The researchers were not interested in settling the macro-sociological debate about whether regionally or nationally televised athletic events trigger widespread increases in the prevalence of domestic violence. Rather, the researchers assumed the legitimacy of clinical claims that in some instances televised sports are among an array of processes that can contribute to men's violence against women. In order to better understand the social-psychological dynamics involved, a descriptive, exploratory approach was used to elicit and analyze women's accounts of such beatings where they did occur.

The research findings lend credence to theoretical arguments that sports media can inform and inflame the social construction of violent masculinity. They concluded that sports media are not so much the "cause" of the violent actions of the men under study, but more as the "carrier" of psychosocial meanings and cultural practices that are linked to men's collective domination and control of women. Televised contact sports operated as part of a cultural setting that is condusive to domestic violence. Also involved were additional contributory factors such as alcohol and drug use, frustration, and gambling. Mediated sports appeared to function for these battering men as a cultural site in which a confluence occurred between psychosocial processes (e.g., boyhood and adult identification with sports and aggression, and interpersonal dynamics in family relationships) and the adoption of cultural scripts that equate manhood to violence proneness and domination over women. These dynamics receive highly ritualized expression in much sports media through production practices that often merge glorification of physical power, patriarchal narratives, and aggressive masculinity with video game sound effects and violence motifs, charged with emotion and drama.

Relationships among sports fandom, media representations of sports, patterns of media consumption, and real-life violence are complex and multi-dimensional and research on their "effects" does not lend itself to simple behavioral analysis. It is likely that the most powerful effects of violence in sports media, like other forms of televisual and filmic violence, may be in the cultivation of values and attitudes towards violence, power, and authority. As Gerbner (1996) points out, representation, *per se*, denotes power. In prime time television, men outnumber women by a ratio of about 3 to 1; moreover they are much more likely than women to play roles where they are the agents of dramatic action including perpetrators of violence. In prime time televisual coverage of professional sports, men may well outnumber women by a ratio of 100 to 1 or more. This simple fact tells us more than any other research finding about how televised sports programming cultivates the values of hegemonic masculinity among sports fans and within American culture more generally. The pervasive presence of the big men who are the big performers in big sports – their celebrity and Promethean charisma – communicate that the world of big men is still where the real action is. It is the arena of power and women are excluded from it.

INJURY, SACRIFICE, & MASCULINITY

Injury is everywhere in sport. Its ubiquity is evident in the lives and bodies of athletes who regularly experience bruises, torn ligaments, broken bones, aches, lacerations and muscle tears. "Injury reports" appear daily in local newspapers and in the analyses of television and radio commentators. *Sports Illustrated* markets its subscription campaign by giving new subscribers videotaped highlights of football players smashing one another's bodies. Injury is presented as entertainment, as spectacle. Television cameras regularly frame injured players and slow motion replays are used to allow viewers to see how an injury occurred and commentators to estimate the location or extent of the injury. Commentators sometimes comment on cuts and bleeding as a verbal supplement to depictions of bloodied athletes on the screen. Players who are shown being taped up on the sidelines or led into the locker room to be checked by the team doctor at half time are often praised by commentators upon returning to the action with words such "brave," "determined," "courageous," and "tough."

Despite the omnipresence of injury in sport media, there has been no research that searches out its cultural meanings or gendered dimensions. Sabo (1994) has speculated that the cultural fascination with injury in sport and sport media is related to the "Pain Principle," which is defined as the patriarchal cultural belief that pain is inevitable and that the endurance of pain enhances one's character and moral worth" (p. 3). He argues that the Pain Principle is an overarching narrative (or "metanarrative" in Lyotard's sense) or cluster of meanings that became installed in western Judao-Christian cultural traditions and, ultimately, fused with cultural practices surrounding traditional men's sports. The Pain Principle is simplistically evident in locker room slogans such as "No pain, no gain," "Sacrifice your body," "You gotta pay the price of victory," or "When the going gets tough, the tough get going." As an ideological process, the Pain Principle is closely tied to the construction of hegemonic masculinity, encouraging lesser-status males to comply with the expectations of dominant-status males, thereby preserving and shaping hierarchical relations among male groups in the larger gender order. The Pain Principle encourages boys and men to suffer through and play along with the hierarchically organized power relations that often do not serve their immediate interests.

Sports media valorize the athletes who surmount injury, endure pain, and return to the field of hierarchical endeavor. Ironically, as the athlete's body is "built up" in order to "move up" the competitive hierarchy, it is increasingly worn down. Many athletes are thus embroiled in a larger set of power relations inside and outside sport that are often exploitative and lead to physical entropy. Within the context of the competitive hierarchies that comprise late twentieth century gender regimes, athletes may be cultural prototypes modeling the behavior of (and for) the tough-minded, success-striving but increasingly expendable middle-managers of the post-Fordian economy who drive themselves day after day, only to be "benched" by stress-related illness or corporate downsizing or replaced by cybersystems. These portrayals may also be modeling stoicism and resilience for factory and service workers who must do more for less because they are "lucky enough" to have jobs in an economy that thrives on impermanence and liquidity. In short, we suspect that the media representations of pain and injury among athletes, particularly in televised productions, are ritualized expressions of more subtle relations of power that tap the Pain Principle and hegemonic masculinity for cultural and political legitimacy.

Within the commercial imperatives of television, the blood sacrifice of the athlete performs the same function that it does in dramatized violence. The camera briefly indulges the voyeurism of viewers, arouses their primal fears, then delivers them, in this emotionally vulnerable state, to commercial sponsors who offer the immediate relief of a Miller Lite beer or Big Mac (Goldsen, 1978). In short, blood sports trigger primal anxieties, and consumerism comes to the rescue with a quick fix.

Sports media may serve as a theater for male sacrifice. Like other forms of televisual violence, action, adventure or cartoons, violence on the playing field is too often presented as violence without consequence. Five big men sack the quarterback, plummeting him to the ground. His face is contorted in pain as the trainers attend to his sprained ankle. The camera demurely turns away and cuts to a commercial – lest we see the tears running down the face of Saturday's hero. Ten minutes later, however, taped and anesthetized, our hero is back at his post throwing the game-winning touch-down. Prometheus rebounds. In sport, unlike other television entertainments, the mayhem is real, not feigned or animated, and the action has real consequences for the athlete long after "the show" is over. The superhuman behavior modeled on screen is not behavior that any mortal, including the bravest quarterback in the history of football or the toughest of world heavyweight champions, can successfully emulate off screen. Yet, it has been a central model of heroic masculinity available to men and boys in Western popular culture.

The role that Mohammed Ali, the hero who too "courageously" fought too many rounds, played in lighting the Olympic Torch at the opening ceremonies of the 1996 Olympics seemingly confounded this venerable convention. Audience responses to Ali's presence in the pageant were mixed and frequently emotionally charged. President Clinton applauded the mainstreaming of the disabled. Some saw Ali as a false hero: not Prometheus with a broken wing, but an unpatriotic draft-dodger who surrendered his right to the golden circle long ago. Some, black and white, remembered him as a "black power" advocate, and interpreted his presence in racial terms rather than in terms of disability. Ali's real-life pain, however, the fact that his brain and health were basically destroyed by a brutal sport wherein mostly poor men bludgeon one another in search of fame and fortune remained obscure. The tidal flows of heroic disability and racial struggle hid the undertow of patriarchal intermale violence and blood sacrifice.

Finally, we wonder if the battery of men's bodies in televised contact sports may give men glimpses into their own vulnerability and victimization, especially poor and working-class men and men of color. The psychodynamic inference might read, "Since the men on the screen are vulnerable and beaten, so am I." McBride's (1995) analysis of the psychodynamics of sacrifice in contemporary patriarchal culture contends that sports provide a cultural theater for men to identify with the victims of violence which, in turn, generates rage and anguish that gets projected on to the female other. Drawing on the theories of Bataille (1985) and Irigaray (1985), he argues that within the "masculinist psychic economy" of American culture, war, football, and battery are interrelated expressions of men's need for power and control. However, the suppression of men's needs for intimacy necessitated by conformity to traditional masculinity results in emotional ambivalence and deep-seated frustrations which, in turn, are channeled individually through battery and collectively through gang rape or war. The links between aggression in sports media and men's rage, anxiety, and violence remain under-researched and unknown.

EROTICIZATION OF MALE ATHLETES

Feminist critiques of representations of female athletes focus on the sexualization and ojectification of female athletes especially gymnasts, swimmers, divers and figure skaters. Vertical camera pans of the young, scantily-clad, bodies of gymnasts and divers posed to perform reproduce the clichéd conventions soft-core pornography, but do so in concert with voice-overs that extol the child-like innocence and vulnerability of the athlete. These are the sports that draw big audiences for female athletes – individual, rather than team competitions, where pretty faces, supple bodies and moving narratives provide the media frames.

In contrast, men who achieve in contact team sports draw the big television audiences. In contact sports where male bodies are not protected by padding and multiple layers of clothing (e.g., boxing, wrestling, and basketball), a highly articulated set of rules polices the zones of contact and athletes who cross the boundaries are charged with fouls. A curious kind of dance of intimacy and retreat is played out in these sports – a dance that is pragmatically designed to protect against injury, but does so with a hyperbolic symbolic excess that seems to both gesture to and issue interdictions against homeroticism. One cannot, for example, imagine wrestlers regularly patting each other on the buttocks the way football players do. Football uniforms, pads, helmets, cleats, and an array of face and neck guards are designed for protection against injury in this dangerous contact sport. But the visual impact of the pragmatics of these designs amplify the ritualized displays of hegemonic masculinity by making big men even bigger, larger than life. Like gladiators of old, they are literally men of steel, armoured and posed. Because the bodies of football players are protected by armor, the touch zones are more fluidly defined. Direct body contact is the point of the game, and men make physical contact with other men on the playing field in ways that are rigidly proscribed by heterosexism everywhere else.

In this respect, football might be thought of as a kind of medieval carnival ritual where inversion of the rules on the field emphasizes their pervasive intractability everywhere else. The media frames that are used to represent this carnival exaggerate the effect; e.g., low camera angles further amplify the already exaggerated bulk of the players, the hyperbolic language of sportscasters exaggerate the significance of the contest, the roar of the crowd and the fans mugging for the camera become part of the performance, the spectacle. The camera romances glamorous women in the stands or scantily-clad cheerleaders that perform just beyond the boundaries that separates the Promethean realm of hyper-masculine men from the mundane realities inhabited by ordinary mortals.

THE "WOMAN QUESTION" IN SPORTS MEDIA

Sport has remained a remarkably resilient bastion of hegemonic masculinity despite the fact that in the last twenty-five years women athletes have rewritten all the record books and defied all of the conventional wisdom about the limits of female athletic performance. Although women's record-breaking achievements have been the real sporting news of the late twentieth century, these achievements were virtually unreported by mainstream media until very recently. Indeed, 1995 was the first year that newspaper coverage of women's athletics exceeded that of "dogs and horses" (Lopiano, 1996). As a result, when critical feminist media research has examined representational practices in sports media, it has focused almost exclusively on the ways sports media stereotype, trivialize, marginalize or ignore women's athleticism.

This focus has made good political sense. It has provided activists with a knowledge base that has brought about changes in the ways that women are represented in sports media. The impact of these efforts was dramatically demonstrated in the production decisions that went into United States television coverage of the 1996 Centennial Olympic Games in Atlanta.

NBC Television, which won the United States broadcast rights for the Olympics, consciously choreographed a production plan that was designed to target a female audience. In doing so, NBC attracted the largest Olympic television audience since 1976; midway through the seventeen day coverage, the audience was 50 percent female, 35 percent male, and 15 percent children and adolescents of both genders (Remnick, 1996). NBC's Director of Research, Nicholas Chiavone, actually drew on feminist theory in devising the production plan, albeit an essentialist reading of Carol Gilligan's *A Different Voice* that might drive many feminist theorists to exchange their pens for swords (Remnick, 1996). Yet, despite the retrorationale, the soap-operatization of the "up close and personals" and the camera's persistent romance with women in spandex and leotards, NBC's 1996 production did put more high-achieving women athletes on camera in front of more viewers than ever before, and it did feature a long, serious, interview with Anita DeFrantz, International Olympic Committee member and President of the Amateur Athletic Foundation of Los Angeles, conducted by Bob Costas, arguably the most influential and respected commentator in sports broadcasting today.

There were sound commercial reasons for NBC's "scientific campaign to shape their broadcasts to a feminine sensibility" (Remnick, 1996, p. 26). Men control the remote control in most households (Gray, 1992). When sports is "on," especially the highly publicized and widely discussed Olympics, NBC could assume that, as David Remnick (1996) put it, "Men, being men, would be there already, a Bud in one mitt and the clicker in the other" (p. 27). If the female audience could also be delivered to advertisers, however, program ratings and network profits would go up; and, not incidentally, women viewers would serve to inhibit the clicks in the mitts. NBC was responding to both sports marketing research and its misreadings of feminist research in designing a production that would "go for the gold" by showcasing United States women's Olympic performances. Commenting on the coverage, broadcaster, former Olympian, and President of the Women's Sports Foundation, Wendy Hilliard, stated:

> Sports coverage is becoming more inclusive – no longer is it a predominantly male domain, from both the participant and spectator perspective . . . NBC's programming decision would not have occurred without the support of corporate advertisers who are increasingly using sports and female athletes to appeal to female consumers.
>
> (Women's Sports Foundation, September 23, 1996, p. 1)

Women's sports advocates recognize that the increases in girls' and women's participation in sports and fitness activities since 1972 has been simultaneously fed by
legal pressures wrought by the passage of Title IX, the activism within the women's
sports movements, and the accelerating efforts by corporations and entrepreneurs
to tap opportunities for profit-making. As Hilliard (1996, p.3) notes,

> These female consumers are now active recreational and competitive sports-
> women, thanks to Title IX. In 1970, only one out of 27 high school girls
> played varsity sports. Today the figure is now one of three!

From the corporate perspective, fans are consumers. Professional football
player representative, David Meggesey (1993) reported that National Football
League management sometimes refer to fans as "fannies in the seats." Sports media
cultivates fans by feeding their passion for sport between games and seasons.
Media furnish Monday morning quarterbacks with ammunition and authority. Above
all, however, they sell fans to advertisers. According to Rosner (1989), sports media
are expected to generate a gross national sports product of $121.1 billion by the
year 2000, while projections for sports advertising revenues on television are $11.5
billion and, for all advertising revenues combined, $25 billion.

The sports entertainment industry has nearly saturated the domestic male
market. Females now constitute the major growth center in the United States for
sports, fitness, and sports media and sports-related purchasing. A related demographic phenomenon can be observed in the computer industry, which ignored
women consumers in its advertising and marketing campaigns until upscale,
domestic, male markets began to stagnate. In "going for the gold" of women's
sports, corporations are acting out of enlightened self-interest; in doing so, they are
also advancing some of the goals of women's sports activists.

Given that, in other parts of American popular culture, corporate sponsorship
routinely cultivates artificial, unhealthy, and racist stereotypes of idealized female
bodies, some critical feminists are understandably uncomfortable riding the tide
of this contradiction of capitalism (Kilbourne, 1995). Yet, this uneasy partnership –
Herbert Marcuse (1964) would have called it "co-optation" – of women athletes'
goals and corporate goals is a pragmatic accommodation to the realities of the post-
Fordian economy. In this new world order, global corporations, not nation-states,
have become the new arbiters of power. Some of us are deeply troubled by these
developments (Jansen, 1988, 1991). However, asking women's sports advocates to
renounce such partnerships is asking them to sacrifice their cause and resources
to the purity of a retro-utopian politics. Building a better world does require sacrifice, but it also requires realistic assessments of what sacrifices constitute meaningful resistance and what sacrifices simply do our opponents work for them. The old
lifeboat ethic, "women and children first," usually meant they were the first to drown.

GAY ATHLETES IN SPORT

Why are sports journalists simultaneously so attuned to the presence of lesbians in
sport, but so oblivious to the presence of gay men in athletics? The issue of lesbian

athletes has not been covered by television as much as by radio and print media. Radio talk shows, maudlin and occasionally upfront gross, are sometimes eardrum forums for men lamenting and demonizing lesbians or "dykes" in sport. While feminists have accused sports journalists of end-stage homophobia, Crosset's ethnographic research of the Ladies Professional Golf Association (LPGA) shows that male journalists are curious about the personal lives and sexuality of the women professionals. He asserts that many of the men journalists who cover the LPGA tour seem to envy women's athleticism. Some male sport journalists use lesbian-baiting as a device for discrediting women's athletic performance and ability. But, as Crosset (1995) explains, the lesbian-baiting goes further than woman-jock envy:

> The pursuit of stories about lesbians on the tour serves to preserve golf as a "naturally" manly pursuit. This sort of coverage ensures the comfort of the sports media's primary market – men. The media industry has a stake in maintaining the image of sport as a resource for doing masculinity. It sells.
>
> (p. 126)

Put another way, lesbian-baiting preserves male hegemony in sport and society.

In contrast, sports writers largely ignore the presence of gays and bisexuals as if they hardly exist in sports or only exist in "feminized" sports like figure skating. This same pattern of hyperawareness of lesbians and "look-the-other-wayism" in relation to gay and bisexual men athletes is also evident among sports scientists and critical scholars. Academic focus has been mainly on lesbian athletes. Why?

It may be that gay men represent a unique threat to the maintenance of male hegemony in sport when compared to that of lesbian women. Just as Prometheus challenged the Gods of Olympus by stealing their fire, gay athletes may challenge the logic of the gender regimes of contemporary Western culture. Not only is the gay male athlete perceived as a defecting from heterosexual models of masculinity, but his presence in the theater of sport ruptures cultural associations among masculinity, athleticism, hardness, toughness, and heterosexual potency. The gay male athlete is not only a traitor or transgressor, but the mere acknowledgment of his presence in the locker room symbolically erodes the efficacy of men's fantasies about a unitary or monolithic hegemonic, heterosexual masculinity.

The comparative silence of sports media professionals and sports scholars around gay male athletes mirrors the "don't ask, don't tell" policy on gays in the military. Few, it seems, are willing to acknowledge that presence of gays in the proverbial shower. This reticence affirms Simone de Beauvoir's (1974) assertion that denial is the first principal of patriarchy. Hegemonic masculinity's idealizations of "manly men" are extraordinarily fragile constructs. Made of myth, these ideals are constantly contradicted by reality, and, as a result, they constantly require aggressive reaffirmation. Prometheus, it seems, can only be apprehended through the mist by "wannabees" who keep one eye closed.

MEN OF COLOR, COLORLESS MEN

Contrary to previous research on media representation of African-American athletes, Sabo, Jansen, Tate, Duncan, and Leggett (1996) found that producers of televised international athletic events now appear to be generally attuned to issues of racial representation and cultural diversity. They showed that commentators did not construct negative representations of black athletes. Content and rhetorical analyses revealed that black athletes were significantly less likely than Asian and white athletes to receive negative evaluations from commentators. Additional qualitative analyses of the personal interview segments showed that race, ethnicity, or nationality did not appear to determine the types of stories or metaphors that producers and commentators used to frame athletes. In relation to black athletes, media professionals appear to be consciously and purposively responding to past criticisms of prejudicial treatment of blacks in sport media and televisual media in general (Dates & Barlow, 1990; Riggs, 1991).

The less frequent use than in the past of physical descriptors and negative evaluations with reference to black athletes suggests a heightened sensitivity, or perhaps a guardedness among commentators, concerning negative representations of black athletes. Other research also suggests greater sensitivity in televisual portrayals of African-American males (Gerbner, 1993), although this sensitivity frequently lends itself to multiple and multiply coded readings (Jhally & Lewis, 1992). Within broadcast sports media, it may be that producers are genuinely responding to pleas by civil rights advocacy groups for fair treatment. This responsiveness also has pragmatic advantages both domestically, where the demographics of US network television audiences are becoming less white and less affluent, and internationally, where US television programmers seek to cultivate new markets for exports of US sports media and products.

Nevertheless if, as we have suggested, representation on the screen communicates power and absence communicates powerlessness, then African-American male athletes have to be conceived as a powerful presence in US sport and sports media despite the fact that they remain grossly underrepresented in positions of authority in the US including management positions in sports and media industries (Melnick & Sabo, 1994). How can this apparent conundrum be explained? Black athletes are, in fact, much more of a presence in professional sports in the US than would be predicted based upon their presence in the American population at large. They are a dominant presence (in sheer numbers as well as prominence as "stars" in professional basketball; they are also a powerful presence, and on some teams the dominant presence, in football and baseball.

In short, some (perhaps even most) of the leading stars in the big three professional men's sports in America are black men. They have symbolically stolen the fire of Prometheus. But what black men achieve on the field – in sport and sports media – they are still largely denied in other spheres of American life. Jhally and Lewis (1992) describe this contradictory acknowledgement and denial of black agency as "enlightened racism". Representations of black male athleticism draw on uniquely American representational practices that have their roots in the stereotypes that emerged out of the Reconstruction, which politically empowered and then culturally disenfranchised black males. Eugene O'Neill's (1972) character,

Emperor Jones, is a prototype embodiment of this stereotype. Powerful but dangerous, his fire burns briefly and eratically; and, if this fire is not domesticated by accommodation to the rules of white culture, it usually comes to a tragic end. Indeed, O. J. Simpson's rise to celebrity status during the 1970s and 1980s was predicated on his enculturation into white corporate culture, while his disgrace as an accused murderer was often grounded in a black racial identity.

Leola Johnson (1996) has analyzed the print and electronic media texts that at once framed and facilitated O.J. Simpson's success at marketing himself as a "colorless commodity in American culture." She docments how "O.J." became the first black athletic hero who "crossed over" into the world of major corporate sponsorship, paving the way for black male advertising icons Michael Jordon and Shaquille O'Neal. Black male superathletes such as Jackie Robinson, Wilt Chamberlain, Kareem Abdul Jabbar, Arthur Ashe, and Mohammed Ali achieved heroic status but with little financial returns vis à vis corporate advertising. Like Asians are sometimes described today, O.J. Simpson became a "model minority" for corporate America, who rejected his ghetto roots and embraced materialist culture with both arms. Johnson's analysis of Simpson's career reveals that his credentials as an athlete role model were bolstered by his public condemnation of the black athlete revolt of the late 1960s and refusal to smoke marijuana (he tried it but "didn't inhale"). Simpson also smooth-talked to the press about his love of family though his sexual exploits with women were also borderline legendary among the male journalists who hung out in the locker room subculture. Simpson was forever affable, echoing the "smiling Negro" tradition in American culture (e.g., Aunt Jemimah), which allowed the press and whites to feel good about race relations and safe in their beds and living rooms. Simpson's image of "easygoing super-manhood" was further amplified by televisual devices that permitted viewers to get "up close and personal" with "O.J." and slow-motion replays of his running exploits. In short, Johnson's deconstruction shows how Simpson's success among media was based in his image as a colorless male supremacist, the "white man's Negro and a man's man."

It is ironic that, amidst the media coverage of Simpson's trial for murder, the auras of corporate colorlessness and socially-acceptable male supremacy largely evaporated. The "race card" was so easily played in the racially divisive O.J. Simpson trial because these stereotypes lie close to the surface of the American subconsciousness, a fact which also explains the obsession of both white and black Americans with the case and their disparate interpretations of it.

This is not to suggest that the new sensitivity that television brings to its representations of black male athletes is less than laudable. To the contrary, it marks a significant improvement over the representational practices of the past, but it remains what Marlon T. Riggs (1991) called a "color adjustment"; i.e., an improvement of images of blacks on-screen that allows white audiences to deny the effects of racism off-screen. Improvement in the representational practices used to cover black athleticism is therefore a partial victory in both senses of the term. It is not a victory that has wrought any significant improvements in the conventions used to represent black women (Dines & Humez, 1995). Moreover, the new racial consciousness of sports broadcasters has not yet led to modifications in the conventions used to represent Asian or Hispanic athletes; these groups continue to be

represented in ways that resonate closely with American racial and ethnic stereotypes about these groups (Sabo, Jansen, Tate, Duncan, & Leggett, 1996).

CONCLUSION: PANDORA'S FIRE?

No feminist archeology has exposed the deep structure of the gender politics of
Western sports discourse. Feminist sports media research has yet to produce its
Mary Daly (1973). Our analysis of the ways in which deeply embedded cultural
myths and stereotypes continue to resonate within the semiotic resources from which
sports media draw its language and images is intended to be suggestive rather than
definitive. We believe it does, however, demonstrate that sports talk, fandom, media,
and celebrity are potent forces in resisting challenges to hegemonic masculinity.
Yet, we also acknowledge that there are fractures in the prevailing gender order,
which these discursive practices can only partially repair.

The future is not assured but political activism and critical scholarship have
made a difference in sports and sports media during the past two decades. Lest we
forget or underestimate the significance of these achievements, this has been
a period when the Right has dominated political and economic life in America, a
time when many of the egalitarian initiatives of the 1950 and 1960 stalled or
reversed course. Pandora may yet claim the fire.

NOTES

1   Goffman (1979) both problematized and relied on a form of content analysis in his
    analysis of gender relations in print advertisements.
2   Sophisticated forms of content analysis avoid this trap by using intermediate interpre-
    tive methods (for example, semantic differential tests), reflexive coding conventions, and
    independent coders in constructing categories of analysis.
3   This statement is not intended to imply that media researchers are more prescient than
    sports sociologists, but rather that they bring different conceptual apparatus to the enter-
    prise. Where sociologists think in terms of social institutions, sport, politics, the family,
    church, business, etc., which make multiple claims on individuals, media research focuses
    its attention more narrowly on media institutions. In the US that means media researchers
    study a commercial system, and that the profit principle is therefore foregrounded in
    their analyses. The conceptual distinction is subtle but consequential. Sociological
    analysis of sport provides a framework for imaginative historical and comparative explo-
    rations of the institution of sport, while media research secures a more pragmatic micro-
    analysis of how cultural production actually works within a commercial system.

Part four

MediaSport

Audiences

Chapter 14

Reading the Sports Media Audience

Garry Whannel

> Given television's conspicuousness in contemporary culture and society, this poverty of discourse, this lack of understanding is rather embarrassing indeed, if not downright scandalous.
>
> From *Desperately Seeking the Audience* (Ang, 1990, p. 53)

Despite decades of media research, the audience is still a remarkably difficult area of analysis. A long tradition of effects research had difficulty finding convincing evidence to support the more morbid fears about the impact of portrayals of violence. Research into the uses to which the media has been put provides evidence of an "active" audience, but at the same time this research raises questions about whether simple categorizations of use can adequately represent the complexities of lived experiences with media. Research within the media industry has been instrumental in producing detailed and (presumably) accurate information about patterns of consumption, but is far less revealing about the motives, feelings and pleasures of viewing.

Cultural studies has generated two distinct approaches to the audience. The first, influenced by Foucault and other post-structuralists, is that as the world can only be understood in and through discourses, and individuals cannot be seen as unified, enunciating subjects, the audience is best understood through analysis of texts. To some, indeed, the audience itself is radically unknowable. The second approach seeks to draw on ethnographic methods – participant observation, open-ended interview – in order to build up a more elaborate picture of the place of television and other media in people's whole way of living.

In this chapter, I will concentrate on the television audience, and the various ways in which people have tried to understand it. I will review some media industry material, outline trajectories in media and cultural studies, and finally explore in greater detail the application of developments in cultural studies to analysis of media sport audiences.

Even though sport on television can win huge audiences it still has relatively low status as a cultural form. When television critics discuss sport coverage it is typically either in the form of satire and parody, as in the writing of Clive James, or derision of the large amounts of air-time devoted to it (e.g., Shulman 1973). While such criticism has little to do with the expectations of audiences, the low status of television forms such as game shows, soap operas and sport is constantly marked and underlined by journalistic writing on television. The media industry in general, on the other hand, takes a great interest in the size and composition of its audience and this is particularly true of television sport producers (McVicar, 1982).

THE MEDIA INDUSTRY

The media industry focuses on the size, habits and demograpic profiles of audiences, for obvious reasons. Newspaper circulation figures and television viewing figures are available, usually with break-downs into age class, gender, age and region. This information in itself tells us a certain amount about the media sport audience. Sports pages of newspapers are, not surprisingly, read far more heavily by men than women, and in Britain the distinction between tabloid and broadsheet newspapers produces a strong class distinction. The larger circulation tabloids, with a working class readership, focus largely on soccer, boxing and racing, while the broadsheets cover a wider range of sports.

On television, some sporting events – the Olympic Games, the World Cup, the Super Bowl and the World Series – have a unique ability to win and hold large audiences, and the neat regularity of television's schedules will be torn apart to cover them. Much sport, though, only has a relatively small appeal, and its place outside of peak-time reveals that it is there partly to provide cheap programming to balance the more expensive drama and light entertainment material.

Sport audiences divide along gender lines more markedly than most program forms, which have a relatively even gender balance. Only sport and soap operas show a marked gender preference, with more men for sport and more women for soap operas. Even here, gender difference is rarely much more than 60 to 40. Such figures, however serve to obscure the actual nature of the viewing experience. People recorded in audience figures as present in the room with the set turned on are not necessarily actively watching, nor have they necessarily chosen the program, as Collett's research vividly demonstrated (Collett & Lamb, 1986). The video material from Collett's research (some of which was included in the Channel 4 series *Open The Box* in 1986), portrays living rooms with a wide range of activities going on while the set is tuned in. At times programs are watched with intensity, but sometimes no-one in the room is paying any attention at all. People iron, read, run the vacuum cleaner, practice the flute, dance, kiss and sleep in front of the television set. Of the 40 percent of women recorded amongst the typical sports audience, we have very little evidence as to the proportion of them who are active and selective viewers.

Viewing, as Morley has argued, is always the outcome of domestic practices in which some are making active choices and some are acquiescing (Morley,1986). Leisure studies research has suggested that women and men experience leisure time differently. Typically, men experience a sharp division between work and leisure. Women, for whom the home is seen more typically as a sphere of production as well as consumption, are more likely to experience a blurred distinction between work and leisure. Domestic labor is, still, mostly performed by women and consequently television watching is often combined with household chores like ironing or mending clothes.

Major sport events are a common pretext for popular journalistic renditions of the anger of non-sports fans, often women, at finding favorite programs displaced for sport. Media industry research has in the past probed the impact on audiences of such events. The BBC Audience Research Department reviewed findings about audience attitudes and viewing patterns during three soccer World Cups (BBC, 1976). In 1966, England's appearance in a match could add around 10 percent to the viewing figures. In 1974, when England had failed to qualify, Scotland's appearances added 5–6 percent to the audience. Men were, in 1974, much more likely to watch than women – 36 percent of men, 18 percent of women (a split of 66 to 33). But the ratio changed during competition – it started at 75 to 25, and by the end was nearer 60 to 40.

BBC research in the mid-1980s reported that 75 percent of men and 45 percent of women had an interest in one or more sports. 70 percent of middle class and just over 50 percent of working class respondents expressed a sports interest. Since 1979 there has been a decline in the proportions of sports enthusiasts expressing interest in each of the sports covered in the survey, with the single exception of snooker (Marles, 1984). Variations in audience size mean that a small proportion of women in a big audience is of greater significance than a large proportion of a small audience. In 1988 the sports in the UK with the highest proportion of adult male viewers were rugby, cricket, baseball, soccer, American Football and golf, but in no case were adult men more than 56 percent of the total audience. The sports with the highest proportion of women in the audience were skating, tennis, and equestrian sports, all with audiences including over 53 percent adult women. This appears to echo the supposed masculine/feminine orientation of these sports. Yet if audience size is taken into account, far more women watched the major sports, soccer, cricket, athletics, snooker, golf and racing. Only tennis had both a high proportion of women and a high overall audience. (*Independent*, April 4, 1989)

There were also marked differences in class. The audience for television sport, like the population as a whole, is predominantly working class. The largest proportions of social class AB (middle class) were to be found in the audiences for rugby, skiing, tennis, golf and cycling, while those sports with the largest proportion of CDEs (working class) were wrestling, darts and boxing. Young (16–24) viewers had a marked preference for baseball, swimming, American Football, sumo wrestling and cycling, almost exclusively Channel 4 sports (*Independent*, April 4,1989). Yet these percentage figures can be misleading. The 1988 total figures suggest that in every demographic category the most watched sports were snooker and soccer, along with the Olympic Games and multiple sports programs such as Grandstand and Sportsnight. Among both men and women, and in social classes

AB, these four were followed by cricket, athletics, racing, tennis and golf. We need to know far more about which members of households choose to tune in to which sports, and what degree of resistance this produces from other members.

Barnett (1990, p. 80) argues that the ratings conceal considerations such as time of day and day of week that are key determinants on the availability of viewers. Cricket, shown on summer afternoons, can rarely get a big audience, whereas snooker, shown on winter evenings, has greater potential. Channel loyalty, the inheritance factor, and the range of channel choice also intervene, as Goodhart (1975) established,while Barnett argues that watching television sport is increasingly a default activity . . . "when there is nothing else to do, television takes over" (1990, p. 85). The ratings figures also conceal activity within programs – there is a substantial audience turnover during programs. In some soccer broadcasts, 90 percent more watch the last 5 minutes than the first 15 minutes.

Barnett identifies familiar problems with survey information; reliable data collection is expensive and is limited to occasional ad hoc studies; question standardization between different research is rare; sample sizes of 1000 only give accuracy with 3–4 percent variation; and responses to sport related questions are greatly affected by the time of year. However, he suggests that the Target Group Index figures do allow for some comparisons. These figures suggest that between 1969–89 in the UK there appears to be a substantial decrease in levels of absolute interest. With one notable exception, every major sport has experienced some decline in television popularity over the years. This downward trend is mitigated by periods of national success or the popularity of outstanding individuals.

Barnett suggests that this is not because of a change in sports – it is highly unlikely that all have become less interesting. Nor is it because of changes in the coverage as technical and professional standards have risen. Rather it is due to changes in the audience, for whom television is increasingly a default activity. Changes in scheduling do contribute. There has been an extension of television into the night and morning – periods with low audiences; the amount of sport in peak time has diminished, and there are an increasing number of minority sports. The age and gender differences in popularity of particular sports make scheduling in peak time unlikely. Barnett suggests that the American experience is somewhat different, suggesting "a great deal less antipathy among American women towards television sport than among British women" (1990, p. 104).

Ien Ang has argued that in their practices media industries construct an object, the television audience, that does not exist and fail to take account of very real diversities and complexities. She argues that "institutional knowledge is not interested in the social world of actual audiences; it is in 'television audience' which it constructs as an objectified category of others to be controlled" (Ang 1990, p. 154). Ang asserts that "academic researchers have often all too easily complied with the institutional point of view in their attempts to know the television audience" (1990, p. 155).

THE EMERGENCE OF MEDIA AND CULTURAL STUDIES

In the last forty years academic analysis of the media has developed from a small sub-branch of sociology into a large, diverse and complex field of analysis in its own right. Yet this increasingly sophisticated body of work has had remarkably little impact on a public agenda that is still dominated by the "effects" problematic. Popular concerns over the power of the media, characteristically centered upon sexuality, violence, morality, and impact on the young, continually re-emerge despite the general tendency of media research to refute the "direct effects" hypothesis.

Early study of the media, framed by concern over the role of propaganda in the rise of European fascism and Stalinist communism in the 1930s, and by the use of propaganda in the Second World War, was dominated by the hypodermic needle model. This stimulus-response model aimed to test, sometimes in laboratory conditions, the audience reaction to specific messages. It soon became clear that the message could not be considered in isolation, and the impact of peer groups, and other associates on the reception of messages needed to be taken into account (see for example, Lazarsfeld et al., 1944).

The effects studies of the 1950s suggested that certain people within any group, often those with greater status, intellectual grasp, or simply more media exposure, functioned as opinion leaders, and that media messages worked through them, in what became termed the two-step flow (Katz & Lazarsfeld, 1955). Much of this research centered on political messages and on the measurement of attitude or voting intention. However attempts to "prove" this more sophisticated variant of the stimulus-response model typically found that media messages were more likely to produce a reinforcement than a change in attitude (Klapper 1960). While the media did not appear to have fabulous powers to determine what people thought, it did however appear to have a power to determine what people thought about. Consequently, research began to focus on the role of cultural producers as gatekeepers (Breed, 1955; white, 1964) and agenda-setters (Cohen, 1963).

While work within this tradition has continued, a counter-tradition developed in the 1960s that invited us to re-frame the question and, rather than asking "what do the media do to people?", asked "what do people do with the media?" This form of research, which focused on the uses of the media and the gratifications it provided, became known as uses and gratifications research (see, for example, Blumler & Katz, 1974).

Others were critical of the dominance of quantitative method (Lull,1990) and attempted to draw on a different qualitative empirical alternative, rooted in the work of Garfinkel on ethnomethodology, Edmund Husserl on humanistic phenomenology, and Alfred Schutz on social intersubjectivity. The qualitative strand produced work in the 1960s and 1970s that encouraged the integration of the study of interpersonal communication and the media (for example, Blumer, 1969; Goffman, 1959; Hymes, 1964).

In the 1960s the vast majority of this research was located within sociology; media and cultural studies were still not well established as distinct academic fields. In the process of their formation as interdisciplinary fields, they incorporated and borrowed from other academic disciplines, notably history, literature, and linguistics. Developments in Britain from the late 1960s provided key moments. The study of media and film, hitherto largely shaped by the precepts of either sociology or literary criticism, was being revolutionised by the impact of French structuralism, most notably the anthropology of Levi-Strauss (1967), and the linguistics of Saussure (1959), as fused in the semiology of Roland Barthes (1967). These developments, which took place primarily in the journal *Screen* and the work of the British Film Institute, had a formative impact on the field of media and cultural studies which remains profound and central.

During the 1970s, as film and media studies developed, Birmingham University's Centre for Contemporary Cultural Studies (founded in 1964) attempted to find a satisfactory synthesis of culturalist and structuralist traditions. For some, this synthesis was shaped and informed by the work of the Italian Marxist Antonio Gramsci. Others, accepting the force of the structuralist critique of "agency," and its insistence on the power of language and ideology, progressed to the post-structuralist work of Foucault and others. These analyses regarded human subjectivity as constructed by discourses and hence "audience" was best understood as a product of discursive formations. An alternative culturalist strand, which rejected the individualized and empiricist precepts of mainstream quantitative sociology, advocated the use of ethnographic and participant observation methods as ways of exploring people in their cultural contexts (see Hebdige,1979; Hobson 1982; Morley, 1980; Willis, 1978).

Stuart Hall's elaboration of the encoding–decoding model theorized the possibility of a range of audience readings, while retaining the determinant influence of the text (Hall, 1980). While alternative or oppositional readings might be possible, the text had a systematic tendency to produce a dominant, or preferred reading. This model was explored in the work of David Morley, who followed up text analysis of the program *Nationwide* (1980) with extensive research into the ways in which the program could be "read" by a range of audiences (Morley, 1981). The problematic here centered not so much on what the media do, but rather on how the consumption of media texts involved the activity of decoding to produce meaning.

This pioneering work on decoding had two notable features. First, the subjects viewed the program in groups in non-domestic situations, a limitation that Morley (1981) acknowledged (see also Jordin & Brunt, 1986; Lewis; 1983). Second, the concept of decoding worked best with those areas of media production – news and current affairs – where meaning and the cognitive dimension are of prime importance. Analyzing baseball, Roberta Pearson (1986) has argued that, just as the texts of sport are more open-ended, so is the audience a more active one, more involved with the process of offering or producing alternative interpretations of the action. With sport, to a greater extent than in news and current affairs, feeling, emotion and the affective dimension are an important part of the experience. The pleasures of viewing are complex and multifaceted and cannot be totally understood from within a decoding model.

The trajectory Morley established has been pursued by, among others, Dorothy Hobson (1982), Ann Gray (1987), Ien Ang (1985) and James Lull (1990). Morley's subsequent work on family viewing (Morley 1986) argues that for men, typically, the home is a leisure site. They plan viewing carefully, watch with attention and are more likely than women to control the television and to possess the remote control. In contrast, women, for whom the home is also a site of domestic labor, typically watch with less attention, and have less say in selection. There is a clear need for study of the audience to be culturally and socially situated (see Critcher, 1992).

MEDIA SPORT, AUDIENCES, AND PLEASURES

Analysis of media sport has tended to focus more on texts and/or production practices rather than the audience. A distinction can be made here between different traditions: the sociological route has produced research into the ways in which media sport is consumed, while the semiological route has produced models, such as the encoding–decoding one, that have in turn produced a research trajectory involving ethnographic enquiry into viewing. Such initiatives have not as yet resulted in much empirical work on audiences for sport.

It has long been acknowledged that audience behavior is not uniform, and different audience members may read events differently. Hastorf and Cantril (1954) concluded that there was no such thing as a pre-existing event that people merely observe, but that the event was a product of the activity of the onlooker. A line of experimental research on sports violence and commentary supports this view. Jennings Bryant (1989) found that among aggression-prone subjects, sports violence might indeed yield maximal enjoyment, but among more mild-mannered peers, excessive violence in sports might be somewhat of a turn-off (1989, p. 280). The disposition of fans towards particular teams and players was consistently a potent predictor of their enjoyment of sports violence. Commentary seems to play a role. Evidence suggests that commentary contributes most to the enjoyment of a televised sports event where opponents are perceived as hated foes rather than as good friends or as neutral and commentaries that stress violence provide more entertainment than commentaries that de-emphasize violence (Comisky, Bryant & Zillmann, 1977; Bryant & Zillmann, 1982).

Dispositional and situational factors influence enjoyment in a variety of ways. Gantz (1981) found that the strongest motivations for sports viewing were the desires to thrill in victory and to let loose. This is reinforced by Wenner and Gantz's (1989) broad study of behaviors and attitudes of sports viewers. They found following a favorite team or player one of the strongest motives, as are finding the drama and tension of the contest appealing. Sapolsky and Zillmann (1978) found that the social controls exerted by fellow viewers influenced perception. In a USA versus Yugoslavia basketball game watched by groups of friends, the social control of the group ensured that Yugoslav baskets were not enjoyed. In a larger group, with friends in the minority, Yugoslav baskets got more enjoyment. This is reinforced by Wenner and Gantz's (1989) finding that a favorite's produced success was a big motivator for viewing, with people enjoying basking in reflected glory. They stated that "Because many aspects of audience experience with televised sport are distinct from experiences with the rest of television, we are convinced that future research needs to look beyond social psychological concerns to the subcultures behind fanship of different sports" (1989, p. 268).

In looking at cultural differences, a good place to start may be gender. Sullivan (1987) found that commentary style significantly influenced perceptions of the degree of aggressiveness of the sports contest, with men enjoying aggressive play more than women. This notion is supported by Wenner and Gantz (1989) who found men gravitated to contact and fast-paced sports, while women preferred more "slow paced" baseball and "less brutal" tennis. James Lull (1990) has suggested that gender difference appeared common to many societies independent of political

system type, stating that "Men everywhere prefer sports, action-oriented programmes and information programming (especially news) while women prefer
dramas (including serials, soap operas, and films) and music/dance/comedy based
programmes" (p, 161). While Lull notes that a man's disinterest in sports may call
traditional masculinity into question, he argues that sports programs must be viewed
as stories that provoke emotional reactions and that audience researchers need to
understand variations in interpretive strategies by cultural position.

Laura Mulvey (1975) has analyzed narrative cinema in terms of a dependence
on scopophilia and voyeurism, which produces a spectacularization of women for
the male gaze. But television sports places male bodies on display, and renders
them available for both a female and a male gaze. Indeed, on the visual level,
athletic bodies are not simply displayed but almost lovingly dwelt over, repeatedly
and in slow motion. Drawing on Laura Mulvey's work on visual pleasure,
Duncan and Brummett (1989) have discussed TV sport in terms of fetishism,
voyeurism, and narcissism.

Similarly, Margaret Morse (1983) has argued that sports discourse is unique
in that its object is the male body. She attributes cultural inhibitions about gazing
at male bodies to a reluctance to make the male body the object of scopophilia –
erotic pleasure in looking. How, she asked, can spectator sports license such a gaze
and render it harmless? She posits a careful balance of play and display in which
voyeurism was transformed into scientific enquiry. Morse argued that where the pleasures of the stadium are communal, a football game on TV is received in privacy
by an isolated, usually male viewer who must forego the pleasures of the crowd.
The extremely long lenses, with narrow angles, flatten space, and along with instant
replay, contribute to a considerable deformation of the stadium point of view: spatial compression, temporal elongation and repetition emphasising only points of
action and body contact to the detriment of the overall geometry of the game.

The frequent repetition means that the game is no longer occurring in a world
subject to the laws of ordinary linear and unidirectional time, and this transforms
a world of speed and violent impact into one of dance like beauty. Where the
stadium-goer is a participant in a ritual, the TV viewer looks at a phantasmatic
realm never seen in any stadium. This fantasy has to do with the passage into
manhood, a period of ambiguous sexual identity. The construction of a masculine
image of power and beauty play an important role in that passage. Sports on television offers a ritual space where man can overcome his separateness from nature,
God, other men and his own body and achieve grace, signified by slow motion.
Slow motion, then, realises the fantasy of the body as perfect machine with an aura
of the divine. The most typical relation of women to sports and this phantasm of
male perfection is avoidance through lack of interest – but women are also unwel-
come in the inner sanctum of sport; the female gaze is that of an outsider.

Morse offers a complex account that warrants further debate and exploration.
The opposition between the communal stadium experience and the isolated male
television viewer has problems. Much television is watched in groups – sports
probably more so, indeed sport, is more likely to be watched in communal viewing
situations, whether in living rooms, or bars, than most forms of television. Morse's
analysis discounts the important social dimension of television – watching it with
others, and talking about it the next day. The pleasures of television sports viewing,

while built around this identification seem to me to be many and various, and cannot be reduced to the scopophilial gaze of the spectator, male or female, at the body.

Pleasures are peculiarly resistant to analysis, present particular challenges to empirical testing, and have both a psychic and a social dimension. Psychoanalytic accounts of pleasure, applied to popular culture, have led to significant insights and influential arguments (Marcuse, 1955; Mulvey, 1975). The use of psychoanalysis alone, however, can be prone to transcultural, transhistoric tendencies, and risks the danger of a psychic reductionism, in which all ideological domination stems from entry into language, or from acquisition of gendered subjectivity (Hall et al., 1980b, pp. 117–176).

It is crucial to retain the social dimension of pleasures, which never appear in abstract form, but always in the shape of particular structured experiences, specific cultural forms, with specific histories and particular modes of production and consumption. Dyer discusses entertainment in terms of energy, abundance, intensity, transparency, and community, categories that clearly provide a way of analyzing the sport experience (Dyer, 1978). Of course, for the typical sports fan, failure is a more common experience than success – sport entertains, but can also frustrate, annoy and depress. But it is precisely this uncertainty that gives the unpredictable joys their characteristic intensity. Sports events offer a liminal moment between uncertainty and certainty; unlike fictional narrative, they are not predetermined by authorship, nor can they be predicted by cultural code or even specialized knowledge. They offer the rare opportunity to experience genuine uncertainty. This is part of the unique fascination of genuinely live events as opposed to those that merely offer the appearance of liveness.

Terry Lovell (1980, 1981), drawing on Raymond Williams' elusive and allusive term, "structures of feeling," proposes the concept of structures of pleasure. Soap operas, for instance, offer a female audience validation, reassurance, and utopianism (Dyer, Lovell, & McCrindle, 1977). If the pleasures of sports viewing have a structure, then identification is central to it. While there are aesthetic pleasures in merely watching a sports performance, the real intensity comes from identifying with an individual or team as they strive to win. Alan Lovell (1975) talks of pleasure points, and a taxonomy of the pleasures of viewing television sport is clearly needed. Such a taxonomy can certainly start by listing the forms of pleasure that can be identified in textual analysis but such a list must be subject to reformulation in the light of audience response.

PROBLEMS OF "AUDIENCE"

Audience research is beset with problems of method, theory, and epistemology. The problems of method stem from our lack of a reliable and verifiable means of getting at the complexities of response that we may have to media images. We can, with a reasonable degree of reliability, ascertain who watches television. What goes on in their heads as they watch is a process that is peculiarly resistant to analysis. Neither effects research, the uses and gratifications approach, the decoding model, nor ethnographic observation and open-ended interview are fully adequate to the task. Pleasures cannot simply be articulated. The utterances of people in interviews and questionnaires, cannot be taken, in the simple sense, as evidence for two reasons.

First, the responses of people to researchers, to questions, and to questionnaires might or might not be accurate renditions. Second, we do not necessarily have the language to express our pleasures; not simply because we lack the vocabulary or verbal dexterity, but because pleasures may well elude the categories of language. How often do we say, "it was indescribable," "beyond words"? The French have a word, "jouissance," to denote that engulfing, unsettling, orgasmic form of pleasure, that precisely disrupts the ability of language to describe and fix (Barthes, 1975). While viewing pleasure, of course, rarely reaches this intensity (although fans have been known to comment that "when they scored it was better than sex") it does highlight the problem that our pleasures are not readily reducible to language.

Theoretically, a lot depends on our model of how audiences work. The crudity of the stimulus-response model was rightly discarded, while the underlying logic of uses and gratifications opened doors to understanding individualized relativism. Decoding studies were always potentially in danger of either an overly mechanical dependence on theories of social stratification, as in Morley's early work, or a collapse into the small scale, self-confirming arbitrariness of Hobson's (1982) *Crossroads* study.

Epistemelogically, we have to ask ourselves carefully what we mean by audience. Ien Ang argues that the audience does not exist as such:

> We must resist the temptation to speak about the television audience as if it were an ontologically stable universe that can be known as such; instead our starting point must be the acknowledgement that the social world of actual audiences consists of an infinite and ever expanding myriad of dispersed practices and experiences that can never be and should not be, contained in any one total system of knowledge.
>
> (1990, p. 155)

If the status of the audience is unclear, the status of the text is also increasingly so in these post-modern times, a complex one. A joke went around at the time of the O.J. Simpson trial:

> "Knock knock"
> "Who's there?"
> "O.J."
> "O.J. who?"
> "You're on the jury."

This joke addresses one problem of audience research – who is the audience and what is the text? It would be very hard to locate anyone who, during 1994–5, had not heard of O.J. Simpson. Major media stories like the O.J. case are everywhere – we don't just consume them, we absorb them by osmosis – they are part of the air that we breathe. A boxing match featuring Mike Tyson cannot be isolated from all the other media images of Tyson which we may have consumed. The meanings that may be embodied in Tyson are a product of this, and also a product of the history of representation of boxers, the heavyweight championship, black versus white and so on. Jack Johnson, Martin Luther King, Malcolm X and Michael Jackson are all part of the culturally available imagery within which we might make sense of Tyson, and how can the audience for this set of images be defined? Major stars and events get such wide and extensive media coverage that the vast majority of people will have heard of a Tyson, an O.J., a Magic Johnson. They are the subject of everyday conversation. If we wish to pursue the issue of the effects of the Magic Johnson and AIDS story, how can we determine either our texts or our audience?

NEW DIRECTIONS

I do not think that attempts to understand the circulation of meaning in both their production and consumption are redundant. There is a need to bridge the gulf between textual analysis and ethnographic work. It thus requires focus on the discursive – how social factors; producers and consumers of meaning – articulate their practices.

Sports viewing is associated with both information and entertainment. Centrally though, it has to do with pleasure. We need to work towards a more adequate taxonomy of sport viewing pleasures (Whannel, 1994). By working with the utterances and responses of audiences, it is possible to construct the range of terms that people utilize to discuss the viewing experience. In many cases, these will echo the ways in which television sport is encoded. The terms used in framing, agenda-setting, in promoting, and in previewing, are likely to be, in large part, the terms that people use to talk about television sport. However there will also be differences. Presences in one discourse will be absences in another. For example, the routine disapproval of rough, violent or rule-breaking conduct in the televisual discourse may not be mirrored by audiences. Some audiences may well regard the rough tackle, the blind-side incident as part of the pleasure. In working with correspondences and dissonances between the discourses of television and those of audience members, clues can be found towards the construction of a taxonomy of pleasure that does not simply read off from the text.

One useful avenue has been opened up by Eastman and Riggs (1994) in an examination of television sport viewing as ritual. The study examines the meanings ordinary sports fans give to ritualized behaviors in the privacy of the home; the ways rituals fit into everyday life and how they alter the sports viewing experience. Eastman and Riggs' study was domestic-centered, but of all forms of television, sport is perhaps the most likely to be viewed communally, and this opens up possibilities. Ethnographic observation of the audience does not have to be limited as in Hobson's research, to the domestic sphere, or as in Ang's research, to written communication. There are extensive opportunities for participant observation of sports viewing in public places. While these situations are not domestic, and may not necessarily be typical, they may well be suggestive in terms of understanding more about the taxonomy of pleasure, the points of appeal, the modes of identification.

In trying to understand this process, the insights of text analysis can provide much help. Analysis of the narratives, modes of address and points of identification in media sport (see Blain, Boyle, & O'Donnell, 1993; Whannel, 1995) chart a discursive field that may correspond to a greater or lesser extent with analysis of patterns in audience articulations about the pleasures of viewing. An elaborate and painstaking search for gaps, discrepancies, and absences might begin to reveal the distinctiveness of audience activity for particular program forms. The study of gender relations in the domestic context (see Gray, 1987; Hobson, 1982; Morley, 1986) does provide insights of great value into the place of television viewing within the home. A development of this work in the specific context of television sports viewing would be of considerable value in the route ahead.

Chapter 15

Watching Sports on Television: Audience Experience, Gender, Fanship, and Marriage

Lawrence A. Wenner &
Walter Gantz

In North America there is a folklore about watching sports on television. The folk tale weaves gendered myths with those about mildly dysfunctional but amusing sports fanatics. The armchair quarterback is often characterized as the passionate fan perched at the end of "his" seat and consumed by the saga of his team's fate. An essential part of the myth is the opened beer can next to the remote control, ready for a guzzle or a quick look at a game on another channel. The armchair quarterback seizes on the situation as one of the few opportunities for the modern male to show his emotional side. Here he cheers and boos, living and dying with the fortunes besetting his team. It is a chance to look in the mirror and see strapping males on center stage playing out dramas that wax nostalgic for a time when physical dominance more clearly corresponded to cultural power.

A drawing of the football widow fills out the myth. Here, the woman puts up with the man's passion for sports. Some slack may be cut by women for this "boyish" preoccupation. Women wait, perhaps even joining in some viewing of the game amidst other household activities. In this waiting, there is resigned tolerance precariously balanced with the knowledge that the male must "pay" for the sporting excursion by some form of relational servitude. In this gender-typed myth, males pay penance with mowing the lawn, a household repair, an owning up to a deferred parental responsibility, or accompanying his spouse on some feminine-typed activity such as a shopping spree or a night out at the ballet.

The armchair quarterback and football widow have been part of our folk-lore for quite some time. The stereotypes behind these cultural myths have been little questioned. In this chapter we look behind the myths by examining the foundational dynamics of watching sports on television. Our treatment relies on a research program that has looked systematically at audience experiences with viewing televised sports (Gantz, 1981; Gantz & Wenner, 1991, 1995; Gantz, Wenner, Carrico, & Knorr, 1995a, 1995b; Wenner & Gantz, 1989). In a series of studies, we have explored the motives, affective involvement, and behaviors associated with viewing sports on television. We have come to understand that the seemingly simple notion of what it means to be a sports fan is remarkably complex. Fans of different sports are clearly fans of different sorts. Just as important, we have come to understand how it is that not everyone who watches sports on television is a fan. The fan is only one part of the television sports spectator picture. Not all men are armchair quarterbacks, and men are not the only armchair quarterbacks.

Our findings inform us of how it is that women and men often experience sport on television in different ways. At the same time, we have been surprised to find out how similar the sports viewing experiences of men and women can be if their interest and fanship are at similar levels. In looking at the role of televised sport in the larger context of marital relationships, our research unravels some of the myths surrounding the football widow. The discussion that follows assesses some of the key issues we considered in formulating our research program. As we interpret our findings and think about what other research suggests to us, we will offer suggestions about how we might best proceed in answering new questions about the audience experience with sports on television.

APPROACHING AUDIENCE EXPERIENCE WITH TELEVISION SPORTS

Television sports viewing is set in two worlds. On one hand, it is like going to the stadium to see a sporting event. On the other, it is like watching other kinds of television programming. We bring diverse experiences, knowledge, and strategies from both worlds to the sports viewing situation. Our orientation to sports, to a certain sport, to a certain team, or a featured player can shade our experience. We may be a casual spectator or a die-hard fan. Similarly, our orientations to television as a medium, to sports programming as a genre, and to coverage of a particular sport, team, or event affect how we approach viewing.

Research on sports spectatorship and fanship (see Guttmann, 1986; Sloan, 1989) provides a variety of clues about why people are motivated to watch sports. In short, the crossroads of identity and ambiguity draw people to sports spectating. Fans identify and enjoy "rooting" for players and teams (Branscombe & Wann, 1992b; Zillmann et al., 1989). Through this involvement they vicariously "compete."

However, because much of this identification is held at a distance, sports spectating is often constructed as a "no lose" situation and can contribute mightily to self esteem (Branscombe & Wann, 1991). Evidence shows that many "bask" in "reflected glory" when "we win" but disassociate from failure as "they lose" (Sloan, 1989). Beyond the identity that causes spectators to root for favorites is the "exciting" nature of the ambiguity over "who wins." Different from other forms of television, televised sport is a live and unscripted drama, but one that guarantees resolution. Viewing brings stimulative stresses that can be enjoyable for some, while others may enjoy escaping into a more "relaxing" sports world where the stresses are not their own (Smith et al., 1981). Of course, such issues may motivate people to watch other forms of television, such as action-dramas. While sports as programming has some unique aspects, many motives for viewing may be shared with other forms of television. For example, people may be motivated to watch sports as social activity to keep someone company, because they haven't got much else to do, or because it will give them something to talk about.

As we began our research program, we realized that sporting events on television range from the ordinary to the extraordinary. Some sporting events signify what may be thought of as cultural high holy days. The Olympic Games, World Cup Soccer, and the National Football League's Super Bowl are all good examples of what Katz (1980) has called "media events" and what Real (1989) has called "supermedia." In nations all over the globe attention to the fate of national teams in the World Cup brings regular life to a halt. In the United States, "Super Bowl Sunday" is an "unannounced" American holiday (Wenner, 1989) where so many people congregate in front of their television sets that roadways and shopping malls lie empty. Like other holidays, these sports super events come to have their own rituals. Elaborate plans are sometimes fashioned to see the "big game." Rothenbuhler's (1988, 1989a, 1989b, 1995) research on the viewing of the Olympic Games suggests specific ways that watching sports super events is very different from watching everyday television. People alter schedules to gather with the same friends and family members who share other social occasions and holidays, food and drink take on a central role in celebration, and friendships and a local sense of community are reinforced in the course of this kind of shared spectatorship.

We recognize that the cultural splash that sports super events make can be significant. However, we believe that the "constant drip" of sports into everyday experience may be even more important in understanding the cultural baseline. In that vein, we sought to understand the "daily grind" of watching sports on television. We start first by exploring the foundational dynamics of television sports viewing. We then move on to understand how these basic orientations vary by gender and fanship. Finally, we explore television sports viewing within the context of marital relationships.

THE TELEVISION SPORTS VIEWING EXPERIENCE

To start with, we were interested in answering some very basic questions: Why do people watch sports on television? How do people feel and what do they do

1   as they prepare for viewing;
2   while they view; and
3   after they view televised sports events?

It is important to note that we found asking people about a generic – sports on television – was not a fruitful strategy (Gantz, 1981; Wenner & Gantz, 1989). Sports was too broad a concept. People could be passionate about one sport, lukewarm about another, and lack familiarity with a great many. Just as people have favorite television programs and can tell you about those in detail, people can comment reliably only about familiar sports they have seen on television. As a result, our research program relies on a strategy that prompts respondents to focus on experiences with familiar or "favorite" sports. We both contrast these responses and aggregate them, when appropriate, to make generalizations about the audience experience with sports on television.

Motives for Television Sports Viewing

The strongest motives for watching sports on television concern both resolution of ambiguity and identification with competitors. Concerns with seeing "who wins" and how one's "favorite does" are among the strongest individual motivations for sports viewing. These tend to combine with the enjoyment that comes with experiencing the "drama and tension" and the excitement of "rooting" for a player or team to win. Indeed, seeking these experiences, along with looking forward to "feeling good" when wins occur, round out the strongest motives for sports on television. Viewing to learn about players or a sport or to "relax and unwind" tend to be important, but more mid-range, motives. Social interaction motives concerning conversational utility ("something to talk about") and companionship ("something to do with family or friends") fall below the mid-range with boredom reducing or time passing goals, but do not sit at the bottom of the motives list. Motives for cathartic release ("letting off steam") or to hear the announcers' commentary appear consistently of little importance. Of least importance across the populations we surveyed was watching sports on television because it offers an opportunity to have a beer or drink, although there are differences across individuals that will be described later. While this latter finding appears to run counter to the stereotype of the beer guzzling armchair quarterback, it may merely indicate that drinking is not a prime motivator for viewing sports across the population or that drinkers do not need the "excuse" of sports to imbibe (Gantz, 1981; Wenner & Gantz, 1989).

Our findings suggest there are more similarities than there are meaningful differences in motives viewers have for watching different sports on television. In particular, affective motives to seek drama and tension, relaxation, or let off steam showed no differences across viewers commenting about their experiences with one of six major sports. Motives to view for conversation, companionship, to hear announcers, or to drink alcohol seem to be largely the same regardless of the sport being watched. However, some motives appear to differ by sport. Viewers of professional football and basketball appear more motivated to view to get "psyched up," most particularly in comparison to baseball viewers. Professional football viewers seem more likely to watch because nothing else was "going on" or "on TV," especially in comparison to more purposive college basketball viewers. College basketball viewers appear distinct, the most motivated to see how their "favorite team does" and to learn about players and the sport. Finally, our findings with tennis viewers suggest that viewing of individual sports is less motivated by the desire to follow "favorites" than is the case for viewing of team sports. This seems a sensible adjustment because with tournament competition, individual sport viewers have no guarantee that their "favorites" will fare well in the draw or be among the leaders (Wenner & Gantz, 1989).

In comparing factor analytic results in two studies that examine the motivations people have for viewing a variety of sports, we find that the similarities in the underlying motivational structures far outweigh differences among sports. Taking the two studies together, five dimensions of motivations appear to have some stability and, if placed in a certain order, can be seen to move along a continuum from more to less involved fanship. The primary dimension, consistently accounting for the most variance in the factor analytic solutions, characterizes a **fanship dimension** and the desire to "thrill in victory." This dimension centers on the excitement of competition and the desire to identify with a winner. Moving down the fanship continuum, we find a **learning dimension**, anchored not so much in an extant identity with players or teams, but in the acquisition of information about both. This cognitive dimension contrasts with the affective fanship goals in the first dimension. The next two dimensions both speak to the social motivations associated with sports viewing. A **release dimension** characterizes how the opportunity to "let loose" can be a motivator for sports viewing. Typically clustered together in this dimension are the motives to "get psyched up" by viewing sports, to "let off steam," and often, to seize the "opportunity" to have a beer or drink. While some of the "release" in this dimension capitalizes clearly on the sports competition unfolding on the screen, a fourth **companionship dimension** moves further down the fanship continuum. Here, sports are viewed because it is a way to spend time with family or friends, who presumably are going to view anyway. While this dimension references sport in the context of the motivation, fanship may be a long way away. Finally, at the outlying edge of fanship is what could be called a **filler dimension**. Here, people view sports to "kill" or "pass" time because there is nothing else "to do" or "on TV." In this last instance, fanship, identity, and involvement become almost incidental (Gantz, 1981; Wenner & Gantz, 1989).

Behavioral and Affective Correlates of Television Sports Viewing

Motives only tell one part of the experience that viewers have with televised sport. Understanding how people get ready for sports viewing, how they feel and what they do while viewing, and how they are affected afterwards helps round out the larger picture. While getting ready to watch a "big game" might involve considerable planning, most viewing involves little preparation. Even so, people frequently talk to others in getting ready, often read reports about what might take place, and, depending on how important the event is, may kill time waiting for the start or tune in early so they won't miss anything. Some people will even get in the mood by having a drink or two before the game starts. While the evidence about these preparatory behaviors is not consistent in our studies (Gantz, 1981; Wenner & Gantz, 1989), these behaviors seem to differ according to sport. College basketball viewers, and to a slightly lesser degree, pro football and basketball viewers, are likely to engage in conversations with others prior to viewing and to tune in early, especially when compared to tennis viewers. College basketball viewers appear the most likely to read reports in preparation for viewing, while football viewers are most likely to have imported the "tailgate party" analogy to their living rooms and prepare for viewing with a pre-game drink (Wenner & Gantz, 1989).

While watching sporting events, viewers' feelings of euphoria or sadness (and even anger) are accentuated when the focus is on a favorite team or player. "Nervousness" about the contest appears heightened as well when favorites are involved. The most common behavior in companion to sports viewing is "having a snack." The evidence is less clear with regards to drinking behaviors, which we found relatively uncommon in a broad sample but more frequent in a student sample. Communicative behaviors such as "yelling out in response to" and "talking about" the action were also relatively common behaviors (Gantz, 1981; Wenner & Gantz, 1989).

Our findings suggest that most of the feelings people have and behaviors they are likely to engage in during viewing vary according to whether viewing takes place alone, with friends, or in a family setting. Viewers are more excessive and expressive in the company of friends. Communicative behaviors such as "talking about the action" and "yelling out" in response are much more common in the group setting, and viewing amongst friends appears to bolster this more than the family setting. Evidence also suggests that "getting angry" when things are going badly and "pacing the floor" is suppressed when viewing alone and facilitated in the company of friends. A "friends effect" also seems likely in facilitating "gusta-tory" behaviors. Here, there is evidence that levels of drinking, and drinking more than usual, are likely to double, with snack consumption not rising quite as much. One behavior – working on household chores – seems to increase when sports viewing takes place with other family members (Wenner & Gantz, 1989).

Feelings and behaviors while viewing seem to also differ somewhat according to the sport being watched. College basketball viewers, most likely to be watching in a group setting, seem to be the most communicative, "talking" and "yelling out" during broadcasts, while baseball and tennis fans appear the quietest. However, even when the viewing situation is controlled, college basketball fans feel the happiest when their favorite does well, the most nervous as play progresses, and the most likely to pace the floor during viewing. The exact converse appears to be true for those viewing tennis on television (Wenner & Gantz, 1989).

What happens after viewing sports on television? Viewing a close sporting contest can leave one drained. If the outcome is as hoped for, a good mood may linger. A bad loss can put one in a foul mood. One could feel guilty about spending so much time in front of the tube and try to make amends by doing chores, spending time with family, or exercising in response to the athletic spectacle. We find some evidence that people "bask" in the "reflected glory" (Cialdini et al., 1976) of victory after viewing by staying in a good mood and "reliving" the experience by talking about the game, deliberately reading about the contest, and watching high-lights on newscasts. Little evidence seems to suggest that viewing prompts exer-cise, drinking, or staying in a bad mood after a defeat. College basketball viewers appear to engage most consistently in a pattern of "basking," especially in compar-ison to viewers of baseball and tennis. While celebrating a win with a beer or drink is an uncommon basking behavior, it is most closely associated with the viewing of college football in comparison to other sports (Wenner & Gantz, 1989).

GENDER AND AUDIENCE EXPERIENCE WITH TELEVISION SPORTS

While the picture we have painted so far characterizes some overarching experi-ences that viewers have with television sports, there is considerable evidence that suggests that the experiences women and men have with sports are very different. Men and women have traditionally been socialized differently with regard to sports. With sport commonly posed as more "gender appropriate" for males, they receive more encouragement to participate, particularly in aggressive sports, than do females (Greendorfer, 1993). Ideals normally associated with masculinity – aggressiveness, bravery, competitiveness, and strength – are incorporated into sport (King & Chi, 1979). Mediated sport may often reinforce masculine ideals by focusing on indi-vidual exploits over teamwork, outcome over process, and the value of aggressive play (Bryant, Comisky, & Zillmann, 1977; Bryant & Zillmann, 1983; Goldstein & Bredemeier, 1977; Jacobson, Waldron, & Moore, 1980). Television more regularly broadcasts sports with a masculine as opposed to a neutral or feminine gender orientation (Matteo, 1986; Roloff & Solomon, 1989), and further tends to treat the achievements of female and male athletes very differently (see Duncan & Messner in this volume). Given such evidence, we wanted to compare the experiences men and women had with televised sport. We did so partly to see whether differences were as severe "as advertised," but also to build a foundation so we could later study gender dynamics with regards to sports in the context of marital relationships.

Some basic measures of sports interest and related media behaviors suggested to us that the motives for watching sports on television, and the behavioral and affective correlates of such viewing, would be very different for men and women. For example, across a sample population, while over three-fourths were "some-what" or "very interested" in viewing sports events on television and even more considered themselves either "somewhat" or "very knowledgeable" about the sport they watched most, the top ends of these scales showed marked differences between men and women. Over half of the men were "very interested" in sports viewing in contrast to less than a quarter of the women. Differences in perceived knowl-edgeability about their favorite sport were more dramatic; over half of the men considered themselves "very knowledgeable" in contrast to less than a fifth of the women. Almost twice as many men than women indicated that they would suffer withdrawal pains within a week if televised sport were taken off the air. Men's consumption patterns were distinct as well. Men watched a third more sports on television on weekends, and almost double the amount on weekdays, than did women. Men spent almost three times as much time reading the newspaper sports pages and watching sport news summaries on cable than did women (Gantz & Wenner, 1991).

These findings were consistent with scientific and anecdotal evidence about gender differences in following sports. Because men are more interested in sports, they consume more coverage about it, and watch more events on television. Given this, we thought it important to explore whether gendered experiences with sport on television were leveled by the amount of interest that individuals had in viewing sports on television. In the summary below, we compare the experiences of men and women, and then assess how interest levels can change a gender-typed picture.

Motives for Television Sports Viewing

Our early findings with a college sample suggest that women watch sports "as a last resort," doing so because other program alternatives are poor, they have nothing better to do, or because friends or family are viewing. On the other hand, men seem more motivated by the "opportunities" involved in sports viewing – a good time with friends, drinking, letting off steam, getting psyched, experiencing some "excitement," and a way to learn more about players (Gantz, 1981).

These results are largely mirrored in a later study. Women were different from men on nine out of fifteen motivations assessed for viewing a favorite sport on television. However, women rated only two of these motivations significantly higher than men. Here, women were more likely than men to watch because friends or family were watching, and because it gave them "something to do" with friends or family. Men more clearly acted like fans. Compared to women, men were more likely to view sports to get psyched up, relax, let off steam, and drink alcohol. Men were also more likely to watch because they enjoyed the tension and drama of the sporting contest and it gave them something to talk about (Gantz & Wenner, 1991).

With the level of interest in sport statistically controlled, many of these motivational differences between women and men disappear. However, this is not true for the two motives that women rate higher than men as reasons for viewing sports on television – watching because that's what friends or family are already doing and viewing as something "to do" with friends or family. And even with interest controlled, men seem significantly more likely to view sports to relax and unwind and show more concern than women over not missing anything in a sports broadcast (Gantz & Wenner, 1991).

Behavioral and Affective Correlates of Television Sports Viewing

Men appear to prepare for sports broadcasts differently from women. The results from two studies suggest than men are more likely to talk and read about a contest prior to its broadcast (Gantz, 1981; Gantz & Wenner, 1991). Men are also more likely than women to get ready for viewing by tuning in prior to the start of an event. However, when level of interest in television sports is controlled, these differences between men and women become non-significant. Such differences did not disappear when looking at pre-viewing drinking behaviors. We found that men remain significantly more likely than women to have a drink to get ready for a sports telecast (Gantz & Wenner, 1991).

While watching games, women report they are more likely than men to also do household chores; this difference holds significant, even with sport interest statistically controlled. Men seem more likely to "let loose" during broadcasts. More than women, men report having a drink and even drinking more than they normally would. Perhaps as a result, men more likely report "yelling" out in response to action or a bad call, being happy when their team does well and angry when they do poorly. When controlling for level of interest, men remain more likely than women to have a drink and more likely to talk and yell about the action (Gantz, 1981; Gantz & Wenner, 1991).

Gender differences can also be seen in feelings and behaviors after watching a game. Regardless of level of interest in sports, women seem more likely than men to continue to watch television after a game even though they hadn't planned on doing so. Men appear distinct from women in other ways. After a game, they are more likely to watch game highlights on newscasts and to read newspaper accounts of the game. They are also more likely than women to have a drink to celebrate victory and to stay in a bad mood after watching a loss. These post-viewing communicative, drinking, and mood differences between men and women do not appear to hold up when sports interest is taken into account. However, some gender differences in post-game behaviors remain regardless of interest. Men claim to exercise significantly more than women after watching a game and are notably more likely than women to avoid their families in order "to recover" after viewing (Gantz & Wenner, 1991).

FANSHIP, GENDER, AND AUDIENCE EXPERIENCE WITH TELEVISION SPORTS

Having found that many of the gender differences seen in experiencing sports on television are lessened when level of interest in sports on television is taken into account, we sought to understand how a more complex conceptualization, fanship, interacted with experiences women and men have with television sport. Fanship has been a slippery concept in sport and cultural studies. In sport in particular, there is a very gray area between the notions of "spectator" and "fan." The terms have often been used interchangeably, with an assumption that all spectators are fans (Sloan, 1989). However this is not necessarily the case. As Guttmann (1986, p. 6) suggests, fans are more "emotionally committed" and "[i]n practice most fans are spectators and most spectators are fans, but it is logically possible to be one and not the other." A person "dragged" to a sporting event or "captive" in the living room keeping company with one who "has" to watch a game has a very different experience from the fan. Of course, coercion is not necessary to qualify as a "non-fan," there is a continuum from "cold" to "lukewarm" to characterize people that might better be thought of as "merely" spectators.

The term fan derives from fanatic, growing from the Latin *fanaticus*, meaning frenzied (*Webster's Sports Dictionary*, 1976). Others (Rudin, 1969, p. 12) suggest the term grows from the Latin *fanum*, meaning "the sacred, the beneficial, the salvific, the temple, the consecrated place." While there is no denying the enthusiasm and activity of the fan, connotations of fanship are often negative. Fans may be seen as obsessed or deviant, with pathologically unfulfilled fantasies (Jenkins, 1992; Jenson, 1992) Sports fans may be cast as "couch potatoes" or linked to hooliganism. Still, there is much to suggest that fanship is active, participatory, and empowering with the passion, pleasure, and self-esteem it generates (Grossberg, 1992; Fiske, 1992). The emotional involvement and identification of sports fans with teams and players explains greater enjoyment in spectating, improvements in mood and self-esteem, and increased generosity, wishful thinking, and aggression (Babad, 1987; Babad & Katz, 1991; Branscombe & Wann, 1991, 1992b; Cramer et al., 1986; Sloan, 1989; Wann, 1993; Wann & Branscombe, 1992).

While sports fanship has been variantly operationalized, much evidence suggests that sports fanship has cognitive, affective, and behavioral components (McPherson, 1975; Smith et al., 1982). Thus, we define fanship in an index that measures perceived knowledgeability about sports, interest in viewing televised sports, and amount of televised sports viewed (Gantz & Wenner, 1995). Due to a number of factors, we found a healthy group of women fans. We surmise that recent socialization practices encouraging girls to participate in sports have also yielded women fans. In tandem, more women having spent time in spectator roles move to become fans. Finally, our methodological tact of allowing respondents to choose a "most watched sport" may more easily find more women who respond as fans than would be the case if an inquiry was limited to one sport, such as football.

Given our earlier findings (Gantz & Wenner, 1991) about how interest in sports seems to level many of the differences in experiences that men and women have with televised sport, we expected that experiences of male and female fans would be most similar to and contrast with groups of male and female non-fans. When compared to non-fans, we expected male and female fans to be more motivated to view a favorite sport, to engage more often in preparatory activities, to be more engaged and demonstrative during viewing, and to be more affected by the experience after the sports event had ended. The summary below reports on correlations between fanship and sports viewing experiences across a sample of adults and considers differences between four groups – male fans, female fans, male non-fans, and female non-fans – formed on the basis of the upper and lower fanship quartiles of both males and females sampled (Gantz & Wenner, 1995).

Motives for Television Sports Viewing

Significant correlations between fanship and motivations to view televised sports were found for most of the motives we examined. Motives characterizing interest and emotional involvement in sport are most strongly correlated to fanship. Only motives to view as a last resort (i.e., viewing because nothing else was "going on" or "on TV" or as "something to do" with friends or family) are weakly correlated with fanship. With few exceptions, such as viewing to "follow bets" or to have a beer or drink, significantly correlated motives appear more strongly related to fanship for women than for men. Compared to men, women's fanship was much more strongly correlated to motives to "learn more" about players and sport, to see how "favorites" do, and to "not miss a thing." Although less dramatic, women's fanship shows stronger relationships than do men's motives to view to "get psyched up," to relax, to "let off steam," for something to talk about, and because of attractions to the "drama and tension," and even because of interest in listening to the announcers (Gantz & Wenner, 1995).

While fanship is more directly correlated to sports viewing motives for women than for men, another picture emerges as the levels of endorsing motives are compared among groups of male fans, female fans, male non-fans and female non-fans. In general, fan groups were more highly motivated than non-fan groups. Only because of one reason, viewing because friends or family were watching, did non-fans, and most notably female non-fans, seem more motivated than fans to view sports. In all other significant differences observed amongst fan groups, a pattern showed male fans most motivated, with female fans closely following at a slightly less motivated level. Male non-fans are the next least motivated, with a gap between them and female fans being more substantial than between male and female fans. A similar gap was seen between the male non-fans and the female non-fans that were least motivated to view for fanship reasons. *Post hoc* testing indicated that while male non-fans were significantly more likely to view sports for fanship related reasons than female non-fans, differences in the motives that male and female fan groups had for viewing televised sport appear non-significant. A rank order of decreasing endorsement moving from male fans, female fans, male non-fans, to female non-fans appears in motives to view sports for the drama, for conversation, to not "miss anything" and to find out how a "favorite does," and for psychic stimulation as well a way to both relax and "let off steam" (Gantz & Wenner, 1995).

Behavioral and Affective Correlates of Television Sports Viewing

Patterns of getting ready for sports viewing relate to fanship in ways similar to motivations. Compared to men, women's fanship is typically more strongly correlated to preparatory activities such as reading and talking about upcoming contests, killing time beforehand or tuning in early, and even having a pre-broadcast drink. Differences among fanship groups are substantial, with preparatory activities most likely by male fans followed closely by female fans, with male non-fans preparing less, and female non-fans least. However, differences in the preparations that male and female fans say they make are few. Both of these fan groups prepare significantly differently from the non-fan groups, with the sole exception being that male non-fans appear no less likely than other groups to have a drink before viewing. Preparation patterns between male and female non-fans are also non-significant, apart from an indication that male non-fans are more likely to read sports coverage prior to viewing (Gantz & Wenner, 1995).

All of the feelings and behaviors during sports viewing that we asked people about show significant correlations to fanship. The strongest links are to affective responses such as feeling nervous, happy, or angry in response to the action. As in other areas, concomitant feelings and behaviors are generally more strongly related to the fanship index for women than for men. A dramatic difference shows fanship much more correlated to feeling happy when favorites do well for women than men. While differences across male and female fan and non-fan groups seem to largely follow a pattern that mirrors findings concerning motives and preparations, they are more complex. For example, there is some evidence the female fans are more likely than male fans to feel happy and to "talk about the action" as it unfolds. Women fans are also more likely than their male counterparts to report "also working" on household chores while viewing, although the contrast is not statistically significant. Levels of doing household work while viewing are more significant when comparing female non-fans with male fans. Still, for many of the feelings and behaviors during games where there are significant differences, a more typical pattern prevails. For example, male fans report greater nervousness, "yelling out," and likelihood of putting off household chores than women fans; male non-fans followed by female non-fans report less than the fan groups. In these cases, differences between fan groups and non-fan groups are significant, while this is not the case for differences between male and female fan groups. Gustatory activities during viewing take on a similar pattern with male fans drinking and snacking notably more than female non-fans, however the more moderate gustatory behaviors of women fans do distinguish them from male non-fans (Gantz & Wenner, 1995).

After watching games, fanship also makes a difference. With the apparent exception of unplanned television viewing after the sportscast, postgame behaviors and feelings appear significantly related to fanship. Little distinguishes men and women fans after viewing. Their fanship is most correlated to their information-seeking behaviors (i.e., reading sports reports or watching highlights) after viewing. Very similar male and female fan groups contrast in significant ways with both male and female non-fan groups by staying in a good mood after a victory, talking more about the game afterwards, and both reading and watching more sports reports. Male and female fans both say they are more likely than female non-fans to "put off household chores" and "have a drink" after viewing. In addition, both fan groups appear more likely than male non-fans to "make a point" of spending time with their family after watching sports events. Significant differences that distinguish the male fan from the female fan, and also from the non-fan groups, surface in the way the male fan takes defeat. The male fan's predilection to "stay in a bad mood" after seeing a loss and avoiding his family afterward "to recover" is notable. However, on the "pro-social" side of things, the male fan can be distinguished, from the female fan and from male and female non-fans, in reporting that he has been stimulated by viewing to go out and exercise more than usual (Gantz & Wenner, 1995).

TELEVISION SPORTS AND MARITAL RELATIONSHIPS

Our research on gender and fanship in association with orientations to sports on television both reinforces aspects of the football widow myth and raises questions about it. On one hand, it seems that men and women are very different in their basic orientations to sports on television. If one were to look just at gender differences in orientations without considering levels of interest in sport, one might see a wide chasm over sports between the sexes. Men clearly act more like fans. They are decidedly more interested in sports, spend more time watching sports on television, and think of themselves as more knowledgeable about sports than women. On the other hand, if levels of interest in sport are statistically controlled, the gaps that remain seem bridgeable. However, one cannot wave a set of statistical controls over a marriage to level differences in passions about sport.

There are some reasons for hope about marital compatibility over sports. First, based on our findings, male and female fans can be remarkably similar in their orientations to sports. Male and female fans are far more likely to differ from both male and female non-fans than they are from each other. Thus, one may deduce that if marital partners are both fans, there may be little turbulence over sports. Second, if both fall into non-fan groups, our evidence suggests that there may be greater actual differences in orientations to sports on television. However, the gaps between matched male and female non-fans may be less consequential because presumably non-fans hold sports at a lesser salience level than do fans. Even though we haven't examined this directly, we would have little reason to think that marital partners who were relatively matched somewhere in "mid-fanship" would experience much sport-related conflict.

We would look for the most substantial marital problems to be caused by sport only in those cases where there is a significant gap in fanship level such that the salience associated with sport spectatorship is high with one partner and low with the other. Even if marital partners were somehow oblivious to mismatched "sports barometers" as they were courting, or even if they chose to initially ignore such differences, marriages are full of give and take, and sports is only one part of cultural life that might call for accommodation over the course of a marriage.

Still a state of affairs suggests there are more sports-impassioned men out there than women. Finding an evenly-matched "sports spectating partner" may be difficult or a low priority in finding a mate. Even while research suggests that shared television viewing is most often valued as a pleasurable, integrative force, facilitating togetherness in marital relationships (Kubey, 1990), there seem to be greater discrepancies between partners over preferences for viewing sports than for other types of programming (Gantz, 1985). Because sports programming is most likely to be aired on evenings and weekends, it may be most likely to cause disputes between spouses over leisure time. Even when women join in sports viewing, it seems they are more likely to take a "subversive subject position" that could threaten and challenge their male partners (Duncan & Brummett, 1993). When the "carry over effects" of exposure to sports are factored in, the "bad mood" that is more likely to remain for men in combination with the need for "recovery time" may fuel marital conflict.

We summarize highlights below from two studies that take a closer look at the role that viewing television sports plays in marriage. We merge findings from a broader two city survey of about 400 married adults with a derivative "coorientation study" of nearly 100 couples in which we were able to "cross-check" responses from both spouses in a marriage about the role of televised sport in their relationship (Gantz et al., 1995a, 1995b). While randomly selected, the samples in the two studies consists of individuals who, on average, were in long-standing marital relationships and who expressed relatively high degrees of marital satisfaction on a composite index. First, we characterize basic orientations to televised sport and assess reactions individuals have and perceive their spouses have about sports viewing. Second, we look at viewing conflicts over sport in their marriages and how these are handled. Third, we assess characterizations that individuals make about themselves and their spouses about behavioral and affective correlates of sports viewing. Lastly, we assess evaluations made about the role viewing sports plays in their marriages.

Orientations and Reactions to Television Sports Viewing

Following familiar patterns, most men say they were either "very" or "somewhat interested" in watching televised sports compared to over half of women. Men clearly underestimate their spouse's interest in sports, while women only slightly overestimate men's interest levels. Slightly more than half share their partner's choice of a favorite sport, which is most likely to be football. About 80 percent can correctly identify his or her spouse's favorite sport. Men say that they watch about 1 hour a week more of their favorite than women say they do of theirs. However, while women estimate that their partners spent more time than men say they do viewing, men underestimate the amount their wives say they view sports by a similar amount. The gap here seems to mirror one in perceived knowledgeability about one's favorite sport. While individuals in a marriage rating their own knowledgeability points to one sized gap, the gaps in knowledgeability that individuals think there is between their knowledge and their spouses appear quite a bit greater (Gantz et al., 1995a, 1995b).

Evidence suggests almost no "anger" or "resignation" with the spouse's viewing of a favorite sport. Most think such viewing by the spouse is "fine," with little difference in this perception between men and women. This differs somewhat from what individuals think the spouse thinks about such viewing. Here, just over half think their spouse thinks the respondent's viewing is fine and another quarter just accept this as a "fact of life." Very few think their partners are "resigned" to their sports viewing habits. Almost no one perceives anger from their spouse over their sports viewing habits or is angry over a partner's sports viewing. Somewhat telling is that while most women see their husbands as pleased when the women watches TV sports, only half of men see their wives as pleased when husbands watch TV sports (Gantz et al., 1995b).

When they watch their favorite sport, what do individuals think their spouses do? Men are perceived by women to be eager to join them in sports viewing. Most women report their husbands join them in viewing, while about a third of men report their wives join in viewing the husband's favorite sport. Almost as many men report that while they are watching their favorite sport, their wives are doing house chores, engaging in another leisure activity around home, or watching TV on another set. When spouses are viewing their favorite sport, most men report joining in viewing, while half the women report joining their mates.

Thus, a considerable discrepancy can be seen between how few husbands think their wives join them in sports viewing and how many women think they join their husbands in sports viewing. If they do not join in watching their husband's favorite sport, women are most likely to report engagement in other home leisure activities or household chores. Conversely, it is revealing that almost no men say they attend to household chores when the wife is watching the wife's favorite sport (Gantz et al., 1995b).

Conflicts Over Television Sports Viewing

What happens when your spouse schedules something for you to do when you want to watch your favorite sport on TV? Remarkably little conflict grew out of this posed problem with women and men generally responding very similarly. Most commonly, men and women said they would go along with their spouse's plan. The conflict was accommodated in other ways such as taping the game, watching part of it, or postponing the activity. More telling was that a number of women and men said this conflict "never happens" because the spouse knew better than to create such a conflict. While arguments were infrequent, four times as many men than women reported they would watch the game anyway, even it in involved an argument. What if the tables were turned? **What would your spouse do if you've scheduled something else for the spouse to do and he or she wanted to watch a favorite sport on television?** About one in three said the spouse would go along with the other plans, although a gender gap indicates more men believe their wives would abandon their sport viewing plans to go along with them than women who believe their husbands would accommodate them by abandoning viewing plans. Similar to earlier posed conflict, about one fifth of men and women said this conflict wouldn't happen because they "knew better." Still, while one in ten women said their spouse would watch even if it involved an argument, almost no men said their wives would have an argument to get to watch a game (Gantz et al., 1995b).

Similar conflicts can occur over what to watch on television. **What happens when you want to watch your favorite sport on TV and your spouse wants to watch something else on at the same time?** Almost no one argues. Responses suggest that almost half of the time the stresses of this conflict are easily resolved by one partner going to a second television set, although a third-again more women than men say they are the "accommodating" ones going to the second set. Almost twice as many women than men are likely to say this conflict doesn't arise and women are much more likely than men to accommodate and watch what the husband prefers. **What happens when your spouse wants to watch his or her favorite sport on television and you want to watch something else on at the same time?** Again, virtually no arguments are likely to occur. Nearly half the time going to another set provides an easy solution. Once again, a gender gap shows two-thirds of the women believe they would be the ones going to the second set compared to just over a third of men. These men's estimates may seem suspicious to women as very few say their husbands would be the ones moving to the second set to watch their game (Gantz et al., 1995b).

Behavioral and Affective Correlates of Viewing

What do individuals think is likely to happen in the household when they watch their favorite sport on television? Arguments appear to almost never happen. Most likely is an assumption that the spouse will join in viewing, a request made for the spouse to join in viewing, or a query about what the spouse is likely to do while the sports viewer is watching the contest. Women appear significantly more likely than men to assume their spouse will join them in sports viewing, to ask their spouse to join in viewing, and to ask their spouse's opinion while the game was on. During the game, discussion of personal issues is unlikely to occur, and the sports viewer appears reluctant to upset the apple cart by asking the spouse to bring food or drinks. **What do individuals think are the expectations made by the spouse when the spouse watches a favorite sport on television?** Here too, assumptions and queries about the spouse's co-viewing or other planned activities is the norm. Expectations of an argument are negligible. Compared to women's evaluations of their husbands, men seem much more likely to think their wives would expect them to join in viewing and would expect them to answer questions about both the game and personal issues. Women appear more likely to expect husbands watching a game to trade agreeing to do something after the game for the wife's approval for the husband's game viewing. Women are also more likely than men to say their spouses expect to be served food and drink during sports viewing. Even with such perceived imbalances, there appears little need for conciliatory behaviors by the sports viewer with the partner who has not initiated viewing. Nonetheless, men seem to feel more guilt as they are notably more likely than women to say they spend time with and do what the spouse wants after watching sports broadcasts (Gantz, et al., 1995b).

Evaluations of Sports Viewing in Marriage

The role that televised sports plays in marriage is far smaller than the football widow folk tale suggests. Four out of five individuals rate the size of the role that TV sports plays in their marriage as either "small" or "very small." Still, a gender gap is apparent. Men are more likely to downplay the significance of sports in their marital relationships. Evidence suggests that more than half of men, as opposed to about a third of women, see the role of TV sports in their marriages as "very small." Nearly twice as many women as men are likely to evaluate that role as "big" or "very big." Even so, almost all married people describe the role of TV sports in their relationship as either "positive" or "neutral." And more women than men are likely describe that role as "positive." Further, arguments and resentment over TV sports seem uncommon. Most individuals think their spouse considers their needs when sitting down to watch sports. Most married people (and a larger proportion of women than men) say they have never argued about TV sports as a problem in their relationship. Almost all of the men and more than three-quarters of women say they have never resented their spouses for watching TV sports. While there isn't much resentment, there is a gap, and a third of men feel their wives have resented them for watching TV sports, while only a smattering of women feel their husbands harbor resentment for their viewing (Gantz et al., 1995b).

There appears to be a good deal of correspondence between how TV sports is characterized in the context of a marriage and amounts of interest in and viewing of sports. People seeing TV sports playing a positive role in their marriage are more likely to be interested in sports generally, in following a favorite sport and believe their partner has interest in following both sports generally and a favorite sport. On the other hand, marriages where TV sports plays a "negative" role or causes "resentment" in the relationship seem to have more problems than others. Individuals with such evaluations view the relationship with their spouses less positively and judge their marriages as more likely to end sometime in the future. Evidence suggests that those who argue with, resent, or feel resentment from their spouses over sports rate their marriages as notably less satisfying. The more limited "cross-check" data that we have suggests that discrepancies between partners in the amount of time spent watching television sports may be more related to low evaluations of marital satisfaction than discrepancies partners may have in interest or knowledge about sport (Gantz, et al., 1995a, 1995b).

In short, negative perceptions and resentment about the role of television sports in marriage, and discrepancies between partners in time spent viewing sports, can point to a marriage that is unsatisfying or in trouble. While disagreements over television sports are not likely to be the only indicant of such marital troubles, they may be an important element in a measuring stick for some marriages. A far greater amount of evidence argues for the positive or decidedly neutral roles that television sports spectatorship plays in marriage. While there are imbalances in how men and women feel about televised sports in their relationships, these imbalances may be no greater than others that couples have. Especially when spouses share time and interests over televised sports, the role it plays in marital life can be mutually beneficial.

CONCLUSION

The long and winding road that we have taken to review audience experiences with watching sports on television suggests that many of the myths associated with armchair quarterbacks and football widows have less at their foundation than commonly believed. While the evidence challenges many basic elements of the myths that surround television sports spectatorship, it does not rule out that people taken with social stereotypes about sports spectatorship can easily find cases that support their beliefs. The picture we are left with does not negate the possibility of the armchair quarterback guzzling beer and cheering for his favorite team as he watches from an easy chair. The picture also does not call into question the present social reality that women are less interested than men in sports or that the masculine-typed sports that dominate television schedules may be less than attractive to many women. The picture we have tuned in also does little to suggest that it is common to find a woman sports fan who reports being as passionate and knowledgeable about sports as many males seem to feel and believe they are. Finally, the picture does not tune out that there are troubled marriages out there in which arguments and resentment over the role television sports spectatorship plays in the relationship may be very good indicants of the inharmonious climate.

However, we find many cracks in the mythic egg. With regards to the basic nature of television sports spectatorship, the norm does not appear to be a "couch potato" with "spectatoritis." Many sports viewers are active, discerning, engaged, and passionate. Because sports spectators come to the viewing situation with different levels of sporting interest, knowledge, and experience, they look for and receive different benefits from the experience. Interested and passionate fans are likely to identify the most with players and teams and to find excitement as events unfold. Other spectators who identify less with players, and thus the outcome, may be more disposed to learn about a sport and its personalities. Others may come to sport viewing because it represents a socially sanctioned and familiar avenue for letting loose, and allows getting psyched up or having a drink without stigma. As we all do in various parts of our lives, there are times where people tag along with others for reasons that sometimes have little to do with an activity. The companionship that results may be intrinsically satisfying or difficult to otherwise find. Similar to what may drive other activities, people watch television sports for purposeful reasons such as these, and there are even times when some will use sports viewing to kill time or fill a gap that could easily be filled in a variety of ways.

The pattern of orientation to televised sport signals little in itself for concern. Few behaviors and feelings associated with sports viewing are cause for alarm. Excessive drinking of alcohol in preparation, in companion, and following sports broadcasts can be a real problem. While drinking across a broad population during sports broadcasts is reported infrequently, closer looks at problem pockets such as the more likely "tailgate-typed" pre- and postgame drinking by football viewers and the increased drinking that is facilitated by the situation of sports viewing with friends appear warranted.

Some overarching parts of the football widow myth are reflected in differences in how women and men experience sports on television. Women generally are more likely than men to view as a last resort or to keep family or friends company. With greater interest, knowledge, and experience men who are more likely to act like fans, are more motivated by the opportunities that sports viewing offers to experience excitement, get psyched up, let off steam, drink, and spend time with friends. Behavioral and affective correlates associated with sports viewing are similarly distinct between men and women. Yet, because the bulk of these differences between women and men disappear when interest in sports are controlled, the gender difference seems largely attributable to a fanship difference. Some things, however, do not seem go away. Sport interested women are more likely than men to attend to household chores during viewing, and men are more likely to drink. While these differences are evident in the context of sports viewing, they are consistent with more broad-based cultural differences between men and women that have little to do with sports.

Myths associated with sports fanship also give way. We largely concur with Zillmann et al. (1989, p. 249) in their assessment that "the typical sports fan manages his or her own emotions admirably. He or she may yell and stomp the ground but, after the game, he or she usually will be no more vicious than after an exciting movie or stimulating concert." Our findings about the character of fanship in television sports viewing suggest that fanship, like other shared interests and competencies, can both be rewarding and cross gender lines. While it may not be as easy to find women fans, and their favorite sport may be likely to be different from men's, female and male fans largely share in orientations, behaviors, and feelings associated with television sports viewing. Male and female fan groups are closer to each other in basic orientation than either group is to male non-fans, and closer than male-non fans are to female non-fans. Worth noting is that women fans appear more likely than even male fans to feel happy and talk about the action while viewing. This emotional "high" that women appear to get and their willingness to talk about sports portends well for the role that television sports can play in marriage.

More substantial parts of the football widow myth are dispelled by our studies of the role of television sports spectatorship in marriage. Gaps in interest that men and women have in sports seem largely overshadowed by how positively sports viewing is evaluated in most marriages. There is little anger and few arguments over sports viewing. Conflicts that sports viewing on the part of one partner might cause with regards to other planned activities or television viewing preferences are routinely accommodated in most relationships. Awareness of the role that such viewing plays seems so substantial that many individuals just can't see conflicts coming up because of what they know about their partner and how easily these conflicts have been resolved in the past. In the face of the football widow myth, it is striking how little a role most married individuals think television sports plays in their marriages. It is striking as well how positively televised sports are viewed in the context of married life, and notable that women evaluate the role of television sports even more positively than do men.

Do we see some problematic elements associated with sports spectatorship? Yes, there may be too much of it, just as there may be too much time spent in other diversions in leisure time that take people away from social responsibility and active engagement in activities that may be more psychically, physically, and culturally rewarding. However, it would be difficult to single out televised sport for its role as a problematic social opiate. It appears no more used and abused than others. Are there marriages where the negative role or resentment caused by television sports viewing can be a propeller or indicant of marital stress? Certainly, but because of the social myths surrounding sports viewing on television, we suspect that sports viewing takes an undue part of the blame. Differences in sports viewing may be more easily seen by married individuals experiencing marital stress than many other, more fundamental differences, that can cause a marriage to fissure. While future research should look carefully at the role that sports orientations play in troubled marriages, it should do so in the context of other influences. In the meantime, more evidence suggests that the armchair quarterback and the football widow have neither been typecast accurately nor are they experiencing many sport-related marital problems.

Chapter 16

Violence and the Enjoyment of Media Sports

Jennings Bryant, Dolf Zillmann,
& Arthur A. Raney

A man's got to have his football on Monday nights. If I've told you once I've told you a thousand times, we are hunter-warriors and need a little brutality in our entertainment . . . I want to see an Oakland Raider take the head off a Denver Bronco and then drop to his knees to thank Jesus for the maiming.

(Martinez & Martinez 1996, p. 26)

Violence in sports has become commonplace in present-day society, and signs of the symbiotic nature of sports violence and media are increasingly abundant. Why have our sports, games, and play become so laced with violence, and why do violence and televised sports so often go hand in hand? These questions will be addressed more systematically later, but some insight can be gleaned from the following two excerpts, one from the popular press, the other from the "trades." The first is from "Walter Scott's Personality Parade," published in *Parade* magazine:

Q: I recently found my son watching a cable-TV show called "The Ultimate Fighting Championship" and was appalled. Men were beating each other senseless. Why is such a thing allowed on TV? And is it legal? – J. M., Austin, Tex.

A: Dubbed the "bloodiest, most barbaric show in history," the controversial contest . . . combines boxing, martial arts and wrestling. The fight ends when one man surrenders or is knocked out. Why do athletes engage in this blood sport? The latest "winner" got $150,000.

(Scott, 1995, p. 2)

The second is from *Electronic Media*, in which a headline proclaimed, "Return of Mike Tyson to Lead Double-Digit Growth," and the lead sentence indicated, "Mike Tyson's return to boxing helped pay-per-view ring up record revenues this year and has punched up big expectations for next year" (Walley, 1995, p 14). "Iron Mike," a convicted rapist and alleged wife abuser, epitomizes societal violence, in and out of the ring. The bottom line seems to be, violence in sports "sells."

Sports violence has become so prevalent in recent years that it has been a common, almost obligatory, topic for sports journalists and sports commentators. For example, on January 3, 1996, the sports pages of the *Tuscaloosa News* contained six stories that were not related to specific games (e.g., football Bowl games, basketball games). Two-thirds (four out of six) of those stories were about sports violence.

The situation is similar with electronic journalism: For example, during the Fall of 1995, commentator Tim Green contributed a piece that aired on National Public Radio in which he decried the "ugly week in pro football" in which on one day he "had watched Tampa Bay linebacker Hardy Nickerson grab the face mask of Chicago's rookie runner Rashaan Salaam, who was already on his way to the ground, and tear off his helmet like he was ripping open a package" (Green, 1995, p. 1). Then, the next day, he and "a national audience tuned in to see if [Pittsburgh Steeler linebacker] Greg Lloyd would make good on his threat to injure [Miami Dolphin quarterback] Dan Marino. He did!" (p. 1). Green continued with the following:

> But Lloyd was wrong in premeditating Marino's injury and declaring to the media that he would hurt him within or without the rules, because when a player puts violence before the game, he becomes a vigilante – someone who disregards the rules for his own purposes. At that point, the whole concept of a game is lost. The beauty of football, at its best, is the delicate balance of breathtaking athleticism and brute power and aggression. When players disregard the rules, the balance is lost. All you have left is a street brawl, and that isn't, and shouldn't be, football.
>
> (p. 2)

Television journalism seemingly followed NPR's lead. On November 26, 1995, *60 Minutes* aired a segment on sports violence entitled "Unsportsmanlike Conduct!" Four days later, *48 Hours* broadcast "Violent Athletes," which showed how young athletes are socialized by their coaches and parents to be more violent in their play, and examined the place of sports in cultivating an increasingly violent culture.

A major portion of the latter program examined the violent behavior *off the field* of some players from the University of Nebraska's 1995 football team. Following up on this television program, the major AP sportswire story on the day of the 1996 Fiesta Bowl, the game that would determine whether the University of Nebraska or the University of Florida was ranked as the top NCAA Division A football team of 1995, devoted several paragraphs to the Cornhuskers' problems with violence and also brought the University of Florida into the view of the sports violence lens:

Osborne [Coach Tom Osborne, University of Nebraska], meanwhile, has been dealing with his players' off-field problems all season.

In addition to Phillips [running back Lawrence Phillips, suspended from the team for six games after beating his ex-girlfriend], sentenced to one year of probation, reserve receiver Riley Washington is facing a charge of attempted second-degree murder . . .

Four other players on Nebraska's roster of about 150 have made news because of legal trouble in the last couple of years. Two Florida players, defensive end Johnie Church and safety Teako Brown, allegedly struck women in separate incidents.

(Walker, 1996, p. B1)

As might be anticipated by Tank McNamara fans, this contamination of the Bowl Games led to a poignant comic strip. Two sports reporters are shown conversing in a press room:

"Four starters trashed a whole convenience store and beat up the clerk and they're being **released?**"
"What is 'Athletic Immunity'?"
"It's like diplomatic immunity. The legislature passed it so that key f'ball players won't be kept out of our bowl games on trumped-up charges."
"So football's pretty important down here, huh?"
"It's renewable and only morally polluting."

(Millar & Hinds, 1995, p. B8)

The issue of sports violence has reached such critical proportions that not only sports journalists and social commentators are concerned, athletes are also daring to speak out on the plague of sports violence. As former Los Angeles Laker (NBA) great Kareem Abdul-Jabbar stated in a television interview, "Sports is a step away from the rule of the jungle. And they're trying to move it back toward the jungle where the strong survive and misuse the weaker in any way that they want. And that's really unfortunate for our whole system of values here in this country" ("Unsportsmanlike conduct!," 1995, p. 16).

These critics are concerned not only with the escalating quantity of sports violence, they are also concerned with qualitative differences in the way hostility and aggressiveness are being incorporated into modern sports, especially media sports contests. One dimension of this new attitude in sports is what columnist Bob Greene has called "The Deionization of America," after professional football and baseball star Deion Sanders. Greene was interviewed on *60 Minutes*, as this program attempted to explain the "trashing and taunting, dancing and dissing, finger-pointing and free-for-alls" of ". . .television that keeps rewarding the hotdogs and the brawlers with more air time, more attention," and "fights [that] are replayed and analyzed in slow-mo" ("Unsportsmanlike conduct!," 1995, pp. 15, 18). Greene argued the following:

"The Deionization of America" is saying to the country, "This is what's good; this is what'll make you rich; this is what sells." Any instincts you have toward humility, any instincts you have toward not showing someone up; any instincts you have toward not trying to make yourself look good at someone else's expense, those are worthless now. You're invisible . . . You'd better be loud; you'd better be in someone's face, because if you aren't, you can't be seen.

("Unsportsmanlike conduct!" 1995, p. 18)

This issue has become so contentious in some circles that in 1995 the NCAA Football Rules Committee passed rules restricting taunting and celebration of individual achievements in college football. The committee distributed to the Athletic Departments of all NCAA member institutions a videotape entitled *College Football: A Celebration of Teamwork*. This video delineated action that the Rules Committee deemed acceptable versus unacceptable. In the words of Vince Dooley, Chair of the NCAA Rules Committee and narrator of the videotape, "The film clips you just saw illustrate the difference between the type of hard-hitting action and excitement that has made college football one of this country's favorite spectator sports and the taunting and showboating that have threatened to ruin the spirit of teamwork and competition that the game is intended to develop" (NCAA Football Rules Committee, 1995).

Moreover, the NCAA Rules Committee allegedly informed college officials and television football announcing teams that sportscasters should curb coverage and comments of taunting, individual celebration, and acts of violence. This issue was also addressed in the *60 Minutes* report, which presented a sample of offending commentary that warrants repeating here, although it loses impact without television's dramatic voice. These statements from sports announcers and color commentators seem designed to encourage sports violence, to fan the flames of the spectators' enthusiasm for violent play:

"Let's go, baby! Come on! Get the gloves off and let's rock 'n' roll!"
"I mean, that's some good duking."
"Holy mackerel, what a fight!"
"We're going to have a brouhaha."

("Unsportsmanlike conduct!," 1995, p. 18)

Another issue closely related to the "Deionization of America" is "The Lost Art of Losing Well" (Edwards, 1995, November). A new generation of American sports heroes seems to have forgotten how to lose gracefully, to recognize with class a superior opponent. Rather, defeat is met with blame shifting, finger pointing, and misplaced hostility.

We whine, we sulk, we make excuses, we blame others, we plot revenge, we call a lawyer. And why is that? Because the home of the brave has become the land of the bad loser.

Once, bad losing was unacceptably bad form. Now it's the norm, and examples are everywhere . . . The noble champ who takes a lickin' and keeps from noisy politickin' is now history. Today, he's just a chump, seen as too meek to mouth off.

(Edwards, 1995, pp. 25–26)

Even the so-called "genteel sports," like tennis, golf, or polo, are now besieged by vicious sore losers who wreak hostility or even aggression on those who are so unfortunate as to get in their way.

> [Consider] the tennis player's racquet-flinging frenzy when a line call goes against him, barking obscenities, abusing the linesman, the umpire, and anyone else who has dared thwart him. If need be, as happened at this year's Wimbledon, he'll wing a line drive, hitting the head of a ball girl, like Tim Henman, or applaud his wife for administering a slap to those who have wronged him, like Jeff Tarango, whose wife, Benedicte, laid a couple of back-hands to the face of chair umpire Bruno Rebeuh.
>
> (Edwards, 1995, p. 25)

And how many times did the news media treat us to those aggressive displays from sore losers? From CNN, to ESPN, to network news, to local news, the American public was shown those same incidents of bad sportsmanship over and over and over.

"Dissing an opponent is nothing new, of course. Achilles, one of history's most infamous bad winners, dragged the fallen Trojan hero Hector behind his chariot around the wall of Troy – and promptly caught an arrow to the heel from the gods" (Edwards, 1995, p. 25). But presumably the gods did not have instant replay, and slow-mo, and television sports news, and sports pages, and sports magazines, and radio sports shows, and television talk-show hosts to tell and re-tell the story of their poor sportsmanship to mere mortals, who might just incorporate the lessons of "the gods" into their own behavior and cultural values.

THE ORIGINS OF SPECTATORSHIP AND THE ROOTS OF SPORTS VIOLENCE

Consideration of the activities of "the gods" provides a segue to the ancient origins of sports spectatorship, which have been explored in great detail by Guttmann (1986), Crabb and Goldstein (1991), and Zillmann and Paulus (1993), among others. The present synopsis owes much to the last treatment.

Although evidence for organized sporting events can be traced back into Egyptian culture as far as 5,200 BC, evidence for sports spectatorship is extant only from the first century BC. The locus of these reports was the Grecian Olympic Games, which offered dimensions of spectator entertainment as well as opportunities for civic and religious ceremonies (Guttmann, 1986; Harris, 1972).

The Grecian appreciation of athletic grace was soon to be usurped by the spread of the Roman Empire and the accompanying Roman urbanization. According to Midwinter (1986), this urbanization created and nourished a growing appetite for sports spectacles laden with violence. Not only did spectators play a major role in Roman "blood sports" like gladiator matches or violent chariot races, often the most privileged spectators determined whether the losers were sacrificed by the victors – perhaps not the pre-eminent "thrill of victory," but certainly the ultimate "agony of defeat." These blood sports were superspectacles in terms of attendance, even by today's standards for non-televised sporting events. For example, Rome's Coliseum accommodated at least 40,000 spectators, and the largest Roman race-track hosted crowds of approximately 250,000 spectators (Harris, 1972).

THE SCOPE OF SPORTS SPECTATORSHIP

The attendance records for Roman sporting events remained unchallenged until the period of the industrial revolution, although blood sports such as bull-fighting continued to attract large crowds in regions such as the Iberian Peninsula. As it did with many other aspects of society, the industrial revolution dramatically changed things as far as sports spectatorship was concerned. "Lending some degree of support to the orthodox Marxist view that spectatorship, as a significant form of recreation, is an outgrowth of the monotony of machine-dictated labor (Ponomarev, 1974; Sansone, 1988), sports events became the weekend love affair of all those whose workday was strictly regulated by production schedules (Zillmann & Paulus, 1993, p. 601). For example, in 1901 110,000 spectators paid to see the final of the Football Association (FA) Cup in Great Britain (Midwinter, 1986).

Today, of course, going to the game is a major pastime in the United States and throughout much of the rest of the world. In the United States alone, more than 200 million spectators attend college and professional games each year, spending more than $6 billion dollars on spectator sports. Although the portion of the entertainment budget the average American spends on live attendance at sports events is relatively small – less than 2 percent of the average person's total enter-tainment budget and only about one-fourth as much as the average US citizen spends on gambling each year (Bryant & Love, 1996) – avid fans devote a goodly portion of their income to such pursuits. For example, recent telephone surveys of Southeastern Conference Football fans revealed that those interviewees who iden-tified themselves as "avid" followers of either Auburn or Alabama spent an average of $543 in 1992 and $525 in 1994 – in excess of 10 percent of their subjectively defined disposable income during both years – on expenditures associated with attending college football games (Bryant, Love, & Robicheaux, 1996).

THE PLACE OF MASS COMMUNICATION IN
SPORTS SPECTATORSHIP

The nature of spectatorship changed dramatically with the advent of mass commu-nication, especially television. Now, with the 24-hour sports channels nationally (e.g., ESPN) and regionally (e.g., SportsSouth), instead of attending one or two sporting events per weekend, the fan can watch literally dozens of sports events during a weekend, or even on weekdays, for that matter. Moreover, with the development of multichannel direct satellite services, that same fan can choose from numerous live sports events any time games are being played. "The new communication technologies raised sports spectatorship more than a thousandfold" (Zillmann & Paulus, 1993, p. 601).

Nowadays, drawing "crowds" of a million spectators to televised games is routine, and events like the NFL Super Bowl routinely are among the most widely watched events on network television, gradually becoming a National Holiday in the United States. Moreover, World Cup soccer matches are seen by close to a billion spectators around the world. "Sports spectatorship appears headed for a great future. For the coverage of significant athletic events, the world will be a global village indeed" (Zillmann & Paulus, 1993, p. 601).

Audience size is but one index of the ascendancy of sports on television. The pervasiveness of sports programming on television is another useful index, with the 24 hour-per-day sports channels standing tall as a clear indicator of the USA's and, indeed, the world's love affair with televised sports (LaFayette, 1995). By the late 1980s, sports accounted for more than 1,800 hours of network television programming and for approximately 5,000 hours of cable programming; that does not even take into account the amount of syndicated and local sports programming on the air (Eastman & Meyer, 1989). Those figures grow annually.

IS VIOLENCE A FACTOR IN SPECTATOR'S ENJOYMENT OF TELEVISED SPORTS?

With the availability of sports events on television on the rise, especially with the advent of ESPN, ESPN2, regional sports networks, and direct broadcast satellite proliferation of sports coverage, and with the audience for televised sporting events rising concomitantly, it might seem unnecessary to incorporate ever increasing amounts of violence into coverage. However, from the perspective of sports programmers, the proliferation of sports channels makes attracting a sufficiently large audience to satisfy advertisers or marketers even more difficult; therefore elements like violence that are presumed to be an audience draw become more attractive. Obviously this assumes that either producers' gut reactions or their audience research reveal that violence is an important factor in attracting and maintaining a sizable audience of sports spectators. "The persisting popularity of combative sports, and of wrestling and boxing in particular, would seem to give sufficient support to the contention that at least a good portion of sports spectators enjoy bruising activities that often lead to the temporary incapacitation, by knockout or injury, of some competitors" (Zillmann & Paulus, 1993, p. 606).

Several rationales can be offered to explain why sports violence should facilitate the spectator's enjoyment of sports events (see Bryant & Zillmann, 1983b; Zillmann, 1996). Moreover, a few empirical investigations of the enjoyment of watching televised sports contests have shed light on the value of these theoretical rationales as well as on the assumptions of sports producers and programmers (see Bryant, 1989).

Theories of the Enjoyment of Sports Violence

The most commonly offered rationale to explain why violence in sports should facilitate spectators' enjoyment stems from the notion of *catharsis,* that is, a purgation of pent-up feelings of hostility. The most vocal proponent of this view has been Lorenz (1963). His ideas have been summarized in theoretical terms:

> If, following Lorenz, one were to assume (a) that destructive energy spontaneously builds up in the organism, (b) that the performance of aggressive acts reduces such energy to tolerable levels, a process which is pleasantly experienced, (c) that the performance of competitive actions also serves this pleasing outlet function, and (d) that even merely witnessing competitive actions serves this function, one seems to have accounted for the popularity of sports – doing and viewing.
>
> (Zillmann, Bryant, & Sapolsky, 1979, p. 310)

According to this line of reasoning, the more violent the action in a sports contest, the greater the pleasure that should result from the experience of relief. In reality, the catharsis proposal is associated with numerous conceptual difficulties (Zillmann, 1991, 1996), and it is refuted by a wealth of non-supportive empirical or contradictory evidence from a variety of research traditions (e.g., Baron & Richardson, 1994; Geen & Quanty, 1977; Zillmann, 1979). Nonetheless, despite these difficulties, it is clear that this rationale is widely accepted in society.

An alternative explanation for the enjoyment of violence and even hostility in sports can be derived from the work of Hobbes, Nietzsche, Spencer, and others, but especially Adler (1927). These scholars have claimed that humans are constantly motivated to enhance their own power and self-esteem by *asserting dominance* over others. They have argued that this desire for interpersonal dominance is one of the strongest of all motivators. Cheska (1968/1981) considered the concepts of power and dominance to be objectified in modern sports contests. The strongest degree of power and dominance, according to Cheska's argument, is "direct control," which is "dominance by physical qualities, manipulation, or confinement of others by players in the athletic arena" (p. 371). Certainly the taunting, the "in your face" direct threats, the "dissing," and the like of modern sports seem to be perfect examples of this type of direct control. If it can be assumed that the sports fan aligns him- or herself so closely with the athlete dishing out the hostility or aggression before millions of spectators, then sports spectatorship offers a legitimate way of "asserting dominance" over another in rather dramatic form. From this purview, it would be expected that the more obtrusive and decisive the dominance (so long as moral judgmental "filters" of propriety and the like are not invoked), the greater the pleasure for the viewer, at least for the viewer who "is Adlerian" in personality. This rationale often, but not necessarily, assumes that the spectator "identifies with the hero" (a sports hero or a "heroic team"). For example, Cheska (1968/1981) argued that "control may be associated as identification and involvement of spectators with participating athletes in the enactment of the power process" (p. 371). Although such reasoning is very common, it is conceptually troublesome and has received severe criticism (e.g., Zillmann, 1991, 1996).

A third rationale emphasizes competition. Conflict and competition have long been perceived as key elements in the *enjoyment of drama*. Phases such as "the human drama of athletic competition" often highlight such notions. Moreover, it has been argued that vigorous and vicious play, particularly when mutual injury and pain are likely, is the purest, most primitive index of high competitiveness. Therefore, intensely physical, risky, especially violent play stands for human conflict at its peak, and intense conflict is the heart and soul of high drama (Zillmann et al., 1989). Novak (1976) put it very well: "The most satisfying element in sports is spirit. Other elements being equal, the more spirited team will win: the one that hits the hardest, drives itself the most" (p. 149). According to this reasoning, increased interpersonal aggression and hostility in sports prove to the spectator that the players are "giving it all they've got," are "risking their all" for the game. Therefore violence has utility not only for its own sake, but because it is the perfect symbol that the athletes are giving everything they've got for the contest, and, of course, for the spectator. As Ogden Nash (1937/1980, p. 408) so poignantly phrased things:

> With all my heart do I admire
> Athletes who sweat for fun or hire,
> Who take the field in gaudy pomp
> And maim each other as they romp;
> My limp and bashful spirit feeds
> On other people's heroic deeds.

Bentham (1802/1931) labeled sportive action in which the stakes are exceptionally high as "deep play." This phrase and notion have been adopted by anthropologists to explain primitive spectator sports. For example, Geertz (1976) has examined Balinese cockfights as deep play conducted solely for spectators. "In the cockfight, man and beast, good and evil, ego and id, and creative power of aroused masculinity and destructive power of loosened animality fuse in a bloody drama of hatred, cruelty, violence, and death" (p. 658). Geertz's "thick description" of the fight emphasizes the dramatic aspects of deep play: "The cocks fly almost immediately at one another in a wing-beating, head-thrusting, leg-kicking explosion of animal fury so pure, so absolute, and in its own way so beautiful, as to be almost abstract, a Platonic concept of hate" (p. 659).

If this fury, this hostility, this aggression of deep play is so representative of primitive conflict, it should be expected to produce higher drama. As Cheska (1968/1981) noted, "The elements of drama – participants, ritual, plot, production, symbolism, social message – are all brilliantly choreographed in the sports spectacular" (p. 376). And apparently violence works to infuse entertainment value into sports contests, because it elevates deep play to high drama.

Empirical Evidence for the Appeal of Sports Violence

Despite abundant popular claims and theoretical speculation that sports violence enhances spectators' enjoyment of sports contests, pertinent empirical evidence is scarce. Only a handful of investigations have directly assessed the appeal of sports violence for spectators. In fact, only one study has offered a "heads on" comparison of spectators' enjoyment of nonaggressive and aggressive play (Bryant, Comisky, & Zillmann, 1981). In this investigation, a sizable number of plays in professional football were drawn from games telecast throughout an NFL season. The level of aggression of each play (low, intermediate, high) was ascertained via pretesting, and the plays were edited into a random sequence. Enjoyment of each play was assessed, and enjoyment reactions were related to categories of aggressive plays. As can be seen from Figure 16.1, the more violence and roughness, the greater the enjoyment. This relationship was statistically significant for males only; it was not reliable for females, although the overall pattern of responses generally was similar. Male spectators, then, responded in line with the oft-quoted statement of Vince Lombardi, who readily acknowledged that his sport was "violent" and crowed, "That's why the crowds love it!" (cited in Michener, 1976, p. 520).

These findings were supported in a recent macroanalytic study by Zillmann and his associates (Zillmann, 1995), who identified salient characteristics (e.g., violence, action, speed, risk, artistry) in all sports events on television and then examined male and female respondents' ratings of enjoyment of all these sporting events. As can be seen from examining Figure 16.2, the defining salient characteristic of the sports events that received the highest enjoyment ratings was violence. Moreover, male viewers' ratings of enjoyment of sports containing violence were significantly higher than those of female viewers.

Further support for spectator enjoyment of interpersonal aggression comes from a study by DeNeui and Sachau (1996). A sizable sample of male and female spectators at intercollegiate hockey games rated how enjoyable they found sixteen

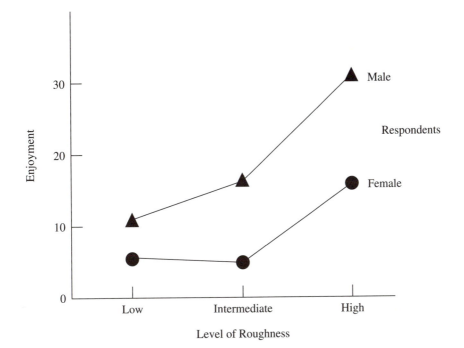

Figure 16.1 Level of enjoyment of sports as a function of perceived level of roughness in play for male and female respondents

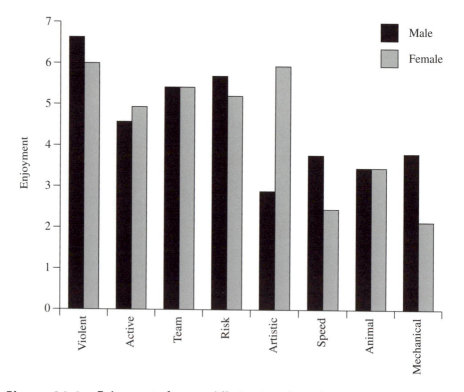

Figure 16.2   Enjoyment of sports differing in salient characteristics as a function of gender of respondents

different games. Their measures of enjoyment were correlated with a variety of game statistics, including variables related to competitiveness (e.g., closeness of the game), game outcome (e.g., home team success), and aggressiveness of play (e.g., penalties, minutes of power play). The only measures that predicted enjoyment reliably were those related to aggressiveness of play.

Corroborating evidence of the enjoyment of rugged play comes from research into the effects of sportscasting. Comisky, Bryant, and Zillmann (1977) drew examples of what appeared to be extremely rough play versus normal play from a professional ice hockey game, and specific video and audio properties were determined in a pretest. The pretest revealed a fortuitous occurrence: One segment in which extremely rough or violent play was presented featured rather bland commentary, and the announcers let the rough action carry the scene without embellishment. In contrast, a segment in which minimally rough play was presented visually was embellished by the announcer and color commentator so as to describe action that threatened to turn into a brawl any minute. This permitted tests not only of broadcast commentary's effects on spectators' perceptions of roughness of action, it also permitted assessments of the effects of perceptions of sports violence on enjoyment of play. In a quasi-experimental design, spectators viewed one of the two selected segments either with or without commentary and rated their enjoyment of the play and then how rough or violent they perceived the action to be. As can be seen from Figure 16.3, the presence and nature of the commentary fundamentally altered perceptions of roughness of play: In the normal-action condition, the commentary stressing violence made the play appear rough, even rougher than the depicted violent play. In contrast, in the rough-action condition, the commentary ignoring roughness made genuinely violent play appear even less rough than the more normal play. This demonstrated that commentary certainly can alter perceptions of play.

More critical for the present discussion, ratings of entertainment value were entirely concordant with the degree to which play was *perceived* to be rough and violent. The condition that was rated as most entertaining was that featuring normal play but that was accompanied by commentary that made the play appear to be rougher than it actually was. Clearly, then, perceived roughness and violence can contribute to viewers' enjoyment of sports contests.

An investigation by Sullivan (1991) provided further confirmation of a portion of these findings. Commentary from a televised basketball game between collegiate foes Georgetown University and Syracuse University was manipulated by professional sportscasters so as to create three commentary conditions (commentary stressing Syracuse aggression, neutral commentary, no commentary). Respondent gender and degree of sports fanship were additional variables employed. Viewers' perceptions of the degree of roughness and violence of play were assessed, as was their enjoyment of the sports contest. Once again, commentary was found to significantly influence viewers' perceptions of sports violence: Viewers of the aggression-suggesting commentary condition saw the Syracuse players as being

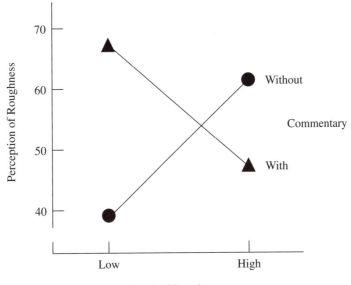

Figure 16.3 Perceptions and actual levels of roughness in play by characterization of roughness in commentary

significantly more aggressive than did viewers in either other condition. As with the study by Comisky et al. (1977), men enjoyed the violent play more than did women. Surprisingly, experienced sports fans' perceptions of play were no less vulnerable to the commentary manipulation than those of less avid fans. Unfortunately, the measures of enjoyment and appreciation were confounded in this investigation, as the commentary merely shifted the locus of the aggression from the less aggressive to the more aggressive team, rather than systematically enhancing or suppressing viewers' perceptions of the overall level of aggressiveness of play. However, trends in patterns of mean scores for enjoyment would seem to support the author's summation that "commentary can facilitate enjoyment of player violence" (p. 502).

A final related investigation featured neither actual nor perceived violence nor roughness; instead, it focused on the animosity between players that increasingly seems to be emphasized in color commentary and sports journalism, as was previously discussed. Bryant, Brown, Comisky, and Zillmann (1982) manipulated the commentary of a televised tennis match so that it appeared to spectators that the two players either loved, hated, or had no particular affective disposition toward each other. As with the previous studies on sportscasting, it was found that commentary was an effective means of altering spectators' perceptions: Compared with presenting the players as best buddies or not specifying their affiliation, reporting that the opponents were arch rivals and bitter enemies made the spectators see the play as more hostile, tense, and intense. Moreover, as indicated in Figure 16.4, spectators who thought the opponents were hated foes, rather than best friends or neutral opponents, reported significantly greater enjoyment from watching the match than did viewers in the other condition. Not only did ratings of entertainment value benefit from the perceived enmity, so did the spectators' degree of excitement, involvement, and interest.

CONCLUSION

The extant evidence clearly indicates that increased player aggressiveness enhances spectators', especially male spectators', enjoyment of watching sports contests. Related evidence from studies of sportscasting reveals that commentary stressing roughness of action can facilitate viewers' perceptions of the violence of the event, which, in turn, can lead to greater enjoyment of the sports contest. And, finally, play-by-play and color commentary that stress hostility and animosity between opponents can cause spectators to perceive play as more violent than it is and also can result in greater enjoyment for spectators.

Does this triangulating evidence provide an unbridled endorsement for increased violence in sports contests and sports coverage? Hardly. Although elevated roughness in play, or spectators' perceptions of more violent play, may contribute to spectator enjoyment, which may be beneficial in its own right, the relative merits of maximizing "the pleasure principle" must be weighed against the relative demerits of potentially contributing to increased societal aggression. If the bulk of the evidence indicates that the immediate gratifications from increased sports violence are associated with concomitant increases in antisocial behavior (e.g,

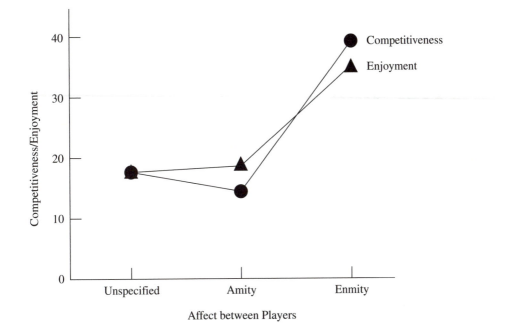

Figure 16.4 Enjoyment and perceived competitiveness of sporting matches as a function of perceived affect between players

Branscombe & Wann, 1992a; Russell, 1992; Russell, Di Lullo, & Di Lullo, 1988–89; Simons & Taylor, 1992; Young & Smith, 1988–89), the court of last resort may decide that the thrills that violent sports events can provide come at too high a cost.

Chapter 17

Extending the Sports Experience: Mediations in Cyberspace

Stephen R. McDaniel &
Christopher B. Sullivan

Just as we begin to develop an understanding of the sports audience experience with print and broadcast technologies, computer mediated sport emerges to offer new challenges. "Cybersport" involves online computing, with interactive multimedia capabilities that transcend the arguably more passive audience experience with traditional media. This chapter explores the relationship between sports and new media by looking at conceptual frameworks that might aid in theory development for cybersport phenomena. An overview of online sports is followed by examples of how computer-monitored data and online surveys can be used to examine sports fans on the Internet, including their usage patterns, demographics and interests. By looking at the various aspects of online sports, it is hoped that this work will help add to the growing knowledge base on sports media and its audience.

SPORTS AND COMMUNICATION TECHNOLOGY

The modern popularity of sports is in many ways related to the development of communication technology. The synergistic relationship that exists between sports and mass media has, along with certain social and economic conditions, greatly influenced the commercial direction of both industries over the past century (McChesney, 1989). As media coverage of athletic contests became an extension of sports spectatorship, the public's appetite for mediated sports helped to increase media diffusion and consumption (cf., McChesney, 1989; McLuhan, 1964). For example, the expansion of professional baseball in the 1870s was accompanied by the speed of the telegraph and of the new rotary press newspapers, both of which allowed fans to keep up with the daily box scores (Betts, 1969; Harris, 1994). During the 1889 heavyweight boxing championship, Associated Press journalists transmitted over 200,000 words across the telegraph wires to newspapers around the world (Betts, 1969).

In the 1920s, radio brought a new dimension to "spectating" as fans could follow a game "live," without leaving home (McChesney, 1989). The sports experience was further transformed with the diffusion of television in the 1950s, the advent of cable networks and direct broadcast satellites in the 1980s and the World Wide Web in the 1990s (Harris, 1994; Zakon, 1996; Cerf, 1994). The dynamics of the sport/media relationship has in many ways helped to transform contemporary sports into mass mediated entertainment; subsequently, both professional and amateur athletes (and coaches) have come to be seen as high profile entertainers, similar to actors/actresses in television and film (Izod, 1996).

Today the World Wide Web (WWW) offers the sports audience more than scores and stories. Sports discussion groups proliferate on the Usenet pages (Malec, 1996). Fans can visit interactive sports sites that offer fantasy games, sports software and player statistics; likewise, they can see photographs, video clips and read feature stories on their favorite teams and athletes (Bruckman, 1996). Sports spectators can become true armchair managers, as they play fantasy games with one another on the WWW. Consequently, today's interactive computer technology offers to take the sports audience experience a step further with its potential to combine the once separate roles of spectator and participant (McDaniel & Armstrong, 1994; Brand, 1988).

One important aspect of the WWW is its relative accessibility to both fans and commercial sports organizations. Its popularity can also be seen in the expansion of traditional sports media, such as publishing houses and broadcast networks onto the Web, as well as the promotion of these Web sites in broadcast and print media at local and national levels (Newcomb, 1996; Berniker, 1995a; Mandese, 1995). With the advent of real-time audio and video over the Web, the sports fan may come to rely even more heavily on the Internet for sports news and coverage of games. Clearly there is a convergence of "traditional" media forms with the newer computer networks, and the outcome seems to be a technological amalgam of interactive multimedia (and in some cases even virtual) sports. Not surprisingly, entertainment content (like sports) is expected to become one of the fastest growing aspects of the Internet in the future (Lohr, 1996).

DELINEATING CYBERSPORT PHENOMENA

The Internet is a unique form of communication because its computer based point-to-point telecommunication infrastructure defines it as a one-to-one medium, like the telephone; yet, it functions like a one-to-many medium, similar to a broadcast station. As December (1996, p. 24) points out, "users of the Internet experience a very different communication context than do non-Internet users." For example, the nature of the network technology allows cybersport fans to be "unencumbered" by geographic boundaries, enabling them to participate more freely in the collective experience that is so endemic to sports fanship (cf. Zillman, Bryant & Sapolsky, 1979). Nevertheless, trying to explain how cybersport fans use the Internet requires that one combine an assortment of theoretical perspectives, each of which was developed to explain a particular medium, generally not the Internet. Looking at the Web as a computer-based communication network, one could draw from network theory (Contractor & Eisenberg, 1990), or from research on the adoption of interactive telecommunications (Sullivan, 1995; Rice, Grant, Schmitz & Torobin 1990; Rice, 1987), or theories about the effects of information technology (Huber, 1990).

Likewise, approaching the Internet as a mass communication technology would also allow us to draw from a considerable body of literature. Morris and Ogan (1996) argue that researchers often fail to see the Internet as analogous to a mass medium and subsequently miss the opportunity to test existing mass communication theory in a network context. They contend that characterizing the Internet as a mass medium would take advantage of many different media theories and permit the use of more critical approaches when examining the production and consumption of programming content, in this instance sports (cf. Jhally, 1989; Trujillo & Ekdom, 1985). Even when limiting the Internet to a mass media context, however, it is important to further specify the nature of communication activity.

The mass media literature offers a number of existing taxonomies with which to approach the initial study of cybersport (cf. DeFleur & Ball-Rokeach, 1989; Wright, 1986; Ball-Rokeach, 1985). Such research might focus on the Internet and the audience experience with online sports content, much like traditional mass communication. Nevertheless, it's clear that new conceptual frameworks are needed to theorize about computer mediated sport. Morris and Ogan (1996, p. 42) characterize the Internet as "a multifaceted mass medium, that is, it contains many different configurations of communication." They outline a typology of network audience to medium relationships based on singular and multiplicative forms of communication, which define Web ("mass") communication as:

- one-to-one asynchronous communication (e.g., e-mail, i.e., electronic mail)
- many-to-many asynchronous communication (e.g., listservers and bulletin boards)
- one-to-one or many-to-many synchronous communication organized around a topic (e.g., MUDs, i.e., Multi-User Dialogues)
- asynchronous communication generally characterized by the receiver's need to seek out the site to access information which can involve any number of variations in source-receiver relationships (e.g., Web sites)

(Morris & Ogan, 1996, p. 42).

Each of these categories addresses a particular feature of the Internet for synchronous or asynchronous communication in both text (e.g., e-mail or gopher) and graphic (e.g., WWW) modes. According to Morris and Ogan (1996), asynchronistic network communication is characterized by a pattern of serial communication in which the user moves sequentially, or "surfs," through a complex set of interlinked Internet sites, each of which offer any number of different possibilities in terms of the number of Web sites, communicators and flow of communication. This hybrid of mass and interpersonal forms of communication requires new perspectives to help explain the dynamics involved in this latest form of interactive telecommunications (Beniger, 1987).

December (1996) proposes an Internet typology arranged according to a hierarchy of network interconnections. He labels the hierarchical levels as: media space, media class and media object. In addition to these three levels he posits two user-oriented concepts that deal with audience perceptions of the Internet: media instance and media experience (December, 1996, pp. 27–28). This typology clearly refers to the Internet; although, each level of the hierarchy could be applied to other media, for example television, so it provides comparability across media systems. Table 17.1 lists these units of analysis along with examples of how December's terminology might be applied in a cybersport context.

The most comprehensive level in December's typology is **media space**, which refers to the interconnection of similar sets of network servers across the Internet; this conceptualization offers some insight into the complexity and inclusiveness of the Internet. An example of media space is the World Wide Web (WWW), which is the set of interconnected servers accessible by Hypertext Transfer Protocol (HTTP) addresses. A comparable media space is the Internet Relay Chat (IRC) which is comprised of the linked networks available through Telnet access. IRC is not accessible through the WWW, so these constitute two separate media spaces. A third media space consists of Gopher servers, which are accessible to Gopher clients and to WWW clients, so these two media spaces overlap; however, IRC clients cannot access Gopher space so these spaces are also separate.

Table 17.1   December's (1996) Units of Internet Analysis Applied to Cybersport Audience Research

Unit/term	Sports example	Research approaches
Media space	World Wide Web	Computer-monitored data to measure number of sites or total volume of Web traffic
Media class	Sports Web sites	Industry analysis (structural-functional or critical perspectives)
Media object	ESPNet or SportsLine	Content analysis or rhetorical criticism
Media instance	ESPNet on Superbowl Sunday 1996	Computer-monitored data to measure site traffic
Media experience	Person "x" logged on to ESPNet on Superbowl Sunday 1996	Online surveys, participant observer, experience sampling, focus groups

December uses the concept of media space to describe the Internet as a multiplistic network of overlapping "spheres of activity." He describes media space as "a seamless forum, in which users can observe any of the content from the servers in that space using their clients" (December, 1996, p. 27).

The **media class** is a subset of media space, referring to the network servers, clients and media content that share similar characteristics (December, 1996). Using this conceptualization, one could posit all network servers dedicated to sports as falling into the media class of "cybersport." This class might cross several different media spaces (e.g., WWW space and Gopher space), but would remain a coherent class by virtue of its sports orientation. An example of the cybersport class can be seen on any sports Web site that provides a set of links to related sports Web sites; the sum total of these sites comprise the cybersport class.

The specific sports Web site, for example, a set of league statistics or a fantasy game, can be defined as a **media object**. For December, media objects are concrete, unambiguous units of observation within a media class, which are tied together by the defining characteristics of the media class. The media class of cybersport, then, is composed of all sports Web sites, sports data sets, games, pictures, stories and information about athletes and athletics; each of these is a cybersport "object." One of the major difficulties in studying cybersport is the rapid proliferation of the media objects within this class, as well as the continual fluctuation of cybersport content, all of which is driven by the ongoing evolution of WWW space.

December deals with the mutable nature of Internet content by proposing the idea of a **media instance**, which is defined as a media object at one particular moment in time. People perceive a media instance, he argues, not necessarily media objects or media classes. An example might be accessing the USA Today Web site (http://www.usatoday.com), with its daily compilation of sports scores, news and features. Another example might be using a fantasy game like SportsLine's Fantasy Football (http://www2.sportsline.com/u/football/fantasy/owners.htm), which allows participants to create rosters of professional football players using game statistics that are updated daily. As these stories and statistics change, so the particular media instance changes, but the media objects (e.g., USA Today online or SportsLine) remain relatively constant. Finally, evoking a uses and gratifications perspective, December argues that each cybersport fan brings his or her individual perception to the Internet, which gives rise to a unique **media experience** for each fan.

One benefit of December's typology for examining online sports lies in the way he separates out categorical units of analysis that can help us to focus on specific elements of cybersport communication. For example, the interaction of network servers in the cybersport media class can be tracked by keeping a log of connection activity from Web client addresses, this can give an indication of user activity within this class. Keeping a record of logins for a particular Web site, tracking how long users stay connected or how many files are downloaded indicates the popularity of particular media objects within the cybersport class, and provides some idea of the consumption patterns of the cybersport audience. These patterns, and others like them, have often been studied in the "traditional" media, but we need to consider them once again in the context of the Internet, bringing us greater understanding of online sport communication.

EXPLORING THE WIDE WORLD OF CYBERSPORT

The Internet provides a daunting number of possibilities in terms of information and entertainment options for sports fans. While many of the sports-related Internet sites are maintained by members of the general public, the traditional print and electronic sports media have also extended their reach into the media space of the WWW (Gunther, 1996; Notess, 1996; Mandese, 1995; Jessell, 1995). In addition to traditional sports media locations, fans can access online information provided by the sport organizations themselves, which includes most major colleges, professional sports teams and leagues (Newcomb, 1996; Pesky, 1995; Waltner, 1995; Lefton, 1995; Berniker, 1995a).

The relatively inclusive nature of Internet communication technology arguably blurs some of the social and commercial boundaries within the mediated sports production complex, as first conceptualized by Wenner (1989). For instance, sports fans are now able to produce sports sites for themselves on the WWW. Meanwhile, some television networks and sports leagues have started to co-promote each other on their sports Web sites, e.g., the NBA and NBC's efforts during the 1996 NBA Finals. The fact that certain owners of professional sports franchises (e.g., Microsoft's Paul Allen, who has interests in both NBA and NFL teams) are also key figures in the high-tech media industry suggests that the distinction between sport and media organizations may continue to blur – a phenomenon that will undoubtedly impact the nature of mediated sport (Katz, 1995).

Sports Media Organizations in Cyberspace

Internet sites maintained by the traditional media are probably one of the most obvious forms of the cybersport media class. Recognizable sports media organizations such as ESPN, *USA TODAY*, *Sports Illustrated*, CBS, ABC and FOX Sports have all developed an online presence as an extension of their print or broadcast formats, which helps to leverage their existing coverage (Gunther, 1996; Baum, 1995; Petrozello, 1995). Even well recognized sports advertisers have established Web sites, as Valvoline did in 1995 during the Indianapolis 500 (Flynn, 1995). Most sites in this media class can be accessed free of charge; although, ESPNet and SportsLine have recently launched subscription-based services (Spiegler, 1996; Berniker, 1995b). Given the embryonic nature of this industry, however, the economic viability of such commercial sites is still uncertain (Lohr, 1996).

The present multimedia characteristics of most Internet sites tend to eliminate some of the typical distinctions found between commercial print and television media. Among the interesting attributes of sports news on the net is the way in which the WWW platform combines the timeliness of electronic media with a potentially greater depth of information than is available from traditional print media (cf., http://www.yahoo.com; http://espnet.sportszone.com; http://www.sportsline.com; http://www.clarinet.com). Moreover, the interactive technology allows the audience more freedom to find information suited to their individual sports interests. ESPNet, for example (http://espnet.sportszone.com), offers links to subsites for specific professional sports pages, such as Major League Ball (http://espnet.sportszone.com/mlb/), college basketball (http://espnet.sportszone.com/ncb/) or sports chat rooms (http://chat.starwave.com). Likewise, *USA TODAY*'s online coverage of college football provides in-depth information on all of the country's major college football programs (http://www.usatoday.com/sports/football/sfc/) and links to other sports-related Web sites (http://www.tcihl.com/~hockey/Coaches/tips.html). This feature has a multiplicative effect, in which the sequential access to different sources of information tends to geometrically increase the amount of information accessible through one Web site.

In another extension of traditional print information, *USA TODAY*'s FanTrack allows sports fans to download statistics on individual athletes. The service provides free tracking software for the user to download, and maintains up-to-date data on professional athletes; the PC software allows a fan to analyze statistics across a league, or to create profiles of favorite players. Another unique feature of many sports media sites (e.g., ESPNet) is that fans are able to communicate via electronic mail with key sports figures and reporters. In this example of asynchronous one-to-one communication, the network technology allows the online fan to bridge some of the communication barriers of conventional mass media, e.g., parasocial relationships with sports figures (cf. Weiss, 1996). It also provides media organizations an efficient feedback mechanism to assess their audiences and markets (Gunther, 1996).

Sports Organizations in Cyberspace

Another example of the fan-oriented cybersport media class can be found in Web sites maintained by the sports organizations themselves. Before the WWW, professional and college sports teams and leagues depended almost exclusively on the mass media to help promote their teams and players (Lever & Wheeler, 1993). The WWW provides a channel for sports organizations to take a more direct approach with community relations, bypassing media organizations and going straight to their fans. Sports fans with online WWW capabilities can now access up-to-date information on their favorite major colleges, minor league and professional sports franchises and athletes. In addition, fans are now able to purchase licensed merchandise and in some cases, even tickets, from the online catalogues of a variety of sports teams (Spiegler, 1996; Ratliff, 1996).

All of the major American professional sports leagues (i.e., NFL, NBA, NHL and MLB) have established Web sites (i.e., http://www.nfl.com/; http://www.nba.com; http://www.nhl.com/; http://www.majorleaguebaseball.com/), which are in turn linked to team Web sites that include schedules, player profiles and statistics (Jensen, 1995; Lefton, 1995). One of the more interesting sports media objects can be found on the NBA's colorful Web site (http://www.nba.com), where fans from around the world can choose among a number of different graphics files, video clips of game highlights and multimedia interviews with star players. As with Web sites maintained by sports media organizations, most sites for sports franchises provide online sports fans a vehicle to communicate with players, coaches and other fans via electronic mail. In addition, sports information on the Net differs from conventional sports coverage by not constraining the sports fan's access to coverage of teams with either local or mass appeal. Rather the WWW media space supports a diversity of sports information from a variety of sources.

Sport Enthusiasts in Cyberspace

Aside from providing information from media and sport organizations, cybersport on the WWW links a community of highly involved sports fans through a number of non-commercial, fan-oriented Web sites. One of the most logical applications of online technology to sports can be found in fantasy leagues, where fans from all over the world can hold mock drafts of professional athletes to create teams that compete for points scored on the basis of individual player statistics (Walker, Rylands, Hiltner & Bellamy, 1993).

Currently, one of the more complex fantasy games on the WWW, Baseball Manager (http://www.baseballmanager.com), allows registered players to manage individual baseball teams made up of professional baseball players whose "play" is based on their real-life statistics. Team standings are constantly changing as different "cyber-managers" take control of team rosters and strategy. Internet access allows such competitions to span geographical boundaries, while maintaining timely access to the statistics that are central to the competition. As previously noted, some commercial sites, like *USA TODAY* (http://www.usatoday.com/sports/baseball/sbfant.htm), currently offer free programs that can be downloaded during a particular sports season, for use in tracking player statistics. Active fantasy game players tend to be heavy users of Web information about sports, much like confirmed gamblers, who not only use this technology to place bets, but seek information (such as point spreads or injury updates on athletes) that can aid their betting (Katz, 1995; Walker et al., 1993). In addition to fantasy league Web sites, non-commercial online bulletin boards and chat rooms provide forums for loyal fans to discuss the specific teams or individual players to which each cite is dedicated, an example of many-to-many asynchronous communication (Malec, 1995a).

While a good deal of Internet sports content is devoted to the fan of spectator sports, the technology is also an important source of information for people who themselves are athletes. As with many sports fan-oriented Web sites, bulletin boards and chat rooms provide athletes from all over the world a platform to share their enthusiasm and involvement, regardless of their skill level or the popularity of their favorite sporting activity (Malec, 1996; Maloni, Greenman & Miller, 1995). The topics currently covered by sporting activity-oriented Web sites are very diverse, ranging from tips on bowling (http://www.bowlingworld.com/) or body building (http://www.frsa.com/bbpage.shtml) to information on Tai Chi (http://www.tai-chi.com/magazine.html) or triathlons (http://www.triathletemag.com/forum/) and any sport in between (http://www.otn.net/onthenet/news/sports.htm).

In addition to fantasy leagues and information for athletes, the participative nature of cybersport can also be found in online computer games. The idea of using the computer to engage in gaming dates back to the first Ataris of the late 1970s. Kids took to onscreen games with an exuberance that made first Nintendo, then Sega, leaders in the electronic game software markets. A generation of young adults has grown up on intensely competitive computer games in video arcades and in their living rooms; the Web currently offers this audience segment another outlet for interactive sports programs (Maloni, Greenman & Miller, 1995).

The move from Nintendo to the WWW is essentially a shift from one multimedia channel to another, one which still has a long way to go to catch up to the fast-paced interactivity of an off-line computer game. At the time of this writing, the Web is currently restricted by the limited bandwidth of the telephone lines which serve as the backbone of the Internet. Therefore, many sports sites confine themselves to still photographs of athletes and textual information predominates. Most of the interactive sports homepages still rely on text-based e-mail for their fantasy games and chat rooms, or listserves for the usenet groups (Malec, 1995b). Yet, interactive games also have a place on the Internet. Multi-User Dialogues (MUDs), for example, have been around since the mid-1980s; they allow two or more players to log onto the same game and then log off as other players arrive to continue the contest (Turkle, 1994). Many bulletin boards allow multiple users to play interactive video games, as well as MUDs, from their home computers (another example of many-to-many synchronous communication). With future increases in telecommunication bandwidth, the use of Web sites for interactive multimedia gaming should increase in both sophistication of computer graphics and speed of response time among players (Bruckman, 1996). The Web may indeed become a new world of virtual sports.

Because of its immediacy and reach, the Internet has obvious appeal to gamblers who wager on sports and this has certain implications in terms of the availability of gambling-related information from media organizations on the Web (Katz, 1995). For instance, ESPN's contracts with major sports leagues influence the amount of gambling-related information it provides in the ESPNet SportsZone, because professional sports organizations want to distance themselves as much as possible from gambling issues. Consequently, SportsZone offers point spreads on a daily basis, while its online competitor SportsLine updates its Las Vegas lines every 15 minutes (Gunther, 1996). In addition to the online gambling-related information provided by media organizations, corporate gambling interests currently maintain Web sites like the Gambler's Corner (http://wwwconjelco.com), which provides links to gambling sites. Sports International (http://www.intersphere.com), a subsidiary of Interactive Gaming & Communications Corporation, offers online gambling using a "virtual" account on the Internet. Likewise, gambling casinos are also sponsoring Web sites, such as Las Vegas Online (http//www.intermind.net/las.vegas.online/homepage.html), Maryland and Atlantic City Casinos (http://www.jaeger.com/~erich/marygamb.html; http://pluto.njcc.com/~lemke/ac/ac.html) and the Hilton at Reno (http://www.sierra.net/Hilton/Reno/). There are even Web sites created by individuals offering anything from lotto opportunities and casino strategies to treatises on how to overcome gambling addiction.

PROFILING THE CYBERSPORT AUDIENCE

As Table 17.1 illustrates, there are a variety of approaches, both qualitative and quantitative, that can be employed to examine cybersport. One method that can be used to better understand the Internet environment and its audience is computer-monitored data collection (Williams, Rice & Rogers, 1988). For example, sports Web sites reside within an expansive "network community" that exists in Internet media space. Therefore, a computer-generated census of sport sites provides an indication of the number of options (i.e., media objects) available to online fans that require him or her to exercise decision-making and employ information-seeking strategies to move through the media objects within the cybersport media class (December, 1996). The Web audience comes to each sports site with an easily recordable address and a presumed interest in the sports content offered at the site – whether graphic or text, linear or interactive; and this allows gauging the volume of connections and the flow of selections at the site, which can also provide important insight on the Internet activity of various cybersport subcultures. In addition to exploring the Internet sports landscape and related usage patterns, computer-monitored data can also be used to examine audience composition and other aspects of the online sport media experience.

Examining Cybersport Objects

One way to develop a better understanding of the sports audience for the WWW is to examine the variety of choices from the user's perspective, which can be accomplished by using an Internet search engine such as InfoSeek, Web Crawler or Lycos to count the available number of sports-related Web sites. A search through sports titles using a search engine will yield thousands of sports home pages and hundreds of thousands of sports-related electronic documents, as shown in Table 17.2. This technique demonstrates the number of outlets for sports stories or for online sports activities, as well as the constantly changing cybersport arena. It also provides an indicator of the diversity of distribution sources that make up the cybersport class on the WWW. Not only does the audience have access to sports stories or related topics from traditional media sources such as *USA TODAY*, CNN, and

Table 17.2   World Wide Web Search Engine Hits for Sports Topics: June, 1996

| Search Term | *Number of different sports documents found by engine* | | |
	WebCrawler	*Lycos*	*InfoSeek*
Sports	41,546	157,554	74,460
College Sports	87,168	300,611	157,026
Women and Sports	3,516	157,554	114,047
Sportszone	2,476	711	3,289
Football	9,428	13,448	15,979
Baseball	7,887	56,873	15,709
Basketball	7,748	4,456	13,753
Hockey	5,996	56,594	9,547
Soccer	5,210	30,421	7,870
Golf	15,245	54,506	23,036
Tennis	7,748	32,747	11,591
Olympics	4,627	14,184	4,627
Totals	198,595	879,659	450,934

Sports Illustrated, but from non-traditional sources as well: for example, fan clubs, individual sports enthusiasts, sports teams, sports marketers and even sports scholars.

When a sports fan uses a WWW search engine to locate Web sites, he or she presents a keyword query to the search engine, which scans its address database for matching terms in the title or body of the Web document. WWW search engines will return sites that match one or all of the query words, indicating the number of keywords successfully matched. As evidenced by the data in Table 17.2, not all search engines are the same; Lycos presents more matches across the board than either Web Crawler or InfoSeek. This is in part due to the 40 million Universal Resource Locators (URLs) listed in its database. Yet, the different databases do not always overlap, as evidenced by the relatively few Lycos matches on the term "sportszone" as compared to results from the other search engines. The media class of cybersport is made up of the total URLs (media objects) locatable by these and all other WWW search engines.

Interesting comparisons can be made (within and) between the search engines in terms of the total number of sports sites available in each URL database. For example, across all three search engines, golf has the most individual Web sites of the sports listed in Table 17.2, followed by football and baseball; yet, soccer probably has a larger international fan base than any of the three. Perhaps, given the costs of computer technology involved in accessing online content, along with the relationship of sport preferences and social class, it is possible that socioeconomics currently dictate the availability of online information for individual sports. While there can be no real certainty in terms of what influences the availability of specific cybersport content, the total amount of sports options on the WWW can seem overwhelming – especially to the fan with only traditional mass media as a referent.

Examining the Cybersport Instance

Tracking the amount and duration of cybersport activity can also help us to understand the sports fans use of new media. One approach consists of counting the number of "hits" or logons for specific sports Web sites, keeping track of data as it is downloaded and the amount of time that each logon spends at the site. Most Web servers employ the "Common Log Format" (CLF) to keep track of logon addresses of the visitor, URL addresses selected and files downloaded to the user; this provides a numeric count of the number of times certain pages or files are accessed, and the length of each visit (Robertson, 1996). Tracking software records the number of times a Web site is visited (i.e., "hits"), as well as the average time each visitor spends at that site and their location. For example, the WWW server log analysis software, getstats, available from Enterprise Integration Technologies (http://www.eit.com) provides hourly to monthly summaries of logons, downloads and domains connecting to the Web site. Such aggregate measures provide data reflecting the popularity or visibility of a specific Web site within a given media class and the number of files (or media instances) downloaded from each site (Robertson, 1996).

The hit method of measuring user access is often employed to provide audits of user activity for many commercial Web sites. *USA TODAY* online, for example, relies on usage data from an auditing program marketed by Internet Profiles Corporation (I/Pro) in conjunction with Nielsen Corporation. The Nielson I/Audit reports usage data aggregated for two 31-day periods. The data are cut to present total and average counts of Web site access over each month and to show access patterns by time of day, day of the week and duration of visit (I/Pro, 1996). Much like television ratings, online media (and sports) organizations use this information for marketing their sites to both audiences and advertisers. Table 17.3 shows a comparison of hit rates between the sports section of the *USA TODAY* site and SportsLine, based on I/Audit data from a 4 month period (I/Pro, Dec.–March, 1996; T. Lieman, personal communication, April 26, 1996). As the table suggests, hits are lowest during the month of December and peak during March. Among the possible reasons for the trends in the audience data, are the large number of college students who regularly access these sites (who are not on campus during most of December). In addition, the increased number of hits from January to March could be due to the interest generated by such major events as the Super Bowl and the NCAA Basketball Championships, which take place during that time period.

The above I/Audit data prepared for *USA TODAY* online and SportsLine provide a set of time-based "snapshots" of Web site traffic, which clearly show that the total number of Web site visits is increasing over time. Other I/Audit data for *USA TODAY* suggest its site receives greater usage during weekdays than on the weekend and this traffic is highest around the noon hour (I/Pro, 1996). Similar to television ratings data, this information helps to illustrate Web site usage habits and preferences of online audiences. I/Audit is but one of several online usage software programs used by Nielsen Interactive Services through its partnership with I/Pro (Krantz, 1995). For example, I/Count tracks the names and geographical locations of organizations whose computers connect to the Web site and the frequency of connection to individual Web pages (Wallach, 1996). Using data from this Web connection auditing software, I/Pro provides a profile of the organizational user of *USA TODAY* and where that user is located.

In an audit report for *USA TODAY*, I/Pro reported that over 60 percent of the Web page usage came from commercial (38.6 percent) and educational (27.6 percent) institutions, and 34 percent of the visits to the Web site come through commercial Internet access providers like America Online and Compuserve. Geographically, 88 percent of the traffic connecting to the *USA TODAY* homepage originated in America, two-fifths of it from the East Coast and one-fifth from the West Coast. In terms of

Table 17.3   Comparison of Web Site Traffic

Avg. Daily hits	USA TODAY Total	SportsLine Total
December 1995	103,399	338,709
January 1996	152,012	387,096
February 1996	200,727	482,758
March 1996	269,405	741,935

the Web site's international appeal, Canadian traffic accounted for about 2 percent of the connections and Australian connections made up almost 1 percent of the total audience (I/Pro, 1996). Those interested in I/Pro, and other types of WWW audience tracking services and software, can learn more about these services by accessing: http://www.naa.org/news/Webcount.html#counting.

Examining the Cybersport Experience

Investigating the demographic makeup of online sports fans is another preliminary step in understanding cybersport. Online survey methodologies are one method currently being used by commercial providers to gather profiles of their audiences and their media experiences. At this time, two of the largest providers of cybersport content are *USA TODAY* online and SportsLine. While both of these commercial sites provide sports content, the general format and content of the *USA TODAY* site is similar to their newspaper. Consequently, it would seem logical that the audience characteristics for each of these two sites might differ. The Web user profile data in Table 17.4 were gathered in separate online surveys conducted by *USA TODAY* online and SportsLine through their respective commercial sites in 1995 (C. Spielvogel, personal communication, February 26, 1996; T. Lieman, personal communication, April 26, 1996). The responses for each company are based on slightly differing methodologies and sample sizes. In some instances categories were collapsed herein to facilitate comparison between the two audiences, and the information regarding *USA TODAY* audiences is not restricted to readers of its sports pages; nevertheless, figures in Table 17.3 suggest its sports site attracts a large audience.

In comparing the demographics of the *USA TODAY* and SportsLine audiences, it is clear that the majority of users are males, of all ages, generally well off financially, who visit these sites two or more times a week. The fact that 89 percent of their online audience are men implies a definite gender orientation to sports, at least on the WWW. Whether this is due to sports per se or access to the necessary technology, or both, is not so clear. While the samples cut across all age groups, it is interesting that about 70 percent of users report making over $30,000 per year. This finding could be related to the availability of computing and online services and that close to 45 percent of all respondents have professional or technical jobs. Based on this data, it appears that the similarities between the two sites' audiences are greater than the differences, which could mean that audience composition may be more endemic to the medium than to the content. Nevertheless, if these findings were projected to users of other cybersport services, one might expect that the majority of online sports fans would be male and have professional backgrounds. Such a finding suggests that the cybersport audience is gender-specific, is less likely to include users from lower socioeconomic levels, and appeals to groups with a fairly good education. Of course, such conclusions are highly speculative given certain methodological limitations with the two online surveys (e.g., respondents' self-selection/self-report biases).

Table 17.4 demonstrates that it is possible to profile the cybersport market by using online surveys to define the audience according to demographic profiles.

Table 17.4   1995 Comparison of Online User Profiles

	USA TODAY	SportsLine
	(N = 2,849)	(N = 1,000)
Gender	%	%
Males	88.5	89
Females	11.5	11
Age	%	%
24 and under	21	39
25–34	30	29
35+	49	32
Income	%	%
$30,000 and under	30.5	27
$30 to $60,000	40	30
$60,000+	29.5	43
Visits per Wk.	%	%
1	12	26
2–3	28	N/A
4+	60	33
Occupation	%	%
Students	22	35
Professionals	29	27
Technical	17	16
All Others	32	22

The online survey is relatively simple and cost-effective to send out; however, it will generally have a low response rate from users (Kryter, 1994; Kim, 1994). Survey samples can be built by compiling a list of e-mail addresses from the logon listings of the Web site or membership of a usenet, as well as by using e-mail addresses from an Internet directory of addresses. Logon listings offer the benefit of a defined user audience based on actual use, though it loses generalizability to a wider market. Using an address directory to create a random sample of Web addresses allows generalizability to a larger set of Internet users, but also runs the risk of sampling respondents who have no interest in sports sites. In either case, the list of potential respondents can easily be randomized, and surveys can be sent electronically in waves until a sufficient number of responses are returned (Kryter, 1994).

DISCUSSION

The computer-monitored data reported herein convey the enormity and relative variety of sport-related information currently available on the Web (see Table 17.2), as well as the growing popularity of such content (see Table 17.3). Although, one potentially disconcerting statistic is the potential lack of diversity in the current cybersport audience (see Table 17.4). According to the online surveys conducted by *USA TODAY* online and SportsLine, the WWW sports arena is almost exclusively a domain for upscale, highly educated, males. Conversely, the Lycos search engine yielded almost 160,000 sites containing the terms: women and sports (see Table 17.1). Therefore, more research is warranted before any strong claims can be made regarding the overall gender orientation of cybersport content and its audience (cf. Greedorfer, 1991; Reid & Solely, 1979).

Because the samples were limited to the users of only two Web sites, with data gathered in the relatively early stages of cybersport development, it is difficult to say if this online audience trend is pervasive (or if it will continue). Nevertheless, because of the already strong commercial orientation of many Web content providers, and the attractiveness of an upscale male audience to advertisers, the potential for the informational interests/needs of other groups (e.g., women) to be ignored should not be discounted. In addition, the costs of computer technology and Internet access create socioeconomic barriers that also prevent many sports fans from participating in the cybersport experience. Since history shows that the commercial aspects of the sport/media relationship have generally dictated the nature of the mediated sport "product" in the past; unless there is a concerted effort to make cybersport more inclusive, there is no real reason to believe that this will not be the case with new media as well (cf. Bellamy, 1989; McChesney, 1989; Jhally, 1989).

One of the current difficulties in studying cybersport and its audience is that the content, technology and usage patterns are never static. Online content (and its producers) are almost totally unregulated at the time of this writing. Consequently, the nature and availability of Web content, as well as the technology (and quite possibly the make-up of its audience) are constantly changing: an assertion that can be easily tested by replicating any of the cybersport key word searches found in Table 17.2. Of course, the evolutionary nature of cybersport creates both challenges and opportunities for those who choose to study this new area of sports communication.

In addition to coping with the rapidly metamorphosing Internet environment, the other potential obstacle to understanding cybersport is the arguable lack of applicable communication paradigms. As previously noted, the qualities of online sport are such that they constitute a meld of mass and interpersonal communication (Morris & Ogan, 1996). Consequently, existing communication theories will in all likelihood need to be overhauled in order to appropriately account for this new communication context (Beniger, 1987). The typologies of December (1996), as well as Morris and Ogan (1996), provide frameworks with which to begin this process (see Table 17.1). The ultimate goal, however, should be to transcend mere categorization of cybersport phenomena and provide a deeper theoretical understanding of the online sports audience.

Just as the multifaceted nature of cybersport dictates the development of new and broader theories; studying this enigmatic form of communication also requires the use of pluralistic methods, as suggested in Table 17.1. Because the Internet simultaneously involves different levels of communication activity (i.e., intrapersonal, interpersonal, group and mass), it seems logical that approaches to its research should be just as varied. While survey data was used herein to profile online sports audiences, future research in this area should not be confined to the use of quantitative methods. Moreover, it is necessary to move beyond mere descriptive studies of audience demographics to examine social and psychological variables, as well as the subcultures, involved in the cybersport media experience (cf. Wenner & Gantz, 1989).

Finally, the role of interactivity and multimedia in shaping the audience experience with cybersport is virtually uncharted territory. Communication technology, like slow-motion video or point-of-view-cameras, has historically influenced the development of the sport media lexicon, and subsequent audience expectation in terms of media conventions (Gruneau, 1989; McDaniel & Armstrong, 1994). Therefore, it remains to be seen how the dynamic properties of cybersport will change, or conform to, traditional media production values. More importantly, we need to understand the implications of new media, in terms of (if and) how it influences the perceptions of cybersport audiences. Likewise, the international implications of cybersport also warrant attention, as the global reach of the Internet allows sport organizations, athletes, media and fans to bridge huge physical distances (cf. Bellamy, 1993; Eastman & Meyer, 1989; Weiss, 1996). However, given the implicit values in sports, combined with the rather ubiquitous nature of the Web, there are also bound to be dysfunctional consequences (e.g., cultural imperialism) associated with the proliferation of this new sports media technology (cf. Trujillo & Ekdom, 1985; Wright, 1986).

References

"A rundown of NFL rights pacts." (1994, January 3). *Electronic Media,* pp. 4, 46.

Adams, B. (1996, October 31). "Airfare: Three new sports channels will attempt to feed growing appetite for sports information." *San Francisco Examiner*, pp. D–1, D–2.

Adler, A. (1927). *Practice and theory of individual psychology*. New York: Harcourt, Brace, & World.

Anderson, B. (1993). *Imagined communities: Reflections on the origins and spread of nationalism*. London: Verso.

Andrews, D.L. (1994). "Michael Jordan: A commodity-sign of [post]Reaganite times." Working Paper (Series II) in *Popular Cultural Studies, No. 1* (Manchester Institute for Popular Culture).

Andrews, D.L. (1996a). "Deconstructing Michael Jordan: Reconstructing postindustrial America." *Sociology of Sport Journal*, 13, 315–318.

Andrews, D.L. (1996b). "The fact(s) of Michael Jordan's blackness: Excavating a floating racial signifier." *Sociology of Sport Journal*, 13, 125–158.

Ang, I. (1985). *Watching Dallas*. London: Methuen.

Ang, I. (1990). *Desperately seeking the audience*. London: Routledge.

Ang, I. (1995). *Living room wars: Re-thinking media audiences for a post-modern world*. London: Routledge.

Ang, I. (1996). *Living room wars: Rethinking media audiences for a postmodern world*. London: Routledge.

Araton, H. (1996, June 18). "Jordan puts his family first." The *New York Times*, p. B13.

Arendt, H. (1958). *The human condition*. Chicago: University of Chicago Press.

Armour, T. (1996, March 30). "The enigma: The puzzle that is Bulls forward Dennis Rodman." *The Chicago Tribune*. http://cmr.sph.unc.edu/–deano/bball/articles/rodman.html.

Armour, T. (1997, January 18). "NBA dresses Rodman down: 11-game suspension will cost him $1 million." *The Sacramento Bee*, Sec. F, pp. 1, 4.

Armstrong, E.G. (1996), "The commodified 23, or, Michael Jordan as text." *Sociology of Sport*, 13, 325–343.

Babad, E. (1987). "Wishful thinking and objectivity among sports fans." *Social Behavior*, 2, 231–240.

Babad, E., & Katz, Y.(1991). "Wishful thinking – against all odds." *Journal of Applied Social Psychology*, 21(23), 1921–1938.

Baitaille, G. (1985). *Visions of excess: Selected writings, 1927–1939*. Minneapolis: University of Minnesota.

Baker, J. (1995, August 25). "Who rules the beach?" *TV Guide*, 43(34), p. 30.

Baldwin, P. (1990, July 10). "Pitchman: Rangers pitcher Ryan expected to be drafted by more advertisers." *The Dallas Morning News*, pp. 1A, 6A.

Ball-Rokeach, S. J. (1985). "The origins of individual media-system dependency: A sociological framework." *Communication Research*, 12, 485–510.

Banks, D. (1993). "Tribal names and mascots in sports." *Journal of Sport and Social Issues*, 17(1), 5–8.

Barber, B. (1995). *Jihad vs. McWorld: How globalism and tribalism are reshaping the world*, New York: Random House.

Barnes, J. (1988). *Sports law in Canada* (2nd edn). Toronto: Butterworths.

Barnett, S. (1990). *Games and sets: The changing face of sport on television*. London: British Film Institute.

Barney, R.K., & Barney, D.E. (1989, May). "Night of heroes: Flags, flowers, and last hurrahs." Paper presented at the meeting of the North American Society for Sports History, Clemson, SC.

Baron, R.A., & Richardson, D.R. (1994). *Human aggression* (2nd edn.). New York: Plenum Press.

Barrow, L.C. (1991). Black colleges not sharing in the gold. *Crisis*, 98(9), 15–19.

Barthes, R (1967). *Elements of semiology*. London: Jonathon Cape.

Barthes, R. (1973). *Mythologies*. London: Paladin.

Barthes, R. (1975). *The pleasures of the text*. London: Jonathon Cape.

Barthes, R. (1984). *Camera lucida: Reflections on photography*. London: Fontana Flamingo.

Bateman, J. K. (1977). "Billie Jean King's publishing adventure: A documentary on the evolution of womenSports magazine from March 1973 through May 1973." Unpublished master's thesis, University of Oregon, Eugene.

Bates, N. (1994, July 26). "Fuss good news for women's sport." *Maryborough Chronicle*, p. 6.

Baudrillard, J. (1983). *Simulations*. New York: Semiotext(e).

Baughman, C. (Ed.). (1995). *Women on ice: Feminist essays on the Tonya Harding/Nancy Kerrigan spectacle*. New York: Routledge.

Baum, D. (1995). "Sports Illustrated swimsuit edition makes waves on the web." *Infoworld*, 17, 82.

Bayless, S. (1989, July 10). "Need a hero? Just send for 'old gun Ryan'." *Dallas Times Herald*, p. D-1.

BBC (1976). "Public opinion about the television & radio coverage of the 1974 World Cup." In *Annual review of Audience Research Findings* (number 2). London: BBC.

Beamish, R. & Borowy, J. (1988). *Q. What do you do for a living? A. I'm an Athlete*. Kingston: The Sport Research Group, Queen's University.

Beasley, M. (1993). "Newspapers: Is there a new majority defining the news?" In P.J. Creedon (Ed.) *Women in mass communication: Challenging gender values*, pp. 118–133. Newbury Park, CA: Sage.

Beauvoir, S. de (1974). *The second sex*. New York: Vintage Books.

Bell, D. (1975). *Power, influence, and authority: An essay in political linguistics*. New York: Oxford.

Bellah, R.N., Madsen, R., Sullivan, W.M., Swidler, A., & Tipton, S.M. (1985). *Habits of the heart: Individualism and commitment in American life*. Berkeley, CA: University of California Press.

Bellamy, R.V., Jr. (1989). "Professional sports organizations: Media strategies." In L.A. Wenner (Ed.), *Media, sports, & society*, pp. 120–133. Newbury Park, CA: Sage.

Bellamy, R.V., Jr. (1993). "Issues in the internationalization of the U.S. sports media: The emerging European marketplace." *Journal of Sport & Social Issues*, 17, 168–180.

Bellamy, R.V., Jr., & Walker, J.R. (1995). "Foul tip or strike three? The evolving 'partnership' of Major League Baseball and television." *Nine*, 3, 261–275.

Bellamy, R.V., Jr., & Walker, J.R. (1996). *Television and the remote control: Grazing on a vast wasteland*. New York: Guilford.

Beniger, J. (1987). "Personalization of mass media and the growth of pseudo-community." *Communication Research*, 14, 352–371.

Benjamin, W. (1969). "The work of art in the age of mechanical reproduction." In *Illuminations*, trans. J. Zohn. New York: Schocken.

Bennett, R., Whitaker, G., Smith, N., & Sablove, A. (1987). "Changing the rules of the game: Reflections toward a feminist analysis of sport." *Women's Studies International Forum*, 10(4), 369–380.

Benns, M. (1994, January 16). "Bias claim by axed cricketer." *Sunday Mail*, p. 2.

Bentham, J. (1931). *The theory of legislation*. London: Kegan Paul. (Originally published 1802).

Berkow, I. (1995, May 13). "Making a misguided approach." *New York Times*, p. 25.

Berkowitz, H., & Zipay, S. (1996, March 7). "Madison Ave. going to bat for baseball." *Newsday*, p. A47.

Berniker, M. (1995a). "Broadcast networks jumping aboard the Internet." *Broadcasting & Cable, 125*, 29–30.

Berniker, M. (1995b). "NBA gets on web with Starwave's ESPN SportsZone." *Broadcasting & Cable*, 125, 69.

Best, S., & Kellner, D. (1991). *Postmodern theory: Critical interrogations*. New York: The Guilford Press.

Betts, J. R. (1969). "The technological revolution and the rise of sport, 1850–1900." In J.W. Loy & G.S. Kenyon (Eds), *Sport, culture, and society: A reader on the sociology of sport*. Toronto: The Macmillan Company.

Bierman, J.A. (1990, Fall). "The effect of television sports media on black male youth." *Sociological Inquiry*, 60(4), 413–428.

Birkhead, D. (1991). "An ethics of vision for journalism." In R. Avery & D. Eason (Eds), *Critical perspectives on media and society*, pp. 226–239. New York: Guilford Press.

Birrell, S. (1989). "Racial relations theories and sport: Suggestions for a more critical analysis." *Sociology of Sport Journal*, 6(3), 212–227.

Birrell, S. & Cole, C.L. (1990). "Double fault: Renee Richards and the construction and naturalization of difference." *Sociology of Sport Journal*, 7(1), pp. 1–21.

Blain, N., Boyle, R., & O'Donnell, H. (1993). *Sport and national identity in the European media*. Leicester, England: Leicester University Press.

Blais, M. (1995). *In these girls, hope is a muscle*. New York: Atlantic Monthly Press.

Blinde, E. (1990, March). "Pressure and stress in women's college sports: Views from athletes." Paper presented to the annual meeting of the American Alliance for Health, Physical Education, Recreation and Dance, New Orleans.

Blinde, E.M., Greendorfer, S.L., & Sankner, R.J. (1991). "Differential media coverage of men's and women's intercollegiate basketball: Reflection of gender ideology." *Journal of Sport & Social Issues*, 15(2), 98–114.

Blinde, E., Taub, D.E., & Han, L. (1994). "Sport as a site for women's group and societal empowerment: Perspectives from the college athlete." *Sociology of Sport Journal*, 11, 51–59.

Blue, A. (1987). *Grace under pressure: The emergence of women in sport*. London: Sidgwick & Jackson.

Blumenstyk, G. (1995, February 3). "Georgia Tech and MacDonald's sign $5.5-million deal." *Chronicle of Higher Education*, p. A44.

Blumer, H. (1969) *Symbolic interactionism*. Englewood Cliffs, NJ: Prentice-Hall.

Blumler, J. & Katz, E. (Eds) (1974). *The uses of mass communications*. London: Sage.

Bogart, L. (1995). *Commercial culture: The media system and the public interest*. New York: Oxford University Press.

Boorstin, D.J. (1978). *The image: A guide to pseudo-events in America*. New York: Atheneum.

Bordo, S. (1987). *The flight from objectivity: Essays on Cartesianism and culture*. Albany: SUNY Press.

Boseman, K. (1994, March 6). "Coca-Cola and the NBA team up globally." *Chicago Citizen*, p. 2.

Bourdieu, P. (1978). "Sport and social class." *Social Science Information*. 17, 819–840.

Boutilier, M.A. & SanGiovanni, L. (1983). *The sporting woman*. Champaign, IL: Human Kinetics.

Braddock, J.H. (1978a). "The sports page: In black and white." *Arena Review*, 2(2), 17–25.

Braddock, J.H. (1978b). "Television and college football: In black and white." *Journal of Black Studies*, 8(3), 369–380.

Brand, S. (1988). *The media lab: Inventing the future at M.I.T.* London: Penguin Books.

Brannon, R. (1978). "The consequences of sexist language." Paper presented at the American Psychological Association Meetings, Toronto.

Branscombe, N.R., & Wann, D.L. (1991). "The positive social and self-concept consequences of sports team identification." *Journal of Sport & Social Issues*, 15, 115–127.

Branscombe, N.R., & Wann, D.L. (1992a), "Role of identification with a group, arousal, categorization processes, and self-esteem in sport spectator aggression." *Human Relations*, 45, 1013–1033.

Branscombe, N.R., & Wann, D.L. (1992b). "Physiological arousal and reactions to outgroup members during competitions that implicate an important social identity." *Aggressive Behavior*, 18, 85–93.

Breed, W. (1955). Social control in the news room. *Social Forces*, 33, 326–335.

Brennan, C. (1996). *Inside edge: A revealing journey into the secret world of figure skating*. New York: Scribner.

Breznick, A. (1994, May 23). "Good sports?" *Cable World*, pp. 124–126.

Briggs, A. (1994). "The media and sport in the global village." In R.C. Wilcox (Ed.), *Sport in the global village* (pp. 5–20). Morgantown, WV: Fitness Information Technology.

British Film Institute (1986). *Open the box: Take the money and run*. Videotape (Direction, M. Dibb. Script, J. Root).

Brod, H. (1987). *The new gender scholarship*. Newbury Park, CA: Sage Publications.

Brown, J.(1985). Foreword. *In Department of Sport, Recreation and Tourism and Australian Sports Commission, Australian sport: A profile*. Canberra: Australian Government Publishing Service.

Browne, R.B. (1983). "Hero with 2000 faces." In R.B. Browne & M.W. Fishwick (Eds), *The hero in transition*, pp. 91–106. Bowling Green, OH: Bowling Green University Popular Press.

Brownell, S. (1995). "Cultural variations in Olympic telecasts: China and the 1992 Olympic games and ceremonies." *The Journal of International Communication*, 2(1), 26–41.

Bruce, T. (1995, Nov.). "Race and gender in televised basketball commentary: Patterns at the professional and collegiate level." Paper presented at the meeting of the North American Society for the Sociology of Sport, Sacramento, CA.

Bruckman, A. (1996). Finding one's own space in cyberspace. *Technology Review*, 99, 48–55.

Brugnone, D. (1995, May 18). "Personal communication." Director of Affiliate Sales and Marketing, Prime Sports KBL Network, Pittsburgh.

Brummett, B., & Duncan, M.C. (1990). Theorizing without totalizing: Speculary and televised sports. *Quarterly Journal of Speech*, 76, 227–246.

Bryant, J. (1989). "Viewers enjoyment of televised sports violence." In L.A. Wenner (Ed.), *Media, sports and society*, pp. 270–289. London: Sage.

Bryant, J., Brown, D., Comisky, P.W., & Zillmann, D. (1982). "Sports and spectators: Commentary and appreciation." *Journal of Communication*, 32(1), 109–119.

Bryant, J., Comisky, P., & Zillmann, D. (1977). "Drama in sports commentary." *Journal of Communication*, 27 (3), 140–149.

Bryant, J., Comisky, P., & Zillmann, D. (1981). "The appeal of rough-and-tumble play in televised professional football." *Communication Quarterly*, 29, 256–262.

Bryant, J., & Love, C. (1996). "Entertainment as the driver of new information technology." In R.R. Dholakia, N. Mundorf, & N. Dholakia (Eds), *New information technologies in the home: Demand-side perspectives*, pp. 87–108. Mahwah, NJ: Lawrence Erlbaum Associates.

Bryant, J., Love, C., & Robicheaux, R.A. (1996). "Two telephone surveys of Alabama residents on the social and economic impact of Alabama and Auburn football". Unpublished data.

Bryant, J., Rockwell, S.C., & Owens, J.W. (1994). "'Buzzer beaters' and 'barn burners': The effects on enjoyment of watching the game go 'down to the wire'." *Journal of Sport & Social Issues*, 18(4), 326–339.

Bryant, J., & Zillmann, D. (1983a). "Drama in sports commentary: An update on NFL telecasts." Unpublished data; as cited in Bryant, J., & Zillmann, D., "Sports violence and the media." In J.H. Goldstein (Ed.), *Sports violence*, pp. 195–211. New York: Springer-Verlag.

Bryant, J., & Zillmann, D. (1983b). "Sports violence and the media." In J.H. Goldstein (Ed.), *Sports violence*, pp. 195–211. Berlin: Springer-Verlag.

Bryson, L. (1987). "Sport and the maintenance of masculine hegemony." *Women's Studies International Forum*, 10, 349–360.

Bryson, L. (1994). "Sport and the maintenance of masculine hegemony." In S. Birrell & C.L. Cole (Eds), *Women, sport, and culture*, pp. 47–64. Champaign, IL: Human Kinetics.

Burgi, M. (1994, January 17). "ESPN establishes global advertising sales unit." *MediaWeek*, reprint.

Burnett, J., Menon, A., & Smart, D.T. (1993). "Sports marketing: A new ball game with new rules." *Journal of Advertising Research*, 33(5), 21–35.

Burroughs, A., Ashburn, L., & Seebohm, L. (1995). "Add sex and stir: Homophobic coverage of women's cricket in Australia." *Journal of Sport and Social Issues*, 19, 266–284.

Buscombe, E. (Ed.). (1975). *Football on television*. London: British Film Institute.

Butler, J.G. (1994). *Television: Critical methods and applications*. Belmont, CA: Wadsworth Publishing Co.

Byers, W. (1995). *Unsportsmanlike conduct: Exploiting college athletes*. Ann Arbor, MI: University of Michigan Press.

Cady, S. (1979, Aug. 11). "Basketball's image crisis." *The New York Times*, p. 15.

Cahn, S.K. (1994). *Coming on strong: Gender and sexuality in twentieth century women's sport*. New York: The Free Press.

Campbell, J. (1968). *The hero with a thousand faces* (2nd edn). Princeton, NJ: Princeton University Press.

Canadian charter of rights and freedoms. (1982). Ottawa: Ministry of Supply and Services.

Canadian Press [CP: Taylor, B. (Ed.)]. (1989 Revised Edition). *The Canadian press stylebook*. Toronto: Canadian Press.

Cantelon, H., & Harvey, J. (Eds) (1987). *The sociology of sport*. Ottawa: University of Ottawa.

Capella, J. N. (1996). "Why biological explanation?" *Journal of Communication*, 46(3), 4–7.

Cappron, R.J. (1982). *The word: The Associated Press guide to good news writing*. New York: The Associated Press.

Card, C. (1995). *Lesbian choices*. NY: Columbia University Press.

Carlson, M. (1996, August 5). The soap opera games. *Time*, 148, 48.

Carman, J. (1997, January 24). "Fox goes out for long one on Super Bowl." *San Francisco Chronicle*, pp. D-1, D-10.

Carroll, J. (1995, May 15). "Butch babes in trouble again." *San Francisco Chronicle*, p. E8.

Carter III, H. (1987). Forward. In C.G. Christians, K.B. Rotzoll, & M. Fackler, *Media ethics: Cases and moral reasoning* (2nd edn) (pp. xi-xiii). White Plains, N.Y.: Longman.

Castle, G. (1991, January). Air to the throne. *Sport*, 28–36.

Cavanagh, R. (1989). "Cultural production and the production of power: Political economy, public television, and high performance sport in Canada." Unpublished Ph.D. dissertation. Ottawa: Carleton University.

Cerf, V. (1994). "A brief history of the Internet and related networks." [Online]. Available World Wide Web: gopher://gopher.isoc.org/11/Internet/history.

CFL's future. (1997, April 9). Canadian Football League Official Website. URL: http://www.cfl.ca/CFLNews/apr9 deal.html.

Chalip, L. (1992). "The construction and use of polysemic structures: Olympic lessons for sport marketing." *Journal of Sport Management*, 6, 87–98.

Chalip, P., & Chalip, L. (1989). "Olympic athletes as American heroes." In R. Jackson (Ed.), *The Olympic movement and the mass media: Past, present and future issues*, pp. 11/2–11/26. Calgary: Hurford Enterprises.

Cheska, A.T. (1981). "Sports spectacular: The social ritual of power." In M. Hart & S. Birrell (Eds), *Sport in the sociocultural process*, pp. 369–386. Dubuque, IA: Wm. C. Brown. (Originally published 1968).

Christians, C.G., Rotzoll, K.B., & Fackler, M. (1987). *Media ethics: Cases and moral reasoning* (2nd edn). White Plains, N.Y.: Longman.

Christie, J. (1992, July 7). Telephone interview with *Globe and Mail* journalist.

Christie, J. (1996, April 29). Personal e-mail communication from *Globe and Mail* journalist.

Chroni, A., Bunker, L., & Sabo, D. (1996). "Gender bias and children's perceptions of the 1996 Olympic Games pictograms." *Melpomene*, 15(1), 18–22.

Cialdini, R.R., Borden, R.J., Thorne, A., Walker, M.R., Freeman, S., & Sloan, L.R. (1976). "Basking in reflected glory: Three (football) field studies." *Journal of Personality and Social Psychology*, 34, 366–375.

Claeys, U., & Van Pelt, H. (1986). "Sport and the mass media: Like bacon and eggs." *International Review for the Sociology of Sport*, 21(2/3), 93–101.

Clarke, A., & Clarke, J. (1982). "'Highlights and action replays' – ideology, sport and the media." In J. Hargreaves (Ed.), *Sport, culture and ideology*, pp. 62–87. London: Routledge & Kegan Paul.

Coakley, J. (1988–1989). "Media coverage of sports and violent behavior: An elusive connection." *Current Psychology: Research & Reviews*, 7(4), 322–330.

Coakley, J.J. (1994). *Sport in society: Issues and controversies* (5th edn). St. Louis, MO: Mosby.

Cohen, B.C. (1963) *The Press and foreign policy*. Princeton: Princeton University Press.

Cohn, L. (1990, January 24). "Montana: Ice man cometh." *San Francisco Chronicle*, pp. D1, D4.

Cole, C., & Andrews, D. (1996). "Look – It's NBA showtime! Visions of race in the popular imaginar." *Cultural Studies: A Research Volume*, 1(1), 141–181.

Cole, C.L., & Denny, H. (1994). "Visualizing deviance in post-Reagan America: Magic Johnson, AIDS, and the promiscuous world of professional sport." *Critical Sociology*, 20(3), 123–147.

Cole, C.L., & Hribar, A. (1995). "Celebrity feminism: Nike style post-fordism, transcendence and consumer power." *Sociology of Sport Journal*, 12(4), 347–369.

Cole, C.L., & Orlie, M.A. (1995). "Hybrid athletes, monstrous addicts, and cyborg natures." *Journal of Sport History*, 22(3), 229–239.

Collett, P. and Lamb, R. (1986) *Watching people with television*. London: IBA.

Collins, J. (1995). *Architectures of excess: Cultural life in the information age*. New York: Routledge.

Comisky, P., Bryant, J., & Zillmann, D. (1977). "Commentary as a substitute for action." *Journal of Communication*, 27(3), 150–153.

Condit, C.M. (1989). "The rhetorical limits of polysemy." *Critical Studies in Mass Communication*, 6, 103–122.

Condor, R., & Anderson, D.F. (1984). "Longitudinal analysis of coverage accorded black and white athletes in feature articles of *Sports Illustrated* (1960–1980)." *Journal of Sport Behavior*, 7(1), 39–43.

Connell, R.W. (1987). *Gender and power: Society, the person, and sexual politics*. Stanford, CA: Stanford University Press.

Contractor, N.S. & Eisenberg, E.M. (1990). "Communication networks and new media in organizations." In J. Fulk & C. Steinfield (Eds), *Organizations and communication technology*, pp. 143–172. Newbury Park, CA: Sage.

Cooper-Chen, A. (1994). "Global games, entertainment and leisure: Women as TV spectators." In P.J. Creedon (Ed.), *Women, media and sport: Challenging gender values*, pp. 257–272. Thousand Oaks, CA: Sage.

Cooper, J. (1994, January 31). "ESPN unmasks pro hockey." *Broadcasting & Cable*, reprint.

Corbett, D.R. (1988). "The magazine media portrayal of sport women of colour." In F.A. Carre (Ed.), *I.C.P.E.R./C.A.H.P.E.R. world conference: Towards the 21st century*, pp. 190–195. Vancouver: School of Physical Education and Recreation, Univ. of British Columbia.

Corbett, D.R., & Johnson, W. (1993). "The African-American female in collegiate sport: Sexism and racism." In D.D. Brooks & R.C. Althouse (Eds), *Racism in college athletics: The African-American athlete's experience*, pp. 179–204. Morgantown, WV: Fitness Information Technology.

Cox, II, P.M. (1995). "Flag on the play? The siphoning effect on sports television." *Federal Communications Law Journal*, 47, 571–591.

Crabb, P.B., & Goldstein, J.H. (1991). "The social psychology of watching sports: From Ilium to living room." In J. Bryant & D. Zillmann (Eds), *Responding to the screen: Reception and reaction processes*, pp. 355–371. Hillsdale, NJ: Lawrence Erlbaum Associates.

Craig, J. (1995, May 13). "CBS stands by Wright." *Boston Globe*, pp. 69, 76.

Craig, J. (1995, May 16). "In CBS' eye, Wright wronged." *Boston Globe*, p. 53.

Craig, J., & Blaudschun, M. (1995, May 14). "Wright, paper stay at odds." *Boston Globe*, p. 94.

Cramer, J.A. (1994). "Conversations with women sports journalists." In P.J. Creedon (Ed.), *Women, media and sport: Challenging gender values*, pp.159–180. Thousand Oaks, CA: Sage.

Cramer, J.A. (1996). "'We're here, We're Queer': Breaking the Silence with Gay Games IV." Unpublished dissertation, Union Institute Graduate School, Cincinnati, Ohio.

Cramer, R.E., McMaster, M.R., Lutz, D.J., & Ford, J.G. (1986). "Sports fan generosity: A test of mood, similarity, and equity hypotheses." *Journal of Sport Behavior*, 9(1), 31–37.

Crawford, M., & Marecek, J. (1989). "Psychology reconstructs the female, 1968–1988." *Psychology of Women Quarterly*, 13, 147–165.

Creedon, P.J. (1993a). "Acknowledging the infrasystem: A critical feminist analysis of systems theory." *Public Relations Review*, 19(2), 157–166.

Creedon, P.J. (1993b). *Women in mass communication: Challenging gender values*. Newbury Park, CA: Sage.

Creedon, P.J. (1994a). Women in toyland: A look at women in American newspaper sports journalism." In P.J. Creedon (Ed.), *Women, media and sport: Challenging gender values*, pp. 67–107. Thousand Oaks, CA: Sage.

Creedon, P.J. (Ed.) (1994b). *Women, media and sport: Challenging gender values*. Thousand Oaks, CA: Sage.

Creedon, P.J. (1995). "Women's sports & fitness." In K.L. Endres & T.L. Lueck (Eds). *Women's periodicals in the United States: Consumer magazines*, pp. 458–473, Westport, CT: Greenwood Press.

Creedon, P.J., Cramer, J.A., & Granitz, E.H. (1994). "Pandering or empowering? Economics and promotion of women's sports." In P.J. Creedon (Ed.), *Women, media and sport: Challenging gender values*, pp. 181–203. Thousand Oaks, CA: Sage.

Crepeau, R.C. (1981). "Sport, heroes and myth." *Journal of Sport and Social Issues*, 5, 23–31.

Crepeau, R.C. (1985). "Where have you gone, Frank Merriwell? The decline of the American sports hero." In W.L. Umphlett (Ed.), *American sport culture: The humanistic dimensions*, pp. 76–82. Cranbury, NJ: Associated University Presses.

Critcher, C. (1992). "Is there anything on the box ? Leisure studies and media studies." *Leisure Studies*, 11.

Crosset, T.W. (1995). *Outsiders in the clubhouse: The world of women's professional golf*. Albany, NY: State University of New York Press.

Crossman, J., Hyslop, P., & Guthrie, B. (1994). "A content analysis of the sports section of Canada's national newspaper with respect to gender and professional/amateur status." *International Review for the Sociology of Sport*, 29(2), 123–131.

Csikszentmihalyi, M., & Lyons, B. (1982). "The selection of behavioral traits: Reasons for admiring people." Unpublished manuscript, University of Chicago.

Curtius, E.R. (1963). *European literature and the Latin middle ages*. New York: Harper & Row.

Daddario, G. (1992). "Swimming against the tide: *Sports Illustrated's* imagery of female athletes in a swimsuit world." *Women's Studies in Communication*, 15(1), 49–64.

Daddario, G. (1994). "Chilly scenes of the 1992 Winter Games: The mass media and the marginalization of female athletes." *Sociology of Sport Journal*, 11, 275–288.

Daly, M. (1973). *Beyond God the father: Toward a philosophy of women's liberation*. Boston: Beacon.

Dates, J.L. and Barlow, W. (Ed.) (1990). *Split image: African American in the mass*. Washington, DC: Howard University Press.

Davis, L.R. (1990). "The articulation of difference: White preoccupation with the question of racially linked genetic differences among athletes." *Sociology of Sport Journal*, 7, 179–187.

Davis, L.R. (1992). "The swimsuit issue and sport: Setting a climate of hegemonic masculinity in *Sports Illustrated*." Unpublished doctoral dissertation, University of Iowa, Iowa City, IA.

Davis, L.R. (1993a). "Critical analysis of the popular media and the concept of ideal subject position: *Sports Illustrated* as case study." *Quest*, 45(2), 165–181.

Davis, L.R. (1993b). "Protest against the use of Native American mascots: A challenge to traditional American identity." *Journal of Sport and Social Issues*, 17(1), 9–22.

Davis, L.R. (1997). *Hegemonic masculinity on the hot seat: Sparring with Sports Illustrated over its swimsuit issue.* Albany, NY: State University of New York Press.

Davis, L.R., & Delano, L.C. (1992). "Fixing the boundaries of physical gender: Side effects of anti-drug campaigns in athletics." *Sociology of Sport Journal*, 9, 1–19.

Dayan, D., & Katz, E. (1992). *Media events: The live broadcasting of history.* Cambridge: Harvard University Press.

Debord, G. (1970). *Society of the spectacle.* Unauthorized translation. Detroit: Black and Red Publishing.

December, J. (1996). "Units of analysis for Internet communication." *Journal of Communication*, 46(2), 14–38.

DeFleur, M.L., & Ball-Rokeach, S. (1989). *Theories of mass communication.* New York: Longman Inc.

Deleuze, G., & Guattari, F. (1983). *Anti-Oedipus.* Minneapolis: University of Minneapolis Press.

Deleuze, G., & Guattari, F. (1986). *Kafka.* Minneapolis: University of Minneapolis Press.

Deleuze, G., & Guattari, F. (1987). *A thousand plateaus.* Minneapolis: University of Minneapolis Press.

Dempster, G. (1985) "Challenges." In Department of Sport, Recreation and Tourism and Australian Sports Commission (Ed.), *Australian sport: A profile*, pp. 120–126. Canberra: Australian Government Publishing Service.

DeNeui, D.L., & Sachau, D.A. (1996). "Spectator enjoyment of aggression in intercollegiate hockey games." *Journal of Sport & Social Issues*, 20, 69–77.

Desbarats, P. (1990). *Guide to Canadian news media.* Toronto: Harcourt Brace Jovanovich.

Detenber, B.H., & Reeves, B. (1996). "A bio-informational theory of emotion: Motion and image size effects on viewers." *Journal of Communication*, 43(6), 66–82.

Devine, F. (1994, January 24). "When laws on discrimination don't play fair." The *Australian*, p. 11.

Dickey, G. (1989, August). "Tell a friend: Joe Montana may be the best ever." *Sport*, 55.

Dimmick, J., & Coit P. (1982). "Level of analysis in mass media decision making: A taxonomy, research strategy, and illustrative data analysis." *Communication Research*, 9, 3–32.

Dines, G., & Humez, J.M. (Eds). (1995). *Gender, race and class in media.* Thousand Oaks, CA: Sage Publications.

Donnelly, P. (1996). "The local and the global: Globalization in the sociology of sport." *Journal of Sport & Social Issues,* 20, 239–257.

Donohew, L., Helm, D., & Haas, J. (1989). "Drugs and (Len) Bias on the sports page." In L.A. Wenner (Ed.), *Media, sports, & society*, pp. 225–237. Newbury Park, CA: Sage.

Drucker, S.J. (1994) "The mediated sports hero." In S.J. Drucker, & R.S. Cathcart (Eds). (1994). *American heroes in a media age*, pp. 82–96. Creskill, NJ: Hampton Press.

Drucker, S.J., & Cathcart, R.S. (Eds) (1994). *American heroes in a media age.* Creskill, NJ: Hampton Press.

Dubin, C.L. (1990). *Commission of Inquiry into the use of drugs and banned substances intended to increase athletic performance*. Ottawa: Ministry of Supply and Services.

Dubow, J. (1997, December 10). Total Sports. URL: http:// www.totalsports.net/SG/fbo/nfl/ news/ap/97113.0415.html.

Duncan, M.C. (1986). "A hermeneutic of spectator sport: The 1976 and 1984 Olympic Games." *Quest*, 38, 50–77.

Duncan, M.C. (1990). "Sports photographs and sexual difference: Images of women and men in the 1984 and 1988 Olympic Games." *Sociology of Sport Journal*, 7, 22–43.

Duncan, M.C. (1993). "Beyond analyses of sport media texts: An argument for formal analyses of institutional structures." *Sociology of Sport Journal*,10, 353–372.

Duncan, M.C., Aycock, A., & Messner, M. (1996). "Speaking of sport: Gender, sport, and media in national and global contexts." Manuscript submitted for publication.

Duncan, M.C., & Brummett, B. (1987). "The mediation of spectator sport." *Research Quarterly for Exercise and Sport*, 58, 168–177.

Duncan, M.C., & Brummett, B. (1989). "Types and sources of spectating pleasure in televised sports." *Sociology of Sport Journal*, 6, 195–211.

Duncan, M.C., & Brummett, B. (1993). "Liberal and radical sources of female empowerment in sport media." *Sociology of Sport Journal*, 10(1), 57–72.

Duncan, M.C., & Hasbrook, C.A. (1988). "Denial of power in televised women's sports." *Sociology of Sport Journal*, 5, 1–21.

Duncan, M.C., Messner, M.A., & Jensen, K. (1994). *Gender stereotyping in televised sports: A follow-up to the 1989 study*. Los Angeles: Amateur Athletic Foundation of Los Angeles.

Duncan, M.C., Messner, M., & Williams, L. (1991). *Coverage of women's sports in four daily newspapers*. Los Angeles: Amateur Athletic Foundation of Los Angeles.

Duncan, M.C., Messner, M.A., Williams, L., & Jensen, K. (1990). *Gender stereotyping in televised sports*. Los Angeles, CA: Amateur Athletic Foundation of Los Angeles.

Duncan, M.C., Messner, M.A., Williams, L., Jensen, K., & Wilson, W. (1994). "Gender stereotyping in televised sports." In S. Birrell & C.L. Cole (Eds), *Women, sport, and culture*, pp. 249–272. Champaign, IL: Human Kinetics.

Duncan, M.C., & Sayaovong, A. (1990). "Photographic images and gender in Sports Illustrated for Kids." *Play & Culture*, 3, 91–116.

Duncan, T. (1993, October 11). "To fathom integrated marketing, dive!" *Advertising Age*, p. 18.

Duquin, M.E. (1989). "The importance of sport in building women's potential." In D. Stanley Eitzen (Ed.), *Sport in contemporary society* (3rd edn) (pp. 357–362). NY: St. Martin's Press.

Dwyer, P., Engardio, P., & Grover, R. (1994, December 12). "Rupert Murdoch: The sultan of sweat." *Business Week*, pp. 90–91.

Dyer, R. (1978). Entertainment and utopia. *Movie*, 24.

Dyer, R., Lovell, T., & McCrindle, J. (1977). "Soap opera and women." In *Edinburgh International Television Festival Programme*. Edinburgh: Edinburgh International Television Festival.

Dyson, M.E. (1993). "Be like Mike?: Michael Jordan and the pedagogy of desire." *Cultural Studies*, 7(1), 64–72.

Eastman, S.T., & Meyer, T.P. (1989). "Sports programming: Scheduling, costs, and competition." In L.A. Wenner (Ed.), *Media, sports, & society*, pp. 97–119. Newbury Park, CA: Sage.

Eastman, S.T., & Otteson, J.L. (1994). "Promotion increases ratings, doesn't it? The impact of program promotion in the 1992 Olympics." *Journal of Broadcasting & Electronic Media*, 38(3), 307–322.

Eastman, S.T., & Riggs, K.E. (1994). "Televised sports and ritual: Fan experiences." *Sociology of Sport Journal*, 11, 249–274.

Eberhard, W.B., & Myers, M.L. (1988). "Beyond the locker room: Women in sports on major daily newspapers." *Journalism Quarterly*, 65, 595–599.

Edwards, H. (1969). *Revolt of the black athlete*. New York, NY: Free Press.

Edwards, H. (1984). "The collegiate athletic arms race: Origins and implications of the Rule 480 controversy." *Journal of Sport & Social Issues*, 8, 4–22.

Edwards, O. (1995, November). "The lost art of losing well." *Sky*, 25–26, 28, 31.

Eitzen, D.S., & Baca-Zinn, M. (1989). "The de-athleticization of women: The naming and gender marking of collegiate sport teams." *Sociology of Sport Journal*, 6, 362–370.

Eitzen, D.S., & Purdy, D.A. (1986). "The academic preparation and achievement of black and white college athletes." *Journal of Sport & Social Issues, 10*, 15–29.

Eitzen, D.S., & Yetman, N.B. (1977). "Immune from racism?" *Civil Rights Digest*, 9, 3–13.

Elias, N., & Dunning, E. (1986) *Quest for excitement: Sport and leisure in the civilizing process*. Oxford: Basil Blackwell.

Emerson, M.B., & Perse, E.M. (1995). "Media events and sports orientations to the 1992 Winter Olympics." *The Journal of International Communication*, 2(1), 80–99.

Emert, C. (1997, January 24). "It's super Sunday for TV ads." *San Francisco Chronicle*, pp. B-1, B-1.

Emig, J. (1986). "Barriers of investigative sports journalism: An empirical inquiry into the conditions of information transmission." *International review for the sociology of sport*, 21(2/3), 113–129.

Endel, B.L. (1991). "Working out: The dialectic of strength and sexuality in Women's Sports and Fitness magazine." Unpublished doctoral dissertation, University of Iowa.

"ESPN international passport." (1995). Promotional material. Bristol, CT: ESPN, Inc.

Euchner, C. (1992). *Playing the field: Why sports teams move and cities fight to keep them*, Baltimore: Johns Hopkins University Press.

Fairlie, H. (1978, November). "Too rich for heroes." *Harpers*, 36–37.

"Fans support women's game." (1996, Nov. 22). *Akron Beacon Journal*, p. D6.

Farrell, T.B. (1989). "Media rhetoric as social drama: The winter Olympics of 1984." *Critical Studies in Mass Communication*, 6, 158–182.

Fatsis, S. (1996, Feb. 16). "Women's hoops takes a long-range shot." *Wall Street Journal*, p. B6.

Fayer, J. (1994). "Are heroes always men?" In S.J. Drucker, & R.S. Cathcart (Eds). (1994). *American heroes in a media age*, pp. 24–35. Creskill, NJ: Hampton Press.

Feder, A.M. (1995). "'A radiant smile from the lovely lady': Overdetermined femininity in 'ladies' figure skating." In C. Baughman (Ed.), *Women on ice: Feminist essays on the Tonya Harding/Nancy Kerrigan spectacle*, pp. 22–46. New York: Routledge.

Finkelthal, A. (1994, March 28). "Signage of the times." *Cablevision*, p. 34.

Finney, P. (1995, May 21). "CBS puts blame on messenger." *Times-Picayune*, p. C1.

Fisher, M. (1989). "The failure of Canadian sports journalism in relation to Olympic sports." In R. Jackson (Ed.), *The Olympic movement and the mass media: Past, present and future issues*, pp. 3.19–3.22. Calgary: Hurford Enterprises.

Fiske, J. (1987). *Television culture*. London: Methuen.

Fiske, J. (1989). *Reading the popular*. Boston: Unwin Hyman.

Fiske, J. (1992). "The cultural economy of fandom." In L.A. Lewis (Ed.), *The adoring audience: Fan culture and popular media*, pp. 30–49. London: Routledge.

Flynn, L. (1995). "Valvoline races to the Web during the Indianapolis 500." *MacWeek*, 9, pp. 22–24.

Fornoff, S. (1993). *Lady in the locker room*. Champaign, IL: Sagamore Publishing.

Foucault, M. (1979, Autumn). *On governmentality*. Trans. Pasquale Paquino. I & C, 6, 6–21.

Foucault, M. (1994). *The birth of the clinic: An araeology of medical perception*. New York: Vintage.

Fox, S. (1984). *The mirror makers*. New York: William Morrow.

Francis, M.E. (1990). "Coverage of African American basketball athletes in Sports Illustrated." Unpublished Master's Thesis, Univ. of Oregon, Eugene, Oregon.

Frasier, A. (1988). *The warrior queens: The legends and the lives of the women who have led their nations in war*. New York: Vintage.

"Games girls' fund-raising knocked back by official (1994, July 21)." *Canberra Times*, p. 1.

Gamson, J. (1992). "The assembly line of greatness: Celebrity in twentieth century America." *Critical Studies in Mass Communication*, 9, 1–24.

Gantz, W. (1981). "An exploration of viewing motives associated with television sports." *Journal of Broadcasting*, 25, 263–275.

Gantz, W. (1985). "Exploring the role of television in married life." *Journal of Broadcasting and Electronic Media*, 29, 263–275.

Gantz, W., & Wenner, L.A. (1991). "Men, women, and sports: Audience experiences and effects." *Journal of Broadcasting & Electronic Media*, 35 (2), 233–243.

Gantz, W., & Wenner, L.A. (1995). "Fanship and the television sports viewing experience." *Sociology of Sport Journal*, 12, 56–74.

Gantz, W., Wenner, L.A., Carrico, C., & Knorr, M. (1995a). "Assessing the football widow hypotheis: A coorientation study of the role of televised sports in long-standing relationships." *Journal of Sport & Social Issues*, 19(4), 352–376.

Gantz, W., Wenner, L.A., Carrico, C., & Knorr, M. (1995b). "Televised sports and marital relationships." *Sociology of Sport Journal*, 12, 306–323.

Garrison, B. (1989). "The evolution of professional sports reporting." In R. Jackson (Ed.), *The Olympic movement and the mass media: Past, present and future issues*, pp. 3.23–3.27. Calgary: Hurford Enterprises.

Garrison, B., & Sabljak, M. (1985). *Sports reporting*. Ames, Iowa: Iowa State University Press.

Gary Bettman talks about hockey in the United States. (1996, January 22). *The Charlie Rose Show* (PBS). Transcript available at URL: http://www.elibrary.com/cgi-bin/hhweb/hhfetch? 38617466x0y914:Q002:D021.

Gaston, J.C. (1986). "The destruction of the young black male: The impact of popular culture and organized sports." *Journal of Black Studies*, 16(4), 369–384.

Gatt, R. (1992, July 14). "Socceroos are pawns in Croats' political grandstanding." *Australian*, p. 22.

Geen, R.G., & Quanty, M.B. (1977). "The catharsis of aggression: An evaluation of a hypothesis." In L. Berkowitz (Ed.), *Advances in experimental social psychology* (Vol. 10, pp. 1–37). New York: Academic Press.

Geertz, C. (1973). *The interpretation of cultures*. New York: Basic Books.

Geertz, C. (1976). "Deep play: A description of the Balinese cockfight." In J.S. Bruner, A. Jolly, & K. Sylva (Eds), *Play – Its role in development and evolution*, pp. 650–671. New York: Basic Books.

Gellner, E. (1981). "Nationalism." *Theory and Society*, 10, 753–76.

Gerbner, G. (1970). "Cultural indicators: The case of violence in television drama." *Annals of the American Academy of Political and Social Science*, 388 (March), 69–91.

Gerbner, G. (1993). *Women and minorities on television: A study of casting and fate*. Philadelphia: The Annenberg School for Communication.

Gerbner, G. (1996). "The hidden side of television violence." In G. Gerbner, H. Mowlana, & H.I. Schiller (Eds), *Invisible crises: What conglomerate control of media means for America and the world*, pp. 27–34. Boulder, CO: Westview Press.

Gerbner, G., & Signorelli, N. (1979). *Women and minorities in television drama: A research report*. Philadelphia: University of Pennsylvania, Annenberg School of Communications.

Gillen, P. (1994/5). "The Olympic Games and global society." *Arena*, 4, 5–15.

Gillet, J., White, P., & Young, K. (1996). "The prime minister of Saturday night: Don Cherry, the CBC, and the cultural production of intolerance." In H. Holmes & D. Taras (Eds), *Seeing ourselves: Media power and policy in Canada*, pp. 59–72. Toronto: Harcourt Brace.

Gilligan, C. (1982). *In a different voice*. Cambridge: Harvard University Press.

Gilman, K. (1974). *Inside the pressure cooker*. New York: Berkley Medallion.

Gilmour, K. (1988). "Franchise the Clubs!" *Australian Soccer Weekly*, 9 (no. 348), p. 3.

Giobbe, D. (1996, May 25). "Sports marketing needs a workout." *Editor & Publisher*, pp. 12–13.

Global NBA Programming. (1997, December 13). National Basketball Association Official Website. URL: http://www.NBA.com/global/.

Goffman, E. (1959). *The presentation of self in everyday life*. London: Penguin.

Goffman, E. (1979). *Gender advertisements*. Cambridge: Harvard University Press.

Goldberg, A., & Wagg, S. (1991). "It's not a knockout: English football and globalisation." In J. Williams and S. Wagg (Eds), *British football and social change: Getting in Europe*. pp. 239–253. Leicester: Leicester University Press.

Goldberg, D. (1995, March 16). "Rams: Why no. Associated Press." *Prodigy Interactive Personal Service*.

Goldlust, J. (1987). *Playing for keeps: Sport, the media and society*. Melbourne: Longman Cheshire.

Goldman, A. (1980). *The moral foundations of professional ethics*. Totowa, New Jersey: Rowan and Littlefield.

Goldsen, R. (1978). *The show and tell machine: How television works and works you over*. New York: Dell Publishing.

Goldstein, J.H., & Bredemeier, B.J. (1977). "Socialization: Some basic issues." *Journal of Communication*, 27(3), 154–159.

Goodhart, G.J. et al. (1975). *The television audience*. London: Saxon.

Gordon, A. (1984). *Foul balls: Five years in the American League*. Toronto: McClelland and Stewart.

Gorman, J., & Calhoun, K. (1994). *The name of the game: The business of sports*. New York: Wiley.

Gorn, E. & Goldstein, W. (1993). *A brief history of American sports*. New York: Hill & Wang.

Graham, C.C. (1986). *Leni Riefenstahl and Olympia*. Metuchen, NJ: Scarecrow Press.

Gray, A. (1987.) "Behind closed doors: video recorders in the home." In *Boxed in: Women and television*. London: Pandora.

Gray, A. (1992). *Video playtime: The gendering of a leisure technology*. London: Routledge.

Green, G. (1994, July 26). "Different rules for female athletes?" *Morning Bulletin*, p. 6.

Green, T. (1995, September 22). "Lloyd's injury to quarterback Dan Marino a 'cheap shot'." *Morning Edition* (NPR). (Nexis Transcript #1700–4), 1–2.

Green, T.S. (1993). "The future of African-American female athletes." In D.D. Brooks & R.C. Althouse (Eds), *Racism in college athletics: The African-American athlete's experience*, pp. 205–223. Morgantown, WV: Fitness Information Technology.

Greendorfer, S.L. (1991). "Differential media coverage of men's & women's in collegiate basketball: Reflection of gender ideology." *Journal of Sport & Social Issues*, 15(2), 98–114.

Greendorfer, S.L. (1993). "Gender role stereotypes and early child socialization." In G.L. Cohen (Ed.), *Women in sport: Issues and controversies*, pp. 3–14. Newbury Park, CA: Sage.

Greising, D. (1994, February 7). 19!95!–Hike! *Business Week*, reprint.

Griffin, C. (1982). "Women and leisure." In J. Hargreaves (Ed.), *Sport, culture and ideology*. London: RKP.

Griffin, P. (1992). "Changing the game: Homophobia, sexism and lesbians in sport." *Quest*, 44, 251–265.

Griffin, P. (1993). "Homophobia in women's sports: The fear that divides us." In G. Cohen (Ed.), *Women in sport: Issues and controversies*, pp. 193–203. Newbury Park, CA: Sage Publications.

Griffin, P., & Gebasci, J. (1990). "Addressing homophobia in physical education: Responsibilities for teachers and researchers." In M.A. Messner & D. F. Sabo (Eds), *Sport, men and the gender order*, pp. 211–221. Champaign, IL: Human Kinetics.

Griffith, P. (1996, February 7). "NFL again tries D.C." *Pittsburgh Post-Gazette*, pp. C-1, C-6.

Grossberg, L. (1992). "Is there a fan in the house?: The affective sensibility of fandom." In L.A. Lewis (Ed.), *The adoring audience: Fan culture and popular media*, pp. 50–65. London: Routledge.

Gruneau, R. (1983). *Class, sport and social development*. Amherst: University of Massachusetts Press.

Gruneau, R. (1989). "Making spectacle: A case study in television sports production." In L.A. Wenner (Ed.), *Media, sports, & society*, pp. 134–154. Newbury Park, CA: Sage.

Gruneau, R., & Whitson, D. (1993). *Hockey Night in Canada: Sport, identities, and cultural politics*. Toronto: Garamond Press.

Guinchard, J.-J. (1987). "Le national et le rationnel." *Communications*, 45, 17–49.

Gunther, M. (1996, "March 4). Web + sports = profit. Right?" *Fortune*, pp. 197–198.

Gunther, M. (1996). "Get ready for the Oprah Olympics." *Fortune*, 134(2), p. 62–63.

Gustkey, E. (1996, Jan. 28). "More NBA teams on horizon, but the players will be women." *Los Angeles Times*, C2.

Guttmann, A. (1978). From ritual to record: The nature of modern sports. New York: Columbia University Press.

Guttmann, A. (1986). *Sports spectators*. New York: Columbia University Press.

Guttmann, A. (1988). *A whole new ball game*. Chapel Hill: University of North Carolina Press.

Guttmann, A. (1991). *Women's sports: A history*. New York: Columbia University Press.

Guttmann, A. (1992). *The Olympics: A history of the modern games*. Urbana: University of Illinois Press.

Haag, P. (1996). "'The 50,000-watt sports bar': Talk radio and the ethic of the fan." *South Atlantic Quarterly*, 95(2), 453–470.

Halbert, C., & Latimer, M. (1994). "'Battling' gendered language: An analysis of the language used by sports commentators in a televised coed tennis competition." *Sociology of Sport Journal*, 11, 298–308.

Hall, A., Cullen, D., & Slack, T. (1990). "The gender structure of national sport organizations." Sport Canada Occasional Papers, No. 2, December. Ottawa: Sport Canada.

Hall, A., & Richardson, D. (1982). *Fair ball: Toward sex equality in Canadian sport*. Ottawa: Canadian Advisory Council on the Status of Women.

Hall, M.A. (1993). "Gender and sport in the 1990s: Feminism, culture, and politics." *Sport Science Review*, 2(1), 48–68.

Hall, M.A. (1996) *Feminism and sporting bodies: Essays in theory and practice*. Champaign, IL: Human Kinetics.

Hall, S. (1978). "The treatment of 'football hooliganism' in the press." In R. Ingham, S. Hall, J. Clarke, P. Marsh, & J. Donovan (Eds), *Football hooliganism: The wider context*, pp. 15–36. London: Inter-Action Inprint.

Hall, S., Hobson, D., Lowe, A., & Willis, P. (Eds) (1980). *Culture, media, language*. London: Hutchinson.

Halonen, D. (1994, August 1). "Suit puts ABC deal on record." *Electronic Media*, pp. 1, 31.

Halvonik, S. (1996, February 17). "McClatchy envisions new stadium." *Pittsburgh Post-Gazette*, pp. A-1, A-3.

Hamilton, I. (1993). *Gazza Italia*. London: Granta.

Harari, F. (1994, January 18). "Where the willow weeps unnoticed." *The Australian*, p. 7.

Harari, F., & Smellie, P. (1994, January 19). Lesbianism in sport prevalent but not relevant, says cricketer. *The Australian*, p. 3.

Harding, S.G. (1991). *Whose knowledge? Whose science?: Thinking from Women's Lives*. Ithaca: Cornell University Press.

Hargreaves, J. (Ed.) (1982). *Sport, culture and ideology*. London: Routledge and Kegan Paul.

Hargreaves, J. (1982). "Sport and hegemony: Some theoretical problems." In H. Cantelon & R. Gruneau (Eds), *Sport, culture and the modern state*, pp. 103–140. Toronto: University of Toronto Press.

Hargreaves, J. (1986). *Sport, power and culture: A social and historical analysis of popular sports in Britain*. Cambridge: Polity Press.

Hargreaves, J. (1992). "Olympism and nationalism: Some preliminary consideration." *International Review for the Sociology of Sport*, 27(1), 119–135.

Hargreaves, J. (1994). *Sporting females: Critical issues in the history and sociology of women's sports*. London: Routledge.

Harris, B. (1994, July 28). "Sex sells women's sport: Graf." *The Australian*, p. 22.

Harris, H.A. (1972). *Aspects of Greek and Roman life*. Ithaca, NY: Cornell University Press.

Harris, J.C. (1994). *Athletes and the American hero dilemma*. Champaign, IL: Human Kinetics.

Harris, J.C. (1995). "Athletic cultural performances: local, national, and global." *Proceedings of FISU/CESU Conference, Fukuoka, Japan*, 57–60.

Harris, J.C., & Hills, L.A. (1993). "Telling the story: Narrative in newspaper accounts of a men's collegiate basketball tournament." *Research Quarterly for Exercise and Sport*, 64(1), 108–121.

Harris, J.F. (1991). "Nobody knows her name: The depiction of the black female athlete in national sports telecasts." Unpublished master's thesis, University of Texas, Austin.

Harris, O. (1993). "African-American predominance in collegiate sport." In D.D. Brooks & R.C. Althouse (Eds), *Racism in college athletics: The African-American athlete's experience*, pp. 51–74. Morgantown, WV: Fitness Information Technology.

Harris, R.J. (1994). *Sports and media: Marriage or conquest? In A cognitive psychology of mass communication* (2nd edn), pp. 115–137. Hillsdale, New Jersey: Lawrence Erlbaum Associates, Inc.

Hartley, J. (1992). *Tele-ology: Studies in television*. London: Routledge.

Harvey, J., & Cantelon, H. (Eds) (1988). *Not just a game: Essays in Canadian sport sociology*. Toronto: University of Toronto Press.

Harvey, J., Rail, G. and Thibault, L. (1996). "Globalization and sport: Sketching a theoretical model for empirical analyses." *Journal of Sport and Social Issues*, 23, pp. 258–277.

Harvey, R. (1995, December 13). "Sites unseen, NBC locks in Olympics through 2008." *Los Angeles Times* (Home edition), p. C-1.

Hastorf, A.H., & Cantril, H. (1954). They saw a game: A case study. *Journal of Abnormal and Social Psychology*, 2, 129–134.

Hebdige, D. (1979). *Subculture: The meaning of style.* London: Methuen.

Heisler, M. (1996, February 11). "Happy days return to league that really works." *Los Angeles Times* (Home edition), p. C-8.

Held, D. (1989). "The decline of the nation state." In S. Hall & M. Jacques (Eds), *New times: The changing face of politics in the 1990s*, pp. 191–204. London: Lawrence and Wishart.

Helitzer, M. (1996). *Sports: Publicity, promotion and marketing* (2nd edn). Athens, Ohio: University Sports Press.

Helmbreck, V. (1995, May 12). "Mechem, players dismiss comments." *USA Today*, p. 3C.

Helyar, J. (1994, September 9). "A whole new ballgame." *Wall Street Journal,* reprint.

Henley, N.M. (1977). *Body politics: Power, sex, and nonverbal communication.* Englewood Cliffs, NJ: Prentice-Hall.

Hersch, H. (1996). "Michael Jordan's Return." *SI OnLine.* http://www. sportsillustrated.com.

Hiestand, M. (1995, October 24). "Sponsors bring good news to women's basketball." *USA Today,* p. 3C.

Higgs, C.T., & Weiller, K.H. (1994). "Gender bias and the 1992 Summer Olympic Games: An analysis of television coverage." *Journal of Sport & Social Issues*, 18(3), 234–246.

Hilliard, D. (1995, November). "Race, gender, and the televisual representation of olympic athletes." Paper presented at the meeting of the North American Society for the Sociology of Sport, Sacramento, CA.

Hilliard, D.C. (1994). "Televised sport and the (anti) sociological imagination." *Journal of Sport & Social Issues*, 18, 88–99.

Hills, L.A. (1992). "Mass media portrayals of drug use in sports." Unpublished master's thesis, University of North Carolina at Greensboro, Greensboro, North Carolina.

Hitchcock, J.R. (1991). *Sportscasting.* Boston: Focal Press.

Hobsbawm, E. (1983). "Introduction: Inventing tradition." In E. Hobsbawn & T. Ranger (Eds), *The invention of tradition*, pp. 1–14. Cambridge: Cambridge University Press.

Hobsbawm, E., & Ranger, T. (Eds). (1997). *The invention of tradition.* Cambridge: Cambridge University Press.

Hobson, D. (1982). *Crossroads: The drama of a soap opera.* London: Methuen.

Hodge, R., & Kress, G. (1988). *Social semiotics.* Cambridge: Polity Press.

Hodges, M. (1995, May 13). "Ben Wright's swing at lesbian pro golfers reinforces 'don't ask, don't tell.'" *The Detroit News*, p. C1.

Hoffer, R. (1996, May 27). "Sitting bull." *Sports Illustrated*, 76–86.

Hofmeister, S. (1995, October 31). "Fox, TCI expected to form sports network." *Los Angeles Times* (Home edition), p. D1.

Holmlund, C.A. (1994). "Visible difference and flee appeal: The body, sex, sexuality, and race in the Pumping Iron films." In S. Birrell & L. Cole (Eds) *Women, sport, and culture*, pp. 299–313. Champaign, IL: Human Kinetics.

Hoose, P.M. (1989). *Necessities: Racial barriers in American sports.* New York, NY: Random House.

Hornby, N. (1992). *Fever pitch.* London: Victor Gollancz.

Horovitz, B. (1992, June 9). "In-your-face ads will play a bigger role." *Los Angeles Times* (Home edition), p. D-1.

Hribar, A.S. (1992, November). "Hegemony, racism and sports mascots." Paper presented at the meeting of the North American Society for the Sociology of Sport, Toledo, OH.

Huber, G.P. (1990). "A theory of the effects of advanced information technologies on organizational design, intelligence and decision-making." In J. Fulk, & C. Steinfield (Eds), *Organizations and communication technology*, pp. 237–274. Newbury Park, CA: Sage.

Hudson, M. (1995, May 13). "CBS keeps Wright after he denies remarks on LPGA." *Los Angeles Times*, pp. C1, C10.

Hurst, M. (1988, July 15). "World champs stunned by gallant Socceroos." *Daily Telegraph*, p. 67.

Hutchinson, J. (1992). "State festivals, foundation myths and cultural politics in immigrant nations." In T. Bennett, P. Buckridge, D. Carter & C. Mercer (Eds), *Celebrating the nation: A critical study of Australia's bicentenary*, pp. 3–25. Sydney: Allen and Unwin, 1992. 3–25.

Huxley, J. (1994, July 30). "Sneers, leers but all the girls are good sports." *Sydney Morning Herald*, p. 7.

Hymes, D. (1964). "Towards ethnographies of communication." *American Anthropologist*, 66(6), 1–34.

I/Pro (1996, December – March). I/Audit Statement. Internal report on web usage from Nielsen Media Research and Internet Profiles Corporation for *USA Today*.

Impoco, D. (1996, July 15/July 22). "Live from Atlanta." *US News & World Report*, 121, 36–37.

Inception of the WNBA. (1996, October 30). Women's National Basketball Association Official Website. URL: http://www.wnba.com/news feat/wnba pc.html.

International Olympic Committee. (1990). *Media Guide*. Lausanne: Author.

International TV Schedule. (1997, December 13). National Football League Official Website. URL: http://www.nfl/com/sideline /worldmedia.html.

Irigaray, L. (1985). *Speculum of the other woman*. G.C. Gill (Trans.). Ithaca: Cornell University Press.

Izod, J. (1996). "Television sport and the sacrificial hero." *Journal of Sport & Social Issues*, 21(1), 173–193.

Jackson, D.Z. (1987, June 14). "Stereotyping on the airwaves." *Newsday*, pp. 2–4.

Jackson, D.Z. (1989, January 22). "Calling the plays in black and white." *Boston Globe*, pp. A30, 33.

Jackson, D.Z. (1996, March 27). "Chasing spirits down the court at NCAA tourney." *Charlotte Observer*, p. 17A.

Jackson, R. (Ed.). (1989). *The Olympic movement and the mass media: Past, present and future issues*. Calgary, Alberta, Canada: Hurford Enterprises.

Jackson, S.J. (1992). "Sport, crisis, and Canadian identity in 1988: A cultural analysis." Unpublished doctoral dissertation, University of IL at Urbana-Champaign.

Jackson, S.J. (1993, November). "Life in the faust lane: Ben Johnson and the 1988 crisis of Canadian national identity." Paper presented at the meeting of the North American Society for the Sociology of Sport, Ottawa, Ontario.

Jackson, S.J. (1994). "Gretzky, crisis, and Canadian identity in 1988: Rearticulating the Americanization of culture debate." *Sociology of Sport Journal*, 11, 428–446.

Jackson, S.J., & Andrews, D.L. (1995, November). "Michael Jordan and the popular imaginary of post-colonial New Zealand: The necessary dialectic of global commodity-sign culture." Paper presented at the meeting of the North American Society for the Sociology of Sport, Sacramento, CA.

Jacobson, N.S., Waldron, H., & Moore, D. (1980). "Toward a behavioral profile of marital distress." *Journal of Consulting and Clinical Psychology*, 48, 696–703.

Jalai, R., & Lipset, S.M. (1992–93). "Racial and ethnic conflicts: A global perspective." *Political Science Quarterly*, 107, 585–606.

Jameson, F. (1979, Winter). "Reification and utopia in mass culture." *Social Text*, pp. 130–147.

Jameson, F. (1991). *Postmodernism: or, the cultural logic of late capitalism*. Durham, NC: Duke University Press.

Jansen, S.C. (1988). *Censorship: The knot that binds power and knowledge.* New York: Oxford University Press.

Jansen, S.C. (1991). "Collapse of the public sphere and the emergence of information-capitalism." *Inquiry: Critical Thinking Across the Disciplines*, 8(4), 1, 21–24.

Jansen, S.C. (1993). "The future is not what it used to be: Gender, history, and communications." *Communication Theory*, 6, 136–148.

Jansen, S.C., & Sabo, D. (1994). "The sport/war metaphor: Hegemonic masculinity, the Persian Gulf War, and the new world order." *Sociology of Sport Journal*, 11, 1–17.

Jaret, C. (1995). *Contemporary racial and ethnic relations.* New York, NY: HarperCollins.

Jarvie, G., & Maguire, J. (1994). *Sport and leisure in social thought.* London: Routledge.

Jenkins, H. (1992). *Textual poachers: Television fans and participatory culture.* New York: Routledge.

Jensen, E. (1994, May 24). "Fox to take some affiliates from rivals, stuns industry." Television news. Prodigy Interactive Personal Service.

Jenson, J. (1992). "Fandom as pathology: The consequences of characterization." In L.A. Lewis (Ed.), *The adoring audience: Fan culture and the popular media*, pp. 9–29. London: Routledge.

Jensen, J. (1994, October 24). "All the sports world's a stage." *Advertising Age*, pp. 1, 4–5.

Jensen, J. (1995, March 13). "Nielsen targets media-driven leagues like NBA." *Advertising Age*, p. 36.

Jensen, J. (1996, May 9). "Jones fails to spur more NFL discontent." *Advertising Age* (Online edition). URL: http:// www.whytel.com/home/perrymck/Jones2.html.

Jessell, H. (1995). "Broadcasters approaching the Internet." *Broadcasting & Cable, 125*, 33.

Jhally, S. (1984). "The spectacle of accumulation: Material and cultural factors in the evolution of the sports/media complex." *The Insurgent Sociologist*, 12(3), 41–57.

Jhally, S. (1989). "Cultural studies and the sports/media complex." In L.A. Wenner (Ed.), *Media, sports, & society*, pp. 70–93. Newbury Park, CA: Sage.

Jhally, S., & Lewis, J. (1992). *Enlightened racism.* Boulder, CO: Westview Press.

Johnson, L. (1996, November 14). "Hertz, don't it? Corporate ideas about race in the making of O.J. Simpson." A keynote address presented at the annual meeting of the North American Society for the Sociology of Sport, Birmingham, Alabama.

Jollimore, M. (July 10, 1992). "Telephone interview with Toronto-based CP reporter.

Jordin, M., & Brunt, R. (1986). "Constituting the television audience." In *ITSC Conference Paper*. London: ITSC.

Kamiya, G. (1990, September 9). "One from the heart: In which our reporter meets his idol." *San Francisco Chronicle*, Image Magazine, 13–21.

Kane, M.J. (1988). "Media coverage of the female athlete in the media before, during, and after Title IX: *Sports Illustrated* revisited." *Journal of Sport Management*, 2, 87–99.

Kane, M.J. (1989). "The post-Title IX female athlete in the media: Things are changing but how much?" *Journal of Physical Education, Recreation and Dance*, 60(3), 58–62.

Kane, M.J. (1995). "Resistance/transformation of the oppositional binary: Exposing sport as a continuum." *Journal of Sport and Social Issues*, 19, 191–218.

Kane, M.J. (1996). "Media coverage of the post Title IX female athlete: A feminist analysis of sport, gender and power." *Duke Journal of Gender Law and Policy*.

Kane, M.J., & Disch, L.J. (1993). "Sexual violence and the reproduction of male power in the locker room: The 'Lisa Olsen incident'." *Sociology of Sport Journal*, 10, 331–352.

Kane, M.J., & Greendorfer, S.L. (1994). "The media's role in accommodating and resisting stereotyped images of women in sport." In P.J. Creedon (Ed). *Women, media and sport: Challenging gender values*, pp. 28–44. Thousand Oaks, CA: Sage.

Kane, M.J., & Parks, J.B. (1992). The social construction of gender difference and hier-archy in sport journalism – Few new twists on very old themes. *Women's Sport and Physical Activity Journal*, 1(1), 49–83.

Kane, M.J., & Snyder, E.E. (1989). "Sport typing: The social containment of women in sport." *Arena Review*, 13(2), 77–96.

Kaplan, E.A. (1988). "Whose imaginary? The televisual apparatus, the female body and textual strategies in select rock videos on MTV." In E.D. Pribram (Ed.), *Female spectators: Looking at film and television*, pp. 132–156. New York: Verso.

Katz, D. (1995, July 3). "Welcome to the electronic arena." *Sports Illustrated*, pp. 56–77.

Katz, E. (1980). "Media events: The sense of occasion." *Studies in Visual Anthropology*, 6, 84–89.

Katz, E., & Lazarsfeld, P. (1955). *Personal influence*. Glencoe, IL: Free Press.

Kaufman, M. (Ed.). (1987). Beyond patriarchy: Essays by men on pleasure, power, and change. Toronto: University of Toronto Press.

Kavanagh (1994, January 29). "Let's sidestep the politically correct waffle." *Courier-Mail*, p. 34.

Kellner, D. (1995). *Media culture*. London: Routledge.

Kelly, K.J. (1996, September 23). "Media ponder best ticket into women's sports field." *Advertising Age*, 67(39), p. 61.

Kent Commission. (1981). Report of the Royal Commission on Newspapers, Volume 1. Ottawa: Ministry of Supply and Services.

Kidane, F. (1996). "The mass media in the developing countries." In F. Kidane (Ed.), *The Olympic movement and the mass media*, pp. 213–215. Lausanne: Department of International Cooperation and Public Information, International Olympic Committee.

Kidd, B. (1987). "Sports and muscularity." In M. Kaufman (Ed.), *Beyond Patriarchy: Essays by men on pleasure, power and change*, pp. 250–265. Toronto: University of Toronto Press.

Kidd, B., & Eberts, M. (1982). *Athletes' rights in Canada*. Toronto: Ministry of Tourism and Recreation.

Kilbourne, J. (Producer and Moderator). (1987). *Still killing us softly: Advertising images of women [Film]*. Cambridge, MA: Cambridge Documentary Films.

Kilbourne, J. (1995). "Beauty and the beast of advertising." In G. Dines & J.M. Humez (Eds), *Gender, race and class in media*. Thousand Oaks, CA: Sage Publications.

Kim, Y.J. (1994). "Electronic mail users' perceptions of computer-mediated versus face-to-face communication: A comparative study." Unpublished doctoral dissertation, Florida State University.

Kimmel, M. (1996). *Manhood in America: A cultural history*. New York: The Free Press.

Kindred, D. (1996, June 29). "Voices: He'll always be the greatest." *The Sporting News*, p. 6.

King, J.P., & Chi, P.S.K. (1979). "Social structure, sex-roles, and personality: Comparisons of male-female athletes/non-athletes." In J.H. Goldstein (Ed.), *Sports, games and play: Social and psychological viewpoints*, pp. 115–148. Hillsdale, NJ: Erlbaum.

King, N., & Rowse, T. (1983). "'Typical Aussies': Television and populism in Australia." *Framework*, nos. 22–23, 37–42.

King, S. (1993). "The politics of the body and the body politic: Magic Johnson and the ideology of AIDS." *Sociology of Sport Journal*, 10, 270–285.

Kinkema, K.M., & Harris, J.C. (1992). "Sport and the mass media." In J.O. Holloszy (Ed.), *Exercise and Sport Science Reviews*, 20, pp. 127–159. Baltimore, MD: Williams and Wilkins.

Kitzinger, C. (1987). *The social construction of lesbianism*. Newbury Park, CA: Sage Publications.

Klapp, O.E. (1956). *Ritual and cult: A sociological interpretation*. Washington, DC: Public Affairs.

Klapp, O.E. (1962). *Heroes, villains, and fools*. Englewood Cliffs, NJ: Prentice-Hall.

Klapp, O.E. (1964). *Symbolic leaders: Public dramas and public men*. Chicago: Aldine.

Klapper, J. (1960). *The effects of mass communication*. Glencoe, IL: Free Press.

Klatell, D., & Marcus, N. (1988). *Sports for sale: Television, money, and the fan*. New York: Oxford University Press.

Klein, F.C. (1995, September 22). "Ultimatum '95: Pay for a stadium or lose the team." *Wall Street Journal*, reprint.

Kline, S. (1993). *Out of the garden: Toys and children's culture in the age of TV marketing*. Toronto: Garamond.

Knisley, M. (1995, January 2). "RuperTVision." *The Sporting News*, p. S-2.

Koenig, B. (1996, November 8–14). "Revived 'Game of the Week' highlights new TV deal." *Baseball Weekly*, p. 4.

Kohn, H. (1945). *The idea of nationalism: A study in its origins and background*. New York: Macmillan.

Korporaal, G. (1995, December 18). "Big bucks in TV sport get bigger." *The Sydney Morning Herald*, pp. 29–30.

Kottak, C. P. (1988). "Being versus doing in international sports." *Society*, 25(6), 53–59.

Krane V. (1996). "Lesbian in sport: Towards acknowledgement, understanding, and theory." *Journal of Sport and Exercise Psychology*, 18, pp. 237–246.

Krane, V. (1997). "Homonegativism experienced by lesbian collegiate athletes." *Women in Sport & Physical Activity Journal*, 6(2), 141–163.

Krantz, M. (1995). "The medium is the measure." *Adweek*, 36, pp. IQ20 – IQ24.

Kryter, K.A. (1994). "Examining the usefulness of computer networks for meeting individuals' information needs using media systems dependency theory." Unpublished master's thesis, Florida State University.

Kubey, R. (1990). "Television and family harmony among children, adolescents, and adults: Results from the experience sampling method." In J. Bryant (Ed.), *Television and the American family*, pp. 73–88. Hillsdale, NJ: Erlbaum.

Lafayette, J. (1995, August 14). NBC's Olympics deal blindsides network rivals. *Electronic Media*, pp. 1, 14.

Lafayette, J. (1995, November 20). "SportsCenter on an ESPN roll: Show's popularity soars with fans." *Electronic Media*, 4, p. 30.

Lafayette, J. (1996, January 22). "Twelve to watch in 1996: Fox Sports' David Hill." *Electronic Media*, pp. 126, 145.

Lafayette, J. (1997, November 17). "NBA's ball bounces to NBC, Turner courts." *Electronic Media*, pp. 2, 52.

Lafayette, J. (1998, January 19). "CBS gets back in the game with NFL." *Electronic Media*, pp. 1, 120.

Lafky, S.A. (1993). "The progress of women and people of color in the US journalistic workforce: A long, slow journey." In P.J. Creedon (Ed.). *Women in mass communication: Challenging gender values*, pp. 87–103. Newbury Park, CA: Sage.

Lait, M., & Hernandez, G. (1995, May 20). "Disney teams with Angels." *Los Angeles Times* (Orange County edition), p. A-26.

Lalvani, S. (1994). "Carrying the ideological ball: Text, discourse, and pleasure." *Sociology of Sport Journal*, 11, 155–174.

Lans, M. (1995, June 5). "Sports team logos are big business." *Marketing News*, p. 6.

Lapchick, R. (1995, April 24). "Women's basketball as a hoop du jour." *The Sporting News*, 219(17), p. 8.

Laponce, J. (1984). *Nation-building as body-building: A comparative study of the personalization of city, province and state by Anglophone and Francophone Canadians*. Social Science Information, 23, 977–991.

Larson, J.F., & Park, H.S. (1993). *Global television and the politics of the Seoul Olympics.* Boulder, CO: Westview Press.

Larson, J.F., & Rivenburgh, N.K. (1991). "A comparative analysis of Australian, US, and British telecasts of the Seoul Olympic opening ceremony." *Journal of Broadcasting and Electronic Media,* 35(1), 75–94.

Lash, S., & Urry, J. (1994). *Economies of signs and space.* London: Sage.

Lawrence, E.A. (1982). *Rodeo: An anthropologist looks at the wild and the tame.* Chicago: University of Chicago Press.

Lawrence, G., & Rowe, D. (Eds) (1986a). *Power play.* Sydney: Hale and Iremonger.

Lawrence, G., & Rowe, D. (1986b). "The corporate pitch: Televised cricket under capitalism." In G. Lawrence & D. Rowe (Eds), *Power play: Essays in the sociology of Australian sport,* pp. 166–178. Sydney: Hale and Iremonger.

Lazarsfeld, P., Berelson, B., & Gaudet, H. (1948). *The people's choice.* New York: Columbia University Press.

Lazier, L., & Kendrick, A.G. (1993). "Women in advertisements: Sizing up images, roles and functions." In P.J. Creedon (Ed.). *Women in mass communication: Challenging gender values,* pp. 199–219. Newbury Park, CA: Sage.

Leach, E. (1976). *Culture and communication.* Cambridge: Cambridge University Press.

Leath, V.M., & Lumpkin, A. (1992). "An analysis of sportswomen on the covers and in the feature articles of 'Women's Sports and Fitness Magazine'," *Journal of Sport and Social Issues,* 16(2), 121–126.

Leavy, J. (1990a). "My book tour diary." *Gannett Center Journal,* 4(2), 58–67.

Leavy, J. (1990b). *Squeeze Play.* New York: Doubleday.

Lee, J. (1992). "Media portrayals of male and female Olympic athletes: Analyses of newspaper accounts of the 1984 and the 1988 summer games." *International Review for the Sociology of Sport,* 27(3), 197–218.

Lee, M. (1993). *Consumer culture reborn: The cultural politics of consumption.* London: Routledge.

Lefton, T. (1995). "MCI on the MLB web site." *Brandweek,* 36, p. 41.

Leifer, E. (1995). *Making the majors: The transformation of team sports in America.* Cambridge, MA: Harvard University Press.

Lenskyj, H. (1986). *Out of bounds: Women, sport & sexuality.* Toronto: Women's Press.

Lenskyj, H. (1991). "Combating homophobia in sport and physical education: academic and professional responsibilities." *Sociology of Sport Journal,* 8, 61–69.

Lenskyj, H. (1992). "Unsafe at home base: Women's experiences of sexual harassment in university sport and physical education." *Women in Sport and Physical Activity Journal,* 1, 19–34.

Lenskyj, H. (1994). "Sexuality and femininity in sport contexts: Issues and alternatives." *Journal of Sport and Social Issues,* 18, 356–376.

Lever, J., & Wheeler, S. (1993). "Mass media and the experience of sport." *Communication Research,* 20, 125–143.

Levi-Strauss, C. (1967). *The scope of anthropology.* London: Jonathon Cape.

Lewis, J. (1983). "The encoding/decoding model: criticisms and redevelopments for research on decoding." *Media, Culture and Society,* 5(2).

Lewis, L.A. (Ed.). (1992). *The adoring audience: Fan culture and popular media.* London: Routledge.

Lichtenstein, G. (1974). *A long way baby: Behind the scenes in women's pro tennis.* New York: Morrow.

Liebling, A.J. (1961). *The press.* New York: Ballantine.

Lipsky, R. (1981). *How we play the game: Why sports dominate American life.* Boston: Beacon Press.

Lipsyte, R. (1975). *Sportsworld*. New York: Quadrangle.

Lipsyte, R. (1995, May 28). "The key word should be 'golfer'." New York Times, p. 21.

Lobmeyer, H., & Weidinger, L. (1992). "Commercialism as a dominant factor in the American sports scene: Sources, developments, perspectives." *International Review for the Sociology of Sport*, 27(4), 309–324.

Lohr, S. (1996, June 17). "The great mystery of Internet profits." *New York Times*, pp. D1, D5.

Lopiano, D. (1996, March). "Women athletes deserve respect from the media." *USA Today*, 124(610), p. 74–76.

Lorenz, K. (1963). *Das sogenannte böse: Zur naturgeschichte der Aggression*. Wien: Boratha-Schaelar.

Louw, E. (1995). Introduction. *The Journal of International Communciation*, 2 (1), 1–2.

Lovell, A. (1975/76). "The Searchers and the pleasure principle." *ScreenEducation*, 7.

Lovell, T. (1980). *Pictures of reality*. London: BFI.

Lovell, T. (1981). "Ideology and Coronation Street." In *Coronation Street*. London: BFI.

Loy, J.W., & Hesketh, G.L. (1984). "The agon motif: A prolegomenon for the study of agonetic behavior." In K. Olin (Ed.), *Contribution of sociology to the study of sport*, pp. 31–50. Jyvaskyla, Finland: University of Jyvaskyla Press.

Lucas, J. (1980). *The modern Olympic Games*. South Brunswick, NY: A. S. Barnes.

Lucas, J. (1992). *Future of the Olympic Games*. Champaign, IL: Human Kinetics Books.

Lucas, R.J. (1984). "A descriptive history of the interdependence of television and sports in the summer Olympic games 1956–1984." Master's thesis, San Diego State University.

Lule, J. (1995). "The rape of Mike Tyson: Race, the press and symbolic stereotypes." *Critical Studies in Mass Communication*, 12(2), 176–195.

Lull, J. (Ed.) (1988) *World families watch television*. London: Sage.

Lull, J. (1990). *Inside family viewing: Ethnographic research on television's audience*. London: Routledge.

Lumpkin, A., & Williams, L.D. (1991). "An analysis of *Sports Illustrated* feature articles, 1954–1987." *Sociology of Sport Journal*, 8, 16–32.

Lyotard, J.-F. (1984). *The postmodern condition*. Minneapolis, MN: University of Minnesota Press. (Original French published in 1979.)

Lyotard, J.-F. (1993). "Defining the postmodern." In S. During (Ed.), *The cultural studies reader*, pp. 170–174. London: Routledge.

MacAloon, J. (1981). *This great symbol: Pierre de Coubertin and the origins of the modern Olympic Games*. Chicago: University of Chicago Press.

McBride, J. (1995). *War, battering, and other sports: The gulf between American men and women*. New Jersey: Humanities Press.

McCallum, J. (1993a, June 21). "Triple play." *Sports Illustrated*, 18–25.

McCallum, J. (1993b, June 28). "They're history." *Sports Illustrated*, 14–21.

McCallum, J., & Kennedy, K. (1996, September 9). "A team torn apart." *Sports Illustrated*, 85(11), pp. 9–10.

McChesney, R.W. (1989). "Media made sport: A history of sports coverage in the United States." In L. Wenner (Ed.), *Media, sports, and society*, pp. 49–69, Newbury Park, CA: Sage.

McClellan, S. (1994, June 13). "Advertisers hope to net global Cup audience." *Broadcasting & Cable*, pp. 27–28.

MacDonald, J.F. (1983). *Blacks and white TV*. Chicago, IL: Nelson-Hall.

McDaniel, S.R., & Armstrong, M. (1994, February). "The symbiotic relationship between sports programming and new communication technology: Implications for mass communication research." Paper presented at the annual meeting of the Western States Communication Association, San Jose, CA.

McDonald, M.G. (1995, August). "Clean 'air': Representing Michael Jordan in the Reagan-Bush era." Unpublished doctoral dissertation, University of Iowa, Iowa City, IA.

McDonald, M.G. (1996). "Michael Jordan's family values: Marketing, meaning, and post-Reagan America." *Sociology of Sport Journal*, 13, 344–365.

McGinniss, J. (1990). *Heroes*. New York: Simon & Schuster.

McGuire, B., & Wozniak, J. F. (1987, July). Racial and ethnic stereotypes in professional wrestling, *Social Science Journal*, 24(3), 261–273.

Macintosh, D., & Whitson, D. (1990). *The game planners: Transforming Canada's sport system*. Kingston: McGill-Queen's University Press.

McKay, J. (1991a). "Hawk(e)s, doves and Super Bowl XXV." *Social Alternatives*, 10(1), 58–60.

McKay, J. (1991b). *No pain, no gain? Sport and Australian culture*. New York: Prentice Hall.

McKay, J., & Huber, D. (1992). "Anchoring media images of technology and sport." *Women's Studies International Forum*, 15 (2), 205–218.

McKay, J., Lawrence,G., Miller, T., & Rowe, D. (1993). "Globalization and Australian sport." *Sport Science Review*, 2, 10–28.

McKay, J., & Miller, T. (1991). "From old boys to men and women of the corporation: The Americanization and commodification of Australian sport." *Sociology of Sport Journal*, 8, 86–94.

Mackie, J.L. (1987). *Ethics: Inventing right and wrong*. New York, N.Y.: Viking Penguin.

Mackinnon, C. (1987). "Women, self-possession, and sport," in *Feminism unmodified: Discourses on life and law*. Berkeley, CA: University of California Press.

McLean, L. (1994, July 26). "Lawrence laments calendar coverage." *The Australian*, p. 5.

McLuhan, M. (1964). *Understanding media: The extensions of man*. New York: McGraw-Hill.

McMurtry, R. (1993). "Sport and the Commonwealth heads of government." *The Round Table*, 328, 419–426.

MacNeill, M. (1988). "Active women, media representations, and ideology." In J. Harvey and H. Cantelon (Eds), *Not just a game: Essays in Canadian sport sociology*, pp. 195–211. Ottawa, Canada: University of Ottawa Press.

MacNeill, M. (1992). "Made in Canada: Producing Olympic ice hockey for a national television audience." In R. Horak & O. Penz (Eds), *Sport: Kult and kommerz*. Austria: Verlag fur Gesellschaftskritik.

MacNeill, M. (1995). "Olympic power plays: Televisual labour and the social use of technology by CTV during the 1988 Winter Olympic ice hockey games." *The Journal of International Communication*, 2(1), 42–65.

MacNeill, M. (1996a). "Olympic power plays: Televisual labour and the social use of technology by CTV during the 1988 Winter Olympic ice hockey games." *The Journal of International Communication*, 2(1), 42–65.

MacNeill, M. (1996b). "Networks: Producing Olympic ice hockey for a national television audience." *Sociology of Sport Journal*, 13, 103–124.

McNicoll, D.D. (1994, July 30–31). "Politically correct pin-ups take the risk out of risqué." *The Weekend Australian*, p. 11.

McPherson, B.D. (1975). "Sport consumption and the economics of consumerism." In D.W. Ball & J.W. Loy (Eds), *Sport and social order: Contributions to the sociology of sport*, pp. 239–275. Reading, MA: Addison-Wesley.

McPherson, B.D., Curtis, J.E., & Loy, J.W. (1989). *The social significance of sport: An introduction to the sociology of sport*. Champaign, IL: Human Kinetics.

McVicar, J. (1982). "Playing the crowd." *Edinburgh International Television Festival Magazine*.

Maguire, J. (1990). "More than a sporting touchdown: The making of American football in England 1982–1990." *Sociology of Sport Journal*, 7, 213–237.

Maguire, J. (1991). "The media-sport production complex: The case of American football in Western European societies." *European Journal of Communication*, 6, 315–335.

Maguire, J. (1993a). "Globalisation, sport and national identities: 'The empires strike back'?" *Society and Leisure*, 16, 293–322.

Maguire, J. (1993b). "Globalization, sport development, and the media/sport production complex." *Sport Science Review*, 2 (1), 29–47.

Maguire, J. (1994a). "American labour migrants, globalization and the making of English basketball." In J. Maguire & J. Bale (Eds), *The global sports arena: Athletic talent migration in an interdependent world*, pp. 226–255. London: Frank Cass.

Maguire, J. (1994b). "Sport, identity politics, and globalization: Diminishing contrasts and increasing varieties." *Sociology of Sport Journal*, 11, 398–427.

Malamuth, N.M. (1996). "Sexually explicit media, gender differences, and evolutionary theory." *Journal of Communication*, 43(3), 8–31.

Malec, M.A. (1995a). "Sports discussion groups on the Internet." *Journal of Sport & Social Issues*, 20(1), 106–109.

Malec, M.A. (1995b). "The wonderful World Wide Web of sports: An Internet resource." *Journal of Sport & Social Issues*, 19(3), 323–326.

Malec, M.A. (1996). "Usenet news groups: Another Internet resource." *Journal of Sport & Social Issues*, 19(1), 108–114.

Maloni, K., Greenman, B., & Miller, K. (Eds). (1995). *Netsports*. New York: Random House.

Malscecki, G.M. (1995). "'He shoots! He scores!': The metaphors of war in sport as the political linguistics of virility." Ph.D dissertation. York University.

Mandel, E. (1975). *Late capitalism*. London: New Left Books.

Mandese, J. (1994a, January 3). "How Fox deal aids NFL global aim." *Electronic Media*, pp. 4, 36.

Mandese, J. (1994b, February 28). "Baseball Network fails to wow advertisers." *Advertising Age*, pp. 1, 45.

Mandese, J. (1995). "The webs take to the net: CBS and NBC extend their interactive efforts to the World Wide Web." *Advertising Age*, 66, p. 13.

Marcuse, H. (1955). *Eros and civilisation*. Boston: Beacon Press.

Marcuse, H. (1964). *One-dimensional man*. Boston: Beacon Press.

Markiewicz, D. (1995, May 29). "Oldsmobile sponsorship rarin' to go." *Detroit News*, pp. 1B, 7B.

Marles, V. (1984). "The public and sport." In *BBC Broadcast Research Findings*. London: BBC.

Martin, C. (1987, January 17–18). "Kissing goodbye to cup racing tradition." *Weekend Australian*, p. 18.

Martin, R., & Adam, S. (1989, 1991 Revised Edition). *A sourcebook of Canadian media law*. Ottawa: Carleton University Press.

Martinez, A., & Martinez, J.C. (1996, January-February). "He said, she said: One man's idea of entertainment is one woman's nightmare." *Modern Maturity*, 39, p. 26.

Martzke, R. (1995, May 12). "CBS' Wright: 'Lesbians hurt golf'." *USA Today*, p. C1.

Mathisen, J.A., & Mathisen, G.S. (1991). "The rhetoric of racism in sport: Tom Brokaw revisited." *Sociology of Sport Journal*, 8(2), 168–177.

Matteo, S. (1986). "The effect of sex and gender-schematic processing on sport participation." *Sex Roles*, 15, 417–432.

Meggesey, D. (1993, November). "A decade of agency: The challenge of changing sport." Keynote address at the annual meeting of the North American Society for the Sociology of Sport, Denver, CO.

Melnick, M.J. (1989). "The sports fan: A teaching guide and bibliography." *Sociology of Sport Journal*, 6, 167–175.

Melnick, M., & Sabo, D. (1994). "Sport and social mobility among African-American and Hispanic athletes." In G. Eisen & D. Wiggins (Eds) *Ethnicity and sport in North American history and culture*, pp. 221–241. Westport, CT: Greenwood Press.

Merrill, J. (1974). *The imperative of freedom: A philosophy of journalistic autonomy*. New York: Hastings House.

Messner, M.A. (1988). "Sports and male domination: The female athletes as contested ideological terrain." *Sociology of Sport Journal*, 5, 197–211.

Messner, M. (1996). "Masculinities and athletic careers." In E. Chow, D. Wilkinson, & M. Zinn (Eds), *Race, class, & gender: Common bonds, different voices*, pp. 70–86. Thousand Oaks: Sage.

Messner, M., & Sabo, D. (Eds) (1990). *Sport, men and the gender order: Critical feminist perspectives*. Champaign, IL: Human Kinetics Publishers.

Messner, M.A., & Sabo, D.F. (1994). *Sex, violence and power in sports: Rethinking masculinity*. Freedom, CA: The Crossing Press.

Messner, M.A., & Solomon, W.S. (1993). "Outside the frame: Newspaper coverage of the Sugar Ray Leonard wife abuse story." *Sociology of Sport Journal*, 10(2), 119–134.

Messner, M.A., Duncan, M.C., & Jensen, K. (1993). "Separating the men from the girls: The gendered language of televised sports." *Gender and Society*, 7(1), 121–137.

Messner, M.A., Duncan, M.C., & Wachs, F.L. (1996). "The gender of audience-building: Televised coverage of women's and men's NCAA basketball." *Sociological Inquiry*, 66, pp. 422–439.

Michener, J.A. (1976). *Sports in America*. Greenwich, CT: Fawcett Crest.

Midwinter, E. (1986). *Fair game: Myth and reality in sport*. London: Allen & Unwin.

Millar, J., & Hinds, B. (1995, December 29). "Tank McNamara." *The Asheville Citizen-Times*, p. B8.

Miller Brewing Company. (1983). *The Miller Lite report on American attitudes toward sports*. Milwaukee: Author.

Miller, C., & Swift, K. (1976). *Words and women: New language in new times*. Garden City, NY: Doubleday.

Miller, J.D. (1991, July). "Guts and glory: A super champion and medical marvel." *Sport*, 54.

Miller, T. (1989). "World Series sound and vision." *Meanjin*, 3, 591–596.

Montville, L. (1990, December 24). "An American dream." *Sports Illustrated*, 91–107.

Moores, S. (1993). *Interpreting audiences: The ethnography of media consumption*. Thousand Oaks, CA: Sage.

Moragas Spa, M. de, Rivenbaugh, N.K., & Larson, J.F. (1995). *Television in the Olympics*. London: John Libbey & Company, Ltd.

Morley, D. (1980). *The Nationwide audience*. London: BFI.

Morley, D. (1981). "The Nationwide audience: A critical postscript." Screen Education, 39, pp. 3–14.

Morley, D. (1986). *Family television: Cultural power and domestic leisure*. London: Comedia.

Morley, D. (1991) "Where the global meets the local: notes from the sitting room." *Screen*, 32(1).

Morley, D. (1992). *Television, audiences, and cultural studies*. London: Routledge.

Morris, B., & Nydahl, J. (1985). "Sports spectacle as drama: Image, language, and technology." *Journal of Popular Culture*, 18(4), 101–110.

Morris, M., & Ogan, C. (1996). "The Internet as mass medium." *Journal of Communication*, 46(2), 39–50.

Morse, M (1983). "Sport on television: Replay and display." In E.A. Kaplan (Ed.), *Regan. television: Critical approaches – an anthology*, pp. 44–66. Frederick, MD: America. Film Institute and University Publications of America.

Morse, R. (1995, May 14). "Golf, where the boobs get in the way." *San Francisco Chronicle*, p. A3.

Muller, N. (1994). "Joe Montana: Made in the USA." Unpublished M.A. thesis. Sacramento, CA: California State University, Sacramento.

Muller, N.L. (1995). "As the [sports] world turns: An analysis of the Montana-49er social drama." *Journal of Sport & Social Issues*, 19(2), 157–179.

Mulvey, L. (1975). "Visual pleasure and narrative cinema." *Screen*, 1(3).

Murdock, G. (1992). "Citizens, consumers, and public culture." In M. Skovman & K. Schroder (Eds), *Reappraising transnational media*. London: Routledge.

Murphy, P., Dunning, E., & Williams, J. (1988). "Soccer crowd disorder and the press: Processes of amplification and de-amplification in historical perspective." *Theory, culture & society*, 5, 645–673.

Murphy, P., Williams, J., & Dunning, E. (1990). *Football on trial: Spectator violence and development in the football world*. London: Routledge.

Murrell, A.J., & Curtis, E.M. (1994). "Causal attributions of performance for black and white quarterbacks in the NFL: A look at the sports pages." *Journal of Sport & Social Issues*, 18(3), 224–233.

Nafziger, J.A. (1992). "International sports law: A replay of characteristics and trends." *American Journal of International Law*, 86, 489–518.

Nairn, T. (1993). "Internationalism and the second coming." *Daedalus*, 122(3), 155–170.

Nash, O. (1980). "Confessions of a born spectator." In R. Dodge (Eds), *A literature of sports*, pp. 407–408. Lexington, MA: D. C. Heath. (Originally published 1937).

National Football League Official Website. URL: http://www.nfl/com/sideline/worldmedia. html.

National Sporting Goods Association (1994). *Sports Participation in 1994, Series 1*. Mt. Prospect, IL: Author.

Nattrass, S. (1988). "Sport and television in Canada: 1952–1982." Unpublished Ph.D. thesis, University of Alberta, Department of Physical Education and Sport Studies.

NCAA Football Rules Committee. (1995). *College football: A celebration of teamwork*. Kansas City, MO: NCAA. [Videotape]

Nelson, M.B. (1991). *Are we winning yet?* NY: Random House.

Nelson, M.B. (1994). *The stronger women get, the more men love football: Sexism and the American culture of sports*. NY: Harcourt Brace & Co.

Newcomb, P. (1996). "Entertainment and information." *Forbes*, 157, pp. 128–130.

"1996 Summer Olympics coverage hits its target: Women viewers." (1996, Summer). *Media Report to Women*, 24(3), p. 16.

Nixon, H.L., II. (1984). *Sport and the American dream*. New York: Leisure Press.

Nixon, H.L. (1993). "Accepting the risks of pain and injury in sport: Mediated cultural influences on playing hurt." *Sociology of Sport Journal*, 10, 183–196.

Notess, G. (1996). "News resources on the World Wide Web." *Database*, 19, 12–20.

Novak, M. (1976). *The joy of sports*. New York: Basic Books.

O'Connor, B., & Boyle, R. (1993). "Dallas with balls: televized sport, soap opera and male and female pleasures." *Leisure Studies*, 12, 107–119.

O'Donnell, H. (1994). "Mapping the mythical: A geopolitics of national sporting stereotypes." *Discourse and Society*, 5, 345–380.

O'Neill, E. (1972). *The Emperor Jones*. New York: Vintage Books.

Olympic Communication [Special issue]. (1995). *The Journal of International Communication*, 2(1).

REFERENCES

Olympic marketing and the New Sources of Financing Commission. (1996, May 9). Lausanne, Switzerland: International Olympic Committee. URL: http://www.olympic.org/femkt.html.

Ong, W. (1981). *The presence of the word.* Minneapolis: University of Minnesota Press.

Ordman, V.L., & Zillmann, D. (1994). Women sports reporters: Have they caught up? *Journal of Sport & Social Issues,* 18 (1), 66–75.

Oriard, M.V. (1982). *Dreaming of heroes: American sports fiction, 1868–1980.* Chicago: Nelson-Hall.

Oriard, M. (1993). *Reading football: How the popular press created an American spectacle.* Chapel Hill, NC: University of North Carolina Press.

Ormsby, M. (1995, May 18). "Golf talent should be LPGA's 'right stuff'." *Toronto Star,* p. B8.

Osterland, A. (1995, February 14). "Field of nightmares." *Financial World,* reprint.

Ostler, S. (1995, May 15). "It's all a plot to make them look like boobs." *San Francisco Chronicle,* pp. D1, D9.

Ozanian, M.K. (1995, February 14). "Following the money." *Financial World,* reprint.

Palmgreen, P., Wenner L.A., & Rosengren, K. E. (1985). "Uses and gratifications research: The past ten years." In K.E. Rosengren, L.A. Wenner, & P. Palmgreen (Eds), *Media gratifications research,* pp. 11–40. Beverly Hills, CA: Sage.

"Pass the money." (1998, January 19). *Electronic Media,* p. 120.

Patton, P. (1984). *Razzle-dazzle.* Garden City, NY: Dial.

Pearman, W.A. (1978). "Race on the sports page." *Review of Sport & Leisure,* 3(2), 54–68.

Pearson, R. (1986). "Bats, balls and cameras: Textually extrapolated reader in televised baseball." Paper presented at the annual meeting of the Popular Culture Association.

Peel, A. (1993, November 15). Athletes rights lecture presented to the School of Physical and Health Education, University of Toronto.

Pesky, G. (1995). "Pro leagues join the Internet: Serve up electronic retailing." *Sporting Goods Business,* 28, pp. 22.

Peters, R. (1976). *Television coverage of sport.* Birmingham: Centre for Contemporary Cultural Studies Stencilled Paper.

Petrovic, K., & Zvan, M. (1986). "Trust in crisis." *International Review for the Sociology of Sport,* 21(2/3), 103–111.

Petrozello, D. (1995). "ABC radio enters WWW." *Broadcasting & Cable,* 125, 38.

Phipers, T. (1995, May 16). "CBS placed in no-win situation." *Denver Post,* p. D2.

Pluto, T. (1996, March 1). "Belle's bad act deserves big fine." *Akron Beacon Journal,* p. A1, A4.

Poe, A. (1976). "Active women in ads." *Journal of Communication,* 26, 185–192.

Ponomarev, N.I. (1974). "Some research problems of physical education in the early history of mankind." *History of Physical Education and Sport: Research and Studies,* 2, 27–46.

Poole, D. (1996, June 19). "NBC will warp time to tell Olympic story." *The Charlotte Observer,* p. 2B.

Porter, D. (1994, July 26). "Athletes calendar sparks uproar," *The Age,* p. 2.

Pound, R. (1992, July 10). Telephone interview with I.O.C member to Canada.

Pound, R. (1994). "The commercialism of sport: Dilemma or deliverance?" *Olympic Congress: Centenary 1894–1994 (Bulletin),* pp. 9–11. Lausanne: I.O.C.

Poynton, B., & Hartley, J. (1990). "Male-gazing: Australian Rules football, gender and television." In M.E. Brown (Ed.), *Television and women's culture: The politics of the popular,* pp. 144–157. Newbury Park, CA: Sage.

Pronger, B. (1990). "Gay jocks: A phenomenology of gay men in athletics." In M.A. Messner and D. Sabo (Eds), *Sport, men and the gender order,* pp. 141–152. Champaign, IL: Human Kinetics.

"Questions at LPGA not about game (1995, May 13)." *New York Times*, p. 29.

Rader, B. (1984). *In its own image: How television has transformed sports.* New York: Free Press.

Radway, J. (1984). *Women read the romance.* Chapel Hill: University of North Carolina Press.

Radway, J.A. (1991). *Reading the romance: Women, patriarchy, and popular literature.* Chapel Hill: University of North Carolina Press.

Raglan, F. (1975). *The hero: A study in tradition, myth and drama.* Westport, CT: Greenwood Press.

Rainville, R.E., & McCormick, E. (1977). "Extent of covert racial prejudice in pro football announcers' speech." *Journalism Quarterly*, 54, 20–26.

Rainville, R., Roberts, A., & Sweet, A. (1978). "Recognition of covert racial prejudice." *Journalism Quarterly*, 55(2), 256–259.

Rather, D. (1994, March 19). "Games plans." *Economist*, p. 108.

Ratliff, D. (1996). "Online service targets sports fans." *Discount Merchandiser*, 36, 21.

Real, M.R. (1975). "The superbowl: Mythic spectacle." *Journal of Communication*, 25(1), 31–43.

Real, M.R. (1977). *Mass-mediated culture.* Englewood Cliffs, NJ: Prentice-Hall.

Real, M.R. (1989). *Super media: A cultural studies approach.* Newbury Park, CA: Sage.

Real, M.R. (1996). "The postmodern Olympics: Technology and the commodification of the Olympic movement." *Quest*, 48, 9–24.

Real, M.R. (1996). *Exploring media culture: A guide.* Thousand Oaks: Sage.

Real, M.R., & Mechikoff, R.A. (1992). "Deep fan: Mythic identification, technology, and advertising in spectator sports." *Sociology of Sport Journal*, 9, 323–339.

Real, M., Mechikoff, R., & Goldstein, D. (1989). "Mirror images, the Olympic Games in cold war rhetoric: U.S. and Soviet press coverage of the 1980 and 1984 summer Olympics." In R. Jackson (Ed.), *The Olympic movement and the mass media: Past, present and future issues*, pp. 4/39–4/46. Calgary, Alberta, Canada: Hurford Enterprises.

"Reality check for the potential sports marketer." (1996, May 9). Godfrey Advertising's Helpful Hints- Sports Marketing. URL:http://www.godfrey.com/godfrey/newsletters/gnl6.html.

Reed, S. (1994, June). "Someone's on the fairway with Dinah." *Out*, p. 95.

"Regional sports: Who's watching." (1994, May). *Cable Avails*, p.33.

Reid, L.N., & Solely, L.C. (1979). *Sports Illustrated's* coverage of women in sports. *Journalism Quarterly*, 56, Winter, 861–863.

Reilly, R. (1996, January 29). "Swinging for the fences: Soweto's talented young athletes are striving to excel, but they are hindered by the legacy of apartheid." *Sports Illustrated*, 84(4), p. 122+.

Reinmuth, G. (1995, May 13). "Wright denies saying lesbians hurt LPGA." *Chicago Tribune*, Section 3, p. 1.

Reinmuth, G. (1995, May 17). "For women's sport, it's a constant struggle." *Chicago Tribune*, Section 4, p. 10.

Reisling, R.W. (1971). "Where have all our heroes gone? Some insights into sports figures in modern American literature." *Quest*, 16, 1–12.

Reiss, S. (1989). "City games: The evolution of an urban society and the rise of sports." Urbana: University of Illinois Press.

Reith, R. (1991, December 2). "3 strategies for viewer control." *Electronic Media*, p. 34.

Remnick, D. (1996, August 5). "Letter from Atlanta: Inside-out Olympics." *The New Yorker*, pp. 26–28.

Rice, L. (1996, Aug. 12). "NBC Olympics breaks records." *Broadcasting & Cable*, 126(34), pp. 45–46.

Rice, R.E. (1987). "Computer-mediated communication and organizational innovation." *Journal of Communication*, 37, 64–94.

Rice, R.E., Grant, A.E., Schmitz, J., & Torobin, J. (1990). "Individual and network influences on the adoption and perceived outcomes of electronic messaging." *Social Networks*, 12. New York, NY: North-Holland.

Rich, A. (1993). "Compulsory heterosexuality and lesbian existence." In H. Abelove, M.A. Barale, & D.M. Halperin (Eds), *The lesbian and gay studies reader*, pp. 227–254. London: Routledge.

Riggs, K.E., Eastman, S.T., & Golobic, T.S. (1993). "Manufactured conflict in the 1992 Olympics: The discourse of television and politics." *Critical Studies in Mass Communication*, 10, 253–272.

Riggs, M.T. (1991). *Color adjustment [videotape]*. San Francisco: California Newsreel.

Rintala, J., & Birrell, S. (1984). "Fair treatment for the active female: A content analysis of Young Athlete magazine." *Sociology of Sport Journal*, 1, 231–250.

Rintala, J., & Kane, M.J. (1991, November). "Culturally constructed factors that mediate the media's portrayal of female athleticism: The case of age, race and disability." Paper presented at the meeting of the North American Society for the Sociology of Sport, Milwaukee, WI.

Rivenburgh, N.K. (1995). "Images of others: The presentation of nations in the 1992 Barcelona Olympics." *The Journal of International Communication*, 2(1), 6–25.

Roberts, J.L. (1993, September 2). "News Corp's Murdoch outlines plans for TV programming on global basis." *Wall Street Journal*, reprint.

Robertson, N. (1996, April). "Stalking the elusive usage data." *Internet World*.

Roberston, S. (1996, April 19). Telephone interview with Canadian Olympic Association Assistant Press Officer to the 1996 Atlanta Games team.

Robertson, S.M. (1983). *Media law handbook*. Vancouver: Self-Counsel Series.

Rodman, D. (with Keown, T.) (1996). *Bad I wanna be*. New York: Delacorte Press.

Roloff, M.E., & Solomon, D.H. (1989). "Sex typing, sports interests, and relational harmony." In L.A. Wenner (Ed.), *Media, sports, and society*, pp. 290–311. Newbury Park, CA: Sage.

Romanyshyn, R. (1989). *Technology as symptom and dream*. London: Routledge.

Rosenbaum, R. (1995, June). "The revolt of the basketball liberals." *Esquire*, 123(6), 102–106.

Rosner, D. (1989). "The world plays catch-up." *Sports Inc: The Sports Business Weekly*, 1(1), 6–13.

Rothenbuhler, E.W. (1988). "The living room celebration of the Olympic Games." *Journal of Communication*, 38, 61–81.

Rothenbuhler, E.W. (1989a). "The Olympics in the American living room: Celebration of a media event." In R. Jackson (Ed.), *The Olympic movement and the mass media: Past, present and future issues*, pp. 6/41–6/50. Calgary, Alberta, Canada: Hurford Enterprises.

Rothenbuhler, E.W. (1989b). "Values and symbols in orientations to the Olympics." *Critical Studies in Mass Communication*, 6, 138–157.

Rothenbuhler, E.W. (1995). "The social distribution of participation in the broadcast Olympic Games." *The Journal of International Communication*, 2 (1), 66–79.

Rowe, D. (1994). "Accommodating bodies: Celebrity, sexuality, and 'tragic Magic'." *Journal of Sport and Social Issues*, 18(1), 6–26.

Rowe, D. (1995). *Popular cultures: Rock music, sport and the politics of pleasure*. London: Sage.

Rowe, D. (1996.). "Taming the 'media monsters': Cultural policy and sports TV." *Metro*, 105, 57–61.

Rowe, D., & Lawrence, G. (1986). "Saluting the state: Nationalism and the Olympics." In G. Lawrence & D. Rowe (Eds), *Power play: Essays in the sociology of Australian sport*, pp. 196–203. Sydney, Australia: Hale & Iremonger.

Rowe, D., & Lawrence, G. (1990). *Sport and leisure: Trends in Australian popular culture.* Sydney: Harcourt Brace Jovanovich.

Rowe, D., Lawrence, G., Miller, T., & McKay, J. (1994). "Global sport? Core concern and peripheral vision." *Media, Culture & Society*, 16, 661–675.

Rubenstein, L. (1995, May 13). "Lesbian remarks about LPGA land analyst in hot water." *Globe and Mail*, p. A17.

Rubin, R. (1981). "Ideal traits and terms of address for male and female college professors." *Journal of Personality and Social Psychology*, 41, 966–974.

Rudin, J. (1969). *Fanaticism: A psychological analysis.* Notre Dame, IN: University of Notre Dame Press.

Russell, G.W. (1992). "Response of the macho male to viewing a combatant sport." *Journal of Social Behavior and Personality*, 7, 631–638.

Russell, G.W., Di Lullo, S.L., & Di Lullo, D. (1988–89). "Effects of observing competitive and violent versions of a sport." *Current Psychology: Research & Reviews*, 7, 312–321.

Russell, N. (1994). *Morals and the media: Ethics in Canadian journalism.* Vancouver: University of British Columbia Press.

Rutherford, P. (1978). *The making of the Canadian media*, Toronto: McGraw Hill- Ryerson.

Rutherford, P. (1993). "Made in America: The problem of mass culture in Canada." In D. Flaherty & F. Manning (Eds), *The Beaver bites back? American popular culture in Canada*, Montreal: McGill-Queen's University Press.

Ryan, J. (1994). *Little girls in pretty boxes: The making and breaking of élite gymnasts and figure skaters.* New York: Doubleday.

Ryan, J. (1995, May 17). "'Lesbians' furor? It's all wrong." *San Francisco Chronicle*, p. D3.

Sabatini, R. (1934). *Heroic lives.* Boston: Houghton Mifflin.

Sabo, D. (1994, June 6). "The body politics of sports injury: Culture, power, and the pain principle." A paper presented at the annual meeting of the National Athletic Trainers Association, Dallas, Texas.

Sabo, D., & Gordon, D. (1995). *Men's health & illness: Gender, power & the body.* Newbury Park, CA: Sage.

Sabo, D., Gray, P., & Moore, L. (1997). "Domestic violence and televised athletic events: 'It's a man thing'." Unpublished manuscript.

Sabo, D., & Jansen, S.C. (1992). "Images of men in sport media: The social reproduction of the gender order." In S. Craig (Ed.), *Men, masculinity, and the media*, pp.169–184. Newbury Park: Sage.

Sabo, D., & Jansen, S.C. (1994). "Seen but not heard: Black men in sports media." In M.A. Messner & D.F. Sabo. *Sex, violence & power in sports: Rethinking masculinity*, pp. 150–160. Freedom, CA: The Crossing Press.

Sabo, D., Jansen, S.C., Tate, D., Duncan, M.C., & Leggett, S. (1996). "Televising international sport: Race, ethnicity, and nationalistic bias." *Journal of Sport & Social Issues*, 20(1), 7–21.

Sabo, D., & Messner, M. (1993). "Whose body is this? Women's sport and sexual politics." In G. Cohen (Ed.), *Women in sport: Issues and controversies*, pp. 15–24. Newbury Park, CA: Sage Publications.

Sage, G.H. (1990). *Power and ideology in American sport: A critical perspective.* Champaign, IL: Human Kinetics.

Sage, G.H. (1996). "Patriotic images and capitalist profit: Contradictions of professional team sports licensed merchandise." *Sociology of Sport Journal*, 13, 1–11.

Samuelson, R.J. (1989, September 4). "The American sports mania." *Newsweek*, p. 49.

Sandomir, R. (1995, May 13). "Golf reporter and CBS deny remarks on lesbianism." *New York Times*, p. 25.

Sandomir, R. (1995, May 16). "'He said, she said,' with a twist." *New York Times*, p. B15.

Sands, J., and Gammons, P. (1993). *Coming apart at the seams*. New York: Macmillan.

Sanger, E. (1995, November 1). "Cablevision's clout in the global game." *Newsday*, p. A37.

Sansone, D. (1988). *Greek athletics and the genesis of sport*. Berkeley: University of California Press.

Santina, W. (1988). "Move to better administration." *Australian Soccer Weekly*, 9 (no. 342), p. 17.

Sapolsky, B.S., & Zillmann, D. (1978). "Enjoyment of a televised sporting contest under different conditions of viewing." *Perceptual and Motor Skills*, 46, 29–30.

de Saussure, F. (1959). *Course in general linguistics*. New York: McGraw-Hill.

Schaaf, P. (1995). *Sports marketing: It's not just a game anymore*. Amherst, NY: Prometheus.

Schiller, H. (1989). *Culture, inc.: The corporate takeover of public expression*. New York: Oxford University Press.

Schlesinger, P. (1987). "On national identity: Some conceptions and misconceptions criticized." *Social Science Information*, 26(2), 219–264.

Schlesinger, P. (1991). *Media, state and nation: Political violence and collective identities*. London: Sage.

Schweitzer, K., Zillmann, D., Weaver, J.B., & Luttrell, E.S. (1992). "Perception of threatening events in the emotional aftermath of a televised college football game." *Journal of Broadcasting and Electronic Media*, 36(1), 75–82.

Scott, W. (1995, December 10). "Walter Scott's Personality Parade." *Parade Magazine*, p. 2.

Segrave, J., & Chu, D. (1981). *Olympism*. Champaign, IL: Human Kinetics.

Seigel, A. (1983). *Politics and the media in Canada*. Toronto: McGraw-Hill Ryerson.

Seiter, E. (1995). "Different children, different dreams: Racial representation in advertising." In G. Dines & J.M. Humez (Eds), *Gender, race and class in media: A text-reader*, pp. 99–108. Thousand Oaks, CA: Sage.

Shanklin, J. (1992, January 1). "Buying that sporting image." *Marketing Management*, p. 58.

Sheeley, G. (1995, May 19). "Ritts calls lesbianism non-issue." *Atlanta Constitution*, p. D8.

Shelton, C.M. (1993). "Hard work paying off." In G.L. Cohen (Ed.) *Women in sport: Issues and controversies*, pp. 275–285. Newbury Park, CA: Sage.

Shifflett, B., & Revelle, R. (1994). "Gender equity in sports media coverage: A review of the NCAA News." *Journal of Sport & Social Issues*, 18(2), 144–150.

Shoemaker, P.J. (1996). "Hardwired for news: Using biological and cultural evolution to explain the surveillance function." *Journal of Communication*, 46(3), 32–47.

Shoemaker, P.J., Danielian, L.H., & Brendlinger, N. (1992). "Deviant acts, risky business, and U.S. involvement: The newsworthiness of world events." *Journalism Quarterly*, 68, 781–795.

Shulman, M. (1973). *The ravenous eye*. London: Cassell.

Simons, Y., & Taylor, J. (1992). "A psychosocial model of fan violence in sports." *International Journal of Sport Psychology*, 23, 207–226.

Sloan, L.R. (1989). "The motives of sports fans." In J.H. Goldstein (Ed.), *Sports, games, and play: Social and psychological viewpoints* (2nd edn), pp. 175–240. Hillsdale, NJ: Erlbaum.

Smale, D.D. (1990). *Continuing the ascent*. Overland Park, KS: National Collegiate Athletic Association.

Smith, A.D. (1990). "The supersession of nationalism?" *International Journal of Comparative Sociology*, 31(1–2), 1–31.

Smith, E. (1990). "The genetically superior athlete: Myth or reality." In T. Anderson (Ed.), *Black studies: Theory, method, and cultural perspectives*. pp. 120–131. Pullman, WA: Washington State University Press.

Smith, G. (1973). "The sports hero: An endangered species." *Quest*, 19, 59–70.

Smith, G. (1996a, June 24). "Crime and . . ." *Sports Illustrated*, 66–88.

Smith, G. (1996b, December 23). "The chosen one." *Sports Illustrated*, 28–52.

Smith, G., & Blackburn, C. (1978). *Sport and the mass media*. Ottawa: CAHPER Sociology of Sport Monograph Series.

Smith, G.J., Patterson, B., Williams, T., & Hogg, J. (1981). "A profile of the deeply committed male sports fan." *Arena Review, 5*(2), 26–44.

Smith, G.J., & Valeriote, T.A. (1983). "Ethics in sports journalism." *Arena Review, 7*(2), 7–14.

Smith, M. (1983). *Violence and Sport*. Toronto: Butterworths.

Smith, W. (1994, July 28). Good s(p)orts. *Courier-Mail*, p. 9.

Smith, W., & Hudson, T. (1994, January 30) "Just not cricket." *Sunday Mail*, p. 97.

Snider, M. (1996, July 19). "Michael Jordan's bigger than basketball; he's a pop icon." *USA Today*, p. 3D.

Sparks, R. (1992). "'Delivering the male': Sports, Canadian television, and the making of TSN." *Canadian Journal of Communication*, 17, 319–342.

Spiegler, M. (1996). "Betting on Web sports." *American Demographics*, pp. 24–30.

Sportel (1994). "TV gets sports. Sports gets viewers. Channels get ads." *Video Age International*, 14(7), 16–17.

Sports Broadcasting Act (1961). P.L. 87–331, 75 Stat. 732.

Sports Programming Interim Report (1993). 8 FCCRcd. 4973.

Staples, R., & Jones, T. (1985). "Culture, ideology and black television images." *The Black Scholar*, 16(3), 10–20.

Starr, M., with Heath, T. (1995, February 6). "Out with the new." *Newsweek Interactive*. Prodigy Interactive Personal Service.

Starr, M. (1996, September 30). "Cash and Kerri." *Newsweek*, 128(14), p. 67

Stockman, M. (1996, May 13). "Two leagues of their own." *Business Week*, p.52.

Stoddart, B. (1994). "Sport, television, interpretation, and practice reconsidered: Televised golf and analytical orthodoxies." *Journal of Sport & Social Issues*, 18(1), 76–88.

Strate, L. (1985). "Heroes, fame, and the media," *Et cetera*, 42, 47–53.

Strate, L. (1992). "Beer commercials: A manual on masculinity." In S. Craig (Ed.), *Men, masculinity, and the media*, pp. 78–92. Newbury Park, CA: Sage.

Strate, L. (1994). "Heroes: A communication perspective." In S.J. Drucker, & R.S. Cathcart (Eds), *American heroes in a media age*, pp. 15–23. Cresol, NJ: Hampton Press.

Strutt, S., & Hissey, L. (1992). "Feminisms and balance." *Canadian Journal of Communication*, 17, 61–74.

Sullivan, C. (1995). "Preferences for electronic mail in organizational communication tasks." *The Journal of Business Communication*, 32, 49–64.

Sullivan, D.B. (1987). "The effects of sports commentary on viewer perception of overt player hostility." Unpublished master's thesis, San Francisco State University.

Sullivan, O.B. (1991). "Commentary and viewer perception of player hostility: Adding punch to televised sport." *Journal of Broadcasting and Electronic Media*, 35(4), 487–504.

Swenson, J.D. (1995). "Narrative, gender, and TV news: Comparing network and tabloid stories." In C. Baughman (Ed.), *Women on ice: Feminist essays on the Tonya Harding/Nancy Kerrigan spectacle*, pp. 204–218. New York: Routledge.

Tannen, D. (1993). "What's in a frame? Surface evidence for underlying expectations." In D. Tannen (Ed.) *Framing in discourse*, pp. 14–56. New York: Oxford University Press.

Taub, S. (1995, February 14). "Hypocrisy on ice." *Financial World,* reprint.

Taylor, P. (1996, June 17). "Slammed!" *Sports Illustrated*, 38–46.

Telander, R. (1984). "The written word: Player-press relationships in American sports." *Sociology of Sport Journal*, 1, 3–14.

Telander, R. (1996). "Old bulls essay." *SI OnLine*. http://www. sportsillustrated.com.

Theberge, N. (1981). "A critique of critiques: Radical and feminist writings on sport." *Social Forces*, 60, pp. 341–353.

Theberge, N. (1986). "Toward a feminist alternative to sport as a male preserve." *Sociology of Sport Journal*, 3, 193–202.

Theberge, N. (1989). "A feminist analysis of responses to sports violence: Media coverage of the 1987 World Junior Hockey Championship." *Sociology of Sport Journal*, 6, 247–256.

Theberge, N., & Cronk, A. (1986). "Work routines in newspaper sports departments and the coverage of women's sports." *Sociology of Sport Journal*, 3, 195–203.

"This time Katarina bears witness." (1992, February 10). *Australian*, p. 18.

Thomas, R. (1996). "Black faces still rare in the press box." In R. E. Lapchick (Ed.), *Sport in society: Equal opportunity or business as usual?*, pp. 212–233. Thousand Oaks, CA: Sage.

Thorngren, C.M. (1990). "A time to reach out-keeping the female coach in coaching." *Journal of Physical Education, Recreation and Dance*, 61(3), 57–60.

Tomlinson, A. (1989). "Representation, ideology and the Olympic Games: A reading of the opening and closing ceremonies of the 1984 Los Angeles Olympic Games." In R. Jackson (Ed.), *The Olympic movement and the mass media: Past present and future issues*, pp. 7/3–7/11. Calgary, Alberta, Canada: Hurford Enterprises.

Tomlinson, A., & Whannel, G. (Eds) (1984). *Five ring circus: Money, power and politics at the Olympic Games*. London: Pluto Press.

Torry, J. (1995, November 7). "Browns bolt for Baltimore, could end 50-year tradition." *Pittsburgh Post-Gazette*, pp. A-1, A-9.

Toulmin, S. (1986). *The place of reason in ethics*. Chicago: University of Chicago Press.

Trujillo, N. (1991). "Hegemonic masculinity on the mound: Media representations of Nolan Ryan and American sports culture." *Critical Studies in Mass Communication*, 8, 290–308.

Trujillo, N. (1994). *The meaning of Nolan Ryan*. College Station, TX: Texas A & M University Press.

Trujillo, N. (1995). "Machines, missiles, and men: Images of the male body on ABC's Monday Night Football." *Sociology of Sport Journal*, 12, 403–423.

Trujillo, N., & Ekdom, L.R. (1985). "Sportswriting and American cultural values: The 1984 Chicago Cubs." *Critical Studies in Mass Communication*, 2, 262–281.

Trujillo, N., & Vande Berg, L.R. (1994). "From wild western prodigy to the ageless wonder: The mediated evolution of Nolan Ryan." In S.J. Drucker, & R.S. Cathcart (Eds), *American heroes in a media age*, pp. 221–240. Creskill, NJ: Hampton Press.

Tuchman, G. (1978). *Making news*. New York: Free Press.

Tudor, A. (1992). "Them and us: Story and stereotype in TV World Cup coverage." *European Journal of Communication*, 7, 391–413.

Turkle, S. (1994). "Constructions and reconstructions of self in virtual reality: Playing in the MUDs." *Mind, Culture, and Activity*, 1, 158–167.

Turner, G. (1994). *Making it national: Nationalism and Australian popular culture*. Sydney: Allen and Unwin.

Turner, G. (1997, January 20). "The ad game." *Newsweek*, pp. 62–63.

Turow, J. (1992). *Media systems in society: Understanding industries, strategies, and power*. White Plains, NY: Longman.

"TV pays the way." (1994, October 21). *USA Today*, p. 2C.

"TV Sports: The $35 billion ticket." (1996). *Broadcasting & Cable*, 126(21), pp. 34–39.

Tyrer, T. (1994, January 3). "O&Os, ratings will get NFL boost, says Fox." *Electronic Media*, p. 47.

Tyrer, T. (1995, January 23). "12 to watch in 1995: Chase Carey." *Electronic Media,* pp. 110, 144, 148.

"Unsportsmanlike conduct!" (1995, November 26). *60 Minutes* (CBS News). Burrelle's Transcripts 28, #11, pp. 15–24.

Urschel, J., & Hiestand, M. (1996, July 16). "Huge salaries 'unfathomable' to many people." *USA Today,* p. 1A.

Vancil, M. (Ed.) (1995). *More rare air: I'm back.* (Text by Michael Jordan; photographs by Walter Iooss, Jr.). San Francisco: HarperCollins.

Vande Berg, L.R., & Trujillo, N, (1989). "The rhetoric of winning and losing: The American dream and America's team." In L.A. Wenner (Ed.), *Media, sports, & society,* pp. 204–224. Newbury Park, CA: Sage.

Verducci, T. (1996, May 27). "A new high." *Sports Illustrated,* 32–39.

Voight, D.Q. (1978). "Myths after baseball: Notes on myths in sports." *Quest,* 30, 46–57.

Volkerling, M. (1994). "Death or transfiguration: The future for cultural policy in New Zealand." *Culture and Policy,* 6(1), 7–28.

Walker, B. (1996, January 2). "Osborne, Spurrier seek perfection on the field (AP)." *The Tuscaloosa News,* p. B1.

Walker, J.R. (1990). "Time out: Viewing gratifications and reactions to the 1987 NFL players' strike." *Journal of Broadcasting and Electronic Media,* 34(3), 335–350.

Walker, J.R., Rylands, C., Hiltner, J.R., Bellamy, R.V. Jr. (1993, November). "Talking about the game: A content analysis of a fantasy baseball bulletin board." Paper presented at the annual convention of the Speech Communication Association, Miami, FL.

Wallach, V. (1996, May/June). "Measuring Web Traffic." *Electronic Retailing,* pp. 17–21, 40.

Walley, W. (1995, November 20). "SET sees record PPV revenue in '96." *Electronic Media,* p. 14.

Waltner, C. (1995). "Trail Blazers score in interactive." *Advertising Age,* 66, 26.

Wann, D.L. (1993). "Aggression among highly identified spectators as a function of their need to maintain positive social identity." *Journal of Sport & Social Issues,* 17, 134–143.

Wann, D.L., & Branscombe, N.R. (1992). "Emotional responses to the sports page." *Journal of Sport & Social Issues,* 16, 49–64.

Warren, J. (1988). "That was the week that was for the Socceroos." *Australian Soccer Weekly,* 9 (no. 346), 11.

Waters, M. (1995). *Globalization.* London: Routledge.

Webster's Sports Dictionary (1976). Springfield, MA: Merriam.

Wecter, D. (1941). *The hero in America: A chronicle of hero-worship.* New York: Charles Scribner's Sons.

Weiss, O. (1996). "Media sports as social substitution: Pseudosocial relations with sports figures." *International Review for Sociology of Sport,* 31(1), 109–116.

Wells, J. (1994, January 17). "Chinese may be telling pork pies about dog stew." *Australian,* p.25.

Wells, J. (1994, July 30–31). "Three cheers for girls with nothing to hide." *The Weekend Australian,* p. 35.

Wells, J. (1994, October 22). "The ethnic riddle still stunting soccer's growth." *Sydney Morning Herald,* p. 70.

Wendel, T. (1996, May 29-June 4). "Will Fox be the fix?" *Baseball Weekly,* p. 4.

Wenner, L.A. (Ed.) (1989a). *Media, sports, & society.* Newbury Park, CA: Sage.

Wenner, L.A. (1989b). "Media, sports and society: The research agenda." In L.A. Wenner (Ed.), *Media, sports and society,* pp. 13–48. Newbury Park, CA: Sage.

Wenner, L.A. (1989c). "The Super Bowl pre-game show: Cultural fantasies and political sub-text." In L.A. Wenner (Ed.), *Media, sports and society,* pp. 157–179. London: Sage.

Wenner, L.A. (1991). "One part alcohol, one part sport, one part dirt, stir gently: Beer → commercials and television sports." In L.R. Vande Berg & L.A. Wenner (Eds), *Television criticism: Approaches and applications*, pp. 388–407. New York: Longman.

Wenner, L.A. (1994a). "Drugs, sport, and media influence: Can media inspire constructive attitudinal change?" *Journal of Sport & Social Issues*, 18 (3), pp. 282–292.

Wenner, L.A. (1994b). "The dream team, communicative dirt, and the marketing of synergy: USA basketball and cross-merchandising in television commercials." *Journal of Sport & Social Issues*, 18(1), 27–47.

Wenner, L.A. (1994c). "Loving the game to death: heroes, goals and spectator emotion." *Journal of Sport and Social Issues*, 18, 299–302.

Wenner, L.A. (1994d). "What's sport got to do with it? Race and the problem of paradigm." *Journal of Sport and Social Issues*, 18(3), 203–206.

Wenner, L.A., & Gantz, W. (1989). "The audience experience with sports on television." In L.A. Wenner (Ed.), *Media, sports, & society*, pp. 241–269. Newbury Park, CA: Sage.

Wernick, A. (1991). *Promotional culture*. Newbury Park, CA: Sage.

Whannel, G. (1979). "Football, crowd behaviour and the press." *Media, Culture and Society*, 1, 327–342.

Whannel, G. (1982). "Narrative and television sport: The Coe and Ovett story." In *Sporting fictions: Proceedings of a conference organized by the Centre for Contemporary Cultural Studies and the Department of Physical Education in the University of Birmingham, Birmingham*, England, 209–230.

Whannel, G. (1983). *Blowing the whistle*. London: Pluto Press.

Whannel, G. (1990). "Winner takes all: Competition." In A. Goodwin & G. Whannel (Eds), *Understanding television*, pp. 103–114. London: Routledge.

Whannel, G. (1992). *Fields in vision: Television sport and cultural transformation*. London: Routledge.

Whannel, G. (1994). "Sport and popular culture: the temporary triumph of process over product." *Innovations*, 6(3).

Whannel, G. (1995). "Sport, national identities and the case of Big Jack." *Critical Survey*.

White, D.M. (1964). "The gatekeeper." In L.A. Dexter and D.M. White (Eds), *People, society and mass communications research*. New York: New American Library.

White, P.G., & Gillett, J. (1994). "Reading the muscular body: A critical decoding of advertisements in Flex Magazine." *Sociology of Sport Journal*, 11, 18–39.

Whitson, D. (1995). "Sport and civic identity in the modern Canadian city." *Canadian Review of Comparative Literature*, 22,125–147.

Whitson, D., & Macintosh, D. (1996). "The global circus: International sport, tourism, and the marketing of cities." *Journal of Sport and Social Issues*, 20, 278–295.

Wideman, J.E. (1996, April 29 & May 6). "Playing Dennis Rodman." *The New Yorker*, 94–95.

Wieberg, S. (1995, August 9). "Frito-Lay adds crunch to Fiesta Bowl." *USA Today*, p. C1.

Wildman, S.S., & Siwek, S.E. (1987, Fall). "The privatization of European television: Effects on international markets for programs." *Columbia Journal of World Business*, pp. 71–76.

Wiley, R. (1991). *Why black people tend to shout: Cold facts and wry views from a black man's world*. New York: Birch Lane Press.

Williams, B.R. (1977). "The structure of televised football." *Journal of Communication*, 27, 133–139.

Williams, F., Rice, R.E., & Rogers, E. (1988). *Research methods and the new media*. New York, NY: The Free Press.

Williams, J. (1994). "The local and the global in English soccer and the rise of satellite television." *Sociology of Sport Journal*, 11, 376–397.

Williams, L.D. (1994). "Sportswomen in black and white: Sports history from an Afro-American perspective." In P.J. Creedon (Ed.), *Women, media and sport*, pp. 45–66. Thousand Oaks, CA: Sage.

Williams, P. (1996, January 24–30). "Only the designated hitter stands in the way of inter-league play." *Baseball Weekly*, pp. 3–4.

Willis, P. (1978). *Learning to labour: How working class kids get working class job*. Hants: Saxon.

Willis, P. (1982). "Women in sport and ideology." In J. Hargreaves (Ed.), *Sport, culture and ideology*, pp. 117–135. London: Routledge & Kegan Paul.

Willis, S. (1993). "Disney World: Public use/private space." *South Atlantic Quarterly*, 92, 119–137.

Wilson, C. (1994, January 23). "Criket's battle of the sexes." *Sunday Age*, p. 13.

Wilson, J. (1988). *Politics and leisure*. Boston: Unwin Hyman.

Wilson, J. (1994). *Sport, society, and the state: Playing by the rules*. Detroit, MI: Wayne State University Press.

Wilson, S. (1995, December 15). "How IOC will divvy up TV pot. Associated Press." *Pittsburgh Post-Gazette*, p. B-12.

Wilstein, S. (1993, January 28). "Wanna bet on sports? Many do." *San Diego Union-Tribune*, pp. D1, D4.

Wittig, M. (1993). "One is not born a woman." In H. Abelove, M.A. Barale, & D.M. Halperin (Eds), *The lesbian and gay studies reader*, pp. 103–109. London: Routledge.

Wolfson. N., & Maines, J. (1980). "Don't 'dear' me!" In S. McConnell-Ginet, R. Borker, & N. Furman (Eds) *Women and language in literature and society*. NY: Praeger.

Women's Sports Foundation (1996, September 18). "Advertisers and marketers embrace 1996 Olympic female athletes." Press release.

Women's Sports Marketing Group (1996, September/October). *Women's sports market report*. Marblehead, MA: Women's Sports Marketing Group.

Wong, W. (1997, January 17). "Football's holy temple of sleaze." *San Francisco Examiner*, p. A-21.

Wonsek, P.L. (1992). "College basketball on television: a study of racism in the media." *Media, Culture and Society*, 14, 449–461.

Worsnop, R.L. (1995, February 10). "The business of sports: The issues." *CQ Researcher*, pp. 123–129.

"Wright no stranger to controversy" (1995, May 17). *Chicago Tribune*, Section 4, p. 10.

Wright, C.R. (1986). *Mass communication: A sociological perspective* (3rd edn). New York: Random House.

Young, G. (1989). "The role that radio plays in Olympism." In R. Jackson (Ed.), *The Olympic movement and the mass media: Past, present and future issues*, pp. 3.15–3.17. Calgary: Hurford Enterprises.

Young, G. (1992, July 6). Telephone interview with radio sports reporter for the Canadian Broadcasting Corporation.

Young, I.M. (1980). "Throwing like a girl: A phenomeology of feminine bodily comport-ment, motility and spatiality." *Human Studies*, 3, 137–56.

Young, I.M. (1990). "Polity and group difference: A critique of the ideal of universal citi-zenship." In C.R. Sunstein (Ed.), *Feminism and political theory*, pp. 117–141. Chicago: University of Chicago Press.

Young, K. (1986). "The killing field': Themes in mass media responses to the Heysel Stadium riot." *International Review for the Sociology of Sport*, 21, 253–265.

Young, K. (1991a, November). "Making violence news: A case study of Canadian media coverage of football and hockey." Paper presented at the meeting of the North American Society for the Sociology of Sport, Milwaukee, WI.

Young, K. (1991b). "Sport and collective violence." *Exercise and Sport Sciences Reviews*, 19, 539–586.

Young, K., & Smith, M.D. (1988–89). "Mass media treatment of violence in sports and its effects." *Current Psychology: Research & Reviews*, 7, 298–311.

Young, K., & Smith, M.D. (1989). "Mass media violence in sports and its effects." *Current Psychology: Research and Reviews*, 1, 298–312.

Zakon, R.H. (1996). Hobbes Internet Timeline v2.4a. [Online]. Available World Wide Web: http://info.isoc.org/guest/zakon/Internet/History/HIT.html

Zavoral, N., & Blount, R. (1995, May 14). "CBS defends Wright's comments on lesbians." *Minneapolis Star Tribune*, p. 4C.

Ziff, H. (1986). "Practicing responsible journalism: Cosmopolitan versus provincial models." In D. Elliott (Ed.), *Responsible journalism*, pp. 151–166. Thousand Oaks, CA.: Sage.

Zillmann, D. (1979). *Hostility and aggression*. Hillsdale, NJ: Lawrence Erlbaum Associates.

Zillmann, D. (1991). "Empathy: Affect from bearing witness to the emotion of others." In J. Bryant & D. Zillmann (Eds), *Responding to the screen: Reception and reaction processes*, pp. 135–167. Hillsdale, NJ: Lawrence Erlbaum Associates.

Zillmann, D. (1995, November). "Sports and the media." Keynote address presented at the International Congress on "Images of Sports in the World." Cologne, Germany.

Zillmann, D. (1996). "The psychology of the appeal of portrayals of violence." In J.H. Goldstein (Ed.), *Attractions of violence*. New York: Oxford University Press.

Zillmann, D., Bryant, J., & Sapolsky, B. (1979). "The enjoyment of watching sports contests." In J.H. Goldstein (Ed.). *Sports, games and play: Social psychological viewpoints*, pp. 297–335. Hillsdale, NJ: Erlbaum.

Zillmann, D., Bryant, J., & Sapolsky, B.S. (1989). "Enjoyment from sports spectatorship." In J.H. Goldstein (Ed.), *Sports, games, and play: Social and psychological viewpoints* (2nd edn, pp. 241–278). Hillsdale, NJ: Erlbaum.

Zillmann, D., & Paulus, P. B. (1993). "Spectators: Reactions to sports events and effects on athletic performance." In R. N. Singer, M. Murphey, & L. K. Tennant (Eds), *Handbook of research on sports psychology*, pp. 600–619. New York: Macmillan.

Zipay, S. (1995, August 9). "Putting a lock on major TV rights." *Newsday*, p. A61.

Zipter, Y. (1988). *Diamonds are a dyke's best friend*. Ithaca, NY: Firebrand.

Index

GENERAL REFERENCE

"subversive" or "empowering" reading positions. As the cultural turn in MediaSport audience study moves ahead, researchers using both culturally "sensitive" qualitative methods and those using more traditional survey methods or empirical analysis will need to recognize the artifacts that come with their methodological choices. In observational settings people are changed and in interview settings people often respond as they like to see themselves as opposed to how they really are. Hindsight, as it is often said, is "20/20." A corollary to this well may be that hindsight also sees far more polyvalence and resistance to texts than would be there without the researcher's query.

Just as audience research has some dangers, it has some real benefits. In particular, research on how fanship and gender interact with audience experience holds real promise. What are the contours of sports fanship and what role does media play in defining these? With rapid changes in how girls and women experience sport, how has this changed audience experience? In pursuing questions like these, it will be important to recognize that we will need to understand not only the texture of these experiences in limited qualitative settings, but do more to make generalizations based on broader survey samples. With the cultural turn, interest in qualitative methods has risen. This was long overdue. However, there remains a continuing need to understand how generalizable some of these thick snapshots are. As oxymoronic as it may seem to some, critically oriented survey research that is methodologically savvy and sensitive to nuance in "reading" the data may lead to our most useful understandings of the MediaSport audience experience.

READING MEDIASPORT

Following an introductory "Playing Field" section, the essays in this collection are placed in three sections, according to whether they most focus on MediaSport institutions, texts, or audiences. In pursuing cultural understanding, such distinctions are often artificial. Readers should join the authors in this collection in seeing MediaSport through linkages amongst institutions, texts, and audiences. While the contributors to this volume touch on major themes in MediaSport inquiry, the expanse of the field is far greater and touches many other cultural borders.

In getting started, the two essays that follow challenge readers to think about the breadth of the social shadow cast by MediaSport. In the first essay, Michael Real places the importance of MediaSport at the cultural crossroads of technology, commodification, and the postmodern condition. Real's essay provides a lens to view where MediaSport inquiry has been and where the "big picture" lies in its global future. The second essay, by Kathleen Kinkema and Janet Harris, rises to the challenge of reviewing and synthesizing broad research and writing on MediaSport. Their essay is an essential starting point for anyone interested in studying MediaSport as a cultural phenomenon. A first reading of the chapter will give you a "macro" view, while later, more selective re-readings of their review will help in framing institutional, textual, and audience issues addressed in later sections of the volume.

MediaSport Institutions are introduced by David Whitson in a chapter that traces fundamental cultural changes in sport to the integrated use of media by a

corporate sphere that manufactures synergies to leverage and expand global markets. In the chapter that follows, Robert Bellamy amplifies many of these themes in examining what he calls a "new oligopoly" of media giants that use sport as a tool for vertical integration. In addition, his analysis highlights how sports organizations use media in their move toward global markets. Pamela Creedon's chapter on women, sport, and media provides important insight into how sport and media are both gendered institutions and how structural biases affect reception of women's sports. Creedon's analysis keys on how market tolerances compromise diversity in the public image of female athletes and their achievements. Margaret MacNeill's chapter on athletes' rights and the ethos of sports journalism raises important new questions to close out this section. MacNeill considers the differential ethos of journalists as they approach sport and coverage of athletes, and more importantly, points to strategic interventions that can help athletes in curbing journalistic abuses of accuracy, privacy, and human rights.

MediaSport Texts are examined in reference to the larger cultural discourses about national identity, celebrity and heroism, race and ethnicity, and gender. This section opens with provocative consideration of mediated constructions of nation and sport by David Rowe, Jim McKay, and Toby Miller. They consider the role of mediated sport in constructing national mythologies, in perpetuating citizenship differentiated by gender, and in co-opting ethnic identity in strategic ways. Leah Vande Berg examines one of MediaSport's key textual artifacts, the sports hero as celebrity. Vande Berg considers how sports heroism has moved other forms of heroism to the margins, and how the social push of marketing has facilitated the traditional modern hero giving way to decidedly postmodern constructions ready-made for the commodity market. Laurel Davis and Othello Harris focus on discourses about race embedded in media treatment of sports in the United States. In a most comprehensive treatment, they illustrate inequities in amount of coverage, the contours of stereotyping, interactions of the coverage of deviance with race, and the heralding of African-American sports success as evidence for the American Dream. Three chapters focused on how gender is constructed in mediated sports texts close this section. In the first essay, Margaret Carlisle Duncan and Michael Messner provide a comparative look at how women and men are treated in coverage by the sports media. Relying on their important series of studies sponsored by the Amateur Athletic Foundation of Los Angeles, Duncan and Messner outline how media differentiates the achievements of female and male athletes through differences in production values, portraits of athleticism, and the symbolic marking of athletes through naming and sexualization strategies. This last issue, the construction of gender identity and sexualities, is given more extensive treatment by Mary Jo Kane and Helen Lenskyj. They examine media treatment of female athletes, extracting how discourses on heterosexual femininity, homophobia, and lesbianism interact with cultural power. In the next chapter Don Sabo and Sue Curry Jansen provide counterpoint in their analysis of constructions of masculinity in the sports media. They use the cultural archetype of the Promethean myth as a point of departure to consider the "binary bind" of gender-typed analysis, the sport media connection to men's violence and the culture of pain, and the marginalization of gay and minority athletes in public discourses of masculinity.

Part two

MediaSport

Institutions

average player salary of $70,000, with stars such as former Stanford standout Jennifer Azzi earning in the neighborhood of $125,000 (Stockman, 1996). Clearly, there's money to be made. CBS purchased the broadcast rights to the NCAA basketball tournament (men's and women's) through to the year 2002 for a reported $1.725 billion dollars (TV sports, 1996). As the women's game "breeds more competitive athletes" and presumably attracts larger, and even more importantly new, audiences, the price tag can only go up.

These indicators suggest that the cream of the crop in women's basketball are starting to earn a living in the institution of sport.[4] Television contracts are increasingly lucrative and promise to bring in additional revenue. In this context, the chicken and egg debate appears to be answered: If you bring them (i.e., fans and/or television audience), we will pay you.

From the standpoint of power, however, control of women's sports remains vested in patriarchal, male-led sport institutions. The male-led NCAA, dominated by the presidents of the football power universities, controls women's collegiate sport. The ABL now faces competition from the NBA for a piece – maybe all – of the action. The NBA launched its eight-team league in 1997 to play during the men's off-season, i.e., a summer schedule. It seems inevitable that only one of the leagues will survive. Stanford Head Coach Tara VanDerveer, who led the US women's team to an Olympic gold medal, sums it up: "If the NBA ran a league on Mars, I think women would go there to play" (Stockman, 1996).[5]

According to the *Wall Street Journal*, the women's game, "emphasizes shot selection, crisp passing and close defense" (Fatsis, 1996, p. B6). But if women "continue the ascent" described by the NCAA, will the game change too? Most of the teams in the women's Top 25 have rosters with more height than the average for a men's high school or NCAA Division III team. Seven of the twelve members of the 1996–1997 Ohio State University women's basketball team, for example, were within an inch of 6-feet or taller.

MASS MEDIA AS A GENDERED INSTITUTION

Equality has been the focus of many critics of mass media coverage of women's sports. They want more coverage – equal coverage – of women's sports. Content studies have argued that female athletes are invisible, ignored and denigrated in the media and the dearth of women's sports coverage functions to symbolically annihilate their existence (Daddario, 1994; Kane & Greendorfer, 1994; Duncan & Hasbrook, 1988).

The number of women enrolled in journalism and mass communication programs has outnumbered men for over twenty years since 1977 (Beasley, 1993). A 1992 study of the journalistic workforce showed that women make up 33.9 percent of the daily newspaper labor force, 44.1 percent of weeklies, 24.8 percent of television and 29 percent of radio (Lafky, 1993). Formed in 1986, members of the Association for Women in the Sports Media, who pronounce their organization's acronym "awesome", are estimated to number five hundred (Cramer, 1994). However, women aren't expected to attain equality in newspaper editorships until 2055 (Beasley, 1993).[6] Radical feminist communication scholars have cautioned,

fed the penis-envy Freudians enough fodder to catch the attention of the TV talk show circuit. Even former President George Bush sent Leavy a handwritten note promising to read her book (Leavy, 1990a). Much of this attention focused on book's first sentence: "You see a lot of penises in my line of work" (Leavy, 1990b, p. 3). Leavy fanned the Freudian flame even more when she acknowledged that the line between fact and fiction in the book was fuzzy at times (Leavy, 1990a).

Sacramento Bee sports reporter Susan Fornoff (1993), who covered the Oakland As for five seasons, describes herself as "a living lab experiment on what would happen to a child raised to dress, think, and act like a woman but sent to live in a world of men . . . of muscle and machismo" (p. xv, xvi). As the only female assigned to a traveling baseball beat during the 1993 season, Fornoff decided she had two options. The first, which she argues many female sportswriters choose, was to "Wear a nun's habit and drink milk and hide in my room" (Fornoff, 1993, p. 4). The second, which she chose, was to "Dress fashionably and drink beer and socialize with the people I covered, with the aim of having a good time getting paid doing something most people would pay to do" (p. 4). Fornoff, a self-described "token" female sportswriter who started her career aged 21 with the Baltimore *News American* in the early 1970s and was hired by *USA Today* one month before it was launched in 1982, fought for equality in the "locker room in the newsroom" (p. 55). At the *News American*, she would occasionally insert a sentence in her post game story asserting that player so-and-so was "unavailable for comment to women sportswriters" (p. 68) to get her editor's attention. At *USA Today*, she protested the fact that women only covered tennis, amateur and women's sports (p. 65). At the *Sacramento Bee*, she outlasted the harassment of slugger Dave Kingman and was rewarded by being the first woman asked to serve on the Board of Directors of the Baseball Writer's Association of America (p. 97). When she left her baseball beat in 1990, her concluding sentiments reveal that while she fought for equality, it was the gendered media system that wore her down: "It wasn't those little locker rooms that drove me away from sportswriting. It was that big locker room" (Fornoff, 1993, p. 227).[8]

A complete case-study analysis of the "big locker room" by Mary Jo Kane and Lisa J. Disch (1993) explores how male athletes sexualize the locker room environment to reinforce the power struggle between men and women. In their analysis of the 1990 Lisa Olson "incident," in which the then *Boston Herald* sports-writer was sexually harassed in the New England Patriots' locker room, the authors detail how media reports constructed Olson as either a classic rape victim (i.e., she asked for it by being there) or a classic hypersensitive female (i.e., she can't take a joke).

The battle continues to rage. Before the start of Game 3 of the 1995 World Series, NBC's Hannah Storm, who has been in the business long enough to be recognized and respected, was verbally harassed. Storm was in the corner of the Cleveland Indians dugout – not the locker room – with a camera crew waiting to conduct an interview. Indians outfielder, Albert Belle, who mistook her for CBS's Lesley Visser, started shouting obscenities at her. As one sportswriter put it, "Apparently, all those women sportscasters look alike to Belle" (Pluto, 1996, March 1, p. A1). Belle ended up with a $50,000 fine, the largest fine in baseball history.